UNDETERRED

A Rural Boy's Journey to the Pinnacle of Academia

John Sorana Akama

with

Joshua Araka

Copyright © 2021 John Sorana Akama

All rights reserved.

This publication may not be reproduced, in whole or in part, by any means including photocopying or any information storage or retrieval system, without the specific and prior written permission of the publisher.

This book is sold subject to the condition that it shall not, by way of trade or otherwise, be re-sold, hired out, or otherwise circulated without the author's or publisher's prior consent in any form of binding or cover other than that in which it is published and without a similar condition including this condition being imposed on the subsequent purchaser.

First Edition: March 2021

Published by Nsemia Inc. Publishers (www.nsemia.com)

Cover Concept: Author

Cover Design: Linda Kiboma

Layout Design: Bethsheba Nyabuto

Project Consultant: Matunda Nyanchama

Note for Librarians:

A cataloguing record for this book is available from Library and Archives Canada.

ISBN: 978-1-989928-08-0

DEDICATION

In memory of Mum and Dad.

About Undeterred

"The fact that Prof. Akama continually snatched what was rightfully his at various levels, as he strived to climb the ladder, encourages us young people to keep on pushing and not take things with ease. His manner of appreciating how life unfolded its chapters to him, favourably and otherwise, is quite motivating." – **Rose Keya Kong'ani, Book Editor.**

"This is more than Prof. Akama's biography as it encapsulates historical, cultural, academic and indeed political experiences of his generation. It is a commentary on a life lived with steadfast focus on succeeding even in the face of challenges encountered, affirming that 'where there is a will, there is a way'." – **Matunda Nyanchama, ICT Consultant and Book Publisher.**

About the Biographer

Apart from doing biographies, Joshua Araka is a multi-skilled and award-winning Kenyan journalist, satirist and novelist. He is the author of *Peppered Path*, *Chronicles of the Idler Volume One*; *Beaten Odds* (co-written with Stephen Mabea) and *Korondo-Panic!*

ACKNOWLEDGEMENT

Writing a biography can sometimes be seen as a personalized reflection on how one has walked through one's life journey. This includes one's successes and failures, enculturation, character formation, academic and professional progression, among other perspectives. However, as much as that may be the case, this kind of undertaking may not be exhaustively carried out without the support and input of critical individuals, institutions and groupings one might have interacted with. On the other hand, it may not be possible to acknowledge all of them in the available space.

In this connection, I start by giving my deepest appreciation to Mr. Joshua Araka, an upcoming journalist, satirist and novelist with huge potential. After identifying Mr. Araka's multi-faceted skills, I managed to convince him to participate in this assignment as co-author. Throughout our endless meetings and discussions in my office, home and even in several hospitality establishments in Kisii Town, we were able to, systematically document and compile several revised drafts, eventually giving rise to this biography. Indeed, it was a great pleasure and joy working with this creative and imaginative writer.

Next, I give a lot of acknowledgement to my immediate family. Particularly, my dear wife Mallion became a key pillar in this noble undertaking. As a special person with whom I have shared my life, she was quite handy in filling the gaps and providing detailed information on many of my life events some of which had faded from my mind. Along the way, she became a cheerful critic of the work that eventually evolved into this final product. Perhaps, more importantly, I have to appreciate her patience and tenacity in all facets of life.

My dear children Orang'o, Nyakoinani and Otwori were my immediate motivators who kept giving me encouragement, and informing me that they were, indeed, eagerly looking forward to read their dad's biography.

Acknowledgement

A number of other individuals whom I had interacted with, over the years, took time from their busy schedules to provide insightful narratives on how they knew me as a person, thus, adding much needed flesh to the work. I particularly, appreciate the role of one of my mentors, Celia Nyamweru, Professor Emeritus at St. Lawrence University in the USA. She helped ignite the initial urge to write this biography when she mailed me a file with neatly arranged correspondence that I had written to her during my time in the United States. Prof. Nyamweru encouraged me further by emphasising that my unique life story was worth telling.

Dr. Robert Maxon, a distinguished gentleman and renowned Africanist, currently Emeritus Professor of African History at West Virginia University, graciously agreed to go through the final copy of this biography and wrote an insightful foreword for the book, which I found to be inclusive as much as it is interesting.

Many of my friends, especially those from my time in secondary, high school and university, whom I cannot mention individually, played a very emphatic role in providing validation of the many issues and events that are captured in this book. To all of them I say a special 'thank you'.

My elder sister, Florence Obaga, was extremely helpful, especially in the narration of events that touch on my earlier life at Nyansakia, Changoi and Borabu. Florence, who has taken a very keen interest in my life over the years, validated many incidents touching on my life from that time.

Special thanks go to Dr. Matunda Nyanchama, the Director of Nsemia Inc. Publishers. Dr. Nyanchama is a highly committed and multi-talented scholar who is a major asset to the Kenyan society. He wears many hats as a renowned scholar, computer scientist, ICT consultant and publisher. This unique Kenyan has, over the years, shown unique and rare qualities as an intellectual who has gone out of his way to assist many researchers and academicians such as myself to document, to publish and preserve indigenous Kenyan cultures, histories and biographies. Notwithstanding his extremely busy schedule, Dr. Nyanchama found time to read and provide an insightful critique of this biography. He was particularly helpful in filling gaps on broader and contextual historical, economic, social and political issues that enriched the book. In this regard, I am deeply indebted to him.

Last but not least, I convey my sincere thanks to the committed and hard-working staff at the Office of the Vice Chancellor, Kisii University. These dedicated staff members include Mama Jemimah Nyamweya, Emily Onyancha and Dennis Okinyi. They have always played a critical role in the typing, printing and binding of several copies of my research work and other assignments, including this biography.

John S. Akama
February 2021

TABLE OF CONTENTS

DEDICATION iii
ACKNOWLEDGEMENT v
FOREWORD xiii
PROLOGUE xix
    Contextualizing my Story xxi
    Aspiring to Do Better... xxvii

1. THE START OF MY JOURNEY.................................. 1
    My Birth 3
    Sorana - My Maternal Grandfather........................... 7
    My Recollections as a Toddler.................................. 9
    A Place in the Sun.. 11
    Unwritten Destiny 14
    How my Parents Met 16
    Family Uncertainty 19
    Our New Abode 24
    Humble Schooling.. 27
    Patriarch Otwori, my Pillar 30
    Otwori's Forced Adventures.................................... 34
    A Great Woman in My Early Life............................. 38
    Overcoming Initial Barriers 41
    The Demise of Mum 43
    A Contrasting Spouse.. 46
    My Father's Changed Life 49

GROWING UP.. 53
    My Initiation 53
    Into Seclusion 61
    The FGM Controversy 65
    Leaving Seclusion 67
    My Christian Name 69

Scaling the Heights in Education 77
Remarkable Achievement 82
Conquering Culture Shock 91
Reflections on A-Level Education.......................... 95
Rare Achievement 101
Call to Duty 108
My Initial Lessons on Teaching and Administration 111
Light and Darkness.. 115

ONTO HIGHER EDUCATION **118**

Entering University 118
Experiencing a New Environment 119
Social Life at University.................................... 123
The Big Ideological Divide................................ 127
Living through a Coup Attempt 131
Back on Campus.. 139
The Karumaindo Experience 143
Power to Read 144
My First Posting as a Graduate Teacher 146
My Transfer to Nyamagwa Boys' School........... 148

2. THE AMERICAN DREAM **153**

My USA Scholarship 155
Aborted Fundraising Initiative 157
In the skies 161
Our Arrival in America 162
The American Shocks...................................... 166
Understanding Capitalism................................ 169
In Class at Ohio 172
Social Life in Ohio 176
My Special American Mentors 180
Other Take-Home Encounters 181
Another USA Scholarship................................ 184
Special Thanks to America 190

3. MY TURBULENT TIMES 195
    The Aborted Dream 197
    Picking the Pieces 202
    In Search of a Spouse 203
    Formalizing my Marriage 208
    Starting Work as a Lecturer 210
    Removal from Departmental Headship 216
    Defining my Own Niche 219
    Academic Activism 223
    Washing Dirty Linen in Public 227
    More Academic Publications 233
    Interview for Professorship 237

4. NURTURING KISII UNIVERSITY 249
    Another Academic Move 251
    Managing Kisii University Constituent College 257
    In Search of Lecturers 264
    Developing the University Strategic Plan 272
    Infrastructural Facelift 275
    Curriculum Relevant to the Times 280
    From Constituent College to University 285
    Becoming the Founding Vice Chancellor 286
    Material Day for Award of Charter 291
    Campuses Phase One 297
    Campuses Phase Two 304
    Restructuring the Campuses 313
    Creating a Medical School 323
    Enhancing Research and Innovation 326
    Celebrating University Cultural Week 330

5. THE WAY FORWARD 343
    Corporate Social Responsibility 345
    Upholding Student Discipline 349

When I Exit from Kisii University 355
The University of the Future 359
The Corona Virus Pandemic 369
Last Initiatives 374
Brief on Succession 377
Service to the Community 378

6. EPILOGUE 387

Broader Kenyan Perspective: My Personal Gaze 389
The Nyayo Era 400
The New Order of Governance 407
7. Reflections on Turning Points 416
What if I Was Not Born? 416
Should I Have Married Earlier? 424
Regarding Other Folks on the Road Travelled 426
On Kenya and Africa in the 'Global Village' 428

REFERENCES 437

Books 437
Newspapers 437

FOREWORD

It is an honour and a pleasure to contribute the foreword for the memoir of a most esteemed colleague, Professor John Sorana Akama. As readers will learn, Professor Akama and I initially met at an annual conference of the African Studies Association in the United States. Our shared interest in the history of the people of Gusii in south-western Kenya led to our co-editing a book that encompassed many aspects of Gusii culture as viewed from the perspective of the first decade of this century. Since that time, we have kept in touch, sharing common interests and keeping abreast of changing dynamics in contemporary Kenya. My small contribution to this interesting and instructive narrative will hopefully illuminate certain aspects of the author's life experiences as well as pointing to major contributions to knowledge made by this work.

Any memoir is a highly personal story that is unique in its focus and the life experiences described by the author. The narrative that follows takes readers through the early years of independent Kenya down to the present as the story of a young man coming to adulthood and undertaking a career in education. While this journey is unique in many ways, there are many steps along the way that are typical of the experience of Kenyans traversing the uhuru years. This is well illustrated by the context provided by the author in discussing his life experiences. While much of the narrative is situated in western Kenya, and particularly Gusii (present day Kisii and Nyamira Counties), Professor Akama's life story is one which many Kenyans can relate with as they recall their own past. In this way, books like this have great value for historians and others interested in the everyday experiences of people, no matter where in Kenya they were born or reside. This way, such books help to build a national history and consciousness as each individual story helps to create a better understanding of the whole.

Foreword

    This certainly rang true for me personally for, as I read the manuscript, I was reminded of my own experiences in Kenya, beginning with my first visit in 1961. This especially because two of the institutions mentioned, Kakamega Secondary School and Moi University, played an important part in my academic and personal development. I transferred to Kakamega for my third year of teaching in 1964. I taught English and History in Form 2, Swahili in Form 1, and served as games master in what was my first experience of a Kenyan boarding school. One of my colleagues, among the faculty there, was Gerald Avedi, a distinguished educationalist who was Professor Akama's headmaster at Kakamega more than a decade later. Here, as was the case with Moi University, my first appointment as visiting professor in 1989-90 occurred prior to Professor Akama's appointment as a lecturer. I returned three more times to teach at that institution, overlapping with the tenure Professor Akama describes later in this book.

    Another individual mentioned in the book is someone who had a substantial impact on my career as a specialist in Kenyan history. This is the late Dr. Zachary Onyonka, whose speech to the author and his fellow students at Itibo Boys High School made an impression. An educational pioneer in his own right, Dr. Onyonka and I were fellow graduate students in the Programme of Eastern African Studies at Syracuse University from 1965 to 1967 when he defended his dissertation and graduated with a PhD in Economics. I still remember driving him to the homes of his doctoral committee members so that he could deliver the final copy of his dissertation prior to his defense. Later, he encouraged and assisted me in my interest in studying the colonial history of the Gusii. He aided me to obtain research clearance through the University of Nairobi and allowed me to stay in the new house he had constructed at Mosocho while I carried out my field research.

    Yet the importance of this narrative goes far beyond these personal links. As readers will note, Kenyan education is a significant theme in this memoir. Professor Akama's journey through primary school to the school certificate and A-levels, and to his undergraduate and graduate university experience is a most informative and valuable story. From it, we learn a great deal about independent Kenya's educational history. The path taken by the professor is neither that of 8-4-4 nor of current students making their way through Kenya schools and colleges, and these recollections of a student and teacher provide much food for thought for those seeking the best possible educational experience for all Kenyans.

Particularly significant in this regard is Professor Akama's recollections and reflections on his career as a university teacher and administrator. His experience as an innovator in the field of tourism instruction at the university level is impressive and has contributed to the enhancement of an important sector of independent Kenya's economy. His experience as an innovator as principal and later Vice Chancellor of Kisii University also looms large in the narrative as, indeed, it should be. His careful recounting of his experiences in launching a new institution of higher education, fraught with many challenges, deserves careful study. This portion of the autobiography makes particularly informative reading, especially in the contrast between the eras of presidents Jomo Kenyatta and Daniel arap Moi and the administrations of Mwai Kibaki and Uhuru Kenyatta.

Another theme that I found particularly interesting was the changes taking place in Kisii and Nyamira counties since independence. Most readers will recognize and have opinions as to the political impact of devolution as reflected in the creation of the two counties and fundamental changes in administration that now characterize these two governmental units. As those living through these years recognize, county government contrasts not with Kenya's experience of the first year of independence, but with the centralizing and top-down development initiatives that supplanted it during the first four decades of independence.

Closely related to this, are the author's observation of the economic changes in the Gusii highlands that marked the independence years. This is a truly remarkable story that has yet to be told in detail. The region's economy rapidly expanded in the 1960s and 1970s as it became part of an "agrarian revolution zone." Gusii became Kenya's leading producer of pyrethrum and bananas as well as a major exporter of coffee and tea, to say nothing of maize. These agrarian developments enabled Professor Akama's parents, farming in an area previously set aside for European agriculture, to pay his school fees and enable the achievement of a first-class education. At several points in the manuscript, however, the author reveals his concern for the future of the region as well as similar counties that have been part of the nation's agrarian revolution zone.

Of particular concern is the future of a sustainable rural lifestyle in the face of increased demand on land resources and, of course, in the time of the Covid-19 pandemic. There are economic and scientific reasons for this situation as well as social and cultural as Professor Akama astutely observes at various points in his story. Sub-division of holdings, in accordance with traditional inheritance patterns, can be seen as a critical factor as is the cultural burial practices that require the deceased to be laid to rest in family land holdings.

These are indeed critical issues for the present and future generations to consider. Will pressure on resources lead to increasing poverty due to diminished access to land and an absence of rural industries? My experience in studying the regions has led me to recognize the reality of this dilemma, but it also provides hope for the future. This is because Kenyans in the past have surmounted great obstacles to achieve a better and more secure future for their children. This is a key lesson of Professor Akama's memoir and fits also with what a study of the past helps us to understand.

More than eight decades ago, Mogonga in Kisii County was the first site of legal coffee planting by Africans in Kenya (1934). Coffee growing got off to a slow start there but eventually spread to the rest of the Gusii highlands as thousands of households were able to benefit economically.

By the 1990s, however, coffee was no longer the leading cash earner for the region, as was the case in other parts of Kenya. This was brought home to me when I visited Mogonga in 1998, 30 years after an initial visit. I found little evidence of coffee cultivation and the pulping station was closed down with the electricity lines disconnected. But the local farmers had adjusted to the conditions by planting maize and tea which I saw in farm after farm. This ability to rise to meet changing conditions and new challenges, as demonstrated by this book, gives me hope for the future in spite of the pessimistic voices that predict insolvable problems for rural Africa.

Finally, let me conclude this foreword by again expressing my gratitude for the opportunity to contribute to this important book. The latter is a credit to the author, a distinguished scholar and administrator. In my experience John is an individual to be admired for his achievements and contributions to Kenyan education and for his strong moral principles and compass.

Robert M. Maxon
Emeritus Professor of African History
West Virginia University

PROLOGUE

I have not lived a perfect life. However, I have grown in loving environment, matured in character and advanced professionally in academia and administration. I achieved all this through continuously snatching victory from the jaws of defeat. Over the years, I have learnt that mistakes are mere steps up the ladder of success. Despite the inequities that we live with, I acknowledge that life is beautiful and worth living. I believe that, regardless of the path each of us takes, we all have a personal story that is worth telling.

Perhaps the biggest tragedy that transcends generations is that most human stories and experiences are never told. Many of these stories, as rich as they may be, are interred with the bones of their would-be storytellers. As a result, critical experiences and lessons learnt by individuals or groups are neither shared nor preserved for present and future generations. This leaves those who would wish to learn from those lives scratching their heads in an attempt to piece together the scant knowledge that they may be lucky to come across from undocumented under-documented sources. Inevitably, the outcome is stunted understanding and misrepresentation of the diverse and unique journeys we all traverse as individuals, groups and institutions.

Most leaders in Kenya and Africa, be they politicians, businessmen, industrialists or educationists, have not told enough of their stories for reasons I cannot explain. A good example is that of the Kenyan heroes and heroines who played a critical role in the struggle for independence, nation-building and democratization. Consider these and philanthropists whose works went on to impact the lives of thousands (if not millions) of individuals and communities.

Despite the indelible marks that these unsung legends left behind, many (if not all) never left us their stories from their perspectives. In other words, they left the arena of reconstructing their history, culture and development of our society to others such as elitist educationists, historians and social scientists. The objectivity of many of these second and third-person stories often gets coloured with biases, attitudes and misconceptions. Worse still, the stories documented by this group are not about the majority of Kenyans and their impact on Kenyan society. It is of the 'big' men and women, invariably from the political class who, in most instances, are not representative of the majority of the citizenry.

Due to outright and sometimes unconscious biases, the historians often end up regurgitating literature that is rich in sycophancy and praise-singing of a few privileged individuals in society. In the long run, the real communal history, culture and development of the majority of the citizenry may not be documented in those elitist works of literature.

Let me provoke you with the following questions as I advance this assertion: has anybody managed to capture the essence of Kenyan peasants and the informal histories of the ordinary men and women in the formation of the Kenyan state? Has anyone written intensively and exhaustively about the ordinary courageous Kenyans who have over the years taken part in the democratization process of the Kenyan society? Do we have any meaningful record of the life histories of common Kenyans who struggled for changes in the Constitution that was promulgated in 2010? Have we heard and read the experiences of the common man in 1982 when there was a foiled coup against President Daniel Arap Moi? Do we have an exhaustive account of the 2007/08 ethnic clashes which led to the death, injury and displacement of thousands upon thousands of Kenyan families?

I now turn to the issues concerning the development of our Kenyan education system where I have spent most of my adult life. How much has been written about university education in Kenya? What journey has the Kenyan university system travelled from its normative years in the 1960s through to the 1980s when I was a student in the system? From where I sit, this unique field provides rich fodder that has not been fully exploited. The Kenyan education system remains scantly documented, a scenario that leaves me unhappy. For a fact, very few Kenyans, who have worked in universities as lecturers or administrators, have written about their experiences and lessons learnt.

Without overstating the point, our university education system has expanded over time and exponentially so in recent years. We had one public university in the 1970s and part of the 1980s. Today, there are more than thirty of them, in addition to several private universities. This situation has widened chances for Kenyans' access to university education and met many Kenyans' desire for higher education.

As the sector has made these strides, it has been dogged with concerns, criticism and shortcomings. This scenario precipitates reports that are often inaccurate and/or short-sighted, with harsh judgments made without prior understanding of the core bottlenecks confronting university education. For instance, is it true that Kenyan universities are offering too many courses? Are these institutions providing useful and market-driven training? Are they regurgitating half-baked graduates as some claim? Is the rationale used to raise negative responses to these questions justifiable?

Over time, we have left these stories to be told by sections of the political class, media practitioners and civil servants, some who possess a limited understanding of the way university education works. However, since society and fate have conspired to give them a national platform, they continue to offer generalized statements that are often laced with distortion of facts. Sadly, as Mark Twain says, 'A lie can travel halfway around the world while the truth is still putting on its shoes.'

Contextualizing my Story

It is within this broad context that I resolved to tell my own story. My urge is to share my life history and experience with various people in our country and beyond if only to enrich information about the space I have occupied in my short life on earth. As I tell this story, I know that there are many Kenyans who probably have stories of greater accomplishment than mine. In a way, this is my challenge to them to break their silence about their life experiences.

Prologue

A good example I know is that of one Kenyan politician and pioneer senior civil servant who played a critical role during Kenya's independence. At one time, I believe he was at the centre of suppression of individual freedom and human rights in the country. By virtue of his position, he has with him a story of great essence to the Kenyan society in the nascent years of independence. Sadly, he has sworn that he will neither write nor allow anyone to write his memoirs as long as he lives; he would rather be interred with what he knows. In my view, this is a high level of dishonesty which deliberately denies Kenyans a story that forms part of their heritage, whether perceived negatively or otherwise.

The personal story I provide in this book is highly contextualized for it is personal. One can say that I am talking about the growth and struggle of one in the Kenyan society through my own experience. That experience, spanning over five decades offers a glimpse of how life was in my childhood through my years of youth to the present.

The story starts with my very simple early life; I was born in Changoi area of the present day Kericho County. Soon after, I was taken to my rural home at Nyansakia in Kisii for the initial cultural rites, including shaving of the first hair and naming, in line with the dictates of the community.

At Nyansakia, people lived simple, largely peasantry lives. They did not have many material things and were at ease staying in grass-thatched huts, and fetching water from nearby springs for domestic use. They enjoyed highly nutritious indigenous food, as a result of the sweat of their committed labour in their farms. It is interesting that, notwithstanding the simplicity of life then, the people were happy and contented. Moreover, life was communal with each person being his or her neighbour's keeper. Up to now, I have fond memories of my life as a youth at Nyansakia. Sadly, the area is now confronted with a myriad of challenges including increasing levels of poverty, a surging population, food shortage, malnutrition and unemployment of the youth.

The question is: where did we go wrong? Here was a place that blossomed and people led simple, happy lives at the dawn of independence. Now, many, especially the youth, are increasingly impoverished, hungry and angry. This situation is replicated in many places across Gusii, Kenya and the African continent as a whole and can be retold from such a broader perspective.

In this work, I have chosen to be the central character to paint the image of the kind of world I have lived in this far. Through my experiences, I hope that the story will resonate well with other Kenyans. My story captures the earlier forms of primary and secondary school education in Kenya. It also shows that, at the turn of independence, formal education was majorly influenced by colonial policies and plans. This is so to the extent that it leaned in favour of aligning the learners to adopt foreign values at the expense of indigenous tenets and norms that the system cast as inferior.

My early education experience presents an interesting perspective on how Kenyan youth 'lived' in two worlds. On one hand, the youth were expected to conform to the Western-based formal education. On the other, they had to live as typical Africans in an environment where the people practised remnants of their culture, values and social norms.

My story shows that formal education promoted competitiveness and placed emphasis on passing examinations. If one failed in the Certificate of Primary Education (CPE), the Kenya Certificate of Secondary Education (KCSE) or any other national examination, one got relegated to living in rural areas and (presumably) condemned to a life of servitude. This was an option that did not settle well with many as land was diminishing while the population continued rising exponentially.

From an early age, the concept of white collar jobs, deemed as superior, was deeply inculcated into the minds of the youth. Education was seen as a panacea and gateway to prized white-collar jobs, a view that has been entrenched in Kenyans' collective psyche for many years. Its impact can be seen and felt! Today, we have millions of young people who have completed high school and university training but have no jobs. Many can be found 'tarmacking' in the streets of Nairobi and other major towns searching for elusive white collar jobs. Still, many are found idling in rural areas and are totally disengaged from the realities of life in their environment and cannot fathom working in farms when they are holders of beautiful certificates. Unfortunately, their academic documents continue to gather dust on the shelves. Clearly, to many young people, farming is dirty and laborious work that should be left to those who have not gone to school, and the uncivilized.

In my story, I provide a perspective of Kenya's higher level education system. It shows that many of those who succeeded in passing the national examinations and pursued university education ended up seeing themselves as 'the chosen few'. In my view, they falsely regarded themselves as being above the rest of society. Many of them seemed inclined to believe that the best life could only be found in urban centres. They imagined living lives of comfort with good houses, cars and other luxurious amenities. These conceptions have, in most instances, not been tenable.

My Kenyan education experience is juxtaposed with my postgraduate (Masters and PhD) studies in the United States of America. It is a comparative analysis of the Kenyan and American university systems. Further, I am able to provide the experiences and challenges that foreign (especially African) students of my time faced while in America. As the story pans out, it reveals the concept of meritocracy that is highly ingrained in the American system. However, there is no denying that there are challenges in America too. These challenges include crime and racial discrimination.

What makes the difference is that the American system is hinged on strong systems and well-established institutions that work for the good of the American people. In America, if you work hard and do well in education, farming, industry, business or any other venture, the playground is fairly level. You have got very high chances of succeeding. This is what is called the 'American dream'. Quite often, individuals are given ample opportunity to exploit their potential to the fullest and while at it, promote the social, economic and cultural common good. In fact, America is a country that has largely been built by immigrants from Africa, India, Japan, China, Europe and other parts of the world. These people transformed the US technologically and in all other social, economic and cultural spheres.

As a consequence, some of the best doctors, engineers, researchers and professors in America are of foreign origin. One is left asking: why can't Kenya develop a culture of meritocracy in schools, business, industry and other sectors of the economy? Is it that we do not appreciate the value of such a system? In my view, meritocracy is the only way the country can hasten its advancement to prosperity.

America is a country with well-developed institutions in sectors such as education, politics, economy and health. The institutions are well-grounded and have strong foundations. It is why the country is able to sustain itself economically, socially, politically and culturally, notwithstanding the challenges and problems it faces. As Kenyans, we can learn a thing or two from America without copying the American model in entirety. This is what China has done. The Asian country got ideas from the Western world, adopted and improved them for its own wellbeing. As a result, their economy has soared and their science and technology is booming. China is currently one of the wealthiest countries of the world even as its global power continues to rise.

****

As much as they have borrowed scientific and technological ideas, however, the Chinese are grounded in ideologies ingrained in them by their own legends such as Confucius, Mao Zedong and Deng Xiaoping. I have noted in this book that as Kenyans, we need to ground ourselves in our own values too. This way, we would shun the attempt of copying and aping the Western culture of consumerism and other forms of alien social and cultural values that lead to cultural decadence. Even in as simple an example as the extent to which we give our children foreign names like Reagan, Trump, Saddam and Clinton. These names do not have any significance and bearing on our cultural and social context.

Worse yet, we have completely changed our lifestyles, especially with respect to eating habits. The Kenyan elites want to be seen consuming Western cuisines, served in high-end hotels and restaurants in Kenya's big towns and cities. These food choices are now leading us into a crisis where non-communicable lifestyle diseases are increasingly becoming prevalent in the Kenyan population.

Unfortunately, we are getting deeper into cultural and social decadence. Our youth are hooked onto watching Western movies, dancing to tunes that carry little content and generally imbibing negative cultural values that are propagated in social media via the Internet. I hasten to add that social media and other modern communication channels have a lot of value when utilized appropriately. Indeed, these technological advancements have revolutionized and eased communication as we can share and pass information in an efficient and cost-effective manner.

While telling this story, I have been frank about the many challenges that I have faced in my life. Many of these drawbacks appeared to be insurmountable. They included disease, academic hurdles, career progression impediments and management challenges. A case in point is when I became the Principal and later Vice-Chancellor of Kisii University. Through commitment and God's grace, I have been able to overcome many of the obstacles I have faced and I am keeping on with my life as I serve my last term at Kisii University.

Perhaps, more importantly, reading through my life experience and challenges can serve as an example of how human tenacity, focus and commitment can make one triumph in one's undertakings, notwithstanding the odds. It shows that through focus, discipline and proper counsel, one can overcome daunting life encounters and eventually achieve success in one's endeavours.

In this regard, as much as the story is about me, it also provides an elaborate explanation and understanding of how a human being, faced with ever-changing circumstances in life, can juggle the various options, guided by strong grounding in one's values. All that one needs to understand is where one came from, where one is and where one is going. In fact, this exposition shows that life is a series of challenges and what matters most is how one responds to those challenges. Responding to the challenges negatively, and maybe becoming defensive and giving up in life, may result in failure and the resultant destruction of one's dreams and aspirations.

Aspiring to Do Better

Taking a route of positive thinking, commitment and hard work can lead to success. In other words, in life, we are capable of conquering the challenges we face when guided by determination and commitment.

This book contextualizes the fact that as human beings, we are essentially social animals. There is no way one can succeed as a lone entity where one works in isolation of other human beings. As people, nature has engineered us to work with others in order to build our lives, the lives of the people around us and for the overall good of our communities, and the world.

It has been said that as much as possible, we need to think globally but act locally. If you want to make an impact in your life and society, you may not achieve it by thinking that you can change the country or world at the press of a button. However, if you strategically strive to change the people around you by, say, transforming yourself, your family and the community positively, your actions may likely have an everlasting impact on the community. Over time, the impact may reverberate beyond your community and touch other people beyond your reach. In other words, by acting locally in farming, business, religion or any other sector, you will assert a 'bottom-up' influence on human affairs.

Through this approach, you will be able to transform the lives of others. If you touch, 10, 100, or 1,000 people, the effect will spread, via multiplier effect, to the world where God has placed you. So, for instance, if you are a university lecturer or professor, start by thinking about issues and challenges that your university and immediate community are facing. As a problem solver, seek ways of providing timely solutions to those challenges. Through this, you can then talk about extending your influence through interactions and other forms of research initiatives. Your ideas may then be adopted by others and then, collectively, you can change the country or the world through that very positive impact that you had managed to make in your immediate community.

This reminds me of a man who, while lying in his bed, sick, frail and dying said, "When I was growing up, I thought I would change the world but I was unable to do so. I thought that I would change my country, but I was unable to. Perhaps had I started by changing my own family, it could have acted as an example. It could have touched those around them, who would have also touched the wider society. Through that, I would have changed the world." He also instructed that the words, 'Here lies a man who was unable to change the world' be inscribed on his tombstone.

The point is that, all lives matter. Whatever you are doing, be it as a cleaner, small businessman or church leader, if you show commitment in your work and excel in it, you can become an example to others. Through this, you will inspire others around you to work hard and improve their lives. Whatever fate has thrown before you, be it working on a small scale business or on the farm, always endeavour to give it your best. Have a positive attitude in whatever you are doing and you will always succeed.

In the Bible, the book of Genesis 1:27 says, "So God created human beings, making them to be like him." Sincerely, if God created us in his image, it would imply that, within us, there are latent good attributes and what we need to do is to ignite the Godliness in us and we will succeed. Indeed, God did not create us to fail, but to triumph. When humanity fails in its endeavours, then we can say that we are not fulfilling the purpose for which God created and put us in this world.

I have clearly portrayed in this book that, in my life, I cannot claim that I was in any way exceptional compared to those around me. In fact, throughout my life, I have seen people who are better endowed than myself, be it in education, or other forms of endeavours. However, many of these people did not manage to go as far as I did, mainly due to lack of commitment, dedication, negative thinking and guidance.

The point is, even if you are an average human being, with the right mindset, focus and hard work, you can always achieve your life goals. If one looks at the various stages of my life from home, school, university and overall work environment, you will see how I have lived with hope, resilience, determination and hard work.

However, as I noted, I have imperfections. While alive to this fact, in this book, I have also shown my weaknesses, missed opportunities and misinformation that came my way. I have clearly shown how the death of my mother when I was still a teenager, affected the trajectory of my life up to the present time. I have shown how misfortune struck me after I got a job in the USA after completing my PhD studies and I had to fly back to Kenya while sick. When I got home and recovered, I had to navigate, circumspectly, to regain my focus as far as my pursuit of career advancement was concerned.

I ask myself a number of questions. Had I stayed with the job in the United States, would I have risen to become a Vice-Chancellor of a public university in Kenya? Would I have become a full professor in a university system? Would I have managed to help the less fortunate, the orphans and vulnerable youths as I do now, albeit in a small way commensurate to my ability? Would I have been in a position to write my story and share it with you the way I have managed to do? These are questions that I have tried to address in this book.

Finally, I have to say that in this world, a majority of the people are by nature good human beings. However, it is also true that in any given society, there is a small percentage of the population with dark hearts. These are the very people who do most of harm that ends up destroying society and other people's lives. These are people driven by malice, evil and dark hearts. They are full of envy. They will go any length to destroy other people's lives, especially those they perceive as being more successful than they are.

In this book, I have demonstrated the negative attributes of a few people who are capable of destroying other people's dreams by using all manner of evil mechanisms and schemes. In fact, these people could even kill their fellow human beings whom they perceive as more successful. They can go out of their way to do substantial harm to otherwise innocent people. I met such characters in the journey of my life as expounded in this book.

I have told my story the way I know it and in the best way I could do so. This can serve as a challenge to others. Everyone has a story to tell, to share their unique experiences with the broader society. This way, we will have many stories of us and depart from only reading about selected stories of a few powerful people and individuals.

Thank you!

1. THE START OF MY JOURNEY

My Birth

If I had been born where my umbilical cord was buried as tradition dictated, women of Nyansakia community in Kisii, Kenya, would have ululated three times to announce my arrival in the world. However, as fate would have it, I was born in Changoi Multinational Tea Estates on the outskirts of Kericho Town in present-day Kericho County. Changoi was inhabited by low-income workers in the tea estates owned by multinational companies. The residents came from various parts of the country, forming a mosaic of the Kenyan nation.

My late father, Andrew Akama, worked as a carpenter in one of the tea factories. Like many of his generation, he was forced by circumstances to work for money. You see, colonialists had introduced the money economy. With that, came taxes which every able-bodied male was required to pay. This compelled many young men to move from their rural homes to earn a living and raise money to pay the mandatory taxes.

As history would have it, when labour pangs started to bite my late mother Teresia Kwamboka that day in 1959, fellow women in the estate swung into action and ensured that she safely delivered a bouncing baby boy, the second fruit of her womb. They then ululated in different tongues and danced to welcome me, the newborn, *mosamba mwaye*, as Abagusii would say.

My mother would later tell me that she was extremely elated when she held me in her hands for the first time. She had been sickly throughout the period of the pregnancy. Fearing she might lose the child she was carrying, she acted quickly. She relocated from her matrimonial home in Nyansakia village, where my elder sister, Florence Nyaboke, was born. Later in life, she would divulge to us that her complications with pregnancies were later mysteriously treated by a Gusii herbalist. The herbalist also gave her a chain, which she wore around her belly. She would later give birth to one more son and three daughters after me.

The Start of My Journey

In obedience to the children welcoming ceremony of Abagusii, my mother travelled from Kericho to our ancestral home in Kisii carrying me in her arms. This was a month after I was born. The journey was compulsory and significant as I was to undergo initial rituals, including being given a name and formally getting incorporated in my extended family lineage.

My mother had left home for Kericho while heavy with pregnancy. She was frail. The news that she had returned home with a bouncing baby boy in her hands swept through the area like a bush fire. I am told that our arrival electrified the otherwise sleepy community of Nyansakia as the local people trooped to our homestead. From conversations with my mother later in life, I learnt that this turned out to be a big celebration. I am not sure it would have been of the magnitude it became if the child were a girl.

As I grew up, I learnt that a traditional grass-thatched house with an earthen floor and mud walls was what was home to us. Another structure that stood in the homestead, at the extreme end of the compound, was a pit latrine. Typical of many homes at the time, there was neither running water nor electricity in the place, although these are now available in a few homesteads. In contrast, the house where my father stayed in the tea estate was modest. It had an earthen floor, brick walls and the roof was made of corrugated iron sheets.

I am told that, as family and neighbours gathered and invoked the name of *Engoro* (the name for God in Gusii), a white goat was slaughtered to bestow blessings on me, the newborn. As tradition demanded, elders who were largely my grandfather's age mates sat at the *egesieri kia bweri* (the main entrance to the homestead) facing eastwards as they shared traditional brew from a common pot using *chinkore* (traditional drinking straws).

I have expounded in my book[1] that the design and construction of a typical Gusii homestead was done bearing

---

[1] *The Untold Story: Gusii Survival Techniques and Resistance to the British Colonial Rule* (Nsemia Inc., 2019).

in mind the defence of the people, especially the weak (women, children and those with disabilities) and livestock. Our homestead at Nyansakia was not any different. Where the elders sat gave them a vantage view of the picturesque Emanga (the Manga escarpment). Emanga is still regarded as a holy shrine for the Gusii community. The imposing cliff which is intact to this day overlooks Kisii Town and separates part of Kisii and Nyamira counties. Emanga was of great importance to the community. *Ngoro ya Mwaga* (an underground tunnel) held special significance in the spiritual life of Abagusii. It was believed to an abode of ancestral spirits (*chisokoro*), who were intercessors between the living and the Gusii Supreme being (*Engoro*).

The shrine was regarded highly by the Gusii people in general and members of the broader Kitutu clan where it was situated in particular. There was an intricate religious procedure to be followed for one to get near to the shrine. It was also believed that whoever went contrary to the requisite laid down procedure would fall into the tunnel never to be seen again. It is believed that the tunnel leads directly into Lake Victoria.

To get to the shrine, the procedure entailed tying some special spear grass that grew nearby into matching knots, then carrying a bundle of firewood which one threw into the main cave. It was believed that the departed ancestors would use the firewood to light a fire to keep themselves warm when it got chilly. Stories had it that, in the evening, those at the foot of the hill and further from it in direct line of sight could see sparkling flames of fire from the holy shrine.

All forms of special sacrifices and prayers took place at the shrine. They ranged from those pertaining to women who could not get children to unfavourable weather conditions like drought and more. For example, in the days of yore whenever there was a drought, a rainmaker (*omonyibi*) in tow with respected elderly women would gather near the shrine. The rainmaker would then lead his entourage in performing the 'rain dance' *(ribina)*. For sure, elders will tell you, there would be a heavy downpour following the special *ribina* dance.

Back at home, as members of the Nyansakia community feasted in our homestead, consultations took place on the sidelines. Those involved in the close-knit talks were immediate family members from both my maternal and paternal side. They had to find a name that could be suitable for me.

It was after these elaborate consultations that it was resolved that I be named Sorana, and Sorana I became. The name is special. I was named after my mother's father. He was a religious, enterprising, generous and an outgoing man whose actions have lived beyond his time. He came from Embonga in Bogichora sub-clan of the larger Bogirango clan in present-day Nyamira County.

During the naming ceremony, the elders, led by my grandfather enchanted names of their ancestors. They thanked *Engoro* and the ancestors for their mercies and sought their guidance for survival and continuity of the family. In appreciation, they showered the spirits of their forefathers with praises for accepting me as a new member of the family and lineage.

While the men did their bit, the women did theirs too. The mothers, led by my grandmother, performed a standard ritual meant to protect the new born from the infamous *ebibiriria* (evil eye). It was and it is still believed that some members of the community possess evil powers that can cause sudden illness in children. If left untreated the child can die. *Ebibiriria* remains a mystery given the way it is believed to be transmitted. A person with an 'evil eye' only needs to look at a child for the *ebibiriria* to take effect.

"*Engoro inderere* (God, protect and help raise our child)," they would say, as they tossed me gently while facing the *Ngoro ya Mwaga* shrine. Indeed, birth signalled continuity among the Gusii people. Parents believed they would 'live' through their progeny. It also occupied a very special place in people's hearts.

My maternal grandfather, whose name I carry, was a prominent, promising and upright man who died in the

1940s. History has it that the name 'Sorana' was Omogusii's corruption of 'Soranus', an Italian name that is widely accepted and given to many during the Catholic baptism. Abagusii believed that a child would take the characteristics of the person it is named after; by naming me after a good man, the community hoped that I would take after his good character and deeds.

After acquiring the name, my hair was shaved for the first time. This was a responsibility of high esteem carried out by grandmothers. That day, my grandmother Kemunto took a specially prepared traditional razor blade. Skilfully and gently, I am told, she shaved my head and the hair was later on buried at a particular spot in the homestead. This was in line with the dictates of Gusii tradition. At the same time, part of my umbilical cord, which my mother had preserved after giving birth to me in Kericho, was buried in the right-hand side of the homestead. This sealed the fact that I was now part and parcel of the family and the Gusii community in general. It also meant that I had to live and abide by the dictates of the community.

Interestingly, according to Omogusii folklore, once a child was born, it was presumed that she or he had burnt her or his house. Regardless of gender, the child was referred to as *Mosamba Mwaye*, the "one who had burnt one's house." In this case, the house referred to the mother's womb. For the child to be welcomed to the earthly home and be part of it, it had to undergo these diverse rituals and ceremonies that could go on for days or months.

Sorana - My Maternal Grandfather

When I look at the riveting history of my maternal grandfather, I wonder if I would have really been born into this world and be named after him. I am informed that he was a renowned mason. But prior to venturing into masonry, he had joined the Catholic priesthood. When one becomes a Catholic priest, one leads a life of celibacy. However, my grandfather never graduated to become a priest. This happened because circumstances prevailing at home caused him to abandon the church mission midway.

This is how it happened. Being a young, muscular and energetic young man at the time when Christianity was still new in Gusii, my maternal grandfather was among the first converts to Catholicism. His interest to walk the journey of priesthood led him to a Catholic parish in Kampala, Uganda.

This religious sojourn did not amuse his father Mweberi, and for good reasons. My grandfather, Sorana, was the only son of his mother. In those days, most Gusii men including my great-grandfather had many wives.

Like in most African communities, sons maintained (and continue to have) a special place in the family as they carried the family lineage and heritage. Sons were also charged with taking care of their parents in old age.

Considering he was an only son, the hearts of my grandfather's parents sank when he left home. For several days and months, his father would not work, let alone eat or sleep peacefully. The old man's fears were perched on the fact that once his son joined priesthood, he would not marry and have a family. This carried with it huge cultural ramifications. In fact, it meant that the family lineage stared at an imminent and unavoidable end. This was perceived as an everlasting curse to the extended family. My great grandfather did not want to become the laughing stock of a religion he knew little about.

It was also during a period when Africans highly dreaded and avoided the colonial administrators of the time like a plague. Undeterred by these circumstances, the old man had no option other than directly face the then Kisii District Commissioner. Weary, teary and helpless, he explained to the British administrator his predicament and that of his extended family. My great grandfather must have made a compelling case regarding his son. This convinced the officer to write him an official letter bearing the British Queen's court of arms. My great grandfather then delivered the letter to the Parish in Kampala and, with that, he secured his son's release from becoming a priest.

I value my grandfather Sorana because I carry his name. I am also told that I have some of his character traits. This did not come as a surprise to me because the Abagusii believed that a child's character mimicked that of the person the child was named after. For that reason, few children were named after people with questionable reputation.

While away from home, my grandfather had acquired masonry skills and upon his return, he put these skills to full effect. In the process, he became a famous mason. To date, people marvel at the architectural vigour and mastery of my grandfather's time. His work helped build landmark houses some of which stand to this day. When one looks at these works of my grandfather, one agrees that they stand apart from the rest. The works include the oldest church building in Kisii, Nyabururu Catholic Parish. There is also a shop in his home area at Bonyunyu market. Both buildings imposingly stand strong to this day.

My Recollections as a Toddler

Although Kericho, where I was born, is still considered to be one of the greenest towns in Kenya, its current state is nothing close to what it was in the 1960s and 1970s. In fact, in the earlier years, Kericho was a small paradise, surrounded by sprouting canopies of a tropical forest that teemed with a myriad species of wild animals and indigenous birds. The area was characterized by lush, thick and flourishing indigenous tropical forest vegetation and tall savannah grassland which sandwiched the few tea farms of the time.

Currently, when one visits Kericho, its tranquil and picturesque green landscape is characterized with acres and acres of tea plantations. The breathtaking view of the beautifully manicured tea bushes stretch to the horizon and appear to touch the sky. Of course, there are spots of man-made forests largely comprising of eucalyptus trees. There are also buildings which are abodes for workers or that house the tea factories. These are the only key features that break one's view of the 'green gold' that the tea has become.

My father was an early convert to Catholicism, which made him relatively well-versed with religious and general contemporary issues of the time. The fact that he was a member of the tea workers' union, at a time when the country was under the colonial rule, attests to this fact. According to my father, at the time I was born, the wind of change in Kenya was in the air. The country was on the verge of achieving self-rule, following a fierce struggle that saw many detained, and others lose their lives.

The smell of victory was nigh. Trade unionists and other political elites of the time combed the tea estates, encouraging people not to relent in the struggle. Inevitably, Kenya was headed for self-governance. It was an opportunity for indigenous Kenyans to thrive in various spheres of life and be able to shape their destiny.

The firebrand trade unionists and politicians whose names I heard at the time included Tom Mboya, who later served as a minister in the independent government before he was assassinated. Others were Jomo Kenyatta who would later become independent Kenya's pioneer President, Oginga Odinga who became Kenyatta's Vice-President before the two fell out, Daniel Arap Moi who succeeded Kenyatta in 1978, Bildad Kagia a firebrand left leaning politician at the time, and another trade unionist Fred Kubai.

Many of these politicians belonged to the Kenya African National Union (KANU) led by Jomo Kenyatta. Others had ties to the Kenya African Democratic Union (KADU) led by Ronald Ngala and Moi. KANU and KADU were the dominant political parties. The others were smaller and did not command significant national following.

KANU and KADU leaders tried to outsmart each other. They packaged themselves as the liberators of the nation and sought to endear themselves to fellow Kenyans. They traversed the country holding rallies and counter rallies to the chagrin of the colonial establishment and bemusement of freedom-thirsty Kenyans.

My father would later tell me about some of these encounters. In one peculiar incident Moi (who was in KADU), who hailed from the expansive Rift Valley region where Kericho lies, arrived in Kericho town at the head of an entourage a day after KANU had held a ground-shaking rally at Kericho Green Stadium. During the visit, the future president was carrying a jerrican full of kerosene. In coded language, he uttered to his supporters that time was ripe for parasites (those not towing the KADU line) to be ejected from the Rift Valley.

In Kericho, Moi was literally at home. Despite this, he was given a cold reception. He addressed a stadium which was nearly empty. KANU had entered the blood streams of the people. It had become the most popular party. Indeed, it later went on to form the first independence government. And as history would have it, Moi and Ngala eventually wound up their party and joined KANU, a party which he would later claim that it would be in power for a hundred years.

A Place in the Sun

Whenever the morning sun dazzled in the horizon, its golden petals stretched outwards and into the rich blue sky. Then, the shiny layers of the sky kissed the ground, warming the morning dew upon which infants were trained to rise and make their initial clumsy steps. The invitation of a new day in Nyansakia appeared ordinarily pleasant. In Ekegusii, my native language, the soft morning sun is called *ensakia*. In the etymology of words therefore, this is where the name of our area (Nyansakia) is derived from. My guess is that those who gave the name to the place were influenced by the way the morning sun shone.

In my early years, there were many simple leisure activities for the children. One could be sitting under a tree, then; a bird carrying some piece of dry grass in its beak flew by. If one looked keenly, one could realize that the bird was building its nest. It then left again and returned with another piece of grass moments later. At the end of the day, it had its own brand new, beautifully woven nest. Now the nest was ready for the bird to lay eggs that it would incubate within time to become beautiful featherless chicks.

Children could tag along with their parents to the fields and help with what they could. Children were also sent on errands such as fetching water or food for the working crew. Boys were charged with taking care of the homestead's livestock. They ensured that the animals grazed without getting into farms and had their fill at watering places. Young children were always under the tutelage of older ones who in turn were under the tutelage of their parents and parents' peers.

Watching a bird build its nest may seem foolish. It was not. The key lesson from the bird's activity was that for one to succeed, one had to work hard and be patient. Even so, there was never a man or woman who had enough time to watch birds build their nests. When people worked, it was a taboo for one to appear still for long. When tilling the land, for instance, everyone had to keep working. Those who stood for too long instead of tilling or clearing the bush were shamed. They would be told that a bird might mistake them for a tree on which to perch. Being lazy was not an option unless one wanted to be cursed or condemned by the community. Hard work was the mantra of the community.

At the time of Kenya's independence in 1963, there were approximately 300,000 people in Gusii. That number has increased tenfold to over three million people today. This has put pressure on the once rich, fertile soils of the land. Cultural practices, like land inheritance, has diminished land holdings for many families and affected agricultural activities. Each homestead has a duty to divide and subdivide its land among the sons. The land is currently composed of small plots, yet the subdivision culture goes on unabated.

My place, like many others around it, was sparsely populated in the 1960s. I freely mingled with my peers and played games such as hide and seek in the fields. We chased butterflies, birds, hares and foxes. Sometimes we hunted birds of the air and roasted them for group consumption. We could also fish in the nearby Nyakorogoko River. During the heavy rain, the river swelled to the point of sweeping away domestic animals. The river would drain into the already giant Saosao River, which flowed in meanders and straights. It traversed through the rich agrarian plains and valleys of Gusii before crossing to Luo Nyanza and finally emptying its waters into Lake Victoria.

There were lush bushes, shrubs and thick natural forests especially at the hilltops overlooking our home. The forest canopy seemed to reach the sky and one could be forgiven for imagining that there was no other world beyond that horizon. It took me awhile to discover that there was a world beyond what I could see when I stood at our home.

The soil was rich and fertile. Crops like finger-millet, sorghum and cassava sprung like mushrooms. Within a few weeks of planting, the crops coloured the land green. There was always a bumper harvest. Families stored harvested grains in common granaries from whence they fed themselves throughout the year, each taking according to their needs. It was unheard of for a person in the community to sleep on an empty stomach when the neighbour had food in the store.

Unfortunately, most of the once broad rivers and sparkling springs have shrunk over time. This was inevitable with the unsupervised logging of water-friendly indigenous trees and replacing them with exotic ones like the eucalyptus tree species. Some indigenous trees have actually disappeared altogether. This has reduced the amount of rainfall the area receives and the quality of water available for domestic use. In yesteryears, Gusii was regarded as abundantly blessed. Some argued that Gusii was right under God's bathroom and since he bathed frequently, the water came down as torrential rains. Unlike today, rains were regular and heavier.

In my view, and this is an opinion shared by a number of researchers, Gusii should be the last part of Kenya to experience water shortage. The water levels have gone down to the extent that some springs disappear during dry spells and only reappear when it rains.

Once regarded as a rural area, Gusii is now a sprawling semi-urban sprawl. An aerial view of the countryside shows several roofs separated by fences that run across or parallel to the terrain. Due to connectivity to electricity in rural homes, an evening drive in some parts of Gusii may confuse a visitor to think it's a contiguous urban establishment.

Unwritten Destiny

My love for family has always been my measure of stability. It is from my family that I have nurtured my virtues and sense of purpose. My grandfather Otwori was a great man, according to family lore. His extended family belonged to a section of Abaochi sub-clan. They eventually migrated to Nyansakia in Kitutu after settling at present-day Boochi area. I will expound more about his character, charisma and legacy as the story unfolds.

For now, I have to reveal that my grandfather's towering muscular figure and deep voice reinforced his role as the family patriarch. Like many patriarchs of his time, he rooted for the unity of his family, a role he played very well.

I look back and wonder where the rains started beating modern families. Growing up at home was bliss and lovely since the family bond was strong. Additionally, child upbringing was a communal affair. Reprimanding a child for wrong-doing was not an abomination when any person older than the child did it. This is something no one can dare do today. Our society has since evolved and 'human right systems' have come to bear, undermining our social foundations.

As children, we enjoyed roaming from home to home, devouring meals together. Women took offence when they offered food and you refused. Unlike today when one takes care of only one's children, back in the day, mothers were eager to feed us and we were spoiled for choice. This kind of life made the children to be as generous as their parents. It also built a sense of camaraderie.

Various social and economic dynamics have influenced the change of behaviour. People have been compelled to cut down on the long family linkages. The family chain has become too weak at the joints and, in some cases, got disjointed altogether. Today, we have lost our greatest virtue of community. One would rather think of one's blood children and spouse, while one's siblings and even parents wallow in poverty, diseases and other forms of maladies.

I suspect that if my grandfather resurrects today, he would be taken aback by the status of our home area. The kind of life we lead today may make him want to go back and rest in permanent peace. At the time of his death, families worked in the farm as a group and, typically, had a common granary where the harvest was stored. The food belonged to all of them. From the store, each one took according to one's need. This is no longer the case as each family member wants his piece of land. The sub-division of the land resource has led to land sizes that have no meaningful economic value. The land is split due to inheritance practices but no conversation has arisen in Gusii that there is no more of the resource to be shared. Only education is the viable and formidable legacy that a parent can now leave for his or her children.

My grandfather Otwori had intense love for his family. His three sons had been blessed with notably light-skinned and energetic baby boys. The boys included me. He proudly called us *ebisicha bi'omotombe* (red hot poker tree flowers) because of our light skin colour. As most Gusii patriarchs, he was very proud of his family.

In many instances land was collectively owned and work was done communally in an arrangement called *egesangio* or *risaga*. However, my grandmother had shown my mother when she was newly married a parcel of land where she could grow whatever she wished. Even after this, as tradition demanded, my grandmother took her through an elaborate tutelage up to the time my mother was allowed to start cooking in her own house. This is unlike these days when a newly married couple can move to their own house and prepare their first meal without the blessings of the parents.

It is important to note that unlike now, marriage was a clan affair. This ensured that one got it right from the beginning. It was not even within imagination that a young man could take a walk, find a beautiful lady, seduce her and bring her home as a wife. Marriage had a clearly defined and intricate procedure. As a result, divorce, which is rampant these days, was very rare.

How my Parents Met

My parents would never have met were it not that a go-between, called *esigani* in Ekegusii, was involved. My grandparents had identified the go-between, or sponsor, and gave him the task of finding a suitable girl for my father to marry. It was after the sponsor did due diligence on the girl that the Otwori family, and other members of the lineage, organized for my parents' marriage.

In traditional Gusii society, the role of the *esigani* was onerous and enormous. The *esigani*, who could be a man or woman, had to find out the character of the lady. A lady who was either lazy or rude would hardly meet the cut for marriage to any respectable prospective suitor. If one hailed from a family with a history of vices such as witchcraft, sorcery, revenge, sexual immorality, murder or suicide, one was avoided like a plague. Such a person would be avoided and condemned to age in her parents' home without ever getting married.

By the time of my parents' marriage, Christianity had registered itself in the land. As such, the *esigani* was also required to consider the religious inclination of the girl. As luck would have it, my mother hailed from a family which proclaimed the Catholic faith like my father's.

After the initial introduction, my father was allowed to visit my mother's home in the company of his age mates. The visit, known as *ekerorano* Ekegusii, is a major milestone in the courtship process This visit was significant so they could meet the girl they planned to take home for a wife.

Interestingly, in traditional Gusii society, it was during this visit that the girl and her parents revealed their stand on the impending marital engagement. If they felt uncomfortable with the proposed relationship, they would show unpleasant behaviour. For instance, they would suddenly start sweeping the compound raising dust in the presence of visitors. They would also order the visitors to leave since they were 'derailing the family's activities' of the day. Where the delegation was viewed positively, it was warmly received and sumptuously fed.

Family stories indicate that my father's delegation was not met with resistance from his would-be in-laws. They were warmly received. Soon after, dowry and marriage negotiations started in earnest. My father's family paid sixteen heads of cattle and three goats, the going rate of dowry during the time, to seal the marriage. Now that the marriage had been blessed, the expected fruits were children. And the children were us.

****

By the early 1960s, my parents had settled down well as a couple within the broader extended family. They already had three kids including myself. As time passed, we could see the elderly in the community gather around a radio in our grandfather's compound. Jomo Kenyatta, who would become the first president of Kenya, had been released from prison and Britain was fast losing the battle of retaining Kenya as her colony. Kenyatta would lead Kenya into independence in 1963.

As I later connected, the people in our area were divided on whom, between Jomo Kenyatta and Jaramogi Oginga Odinga was best suited to steer the country forward. For instance, those who did not see Odinga to be the best bet argued that he was likely to introduce communism, which would make Kenyans a poorer lot.

In Gusii, firebrand politicians of the day including Lawrence Sagini, Zephaniah Anyieni, John Kebaso and Henry Nyabuto who are now all deceased became even more vocal. They would later sail through in elective politics, save for Nyabuto, who was allegedly assassinated in his prime age.

The independence celebrations were evident even in my grandfather's homestead. This was reinforced by the fact that he was among those Gusii warriors who battled it out against the British soldiers at the present-day Mosocho. The battlefield was not far from our home at Nyansakia. Here, several members of the King's African Rivals were killed in the combat with Gusii warriors. The former had moved in to establish control of Gusii by the colonial administration. The Gusii warriors suffered more than a hundred casualties during this adversarial encounter.

Even as Kenyans got independence from colonial rule, at individual level, they struggled with personal problems. My mother was not an exception. Yes, she had been shown where to grow her crops and she was doing it with all zeal and zest. Further, she had been blessed with children to feed and bring up and she was doing it well. However, there was a problem: she did not have control over her bumper harvests because it was put in the family's common granary.

She had managed to sell some of the grains and purchased some cattle, but much of it was under the control of her father-in-law, my grandfather. He was the family patriarch; his word and deed were final. This was an unpalatable arrangement to a forward-looking woman like my mother. However, she did not have the audacity to question the family establishment; such an act was unheard of at the time.

One day, my grandfather probably woke up on the wrong side of the animal skin he slept on, drove the heads of cattle my mother had bought and converted them into dowry for one of his sons. However disciplined, down to earth and loving my mother was, she could not stomach this, although she neither confronted nor reported him anywhere.

As tradition demanded, all livestock in the homestead belonged to the patriarch. It could have been an abomination for any woman, let alone my mother, to launch a direct complaint to my grandfather. Whenever my father visited the family, which was usually after one or two months, my mother would apprise him of the happenings. My father could not do much to unburden my mother. According to Gusii tradition, the family patriarch's word was the law in the home. His sons and especially daughters and daughters-in-law could never dream of challenging him.

However, at this time, people were getting enlightened. They were also being influenced by the Western way of life. My mother too was in toe. Having come from a Christian family and with formal education up to Class Three, she intuitively saw the unfairness in the family conduct. She was literally working for others and this was retrogressive in the dawn of a new Kenya. She had to make a decision. The decision would spell a new trajectory for her nuclear family.

Family Uncertainty

One morning, my mother woke me up as roosters crowed. She had lit a kerosene lamp. When I cleared my eyes and stretched, the lamp's smoke blew against the wall and soothed it. I did not enjoy leaving the comfort of the blanket, but my mother had partially opened the window and the morning wind found its way into the room. She told me that it was time for us to move out of the village to join our father again in Changoi Tea Estates in Kericho. This is the place where I was born. At this time, I was around five years old and had two siblings, Florence Obaga and the late Mary Moraa.

All along, my life had revolved around the friends I had grown up with in our neighbourhood in Nyansakia. I wondered how long we were going to take before coming back. This was a non-issue to my mother, going by the instructions she gave me that morning. As we had porridge for breakfast, I could hear birds of the air in frenzy, singing their morning melodies to welcome the new day.

The experience which lay ahead of me that day has stuck with me to date. I had never been in a vehicle, save for when I travelled from Kericho to my home, barely a month after I was born.

Christened *Nyabwansu*, the rickety mini-bus was the only one that plied the only murram road in our home area, picking travellers, enroute to Kericho. My heart beat unusually fast once the vehicle stopped and we got in. The bus was nearly full. Almost every seat had someone who appeared sleepy for the journey and unwilling to create space for new entrants. There was luggage stowed on the walkway, under the seats and on racks on either side of the aisle.

We sat near a window and the hills yonder yellowed in readiness to unmask the morning sun. Then the driver hooted and, in a flash, started the engine. My heart skipped a beat when I realized that, as the vehicle zoomed ahead, trees and the entire landscape seemed to race in the opposite direction. I screamed, fearing that I was in danger, to the bemusement of our fellow travellers who assured me that we were safe. I came to learn later in a science lesson that stationary things seem to move when you are riding in a car because motion is relative. Science tells me that when you are in a car and looking out of it, it seems as if the stationary things are moving because one feels as if he or she is staying still, but in reality, it is the other way around.

During the journey, we covered miles and miles of murram to get to our destination. The road was rough and the bus navigated through potholes, ascended and descended the terrain my anxiety grew by the minute until I unconsciously fell asleep. When I was woken up, we were already in Kericho town, disembarking. The journey had lasted several hours.

Everything at the estate looked different from what I knew back in Nyansakia. Workers and their families lived in semi-permanent houses and even before my father ushered us into his house, I felt homesick. I wondered if I was ever going to get a chance to sit with my grandfather and cousins around a fire in the evening. I was worried whether I was ever going to share a meal accompanied with traditional brew while listening to tales. After dinner, this being my first day ever to sleep on a mattress spread on a bed, I slept soundly. Back home, we slept on an animal skin spread on the floor and we were pleasantly comfortable with it.

****

In beautiful Kericho of the 1960s, the tea plantations were not as extensive as they are now. Then, the plantations were juxtaposed with thick forested indigenous canopies. In the trees, buzzards, kites, quails, crested cranes, swift birds among other birds of the air tweeted all day. Animals like monkeys, baboons, antelopes and even leopards were easy to spot. This is unlike now when perhaps you will only see a few monkeys. Most indigenous trees have also been replaced with tea plantations and eucalyptus trees. The fast maturing hardwoods are ideal sources of fuel used to dry the tea at the many factories.

For the first few days in Kericho, I was out of place. The children who were my age were from various ethnic backgrounds. They included Luo, Gikuyu, Kalenjin and Luhya. I had never uttered a Kiswahili or English sentence. As well, these children were strangers to Ekegusii, which was the only language I was familiar with. Issues of language barrier set in as they spoke to me in Kiswahili. When they discovered that I was incapable of responding, they laughed. This annoyed me and I pelted them with stones in retaliation.

One day, I accidentally hit a girl with a stone. When word of my indiscretion reached my father, he summoned me to lie down for a heavy spanking. This made me hate Kericho even more. However, I did not have anything to do to find the peace and fun I left in my village.

I was enrolled in Standard One at Changoi Primary School in 1964. Here, I got into more trouble since teachers used either Kiswahili or English to teach. A majority of the learners were comfortable with it, making me feel like a fish out of water. I ended up hating school and soon abandoned it. I look back at the irony of life and laugh. That I dropped out of school temporarily yet I could one day become a professor is quite an interesting turn of events.

To address my predicament, my sister Florence was withdrawn from her school back in Nyansakia to join us. Florence was in Class Two and once she came, I got comfortable since we could go to Changoi Primary School together. Her 'protection' enabled me to adapt to the school environment and with time, I was able to communicate with other pupils in Kiswahili.

My father had interacted with people from various backgrounds due to Christianity and his job. This was unlike a number of his peers back at home. So, he took education seriously. In fact, my father enrolled himself for adult classes at the estate to keep himself abreast with knowledge in literacy and numeracy.

Due to these classes, he became very good in reading the Catholic rosary and liturgy. Within a short time, he became a Catechist whose main role was teaching converts and preparing them for baptism. This placed him at a higher social standing in Changoi and its environs than before. Compared to other members of his family, my father had gotten earlier exposure to modernity, especially as concerns the value of formal education.

At some stage, my father who was the second born in his family, thought of influencing his brothers to join him in Kericho to get formal education. Although they came, they disappointed him. They abandoned studies and retreated to the village to get married. This compelled my father to rededicate his energies to the education of his own children.

I salute my late father. He wanted the best out of us. He gave his all to give us a foundation for life. He had made a blackboard and would buy chalks and books to teach us basics like the vowels *(a e i o u)* and the alphabet. However, I appeared to disappoint him because my sister did better than me in studies. This often landed my backside in trouble. He also pinched my ears and rewarded my sister. This made me dislike school even more.

In retaliation, I could do the unimaginable like soiling my uniform early in the morning to have an excuse of not going to school. I became riotous and withdrawn until my mother intervened. From then on, my father toned down the bashing and my love for school was rekindled. I could now play with my peers and do all that appertained to being a lad in a school environment.

With my parents and siblings in Kericho, we were home away from home. While my father worked as a carpenter, he gave my mother some seed money to start a tailoring business. With the capital, she bought three sewing machines and hired three tailors who were of Luo origin. The trio became renowned tailors in the town.

In Kenya, it is often argued that each community has its unique traits. For instance, the Kikuyu and the Gusii people are perceived as being good in business and money making initiatives. In the same breath, the Luo people are believed to be perfectionists in what they engage in. Be it as it may, the Luo community has over the years produced some of the best doctors, teachers, lawyers, professors, politicians, carpenters, tailors and mechanics. Perhaps these stereotypes stem from the effects of colonial rule and are over-generalizations of unique characteristics of the Kenyan people.

My mother's tailoring business became a success story. There was a huge and ready market for the ready-made clothes.

My mother would purchase materials then engage more tailors to sew the clothes that she sold to workers. She grew into a skilled entrepreneur who saw a window of opportunity every time workers got paid at the end of the month. She made good money from the enterprise and encouraged my father to have an account with the Standard Chartered Bank for their savings. As banking history would have it, my parents introduced me to bank with the Standard Chartered Bank where I still have an account.

When I critically look at the character of my father, I see that he was an African socialist. He would occasionally gift his visitors with the clothes sewn by the three tailors. This was contrary to the spirit of entrepreneurship, which ran in my mother's blood. It therefore meant that they would occasionally be silently at loggerheads, although my mother's school of thought prevailed in the long run.

Our New Abode

Our studies in Kericho were soon to be halted. Before Kenya got independence, white settlers occupied huge tracts of land that were exceedingly fertile. The large fertile expanses of lands were referred to as the White Highlands. The tracts were in areas like Laikipia, Nakuru, Nyandarua, Sotik and Kericho. Others were in Trans Nzoia and Uasin Gishu in the North Rift.

With the imminent exit of the colonialists in 1963 and 1964, indigenous Kenyans enjoyed their restored freedom. The tracts of land previously occupied by the white settlers were being disposed of. In a bid to enhance government policy called African socialism, the state encouraged Kenyans to purchase the land and engage in meaningful agricultural activities.

My parents' bank savings enabled them acquire 20 acres of land in Borabu Settlement Scheme which lies astride the current Nyamira-Bomet counties' border. Although my father was particularly not for the idea, he later accepted it anyway.

In 1965, my mother, three sisters, my newly born brother and I moved to our new land. We had literally moved into a forest. Several indigenous trees stood there while animals like foxes and hyenas roamed freely. I have to salute my mother for showing unmatched resilience and big-heartedness that was uncommon of women back in the day. She strove to make the new home habitable by clearing the bushes, fencing and building a hut. She planted tea on two acres of the land and brought in a number of dairy cattle to start our lives off. The tea bushes my mother planted are still there even as I share my story today. They are now owned by my step-mothers who my father married following the death of my mother.

Our next challenge was getting a school for us to carry on with our studies. The nearest one was Tindereti Primary School, which was about 12km away from our home and was accessible after trekking a steep terrain. The school is among the oldest in the area.

The long distance meant that we had to wake up unusually early, navigate the path through bushes to be in school before eight. My sister joined Class Three. I was in Class Two. I remember that, for the first time in my early school life, I topped in my class. This was largely so because I came from an urban school in Kericho with higher standards compared to Tindereti, which was deep in the rural area. It was my turn to get gifts from my parents for the star performance. I was happy and encouraged.

However, the long distance we covered every morning and evening was a concern to our parents. This challenge was solved with the establishment of Mecheo Primary School, which I joined in Standard Four. The school was nearer home. Four years later, I sat for the CPE, obtaining a C+ (plus) which was an average performance.

Adjusting to the new environment at Borabu Settlement Scheme evoked both good and bad memories. However, the sad memories outweigh the good ones. It was a baptism of fire at personal level.

During weekends and holidays, I had to accompany my uncle to the grazing fields then to a constructed dam whose water came from a spring. The water point has now shrunk substantially because of pollution from increased human activities. The activities include encroachment of the riparian area and siltation from farms upstream. The forest destruction and pollution comes from the regular use of chemicals in farming. Some of these get washed into the spring, which dries up during the low rain season. The aquatic life is totally messed up.

Walking under giant trees, the grassland bushes and riparian vegetation was a scary experience. It was even scarier when my uncle tasked me with driving our herd of about twenty cows to and from the river. This is what he did one day before I fully acclimatized myself to the new environment.

Some of the cattle hurried ahead while others dispersed to opposite directions. Then, I met some neighbours' children who insulted and pelted me with stones. However, much as I was agitated and scared, I did not have an option but withstand the harassment. By the time I got all the animals on track and drove them home, the sun was about to reach its destination for the day and pave way for darkness. This earned me a memorable spanking from my uncle.

As a child, I also felt isolated because homes in the settlement scheme were far apart. I could only find my peers and play with them in school. Nevertheless, my early introduction to farm work, like tilling the land using oxen, weeding and picking tea, prepared me to be a responsible person. It also made me appreciate the reward of hard work.

I witnessed my mother turn the land full of acacia trees, savannah grassland and stumps to a farmland. She then erected a barbed wire fence around it to mark out the boundaries of our land and this was an eye opener to me. My mother put in a lot of effort to transform the virgin land into a cultivable resource. This made some men openly envious and would retort that, "*abasacha bande ebakonywoma abakungu bagokora emeremo buna chibarasi* (some men marry women who work like horses)" and my father was one of them.

Even as we adjusted and coped with the new life, my father who we had left behind in Kericho, married another wife. When he brought her to Borabu, my mother welcomed her. Such a gesture is near impossible now in most communities in Kenya because polygamy is regarded old fashioned and unacceptable. However, the new woman (my step-mother) was relatively weak and would not cope with the busy hard working environment our home was. After a few months, she secretly packed her belongings and left, never to return. My father would later blame it on my mother despite her innocence. An attempt by my father to locate the woman who left became a task in futility and he eventually gave up.

Getting late to school earned one several strokes of the cane. I highly dreaded all these. In the evening, we got home and worked again in the farm. This instilled in me the virtues of hard work and resilience. At age 12, I could pick tea, herd cattle and lead the oxen in ploughing the land. Presently, it may appear wild for a parent to subject a school going child to such strenuous work, morning and evening, especially on school days. Activists call it child labour or child abuse. I view it as training; good training.

Humble Schooling

When I reflect on my life at Mecheo Primary School, I conclude that I succeeded through God's grace. While some teachers were good and devoted to their vocation, the school had some teachers who were very lax. Some were immoral and semi-illiterate. They poorly attended lessons and seemed to have reduced caning us into a cherished hobby. The wild caning made some of my fellow pupils either shift schools or abandon schooling for good.

I must emphasise that sexual immorality was high and some teachers were the culprits propagating it. They took advantage of young and innocent school girls, some as young as fourteen years old. The amorous teachers impregnated them and unashamedly got away with it. Some of the girls ran short of options and got married to them as second or third wives despite their tender age.

Some of the teachers' impunity was outrageous and legendary. I remember there was a teacher who was accused of impregnating three girls at once. Nothing was done to him despite the uproar because he managed to bribe his way to freedom. The teacher was very arrogant and would even dare the parents to have their daughters name the newborns after him. This very teacher was completely daft and I cannot remember learning anything positive from him.

Ironically, it appeared that some girls competed for the attention of the philandering teachers. In one year, nearly fifty of them were impregnated by teachers who should have been their second parents. Nevertheless, the alleged teachers never paid for it even as they ruined the lives of innocent girls. Up to this day, it baffles me that these evils went on in a school which was and is still sponsored by the Seventh Day Adventist (SDA) church.

****

Although colonialists had left, it appeared like Kenyans were still nursing fears of allegiance to them. If not, this was a clear sign of brainwashing through the colonial rule. In the assembly every morning, we could sing:

> (London is burning) X 2
>
> (Look yonder) X 2
>
> (Fire fire) X 2
>
> But there's no water...

This followed with the Ekegusii version of the song;

> (London nkoyia ere) X 2
>
> (Rigereria ng'umbu) X 2
>
> (Omorero omorero) X 2
>
> Korende mache taiyo...

Classrooms at the school had mud walls and floors. Often, we were infested with jiggers since we walked barefoot. As much as wearing shoes to school was not illegal, most of our parents did not deem it necessary for us to have a pair or two of shoes. Basically, it was perceived as a luxury during that time. Even so, some teachers never cared that our feet provided residence for the irritating parasites. Some teachers saw themselves superior and intimidated parents whenever they raised concern over their conduct.

I also recall that there was covert segregation along religious denominations. We as Catholics appeared to be out of place in a school that was sponsored by the SDA Church. This covert segregation along religious lines exists even now in a number of schools in Kenya. Some parents can eject a newly posted teacher out of their school on the basis of his denomination. Interventions by government, like the delocalization of teachers, appear to fix this challenge.

The religious discrimination was real to the extent that my friend was once beaten up by his father after he found him playing with me, a Catholic. This compromised my love for education for a number of years, up to upper primary when I woke up to the reality that education was the only thing that took me to the school.

As I observed earlier, I obtained a C+ during my first attempt. That was in 1972 and I was among the top ten performers that year. I was supposed to join secondary school the following year but I did not due to a severe skin disease attack.

When I went back to Mecheo to retake my CPE the following year, I worked even harder and scored grade A. This secured me a place at Itibo Boys' High School, one of the promising secondary schools in Kisii then.

From my days in Mecheo, I recall one Mr. Enock Bogita who was the most devoted teacher. Through his efforts, maths became my favourite subject. I also remember another teacher who handled English which he was not good at. He could insult us "*motichete buna emetimbiri y'enchogu* (you are thick like an elephant's back orifice)".

Through the intervention of some parents like Omosa, Mabea, Nyakundi, Ooga and my father, Mecheo was later streamlined to become a good school. These are the parents who raised their concerns compelling District Education Officers to hold a stormy crisis meeting at the school. The parents accused some teachers of unmatched incompetence and promiscuity forcing the education office to transfer errant ones.

The teachers were replaced by devoted ones including Mr. Henry Nyariki who came in as the Head Teacher. Under his stewardship, sanity was restored at the school. The school could from then on walk in the motto of our sponsor, the SDA Church.

Some notable strides which have transformed our education sector include the enactment of the Sexual Offences Act, abolishment of corporal punishment and improved training of teachers. I strongly detest corporal punishment at home or school. It created an intimidating environment where no student could dare question authority. One was meant to obey in fear and respect. It was a very undemocratic form of punishment because it created an impression that, as a student, you were there to be seen and not to be heard. Surely, this was not a proper strategy of guiding children. In retrospect, teachers took the proverb; 'spare the rod and spoil the child' out of context.

As much as caning made us to think twice about our behaviours, it still was not justifiable. It promoted a culture of conformity and killed creativity, adventure and the desire to discover. It undermined the very cardinal reasons children go to school.

However, I can say that not all teachers were lax and/or badly behaved. We had several teachers who were highly committed to their work. These teachers used to go out of their way to teach us during holidays, especially those pupils in upper classes. The teachers would also teach us during the evening and morning preps. As already mentioned, a notable teacher from the time is Enock Bogita who was a highly dedicated maths teacher. Other devoted teachers like Ezekiel Anyona, Tabitha Ogechi and Peter Maina also did their best to teach and shape our characters.

These dedicated primary school teachers played a critical role in laying a good academic foundation for us. This was particularly for students who were focused and dedicated in their studies. In overall, these teachers were extremely strict and made it clear that any form of wayward behaviour would not go unpunished.

Patriarch Otwori, my Pillar

We all come from a specific family tree. The beauty of traditional African families was that they were bound by strong kinfolk that transcended generations. This is no longer the case in many families now due to change in lifestyles. Modernity, exploration, urbanization, and education, among other factors, have weakened these family bonds.

A lot of members of my family influenced my life trajectory. Of these, my parents and paternal grandfather made a significant impact on my life. It will be a great disservice if I fail to share how their choices in life influenced mine.

My grandfather Otwori's story interests me in monumental proportions. Family history has it that Otwori's great-grandfather, Mokoro, was a Maasai who was found abandoned sitting at a fireside. This was during the infamous Ngarora war that took place around 1820. It involved the Maasai on one side and Abagusii on the other. The inter-ethnic skirmishes happened majorly as a result of cattle theft.

Culturally, the Maasai believed that all cattle belonged to them. As such, Maasai warriors armed themselves to the teeth and would cross the porous Kisii border deep in the night to carry out their raids. To them, the raids were principally intended to capture cattle and return 'their property' home.

The Ngarora war started with an initial attack near the Mara River. There is archaeological evidence showing that Abagusii had settled around the Mara River. The evidence includes pottery associated with the community, which was found at the banks of the river. Here, the Siria clan of the Maasai attacked Abagusii, compelling the latter to retreat to a place called Ngarora in the present Trans-Mara region. It is interesting to observe that this place was named Ngarora after the killing of a famous Gusii warrior called Ongarora. The killing of this lead warrior by the Maasai raiders made the Gusii to retreat from the area. Even to this day, the area occasionally gets volatile as locals fight for land and livestock.

It is during one of these clashes that Gusii warriors repulsed their tormentors and found a boy, about two years of age, abandoned at a fireplace. As it was the norm, warriors neither killed children nor women. Today women and children are vulnerable to conflict outbreaks and in most cases bear the brunt of conflict. Recent examples include the rampant xenophobic attacks in South Africa where women and children frequently get attacked and maimed.

Instead of harming the child, the Gusii warriors carried him home. This alone was a sign of triumph against their aggressors. The child was given to a woman who had no children, after the Gusii elders undertook several magical-religious rituals as culture dictated then. The rituals were meant to cleanse the child against any bad omen. In the rituals, the elders also beseeched the ancestors to accept the alien boy to be a member of the community.

After the magical-religious ceremony, the child was sprinkled with blood and milk on the face and neck. Then, a copper ring was put round his hand to protect him from any malevolent forces. As the instructions were, the bangle was never to be removed unless for re-adjustment as the child grew up.

Family history has it that the left-handed child grew into a skilled warrior who wielded spears and arrows like no other. He fast became an asset to the community and would fight at the frontlines. Every time they went to war he rarely missed a target. Whenever warriors from Gusii went to war, this prized asset took the battlefront position. He was a sharp shooter, very efficient in using spears and arrows. However crude, spears and arrows were the only efficient weapons the communities had then, and skilled warriors rarely missed the target.

The fact that he was left-handed was an added advantage. Many warriors especially from the rival community were right-handed. The rivals could not effectively time and dodge arrows propelled from the left hand. I have a feeling that the narrative is correct and I may have inherited the trait as I am left handed too. I am informed that this trait is genetically transmitted. It could be the reason why quite a number of people in our lineage are left-handed.

Mokoro helped the Omogusii warriors win a contest after another against the Maasai. In turn, this made him famous and his prowess reverberated across the land. When Abagetutu clan of Gusii had problems with their Luo neighbours, Mokoro was brought in to give a hand. This is how Mokoro migrated from his original home in Boochi area of Bomachoge and came to Kitutu Chache. He would later settle in Nyansakia area, never to return to Boochi.

The bangle that Mokoro wore became an heirloom of the family. After he died, it was passed on to his first grandson. When the grandson died, the treasured item was given to his grandson, my grandfather Otwori who wore it to his deathbed in 1974. One of my uncles dared to break the chain and selfishly claimed the bangle for himself. When he attempted to wear it on his wrist, he fell sick and suffered memory lapse. In the process, the bangle got lost. Clan elders had to be called upon to perform a ritual where they asked our ancestors for forgiveness of the transgression. He only recovered after the ritual.

Like his great-grandfather, Otwori became a great warrior of his time and took part in many battles on behalf of the community. Gusii folk history has it that Otwori took part in the Saosao war in 1892 as one of the lead warriors.

His skills would later prove useful in the Abagusii resistance war against the British colonial soldiers. In the emerging combat, Gusii warriors were able to repulse British Colonial Soldiers, the King's African Rifles (KAR). Following this unexpected resistance, British soldiers retreated and sought reinforcement before re-launching the attack. Historically, this was a great achievement for Abagusii considering that British soldiers had superior firearms compared to the spears and arrows of African warriors. It was only after the colonial soldiers received reinforcement that they killed hundreds of people with Abagusii losing good warriors especially from the Bonchari and Bogetutu clans, who were at the epicentre of the Gusii resistance.

Hot in the heels of the bloody attack, Otwori and his fellow warriors waylaid the British soldiers at the present day Mosocho. Although they suffered heavy casualties, they were able to recover over 2000 herds of cattle that had been captured by colonial soldiers. During the attack, the first Kisii District Commissioner, Geoffrey Alexander Northcote, was nearly killed. This information correlates well with a research I carried and published under the title *The Untold Story of the Gusii of Kenya: Survival Techniques and Resistance to the Establishment of British Colonial Rule*.

As my grandfather Otwori would later tell me, with a lot of retrogression Gusii warriors were majorly defeated because they were fighting an enemy with sophisticated weaponry. At first, and unknowingly, the warriors did not regard guns to be dangerous weapons as they appeared to be unique walking sticks. Gusii warriors ended up dying in scores when British soldiers fired and felled them in their numbers. The surviving and wounded warriors could later retort, *"twakaga n'erisosu aani n'omorero* (we thought it was harmless. Apparently, it is fire)" in reference to the dangerous weapons.

Otwori's Forced Adventures

By the time the war ended, almost the entire clan of Abaking'oina had been wiped out and most of their precious livestock had been captured by colonial administrators. From then on, Otwori became a marked man as the case was with most of the other men of his age. One day, he got captured and was taken to offer forced labour during the construction of the Nakuru-Kericho road.

During my interactions with my grandfather, he revealed that the work was torturous and many of the African labourers died from the exacting physical labour. Life in captivity was unbearable.

He recalled how one day, as usual, the siren woke him up in the morning. He had a fever and did not want to leave his bed to go to work. This annoyed the foreman who came to his bed and slashed his back with a whip made out of a hippopotamus' skin. The pain seared through his body like a branding iron. He was unable to resist the urge to revenge.

In a flash, Otwori pounced out of his bed like a tiger, held the foreman at the neck and strangled him. As fate would have it, this happened at Kericho, the very place we could later stay.

When he came to his senses from the rage, the foreman's body was lying lifeless before him. My grandfather quickly decided to escape from captivity in the labour camp and trace his way home. It was one of the riskiest things a human being could do at that time. There were no vehicles, no clear roads and wild animals roamed the land. Additionally, the distance from Kericho to Kisii on foot was not practically achievable.

Nevertheless, his fighting spirit told him to take the risk. For days on end, he trekked in the morning cold and in the scorching sun, occasionally stopping to pluck wild fruits to eat or quench his thirst whenever he came by a river. In the evenings, he climbed on a tree, perched himself there and slept.

When he finally made it home, voices of victory swept through the village. Community members gathered in his home to feast and praise him in song and dance. But unknown to them, Otwori's stay was short-lived. Soon, he would be recaptured and driven back to the labour camp where he would spend several months away from his family.

This time, he was taken to construct the Mai Mahiu-Narok road. The environment was worse than the one he had encountered in Kericho. As it was his streak, he continued to go against the establishment. Although he was physically in captivity, his mind was at home with his people. He never stopped looking for a chance to re-join his kinsmen!

One morning, as he later narrated to me, the labourers were summoned to clear the bushes. Even as my grandfather seemed to be energetic and enthusiastic to do the job, he was pretending. At the back of his mind, he was looking for a chance to escape. That chance came when the foreman barked at him. Agitated, my grandfather lifted his fork and hit him hard. The man fell backwards as my grandfather took to his heels. That marked the start of another journey back to his ancestral land. It took him one and half months to get to Nyansakia.

When he was recaptured for the third time, he was to be taken to fight in the First World War. This was in 1915. But what happened this time is a story that has been told and retold, and I will be glad to see it being retold for many years to come.

This time, his elder brother Obabi stunned all and sundry when he said that he was going to the war on my grandfather's behalf. This sacrifice was unheard of. It was a favour to be repaid later. Such a selfless decision was rare even in an

African community where people were close-knit and cared for one another. They wished Obabi well as he stepped out to join the war. But as misfortune would have it, he was killed by the German soldiers at Tanga in the present-day Tanzania.

It was well understood that when an African warrior went to fight in the World War, chances of coming home alive were embarrassingly low unless one was destined to go to war and come back alive. In rare cases where a warrior returned the community welcomed him with celebrations.

Obabi had tasked his brother Otwori to take care of his newly wedded wife while he went to war. Indeed, Otwori lived up to his promise. Upon the death of Obabi, he took care of his elder brother's wife and sired children for his lineage. Further, he helped the widow to raise the children until the first born married. It was after Otwori assisted the first born son to marry by paying his dowry that he was also able to marry his own wife. This was necessary because although he fathered children with his elder brother's wife, culturally they belonged to his departed brother's lineage.

If this was not an act of love, then I don't know what it was! But all I recall is that in all my interactions with my grandfather, he fondly talked about his elder brother who sacrificed his life so that his younger brother could live and carry on with the family lineage.

I believe that my grandfather had a very rebellious spirit against atrocities perpetuated by colonialists and collaborators from the community. This seems to have been the case with most Gusii men who had witnessed the atrocious acts of the earlier colonial administrators. These intruders destroyed entire villages, killed people, torched houses and raped women. Grandfather Otwori learnt war tactics such as aiming and hitting targets with a spear or an arrow from the mature warriors when he joined the *ebisarate* (special encampments occupied by the warriors of the community). This is where warriors honed their war skills, which prepared them to face and defeat their aggressors in times of conflict.

When Otwori met the love of his life Kemunto who would become my grandmother, there was evidently a yawning age gap. Even so, my grandfather loved her unceasingly and never took in another wife as some of his peers did. With my youthful eyes, I could see the love that bound the couple together. He never rebuked my grandmother openly. Instead, he addressed her as *Mosubati Bw'Orang'o* (Orang'o's daughter) with so much pride and glow in his eyes.

My grandmother's father Orang'o Ondieki was a prominent Gusii elder in the Abaking'oina sub-clan of the broader Abagetutu clan. He was revered and liked by many due to his social standing in the community. He had a large family which he managed with a lot of dexterity and understanding. This made him attract respect as a family patriarch and community elder.

My grandfather underwent a number of challenges in his life. Many of his relatives died when their livestock were taken and their community was attacked by incoming colonial soldiers. He was also targeted by colonialists who captured him twice and subjected him to hard labour. Despite of his tender age, he was tasked to take care of his brother's wife, delaying his own marriage for several years.

Due to this, by the time he started a family, he had not accrued reasonable resources. He had to start from scratch with his youthful wife, my grandmother. They struggled to raise a herd of cattle. Blessings came his way; my grandmother bore him seven sons and three daughters, including my late father.

During my interactions with my grandfather, I learnt that he was a principled and honest man. He disliked rumour mongers and gossipers. Every time he met one he would condemn them with his favourite catchphrase; *"ochaga 'nkoba ibere chikomesere,"* loosely translated, "may violent thunder strike you!"

Otwori upheld traditions and brought up his family on the grounds of *chinsoni* (Abagusii's standard behaviour) as much as he was a Catholic convert. In true sense of the word,

Christianity never impacted him much. Since he strictly followed Gusii culture and tradition, he embarrassed the Rangenyo Parish priest by refusing to remove his bangle to be baptized. He instead walked out of the church never to return. The bangle was removed only when he died in 1974.

Sometimes I miss the good company of my late grandfather and his art of narrating stories. Perhaps what I should have stopped doing with him if he were still alive, was consuming traditional brews and singing *emeino* (traditional songs). I also spent time with him as a young adult whenever he visited us at our second home in Borabu.

Whenever he came to Borabu, he assumed authority as the family patriarch. To my bemusement, he would order my father around in our homestead. This left us bemused because at his family level, my father was an authority unto himself. As tradition had it, my grandfather addressed me as his brother and we were awed whenever he addressed his son as *omoisia oyo* (this lad) and my father would respond in the affirmative, promptly.

Despite his strict respect for Gusii tradition, my grandfather showed his love for education. He had seen that those who got formal education had good jobs in the offices and earned a salary at the end of the month. Therefore, whenever he saw me with a book, he would tell me: *"momura ominto, n'amatonetone ayuo ya Abasongo okorigereria? Igo imbuya kegima."* By this he meant that he was encouraged whenever he saw me studying. He also inquired about my performance in school and encouraged my parents to give me presents whenever I did well.

A Great Woman in My Early Life

In his book, *Ethics in a Permissive Society,* William Barclay says that:
> There are many definitions of man/woman and in the end it may well be true to say that man/woman is naturally a working animal. In every life, there are times for doing nothing. It may be an excellent thing if at some time in every man's life there was such a period; but over the years, man/woman was

meant to do something, and in the end he will not be happy unless s/he does.

My late mother Teresia Kwamboka was a great woman. Mama had a big heart! I have to admit that in my entire life, I have never come across a woman who commits herself to her work the way Mama did. She was blessed with intelligence, wisdom, courage and natural beauty in equal measure.

Her early life must have prepared her for later challenges. Her father Sorana, who abandoned Catholic priesthood to marry, was a mason and wealthy man by the standards of the time. He died at a tender age in 1945.

Sorana is chronicled in the folk history of his home area as the first man to build a permanent house. Some of his best works are the oldest churches in the parishes of Nyabururu and Rangenyo. He erected some of the first brick shops in Bonyunyu trading centre near his home at Embonga. People still marvel at the distinct architectural design and soundness of the structures. They contain heritage and serve as historical landmarks for many people in Gusii.

It makes me proud to say that I am the grandson of an enterprising man who introduced water-powered mills in Gusii. The mills ground finger millet as well as maize. Although dilapidated, one of the mills still stands to this day along the Charachani River, at a place called *Ekeera gia Sorana* (Sorana's Waterfall).

Through the various businesses he started, Sorana became a wealthy person of his time. In fact, community lore has it that he was the first person to be spotted with colonial currency at a time when barter trade was the norm. At a time when many in the community walked barefoot, my grandfather dressed smartly in American khaki trousers and shoes. He became the reference point of the elite of his time in Embonga area and beyond. Another one of his strengths was his ability to read and lead others in saying the Catholic rosary and the liturgy.

It was rather unfortunate that the hand of death took him at a tender age of 37 years. However, it should be noted that the angel of Satan beckoned Sorana in unclear circumstances. Stories abound that he was either bewitched or poisoned, basically to end his shining star. Sadly, it was some extended family members who carried the ugly tag of harming one of their own. However, this assertion should be qualified with the fact that there was no way of proving of these unfortunate allegations.

Although I never witnessed his death, my mother divulged to me that the family was devastated to the core with signs that bordered on witchcraft. At times, when the family woke up in the morning, they found dead lizards, rats and snakes plus other paraphernalia, believed to be witchcraft at their doorstep. While my grandmother and the children would panic, my grandfather would downplay the whole scenario by sprinkling the malevolent items with holy water and reading the rosary. He then invoked the name of the Virgin Mary after burning the paraphernalia.

I have never seen a witch in my life and I am not looking forward to seeing one. Their actions border on supernatural malevolence and are incomprehensible to many. For instance, my mother told me that after the mysterious death of her father, she witnessed unruliness propagated by members of the extended family who should have stood with them in mourning.

Some members of the extended family allegedly broke into my grandmother's home. They made away with several items including clothes, a radio, money, cattle, the stalled watermills and other valuables which belonged to her father. When the widow and her children protested, they were clobbered and harshly rebuked. And this marked the unfortunate start of the fall of the promising Sorana lineage.

My mother sadly recalled how some of her siblings, Abuga and Mweberi, soon followed their father to the grave mysteriously. Her mother got visibly frustrated and sought solace in drinking. This compelled my mother to flee home with her younger brother Onyangi, who is still alive. They moved to stay with their maternal grandmother Maria Kiriago at Ekerenyo in North Mugirango.

Overcoming Initial Barriers

My late mother had to persevere great suffering for her own sake and that of her younger brother, Onyangi. At her grandmother's home in Ekerenyo, my mother ran errands and over time became skilled in chores such as milking cattle, working in the *shamba* and making traditional brew. These challenges made her strong and wise at a tender age. At this time, my mother was around 14 years old.

A time came for my mother and her brother to leave their maternal grandmother's home. They did not have a choice because tradition did not provide any. Tradition demanded that a boy should not be circumcised at his maternal grandmother's home. Onyangi was ripe for circumcision but at the wrong place for the ceremony.

My uncle who was nurtured by Mama would not have survived if she was not there for him. Uncle told me that due to the demise of their father and the drunkenness of their mother, his sister became his salvation.

Ironically, it was their very paternal uncles who organized for my mother's marriage. However, they seem to have done so with ulterior motives because the herds of cattle that were given as bride price did not benefit the intended people. My mother's uncles subdivided the animals amongst themselves. They also took my grandfather's land and left his widow helpless.

I cannot blame culture for all these unfortunate incidences. Some of my mother's paternal uncles claimed to be Christians, yet they did not hesitate to subject their brother's family to unnecessary suffering. Perhaps Christianity had substantially eroded the concept of extended families that glued people together. In this regard, the colonial and Christian influences negated what our forefathers cherished; family bonds.

The challenges my mother faced acted as a springboard for her later life. Although relatively young (she was 18), my mother got married when she was strong willed, focused and aware that life can offer its share of challenges. She learnt that it was upon her to lay a strong foundation for her family.

She therefore grabbed opportunities that came her way and through these efforts she contributed to the positive transformation of her family. Although my parents never became very rich, we never lacked what we needed.

Mama had rare entrepreneurial skills; perhaps due to the early loss of her father and the experiences she faced which, in turn, honed her business skills. This is what enabled her to start the tailoring business in Kericho. The business later gave birth to our second and permanent home in Borabu Settlement Scheme.

Probably, the purchase of the 20 acres of land at Borabu was the turning point for our family in terms of property ownership and economic empowerment. Unlike back in Nyansakia where my grandfather was the family patriarch and had strict control of family resources, my parents were now able to use the land they had acquired the way they deemed fit.

The amount of work my mother did amazes me to this day. From building our first hut, fencing the land, planting tea, introducing grade cattle and subdividing the grazing area into paddocks it was a gruelling undertaking. At times, she could carry tea leaves or huge bags of pyrethrum and walk a long distance to the collection centre. She taught me the spirit of hard work and that I must earn what is duly mine, only after doing genuine work with commitment. In doing all these, she laid a strong foundation for us not to live a life of want.

There is a saying which is popular amongst the Gusii which goes, *'bakungu mbaya ko'menwa yabasaririe* (women are good but they talk too much).' Although it originates in Gusii, it eschews application to my mother's case. My mother never engaged in gossip with other women by the roadside or anywhere else for that matter. She was perpetually busy working in the farm and her pastime activity was listening to the radio and going to church on Sunday. This no-nonsense approach to life made her progress well without being at loggerheads with neighbours.

Through her effort, I recall that by 1967, we were well established in Borabu. The maize, pyrethrum, tea and other crops flourished and we had bumper harvest, year in, year out. She worked up to ten hours a day and she might have overstretched herself for our good.

It was against this backdrop that she later suffered severe sickness. She was rushed to Kaplong Mission Hospital where she was diagnosed with diabetes. I vividly recall that night in 1969. We rushed her to the hospital while she was unconscious. We were all afraid she won't make it. When she regained consciousness after an insulin injection we heaved a sigh of relief. She had survived by a whisker.

From then on, she was in and out of hospital but it did not deter her from working. I have never seen such an optimistic woman. At times, she could go down, get admitted at the Kisii General Hospital (now the Kisii Teaching and Referral Hospital) or Kaplong and get out fairly well, only to resume her duties at home. But as years progressed, the disease took a toll on her.

However, her condition made us wiser. We realized that a medical condition can slow the plans one had. We had to adjust ourselves and work harder to fill in the gap occasioned by her condition. Just the way she acted as matriarch for her younger brother Onyangi, my elder sister Florence stepped in to support us like a mother. She was in high school and this affected her performance in the final national examinations, although she later managed to join college and become a P1 teacher.

The Demise of Mum

By the late 1970s, the disease had made it impossible for my mother to work in the farm. She spent most of her time at home but would give us instructions on what should be done in the farm. Interestingly, in all the years even as she was sick, we never lacked food or fees. Some men in the locality envied my father, saying he was lucky to have my mother for a wife.

It is true that a substantial portion of the family's resources were used for her treatment. Despite this, I never saw her portray any signs of fear or giving up. Her positivity, even in the midst of serious sickness, which was relatively rare during those days, makes me marvel at her bravery to this day.

One thing which evidently devastated her was the abrupt death of my last born sister Martha in 1973. My baby sister came down with a severe case of pneumonia at a time my mother was hospitalized at Kaplong and my father had gone to visit her. When he returned the following day, he found a very sick baby. He rushed her to Kisii District Hospital for treatment. Unfortunately, this was not enough to save the child.

To add pain to injury, several of our dairy cattle mysteriously died one after another. Worse yet, the behaviour of my two younger sisters would worsen the situation later on. Against the family wishes, they dropped out of secondary school and eloped.

All this combined ignited fury and consternation of unfathomable proportions in my heart. It must have been an even heavier emotional burden for our sickly mother. It appeared that a floodgate of misfortunes was now directed at our home, but we had to soldier on.

When I look back, the sad memories of the time still replay in my mind as if it happened yesterday. There is no tragedy that is more heartbreaking than the death of a loved one. Perhaps this is what William J. Brennam meant when he said, "death is not only an unusual severe punishment, unusual in its pain, in its finality and in its enormity, but it served no penal purpose more effectively than a less severe punishment."

During my father's sunset days, and recalling the events of the time, he reminded me how he was touched when he saw me take a hoe, dig and plant kales that supported the family for several months. I was doing that at a time when Mama's health had deteriorated substantially. I had become wiser and realized that I was no longer a child in the true sense of the word. In 1979, under the tutelage of my elder sister, we had close to ten acres under maize. We managed to sell the bumper harvest then used the proceeds to clear the outstanding loan balances the family had incurred, including the outstanding payment for the land we had occupied at Borabu. I used part of the proceeds to buy a piece of land near Kisii Town. I would later dispose it off and use the money to fly to the United States to further my studies.

When I remember the life of my mother, what happened in August 1980 still hurts me to the core. This time, I escorted her to Kisii District Hospital and found that there were very many patients. Some were lying on the floor and it took us a long time to have her attended to. Although she was weak, she never showed any sign of giving up.

However, when we reached home, I realized that her health was fast deteriorating. I remember her frail voice as she asked, "Where are my children?" That was a frightening question, coming from a very sick mother. Before we could engage further, she called my father by his name and told him the words that ended up being her last utterance, "please take care of my children!"

These words hit us hard. And to worsen the situation we were in, she went silent; forever. As we rushed her to Kaplong Mission Hospital, we were not sure what lay ahead of us. She was pronounced dead on arrival at the hospital. I saw darkness! It is an incident I would wish to erase from my memory where it is still deeply anchored, but which I cannot.

My mother's death was a major calamity and another turning point in my life. Inevitably, my life took a different turn. This coincided with the time I was joining Kenyatta University College, a constituent college of the University of Nairobi, now a full-fledged university.

Africa's literary icon Chinua Achebe writes in his seminal book *Things Fall Apart* that, "when mother-cow is chewing grass its young ones watch its mouth." Despite my mother's demise, I had learnt invaluable lessons from her life. However, literally speaking, following her interment, I joined the university a very committed and focused person, well aware that the people I left back home were looking up to me. I recall that when I returned home for holidays, the emptiness occasioned by the demise of our mother was stark. I was hurt even more when I discovered that one of my sisters, who had eloped earlier, had returned home only to die mysteriously. Her grave lay next to my mother's! Worse still, nobody had told or prepared me for this additional calamity. I cannot tell how I overcame the pain I felt during that period.

Due to all these traumatic happenings, the year 1980 is still edged fresh in my mind. It was a watershed in my life. I did a lot of soul-searching and it was by God's grace that I managed to overcome the grief and complete my undergraduate studies. If someone were to bring my mother back, I would treat her like a queen, for a queen she was in our lives. Life is never the same when one loses a loved one, more so one's mother. Up to now, remembering the death of our mother leaves me feeling orphaned!

The death of a loved one bears huge ramifications in the immediate family. You cannot fully explain the feeling when you lose someone close to you. You feel like you are in a ghostly world. It takes time and ages to heal but you can never regain fully. However, as they say, time is the best healer. As a Christian, it is my hope that I will meet with my departed loved ones in the afterlife.

A Contrasting Spouse

My father Andrew Akama was a good man. However, some of his character traits differed substantially from my mother's. I get the feeling that God arranges for people with contrasting, and perhaps complimentary, character traits to meet, marry and live together. Perhaps if you exhibit similar behaviour, married life could become boring and not worth living. Clearly, diversity in people's character is the call of nature and the spice which colours life.

My father came from a poor background. His parents married late without any tangible family investment. They had very few heads of cattle and, as much as the family shared what they had, it was never enough. Later, my father would tell me that his parents were so poor that they slept under a grass thatched roof with gaping holes. In a moonlit night, the house got lit, leaving a feeling that they were sleeping in the open. When it rained, the roof leaked, drenching them in the process. As my father would testify later in life, whenever he spotted thick clouds gathering from Rangenyo hills overlooking Nyansakia, he innocently prayed that strong winds would divert the rains. At times, his prayers got answered; when they did not, they endured the consequences.

I had memorable moments with my father. He could tell me stories about his childhood. A good story teller, he could tell me the same story now and again, but each time it sounded new and more interesting.

There is one story he told me and I have never forgotten it to date, probably because he kept repeating it whenever there was an opportunity. It must have been his favourite because the dramatic images it ingrained in his mind. He used to tell me that since his parents were extremely poor, at times they could go without supper, unless they borrowed flour from the neighbours. My father's narrative went as follows:

> One evening, my mother went to borrow cooking flour from one of her neighbours. When she got there, she found that they were about to go out to execute their evil deeds in darkness. Unknown to my mother, the neighbours were actually witches. Perhaps the neighbours did not expect a visitor at that hour and they cast a spell on her, making her dumb. So, she returned to her house without flour and could not talk. In the morning, my father went out and shouted to the whole world, 'my wife came to your home and lost her voice (referring to the house where my grandmother had gone to borrow flour). If she dies, you will also die.' Some hours later, the woman regained her ability to talk.

My father never saw a witch, just like myself and many other people. However, he believed that some people got bewitched and died. To him, witchcraft was inherited and passed from one generation to the next. If none before you in your family lineage practised witchcraft, you would definitely die if you attempted to be one. The following is another story that my late father told several times:

> There was a woman who was married in a polygamous family. The husband realized that the woman's co-wives were mourning now and again following the death of their children.
>
> Upon scrutiny, the man concluded that it was this particular woman who was responsible for or party to those who were determined to wipe out children of the other wives. One day, the patriarch resolved to apply some traditional skill to trap and kill the person who was causing the deaths of his children.
>
> It was believed that if you applied some herbs at the graveside, the person who bewitched the dead person would be exposed the following morning. The patriarch knew that he needed to sharpen some sticks, rinse them and smear them with poison before strategically placing them at the grave and he did exactly that.
>
> And for sure, as the sun rises from the east and sets to the west, the suspected wife visited the graveside and was injured and became very sick.
>
> Knowing what he had done, the man went around the homestead, inquiring if his wives had woken up. When he reached the suspected wife's house, she told him that she was very sick and dying.
>
> The man took a spear and chased the woman and her kids away. She finally died at her parent's home, leaving behind a very young child. Ashamed, her brothers brought the body at night and left it near the man's homestead. The husband had nothing to do other than bury it.
>
> Meanwhile, the infant grew at his maternal grand parents' home until he became a young adult and was returned to his home where he went through initiation and was allowed to marry. However, the young man could not find happiness because the wife was not giving him children.
>
> With time, older women, contemporaries of his late mother and who practiced witchcraft with the now dead witch, approached the son and revealed to him that his wife was not giving birth because his mother's spirit was unhappy.
>
> He had an option of accepting to become a witch as his mother was by offering his wife as a sacrifice. Indeed, the man accepted

to become a witch and let his wife die. He then married a new wife with whom they got several children. He also married other wives who bore him more children.

As fate would have it, this man who had become a notorious and shameless witch appeared to have decided to fully walk in the footsteps of his mother. Due to envy, he started bewitching his age mates and taking their wives.

Later, he was also brutally killed when he was found red-handed in someone's compound at night with witchcraft paraphernalia. The attackers drove five inch nails into his skull, causing him to succumb to the injuries.

From these two stories that my father told me, it is possible that witchcraft is inherited and passed on from one generation to the next. It is possible that there are families with this evil phenomenon, and it runs and gets perpetuated through generations.

My Father's Changed Life

My father went to Kericho when he was barely 16 years of age and started off as a casual tea picker. With time, he discovered that the work was exacting and trained as a carpenter. He moved from picking tea to making boxes used for packaging processed tea leaves.

He also enrolled for adult classes and became good at reading. This made him appreciate the importance of education which he enticed his brothers to get but they disappointed him. When they abandoned school and went home to get married, he diverted his resources to our education.

My father was a socialist. I feel that, to an extent, he loved outsiders more than he loved his family. He preferred giving out money and clothes as gifts to relatives and even strangers, while disregarding how his actions would impact the family's tailoring business. As well, he initially objected the buying of land in Borabu, but later appreciated that my mother's idea was brilliant.

I have to state that my father's character changed when his second wife left. She had found it difficult to cope with life at our new home in Borabu. He accused my mother of having had a hand in her co-wife's exit. However, my mother had welcomed the lady and did not have any conflict with her.

Over the years, my father gradually took to drinking and could become irritable and quarrelsome. I suspect that he was never able to reconcile the fact that the younger wife had run away and gotten married elsewhere. These frustrations, coupled with my mother's sickness and the demise of my two sisters, substantially lowered his esteem and love of life. Worse still, when my mother died, my father was really hurt and sunk even farther.

I have to state that due to her intelligence and persona, my mother had been a very strong influence over my father. She was a real matriarch in the family. Even when she became ill, she continued to play a critical role in making strategic decisions and assisting my father in the management of the family affairs. So, with her eventual demise we were left with a huge vacuum in the family fabric. That void has never been filled to date. My father must have experienced extreme loss and desperation that I may not be able to express in writing. Indeed, death is neither kind nor bright. If it were, it would not have snatched our mother from us at such an early age.

Despite his flaws, my father was a very generous person. I remember one day I came home and found a very sick man called Oswago, a man from the Luo community, nestled in my small bed. When I asked why my father brought a very sick stranger to our home, he said that this was God's child and should be taken care of. I was afraid that the sick man would die in our home. When my father left for a walk, I chased the man away. The following day, he was found dead by the roadside. I wonder what could have happened had he died in our compound.

Later on, when my mother passed away, my father decided to remarry. So, he got a lady, who was actually younger than me, and married her. As children, we did not like the idea but we had no option. It did not take long before the lady started accusing us of being rude and kept demanding that we should be punished. After some time, she left our home saying life was unbearable to her.

Just around that time, my father got an equally young lady, married her and paid dowry. Upon getting the news, the other lady returned home in a huff. We now had two stepmothers, both of them younger than me. It was difficult, and hence took a while, for us to adjust to this new reality.

The situation also made my father to work harder to meet the daunting demands of two wives, their young children and ourselves. He even sold the trees in the farm and some animals to meet the increasing financial obligations occasioned by the expanded family. Of course, as tradition demands, I had to step in and support him. I did this after I returned from the United States where I had gone for my Masters and Doctorate studies.

I returned from America to find that age was quickly catching up with my father. He was in his 70s and his health was waning. We later took him to a Nairobi hospital to see a specialist doctor. He was later diagnosed with prostate blockage and was operated on by a urologist, Dr. Tinega. He failed to make full recovery due to age and in part due to overindulgence in drinking.

My worst experience resurfaced once again in 2009 when I joined Kisii University. At the time, the institution was a Constituent College of Egerton University. I was the pioneer Principal of the nascent college. One day, I received a call from one of my stepmothers in the wee hours of the night. On the line was my father but the voice did not sound like his. I was terrified to the bones and facilitated his immediate evacuation to Kisii Town for treatment.

When I saw him, he was in a bad shape. He got admitted at Christa Marriane Hospital in Kisii Town for several days before we transferred him to Eldoret Memorial Hospital in Uasin Gishu County. He stayed in the hospital for over two months and was attended to by various specialists before he got discharged.

I thought he had been healed but once again, he was taken ill after a few days and we returned him to the hospital. Here, doctors told me that my father's sickness was terminal and all we had to do is manage the ailment through home care. I was devastated even more! We later moved him to Nairobi to stay with my brother for a while but he was not at ease there. We had to take him home in Borabu.

Once at home, it got more complicated to nurse him because my stepmothers could not agree on how and who should take care of him. This compelled me to take him to Eldoret where my family stayed. By now, he had developed dementia. He lost the battle for his life in December 2011, aged 79.

The loss of a family patriarch, in a polygamous family, left a big vacuum. As the first born son in the family, tradition demanded that I take over the responsibility for the family and provide leadership to my step-mothers and twelve siblings. I have to admit that this has been one of the most difficult tasks in my life. In many instances, my step-mothers and step-sisters and brothers have divergent viewpoints on many family issues. It is also expected that as much as I am now the family leader, I should at all times show utmost respect to all members of the family, especially my step-mothers

However, we have also been lucky that the family has fared on relatively well. Thank God, my brother Mathew from my mother's side and I have shouldered most of the family responsibilities including paying school fees for our step-brothers and sisters. Most of them have now completed school, are working and have established families of their own. Of course, whenever there is any critical family issue, it is my responsibility to ensure that it is sorted out amicably.

Although my father's story started well, it didn't end up being a bed of roses. Just like my mother and my grandfather Otwori, he was not perfect. It is not easy to find a perfect human being in an imperfect world. However, despite their shortcomings, I learnt a number of lessons which have shaped my life.

From my father, for example, I saw how drinking can ruin a person's life. Although I was brought up in an environment where people and even I consumed *busaa*, I have a testimony that drinking can be detrimental to a person's life. Of course, I engaged in drinking and partying as a student at the University of Nairobi and in the United States, but I never let drinking control my life. While studying for my PhD, I realized how involving the work was and did away with distractions such as drinking. No alcoholic drink has ever come anywhere close to my mouth since then.

To me, alcohol is a legalized drink which, in most instances, harms lives. It has negatively affected many people and wrecked their lives, jobs, families and relationships. It stunts progress and limits one from attaining one's maximum potential. However, there is another school of thought which contends that alcohol and other consumptives like cigarettes are major contributors to the economy. Since they create employment and generate tax revenues, they should be a tolerated evil.

GROWING UP

My Initiation

My voice had not broken when my father decided that I was ripe for initiation. This was during Christmas holidays in 1968 and we were now, more or less, fully settled in Borabu.

Christianity as well as colonialism had crept in and altered the script of this ceremony which was very dear to the Gusii people. It was a symbolic milestone and rite of passage in a person's life. Although the ceremony has been eroded over the years, its significance continues to withstand the test of time.

Initially, boys went through this rite of passage when they approached the age of twenty years. It also marked their transition from childhood to adulthood. As I gathered from multiple interviews that culminated in the publication of my book, *The Gusii of Kenya: Social, Economic, Cultural, Political*

& *Judicial Perspectives*, "until an individual underwent all the rites of passage and rituals that marked adolescent life, he or she was perceived as still being a child without clear understanding of the complexities and mysteries of life." This is why after physical circumcision, boys stayed in *ebisarate* (seclusion huts) where they went through extensive training to become responsible young men in society. They also got tips on war techniques while in seclusion. Aside from these skills, the process trained young men to be responsible men. After circumcision one was expected to protect the community, its wealth, and the most vulnerable members of the society; women, children and the elderly. Initiation transformed these young men into warriors who would defend the community against external aggression.

The seclusion huts were not accessible to women and served as what could be viewed as military encampments. During seclusion, the newly initiated young men were trained on how to viciously protect the people and property, especially cattle. These were the very skills that came in handy for the Gusii warriors when they fought back the colonial soldiers who invaded their territory in 1907.

This cultural grounding did not excite colonial administrators who believed that anything culturally African was not civilization. The British banned the practice, saying it was a security threat. And they were right! The teaching the young men went through predisposed them to resist external authority.

A good example is that of Otenyo Nyamaterere who played a major role in resisting colonial incursion into Gusii. Otenyo led a contingent of Gusii warriors in attacking British colonial administrators when they first set foot in Gusiil. He was strongly driven by the urge to protect the people from the foreign intruders. He would later face beheading by the colonial soldiers.

Otenyo, like the warriors he led, went through this rite of passage in its entirety. In other words, Otenyo and other warriors honed their fighting skills and their strong mental disposition when they stayed in the youth encampments. They lived and died by their vow to protect their people.

As per the Gusii culture and history, the initiation of boys into men was critical and memorable. In Gusii community, male circumcision was a holy ceremony. It was conducted early in the morning by *omosari* (circumciser; plural, *abasari*) under ritualistic trees growing in places that were regarded to be sacred. These trees included *emiobo, emekomoni* and *emesocho* (singular *omwobo, omokomoni* and *omosocho,* respectively).

The sacredness of circumcision sites was unequivocally understood by the community. Ordinarily, this is where elders sat to resolve disputes involving members of the clan. They also offered sacrifices at the sites to appease ancestors especially during the occurrence or fear of impeding calamities such as sicknesses, drought and famine.

The circumcisers inherited the skill and blessings from their forefathers. It was believed that they had magical-religious powers that would cast away any bad omen or spirits that could harm initiates during and after the ceremony. One could not become a circumciser without extensive apprenticeship and consecration.

As tradition demanded, the initiates stood stack naked leaning on the ritualistic tree. The circumciser chanted while invoking the name of *Engoro* (God), clearly telling the boys that they were going to become men. The rite of passage entailed surgically removing the foreskin using a knife; no anaesthetic was used. It was a critical test of bravery and courage for the boys. An initiate was not supposed to flinch or make noise of any kind, let alone shed a tear due to the pain.

The detailed tribulation I underwent, like many in my generation and former generations, in the name of becoming a young man is ingrained in my memory. It feels as if it happened yesterday.

When the sun set and darkness struck on the eve of the big day, unmarried young men streamed into our compound. Usually, the boys' hut was close to the entrance of the homestead. It stood a distance away from the parents' and girls' huts. The men lit and sat around a fire in our hut to catch some warmth. By 8pm, their number had swelled to about fifty and they could not fit in our small hut. This compelled some to sit in the darkness outside where another fire was lit.

For the occasion, my father had set aside a bull which was slaughtered. The young men excitedly enjoyed meals, including *ugali* which they escorted down their throats with meat. They were also sparingly allowed to enjoy traditional brew as the night wore itself away.

To undergo the initiation with me the following morning was my cousin who lived with us. We would end up meeting about ninety more boys from other areas at the sacred point. Each of them was eager to face the circumciser's knife to transition into manhood.

On the material day, it appeared that although the young men were only allowed to lightly indulge in drinking, they went overboard and got drunk. At midnight, they dismissed their sanity and became brutal. They ordered my cousin and I to walk out and strip naked and join them later.

When we came back to the house naked, my heart beat unusually fast. Instinctively, I shielded my private parts with my hands. This did not augur well with the men. They took it personally and hurled abusive words at us. We were accused of stinking like porcupines. They also caned us while prohibiting us from rubbing our hurting backsides. Despite of the agonizing pain of canes against our skins, we held our tears back. We had been forewarned not to shed tears regardless of the pain because, culturally, crying was 'a preserve for girls'.

Although the young men were people from our home area, it appeared to me that they had suddenly become insane. They called us unprintable names. We were accused of moving around and having affairs with uncircumcised girls whom they demanded us to name. Deep in my heart, I regarded these as wild allegations. No one had prepared us for this!

We did not have a choice but to succumb to their pressure. God knows what they would have done to us if we did not name names. So I randomly mentioned names of girls in the village to satisfy them. As I mentioned one name, they cheered and jeered at the same time probing me to mention another.

I remember one of the men who mistreated us more than the rest. Onduso was a farm labourer at our home. He was very fierce that evening. It was as if he was on a revenge mission against crimes I was not aware of. He kicked me severally accusing me of always disrespecting him.

The mistreatment hit a climax shortly past midnight when they asked us to chew and swallow some bitter herbs. They also asked us to use our teeth to lift some wooden pegs, which they stuck in the earthen floor near the fire place. They were unrelenting in caning us!

Fortunately for us, and I cannot tell how it happened, my father stormed into the room. He was physically agitated. He either heard the commotion or was informed by someone who was unhappy with the torture we were going through.

"I will chase you out of my compound and ensure my son is circumcised using other alternatives. I will even take him to the clinic," my father said angrily. This threat sounded real. The young men knew very well that I was my father's favourite. They also knew that, unlike years gone, circumcision could be done by trained health workers at the nearby health facility.

The men became remorseful and apologized to my father. From then on, the thrashing came to a halt. They now spoke to us gently, giving us a few tips on the journey ahead and encouraging us to face the rest of the journey with courage.

At cockcrow, we were asked to step out and start the long journey. It entailed running with the other initiation candidates at the front and trying hard not to be caught up by the youthful men who were escorting us to the circumcision site. Another instruction was that the two of us were to dip ourselves in water each time we came across a river or spring. The cold water in a chilly morning basically numbed our bodies. It was a traditional anaesthetic measure which would inhibit excessive pain when the circumciser's knife finally met the skin.

We eventually got to the sacred point in Nyamasibi in the current Nyaribari Masaba Constituency about two hours later. We had covered a distance of almost 15km from my home. Here, alongside other initiation candidates from other parts, we were made to lie prostrate on thick grass covered with early morning dew.

Shortly, the circumciser emerged from nowhere, chanting magical-religious words. Against the instructions from the youthful men, I secretly lifted my head and noticed that the circumciser was carrying a skilfully curved staff. Its handle had the shape of a human head. I later came to learn that he had inherited it from his grandfather who was also a circumciser. This was symbolic that he firmly carried the blessings of turning boys into men through circumcision.

"Swear that you are ready to undergo the cut and you will not scream," he thundered, looking at us. He then warned us of the repercussions of screaming, which included untold suffering and humiliation to our families. Traditionally, a boy who screamed during the circumcision was named *enkuri* (coward). If one were labeled *enkuri*, stigma followed and his family's reputation suffered too. Secondly, it would be very hard for *enkuri* to get a wife; he would be shunned by many would be in-laws as the person who 'cried' during the cut. There were other claims that letting out a cry during the cut would spell a curse. Indeed, even if one were cleansed later on, it only removed the possibility of a curse and not the reputation. This is why it was such an abomination that no family could hear of it. In addition, screaming attracted a heavy penalty from parents of *enkuri*. They had to offer a bull and several goats to the circumciser that would be used for cleansing.

I remember that the circumciser used one sharp knife for the 92 boys who turned up for the cut that day. When my time came, I partly leaned my back against the tree, with my hands stretched up backwards and round it. My eyes stared vacuously ahead. Meanwhile, the tens of men around us sounded rowdy. They lifted their spears, sticks and all manner of weapons and pointed them at me, while repeatedly shouting, "*moisia yaa!* (you lad!)". Although anxiety threatened to betray me, I remained strong and held my heart in one piece. It appeared like the men would injure me if I gave in to the pain.

The circumciser took less than five minutes to finish the job. Surprisingly, I was not gnawing with pain as I had anticipated. First, the noise from all the men and the thought that I must not scream were a major distraction. Second, my body was already numb from the biting cold and the number of times I dipped myself in the water each time we came across a river or stream. In addition, as each of us was waiting for his turn, he lay naked facing down in the cold morning dew. This was the science of tradition, passed down generations; anaesthetics! In all, the circumciser took about four and half hours to process the 92 initiates.

Once we went through the surgical process, the youthful men who had accompanied us uprooted and gave each one of us a herbal plant called *ekerundu*. We were instructed to hold it in one hand. In the other hand, one had to hold one's manhood tightly. It was believed that the dual action stopped bleeding as well as cast away any evil spell. In some cases, the older boys scared initiates that if they didn't hold their manhood tightly enough, it would disappear resulting in the initiate becoming a woman. The point here was that the initiate needed to pay great attention to the instructions; no one would want to turn into a woman when one was born a man!

With the work completed, the circumciser started a ritualistic song called *esimbore* for the event signalling that the parties could set off to their respective places. The song went like this:

> *Oooyo! Oooyo...eee (Here he is, here is!)x2*
> *Omoisia omoke' mbororo bwamorire (he's experiencing pain)x2*
> *Otureirwe ritimo (His spear has been sharpened)x2*
> *Arwane bobisa (Let him battle the enemies)x2*
> *Arwane Sugusu (Fight in the North)x2*

> *Arwane Irianyi (Fight in the South)x2*
> *Arwane Mocha (Fight in the East)x2*
> *Arwane Bosongo (Fight in the West)x2*
> *Moisia omoke 'mbororo bwamorire (The boy is in pain)*

I have written about this song extensively in my book, *The Gusii of Kenya: Social, Economic, Cultural, Political & Judicial Perspectives*. During my research for the book, I confirmed that this was more of a war song. It was sung figuratively to encourage initiates, now that they had become men, to be bold and be ready to defend their families, clans and the Gusii community against external aggression. The song had other symbolisms; for example, *'otureirwe ritimo'* also meant his manhood has been sharpened and that he would soon be ready to 'fight another war', that of procreation and extending the family lineage.

Song as art is a powerful tool for mobilization and promotes the entrenchment of certain behaviours and characteristics. Researchers agree as much. Kichamu Akivaga and Asenath Odaga in *Oral Literature: A School Certificate Course* write that, "...songs are sung with a great deal of expression and feeling. And people dance with vigour and rhythm. Dancing and singing are an experience that nearly possesses the participants." In participating in singing, one is 'transported' to the realm of the spiritual; it can be an entrancing experience! It is a world of surrealism. Quoting Ludwig van Beethoven, "music is the mediator between the spiritual and the sensual life."

In the end, the impact of music leaves permanent, indelible marks on the partakers. Coupled by the aura of the moment, music and its entire experience can be transformative.

Over the years, I have reflected through the origins of this tradition that combined the physical surgery and psychological conditioning. I have come to believe that it is because of Abagusii's experience and struggle to survive.

As mentioned earlier, the community faced repeated attacks and raids from their Nilotic neighbours, especially the Maasai and the Kipsigis. These clashes often degenerated to wars and resulted in perpetual acrimony that threatened the very survival of the Gusii.

To survive required that male youths be trained and be prepared to face the enemy. In part, the ritual of the circumcision rite of passage was intended to harden the initiates, through psychological conditioning and imparting war skills. Initiates had to show bravery even as they internalized their responsibility in the community in the future. In addition, the process was meant to prove that they were ready to take on the challenges which lay ahead of them as adults.

Into Seclusion

On our way home we, the initiates, were shielded by the young fierce-looking unmarried men. It was a three-hour journey without a dull moment. Ordinarily, it should have taken us one hour or less to cover the distance but it went ceremonially slow. They sung the requisite circumcision song, *esimbore*. In the process, they threw and mentioned all kinds of vulgar words as they sang along.

As we approached our home, women led by my mother danced and ululated happily while charging towards us. I peeped through the human shield, out of curiosity, and saw that my mother had a machete in her hand. She also had wound tendrils and flowers around her waist and neck. A number of women had also decorated themselves in a similar manner. It was a carnival like I had never seen before.

The young men escorting us ensured that the women's roving eyes did not meet the initiates. In the back and forth, the women even attempted to break the human shield, only to be dispersed, using canes, by the young men. When I recall that day, I feel that the drama was worth recording. Unfortunately, there was no one there to capture it. It was not like now when people can instantly record and share anything using mobile phone cameras.

It is noteworthy that even as the men uttered things that were vulgar, it only happened at that special occasion. It also ended there. The celebration was one way the community let off 'steam' and came together. Originally, the ceremony was timed to coincide with the end of the harvesting period.

We finally made it to our homestead where there was more dancing and merrymaking. They led us into our seclusion hut where we would spend a good portion of the month as we healed. A fire had to burn throughout that period. According to the Gusii culture and histology, the fire was to keep evil spirits at bay. It was believed that if by any chance it went off, it signalled a bad omen. Left uncleansed, the omen would show its ugly head in the initiate's adulthood. Consequences included, but were not limited to, one failing to get children of one's own. And, if one did sire children, they would die soon after.

In the hut, it was time to start the fire. My cousins took some special sticks and rubbed them together repeatedly until they saw smoke, then sparks of fire. They coaxed this with dry tinder and shortly after, the fire grew bigger and bigger with addition of more and more firewood. To ensure it would last long, they fed it with indigenous tree stumps that had been gathered and piled in the hut.

It was the start of our seclusion period which lasted more than a month. During the time, we were largely fed on meat and traditional vegetables, which were believed to hasten healing.

In case the fire went off, elders were informed to conduct necessary sacrifices to the ancestors on behalf of the initiates. The sacrifices included the slaughtering of a mature cockerel and a he-goat to appease the ancestors. The fire could then be lit once again after the essential ritual. However, regardless of whether the ritual following the extinction of the fire was done or not, the matter carried a stigma in one's entire life. One would be known as the person whose initiation fire went out!

To ensure that the fire kept burning, some young unmarried men were tasked to stay with us. They were also required to give us instructions of life skills such as being well mannered as adults and how to relate with girls. They also narrated key historical events and the stories of the community's gallant heroes of yesteryears.

Egesimba (mongoose) was the name we were branded during that period because we were allowed to move around, hunting. We could also be mischievous. We could steal hens from the neighbourhood and convert them into meals. I can attest that my cousin and I killed several hens from the neighbouring homes. By the time our seclusion ended, we had noticeably gained weight.

During the idle moments in seclusion, we also fought with fellow initiates from the neighbouring homes whom we encountered as we wandered around. I remember one day, the mock fights degenerated into a brawl that drew the attention of young men, older than us, who came and separated us.

Despite all this, I believe that the experience was worth it. We learnt moral values that held our people together; we had lessons about family and relationships; we learnt what it meant to be men in the community. In particular, my special training and life lessons came from our main instructor (*omosegi*) and an elder who continuously taught us what it meant to be a man. His teachings influenced how I interpreted life henceforth. We were instructed on the virtues of honesty, bravery and respect for women. We were also taught to respect our parents and to be of help to others who may be in need.

I have kept many of the lessons up to my adult life. For example, I never stepped in my parents' bedroom after I was initiated into manhood because this was a taboo. I had fundamentally been trained to become a young honourable man who clearly understood existing social boundaries among family members and the community in general.

Another thing I recall from the period is a strange animal that never was. Young men took sticks and a cow skin to make an instrument dubbed *enyabubu,* a mimic of a mysterious wild animal which made beastly sounds. When it was played, even the boldest of them all trembled. Done in the dark of the night, the feeling of fear was amplified! It was meant to test the courageousness of the initiates.

Part of the training included the gender responsibilities in a home. Men took care of cattle, cleared and worked in the farms, among other things. Issues pertaining to the kitchen were for women, girls and lasses. We had express instructions not to be involved in the things women were supposed to do like fetching water from the river.

This last instruction would soon put us to the test when schools reopened in January, 1969 when I joined Standard Five.

About six of us who had been circumcised in the same season got admission to the same school. One day teachers gave us containers and asked us to fetch water from the stream for their use. We adamantly refused for this was not a chore meant for men. This did not go down well with our teachers. They severely punished and instructed us to fetch the water or be in more trouble.

We reluctantly fetched the water but the news spread like bush fire through the village. Our parents streamed into the school compound, one by one. They unanimously protested against the teachers' act of 'humiliating' us. They also warned the teachers that culture had to be upheld even as they imparted formal education on us.

The teachers stopped sending us to the river only for a short while. When they started again our parents stood by the community's culture that initiated boys should not be fetching water from the spring or doing kitchen work for staff.

****

I grew up at a time when there was confusion occasioned by indigenous social and cultural values on one side and Western civilization on the other. Tradition was telling me to be a warrior who at times forces his way while Western values demanded that I be gentle, and that boys and girls enjoyed equal rights.

Many of these conflicts persist to this day. A man goes to church where he is told that his wife is not his servant but when he gets home, he is supposed to look at life with traditional lenses and behave differently. You can hardly find a man in the Gusii community who openly assists his wife to fetch water from the stream or cook for the family. Information about such a person easily spreads like wild fire and his reputation gets 'tarnished'.

Looking back now, I can say that traditional circumcision among the Gusii bordered on cruelty. As already shown, there was a lot of beating and harassment by youthful men who escorted us to the circumciser. Also, the cut was done without anaesthesia. However, all these acts correspond to military training, which in most cases is painful and torturous. It was purposely intended to harden us. This way, it prepared us to fight the enemy and defend the community against any form of internal and external aggression. However, some of these practices are no longer tenable in contemporary Kenya.

The indigenous practice of the cut does not exist anymore because many of the circumcisers have died without passing down the art to their progeny. In addition, people have embraced a modern and less painful form of circumcision, which is usually done by trained health personnel. Today, it is illegal to subject a human being to any form of surgery without anaesthesia. As well, health issues like the spread of diseases such as HIV-Aids also hastened the death of traditional male circumcision where one knife could be used on several boys without being sterilized.

The FGM Controversy

The issue of circumcision amongst the Gusii will not be complete if I do not disclose that girls were also subjected to it just like the boys. Just as the boys went through initiation when they reached a certain age, so did girls. Circumcision of girls amongst the Gusii was, essentially, clitoridectomy and tailed the removal of the tip of the clitoris[2].

---

2   Editor's note: for a complete treatise of female circumcision in Gusii, see Daniel Momanyi Mokaya's *Female Circumcision among the Abagusii of Kenya*, 2nd Edition (Nsemia Inc.2012).

Human rights activists call it Female Genital Mutilation (FGM). However, without any fear of contradiction, I must say that what Gusii girls underwent was not FGM as sometimes understood. It was a symbolic procedure, which was less harmful than that practised by some communities. When I read about what those communities call circumcision, it is clear that theirs is rather crude. Thus, as much as it may currently appear to be unwarranted and/or repugnant, girl circumcision amongst the Gusii entailed a simple procedure of incision at the tip of the clitoris. It did not involve removal of entire genitalia as was practiced by some communities.

However, whichever way and whichever term we call it, the practice has been overtaken by time. It is now illegal and it is almost dying in Gusii because of the heavy penalties imposed and the community's acceptance to stamp it out following public sensitization.

However, my point of departure on the abolition of female circumcision is that we have not yet found an effective rite of passage for girls. In the past, following the physical act, girls were taken into seclusion just as the boys were. During that time, they were trained on many things, including personal health, body maturity issues and how to be responsible young women. They were also given critical sex education tips and body hygiene guidelines.

A vacuum created by the abolition of female circumcision and the negative outcomes are there for all of us to see. Immorality today is a notch higher than it was in our time. Several girls continue to bear children out of wedlock, even as many end up in the business of the flesh. Minors not only have sex but do so unprotected and end up contracting diseases. Some of these have devastating impact on not only the girls but also their families and those they have liaisons with. This was unheard of in the past. The traditional moral fabric is already destroyed and tattered. As renowned Nigerian writer Chinua Achebe would put it, 'things have fallen apart!'

Also, the number of girls dropping out of school is increasing by the day before attaining levels of education that would assure them of meaningful livelihood. This increases the number of liabilities to women. In the past, virginity was something to be proud of for girls and women. A girl who got married while still a virgin, fetched a bigger dowry. Additionally, her name would be invoked as a role model for others.

I strongly believe that women need an alternative rite of passage where they get the education but not the cut. Indeed, this is what Daniel Momanyi Mokaya has proposed in his book *Female Circumcision among the Abagusii of Kenya*. There are others who have also proposed the same.

Leaving Seclusion

Let me take you back to my circumcision story. At the end of the seclusion period, there were certain rituals that initiates were supposed to partake before rejoining the society. On the last day of seclusion, I was led by the main instructor (*omosegi*) to the nearby river where I had a thorough bath. It is important to note that I was not supposed to bathe during the whole of the seclusion period. After bathing, I wore new clothes symbolising that I had been reborn and I was now a 'man' ready to go out and face the world.

As instructed by my *omosegi* and as tradition demanded, I went to my parents' house in the eerie hours of the day and pronounced, "*Tata! Bora ango....Tata! Bora ango!* (Daddy, please speak! Daddy, please speak!" Of course, I had received instruction from my *omosegi* on the significance of this occasion and the specific words to say as it paved way for me to receive special blessings from my parents.

My father said words of blessings to me, "*Twakoire gwasi ya ng'ombe na banto* (We have blessed you with many people and wealth)." The same was repeated, this time by my mother. They then sprinkled milk on the forehead, which was mixed with traditional brew to signify the sealing of the blessings. It meant that I now had the responsibility and blessings of enhancing the family tree.

Part of the behaviour older Gusii men exhibit even to this day can be attributed to the painful experience they underwent during circumcision and the daunting teachings during the seclusion period. Men coming out of initiation were hardened. They were courageous and fearless. In this regard, Gusii warriors never retreated whenever they were in a state of war as this would be seen as a sign of cowardice and betrayal to the community. This is unlike today where one can hardly discern virtues of courage and steadfastness. In traditional society, retreating would be seen as a failure. That sense of duty to society has been eroded by the current social environment of modernity and adoption of alien cultural and social values.

However, I appreciate the government for ensuring that Kenyans, especially those who live along the border with other communities, live in peaceful co-existence. Unlike in the old days when inter-ethnic flare-ups were common, people now live in relative harmony. An example is the Kisii-Nyamira-Bomet-Kericho border which now enjoys relative peace and tranquility. The government has established a number of police posts along the one time volatile and troubled border and earmarked a security road, which has been built along the borderline. This eases the recovery of animals in case of theft.

I have kept some aspects of our culture, which were passed to me during circumcision. Particularly, I was brought up on the basis of *chinsoni*. This was an unwritten code of conduct for raising a responsible person in the Gusii cultural and social context. For example, I addressed and still address my parents and seniors with requisite respect, something I learnt during the circumcision rite of passage. My children have also taken my footsteps and cannot for example call me by my first name John or Sorana or surname Akama to symbolise that I am not just a name to them; I am their father. Furthermore, life's ideals such as perseverance, tenacity, endurance and courage are instilled in me through the various initiation activities discussed above.

John S. Akama

My Christian Name

Although I dropped English Literature after my A-level studies, I am an avid reader of all forms of literature. One of the lucid poems that interests me is authored by Everett Standa. Titled, *A conversation on African Names*, the poem elicits heavy thoughts in my mind.

My dear, I've been thinking
That we should name the baby-
Like it used to be in our grandpa's time-
after somebody in our ethnic line, you know,
Because the child must have some identity
And not just Patrick Johnson,
David Stewbery, Peter Malizzard, Charles Shoemaker,
Kim Peking, Kennedy Dickson....
You see
I know you value these English
Or, Christian names as they are often called,
But we do not want to lose our identity
Like that!
God will not refuse you just because
You are called Ochieng Adaka or Wekesa Makkesi,
Or Wanjiku Kimani, or whatever other,
Or, let us put it this way,
Supposing you were born, say,
One thousand years in the future,
And you went to the future museum
And picked a book
Written by some fellow by the name
'Bogus Crankshaft'
and, on reading, you discover later,
that this was a real name of a famous
African philosopher, engineer, or whatever;
Wouldn't you wish
The man were called Mutali or Okello
Instead of some meaningless so-called Christian
Names
Bogus Crankshaft!

  - **Source:** *An Anthology of East African Poetry*

The poet avers that those who drop their ancestral names completely in place of Christian or English ones stand the risk of being forgotten way after they are dead. The writer contends that contributions of such people in innovation, literature, medicine and any other discoveries may not be appreciated in future or linked to the right cultural identity. I partially agree with the author of this poem.

After 45 days of intense traditional learning in seclusion, my parents who were staunch Catholics made sure that I also underwent rigorous teachings of the church. The teachings related to the mass, the Bible and liturgy.

It is interesting to note that after undergoing circumcision following traditional norms, my parents prepared me to also undergo thorough Christian teaching. Probably to them, since I had been traditionally initiated to manhood, this was the right time for me to get elaborate religious teaching. Thus, to them, after undergoing a traditional rebirth (being circumcised), I also needed to go through a spiritual one through church teachings and baptism.

When schools closed for April holidays in 1969, they ordered me to start attending the church teachings at Ichuni Catholic Parish. The parish is about 15km away from our home. For the entire month of April, I woke up in the morning and headed for the parish. I studied the whole day and returned home in the evening.

The teachings were packaged in Ekegusii and were extremely detailed. According to the dictates of the church, we were required to memorize the teachings and make them part of us. The Parish Priest, Fr. Joseph Oucho as well as the Catholic sisters addressed us regularly and encouraged us to be well rooted in the faith.

The teachings emphasized the Christian mystery, God the Trinity, that is; the Father, the Son and the Holy Spirit. We were particularly taught that on the cross, all our sins were forgiven. However, at the same time, we were told not to commit sin and to always adhere to the Ten Commandments. For instance, one should not kill, commit adultery and worship any other God. One should admit that to a young mind, as much as the whole experience was interesting, some of the teachings were confusing and I sometimes got lost.

As young as I was, I realized that some of the teachings were in conflict with traditional concepts and values. Examples include what we learnt during circumcision and the attendant seclusion period. At the parish, they taught us to always be gentle, loving and forgiving. This went against what I had been taught to be. During the seclusion period, we were told to be strong and ready to fight for ourselves and our people whenever provoked. We were specifically instructed that one should be ready to fight and even kill in defence of oneself and one's community.

Despite these contradictions, we were never given time to ask questions. In fact, we were not required to ask such questions. We did not even question the catechist when he asserted that our birth names were ungodly. My name Sorana was corrupted from Soranus which is Italian. According to the Parish teachings, the Gusii way of pronouncing it made the name sound African and hence 'ungodly'.

At the end of April holidays, we were told that the sessions would resume as soon as the August holidays set in. On resumption, we were given tests like reciting the rosary and church litanies. We were also told that with the assistance of our parents, we should choose Christian names for ourselves. We would then acquire the new names after baptism.

My parents were well versed with Biblical teachings and it was not difficult for them to settle on the name John. They argued that they were always inspired by the work of John the Baptist, and especially touched by the role John played in the Bible. They liked that he prepared the way for Jesus by baptizing new converts on the River Jordan making them ready to receive the Messiah.

At the parish, I gave the name to the catechist and it was pronounced by the priest when he baptized me. From then on, I became John Sorana Akama. It is also interesting that many people call me John Akama but those who know me closely address me as Sorana, which is my real traditional name.

As a youth, I was excited that I had gotten a new, Christian name. The name meant that I had been accepted into the family of the Catholic Church. However, it took time for people to get used to calling me by the Christian name.

Later on, I experienced many contradictions at school but they were denomination based. My primary school, Mecheo, was sponsored by the Seventh Day Adventist (SDA) Church. Learners were expected to follow the SDA doctrines that emphasized that Saturday was the day of worship and rest. As Catholics, we were told to worship and fellowship on Sunday. It therefore took me a while to understand why the two Christian faiths chose separate days for worship and fellowship.

Conflicts between the two denominations occasionally erupted into the open for everyone who had eyes to see. There was an incident when Fr. Joseph Oucho of Ichuni Parish (we later came under Nyansiongo Parish), wanted to start a dispensary near my home at a place called Endemu. This is an area that was predominantly occupied by SDA church members. The residents vowed that the priest would not have his way. On a planned visit to the area, the residents dramatically stoned his car and chased him away.

In a separate incident, the Catholic Church opened a secondary school at Raitigo. This was against the wishes of the SDA church members from the area. The Adventists stormed the school compound and chased away the newly-hired teachers and students who had reported. To affirm their warning, they burnt the national flag.

They knew little that the flag was an emblem of the nation and not a piece of cloth associated with the Catholic Church. Their act was a serious state offense. Soon, education officers arrived, accompanied by a contingent of policemen. The culprits were rounded up, handcuffed and taken to the police cells where they were held for several days. They were later released after tendering an apology and were warned never to repeat the offence. Ironically, the school today draws a majority of its students from the surrounding homes that are largely of SDA faith.

At Mecheo Primary School, my sister and I suffered and felt humiliated for being Catholic. Shortly before lunch on every Wednesday, classes were suspended to allow SDA preaching by invited pastors. The pastors taught the Adventist Church's doctrines and portrayed Catholicism as inferior and demonic. They painted Catholic followers as a lost lot. They accused parents of Catholic faith of consuming beer and not following simple hygiene and an upright way of life. They added that children from Catholic homes were poorly raised. If that is not humiliation, then I do not know what the term means.

Furthermore, in the school, there was some level of segregation. We from Catholic families were perceived to be from failed homes. My sister and I really got stressed up when we could go to the *shamba* on Saturdays while our schoolmates walked in their best clothes to church. It reached a point where we told our parents that we had faced enough humiliation and we were ready to convert to SDA.

Our parents did not have a better answer to our request other than punish us heavily.

It is my assertion that the teachings offered then were not good for young people. The pastors centred their preaching on materialism. I found these issues to be unnecessary and beyond our imagination and understanding. They painted images of success if one followed the SDA teachings and failure if we went the Catholic way. This, to me, was inaccurate and misleading.

I can also poke holes in the teachings and strictness with which young people from SDA homes were raised. The degree to which children from SDA homes could mingle with the rest of the community was highly restricted by their parents. Most likely, this might have led to lack of development of basic life skills that children acquire through socialization with their peers and others in the broader society. As such, when they got freedom in their later lives, they could not handle it well.

Most of them ended up rebellious to the church teachings. I remember some became notorious drunkards. Some girls became mothers too early and dropped out of school. Sad yet, many of our teachers who proclaimed the SDA faith took advantage of their female pupils and mature women.

In our sphere, matters were not any better for those of us who subscribed to the Catholic faith. We were always told that stepping in an SDA church was sinful. Whenever this happened, you were required to go to the priest and make a confession. I have to confess that I made several such trips to confess in line with this instruction.

I am happy that the situation has improved now. Today, people are enlightened and there are positive interactions across denominations. But there is need for the gaps to be sealed especially in situations where differences in denominations evoke rifts, which hamper not only the smooth running of schools but development in general.

There were also many positive aspects during our time at Mecheo. At the school, we would engage in informal discussions. Those among us who were good in certain subjects would freely share our knowledge with our classmates.

Another aspect was the closeness and intense social interactions and bonding among fellow pupils. I remember some of my best friends at the school, mainly my classmates and/or age mates. I have kept contact with some to this day. The list of my colleagues at Mecheo would be long but I can mention a few, including Huron Obara, Bundi Ondieki, Japhet Omosa, David Maranga, Yabesh Kemoni, Meshack Okero, Ochao Maranga, the late Charles Omariba and the late Ochimbo Nyakundi.

Exciting childhood memories of my days as a pupil at Mecheo still linger in my mind as I tell this story. During out of class hours, in the evenings, we used to engage in various improvised sporting activities such as football, athletics, basketball, long-jump, high-jump and wrestling. We played these games with a lot of enthusiasm and determination.

Indeed, participating in various sporting activities precipitated diverse talents among us. I for one loved athletic activities especially in the short and middle-distance races. However, I have to admit that there were several of my class-mates who were far much better in sports than me.

As youths, we would sometimes engage in intimate and friendly social activities and friendly arguments over different issues. We would debate on who is good in subjects such as English Language and Mathematics. Interestingly, sometimes we would engage one another on the usually cheeky behaviour of boys such as sneaking out of school to go eat fruits like guavas and loquats in farms near the school. Of course, if by bad luck one got caught, one would be punished severely. The worst was when one was sent home to bring one's parent. In such occasions, the parents would tell the teachers to give us even heavier punishment including several strokes of the cane. There were worse punishments like weeding the school garden, uprooting tree stumps and fetching water from the stream.

I remember one morning, on my way to school, an elderly lady whose home was adjacent to the school, had given me traditional brew, *busaa*. When we entered in the classroom for lessons (I was in class 5 then), pupils who were sitting next to me started to complain to the teacher that I was smelling alcohol. Immediately, the teacher swung into action and spanked me several times. As was usual, my colleagues cheered him on while I screamed.

"Go home and come back with your parent," the teacher roared as he hurled one more stroke of the cane that missed me narrowly. If he knew how I dreaded being sent home due to mischief, he would have caned me as long as he wanted. I knew my parents were very strict disciplinarians and would pump a little more sense into my head by chastising me severely.

When my father came to school and was informed what had happened, he shook in deep rage and forced me to the ground where I received additional spanking until I fainted. When I came back to my senses, I found myself outside our classroom away from the punishment scene, surrounded by several teachers and my father. From the corners of my eyes, I could see that although my father had given an okay for me to be punished, my current state had sent panic waves down his heart.

Nevertheless, when I regained normalcy, I swore never to take alcohol again. In other words, the severe punishment from the class teacher and my parent totally transformed my behaviour, at least during my pursuit for basic education. I learnt that beer or any other alcoholic beverage is not good, especially when one is a student.

Biographer's Note: Enock Bogita, a retired teacher and resident of Borabu Settlement Scheme, taught Prof. Akama in primary school. He had this to say:

Although he looked brilliant, I neither knew nor imagined that the young man would become a professor one day. He was a silent, humble and highly disciplined boy. He loved reading and we often told other learners to emulate him. I once told his father that the boy would one day make him proud. It came to pass.

I taught him Mathematics and Geography in Standard Seven at Mecheo Primary School. I am happy that he studied Geography up to university level.

Most of my pupils from the time are now teachers. Some have retired. Prof. Akama's name stands out each time I recall my time at the school.

Biographer's Note: Huron Obara, a retired teacher, lives in Nyansakia village in Borabu Settlement Scheme. A classmate of Prof. Akama at Mecheo Primary School, he had the following in reference to his childhood friend:

Prof. Akama was my classmate in 1971 and 1972, alongside his elder sister Florence who is now a retired teacher. In class, we sat in adjacent rows. I remember that he was very bright and orderly.

We kept the same company most of the time because we came from the same area, Nyansakia in Borabu. Occasionally, we could be caught in mischief and beat-up boys from other villages whenever they ignited trouble.

We have maintained our friendship despite the different

trajectories our lives took. I help him to coordinate activities that are in the interest of our community. He initiated the sinking of a borehole which now serves most homes in our area. In addition, through his efforts, we have a solar drier that helps farmers minimize waste of farm produce, especially traditional vegetables. He also helped us acquire a milk cooler from Poland. These, among other initiatives, indicate that he holds our community close to his heart.

Scaling the Heights in Education

Having a son or daughter in high school was of great importance for a parent as Kenyans acclimatized themselves to formal education in the formative years of independence. As much as I scored an A in my CPE, on second attempt, I did not receive my letter of admission to join high school. This greatly worried my parents and me. It also worried my siblings.

Days were running fast and we all got more anxious. Those from our region who passed received their letters of admission from the Provincial Education Office that was based in Kisumu. That time in 1974, there were very limited means of communication. The main form of communication was letters via the post office. It was unlike now when mobile telephones and the internet have revolutionized communication.

My success in the examinations had stunned everybody, including myself. This is particularly so due to the general poor performance at my school, Mecheo Primary in the national examinations over the years. However, although I expected a good grade, an A was beyond my imagination. This event and several other cases through my academic journey will reveal that I always underestimated myself. Before we sat for the CPE, we selected our dream high schools. The one you settled for as the first option considered you for the opportunity if you met its cut-off mark. If I had estimated better, I would have selected a national school and not Itibo High School, which is located next to my ancestral village of Nyansakia. I have to state that I chose Itibo because it was widely known during that time. It was one of the oldest secondary schools in Kisii region, having been founded in the 1940s.

This notwithstanding, my father knew that if I missed joining secondary school, it would affect my academic journey and probably reduce me into a laughing stock for villagers.

That time, there were people who had evil intentions and could hide or destroy your letter so that you miss joining the high school of your choice. My father suspected that this is what might have happened to my letter. He decided to defeat the devil and avoid the looming embarrassment of his son failing to join secondary school despite my remarkable performance. He travelled to Kisumu, the first time in his life, to find out why I had not received my letter of admission to Itibo. It was a long journey and he did not know anybody there. He just banked his hope in the copy of my result slip he carried and mother's luck.

It was not easy for him to trace the Provincial Education Office since many of the passers-by he met in Kisumu Town were not conversant with Kiswahili. He too could not communicate in Dholuo or proper English. Language barrier stood in his way for several hours before he met a guard, who at first attempted to dismiss him.

"The guard somehow mellowed when I showed him your result slip," my father revealed to me when he came home the following day. It was the guard who showed my father the education office where he learnt that according to the school's Form One selection list, I had indeed been selected to Itibo and my letter of offer had been dispatched alongside others.

The officer was kind enough to give my father a copy of my letter of admission. My father returned home a happy man and we hastily purchased required items like a wooden box, a pair of shoes and other personal items required by the school.

One fine morning in February 1974, I stepped out of our home in a new pair of shorts and wearing shoes for the first time. Excitement swept through my heart and radiated on the face. I once again took a historic ride in a bus christened Getiro, which dropped us in Kisii Town before we connected to the school using another bus, which was known as Mayenga.

I was surprised to find that the school was not as big as its name sounded. Most classrooms and offices had earthen walls, just like my former primary school. The school fee was Ksh. 700 per annum, a huge amount then but my father was well-prepared and he paid it instantly.

When he was informed that the school provided other items such as a bed, mattress, blankets and three meals (breakfast, lunch and supper) daily, my father was happy. We were also to be given uniforms the following day, but this was done almost two months later. With all that the school provided, my father decided that I did not need any money for my personal upkeep, and bid me goodbye with firm instructions that I uphold discipline and work hard in my studies.

I fought back anxiety when he stepped out of the school gate excitedly. I later learnt that he walked down the Manga cliff which separated the school and our ancestral home area and bought his peers beer with what would have been my pocket money. His son had joined high school and this was no mean feat! It called for celebration!

That day, I was all alone, away from my family, in pursuit of nothing but education. It dawned on me that I had started my real academic journey and had transited from a child to a young man. I knew that this new chapter will require me to make crucial decisions that can impact my life positively.

I did not need to be a rocket scientist to tell me that I was once again in a disorganized school environment. The majority of the teachers were habitually absent and some students were extremely undisciplined. I was disappointed to learn that teachers approved bullying of form one students who were pejoratively called 'monos'. We were informed that new comers like me were required 'to be seen and not be heard'.

My first night in the dormitory lasted an eternity. It started with us, the new comers, being lined up. Senior students then shouted in turns, "monos!" and we responded in unison, "Yes, sir." Spending a night in a room full of boys was a new experience for me. But my friend Paul Oseko was more confused as he had never slept on a bed.

"*Ing'ai bakobeeka emetwe gochia* (To which side do we place our heads)?" he asked me. This was the oddest question I ever expected from a boy of his age. It was very difficult for me to restrain myself from bursting into laughter even as I guided him. He continued to be my good friend who later became a teacher.

I vividly recall how our bullies poured cold water on our beds to wake us up the following morning. They then ordered us to remove our shirts, dash to the athletics field and do ten laps. They also read us a code of conduct, which they called the *Monos' Creed*. Among the instructions were the orders that we should never question seniors on any issue, and we should only eat after all seniors had eaten.

I was in deep sleep during the second night when we were woken up again at around 5 am. This time, the instructions were that we run out of the compound, down the Manga cliff through its foot, then up again through Isecha, Enamba then back to the school. We had to obey, lest we face the ire of the senior boys. Some of my classmates could not cover the distance that was over 20 kms and collapsed along the way. Even so, this morning run became a routine for us which lasted several months.

The school did not have piped water and the precious commodity was never harvested when it rained. Students scaled down a cliff and bathed in the spring down below. They also washed their clothes there and hanged them to dry as they basked in the sun especially during weekends. As Form Ones, we had an additional responsibility of scaling the cliff daily to fetch water which was used in the school kitchen for cooking.

Despite the myriad of challenges, it was an abomination for us to be late in whatever we did. We bathed and fetched water quickly to be in time for breakfast at 7.30 am. We then assembled for announcements, mainly from prefects and dispersed for lessons at 8.15 am.

I had a feeling that some of our teachers were ill-qualified to teach. This made me lose interest in subjects like Maths, which had been my favourite in primary school. The situation was aggravated by the conduct of senior students who bullied us.

One day my friend John Ogeka found himself on the receiving end. He told one of the bullies that he came from Nyakoe, near the home of former Kitutu Chache MP, Zachary Onyonka. Ogeka had inadvertently missed the fact that our school was situated a stone throw away from the home of Sagini Ndemo who was Onyonka's sworn opponent.

The political rivalry between supporters of the two leaders usually spilled into the school. In no time, Ogeka was given a severe beating before the bullies made away with his beddings and pocket money. I have to salute Ogeka because despite the hostility he faced, he never quit school. He retired recently from the Ministry of Public Works where he was first employed as a clerk and rose through the ranks to a senior administrative position.

I was most affected when someone stole my shirt, pair of shoes, socks, shirt and shorts. I was only left with the clothes I was wearing that day and that really inconvenienced me. I had to cope by waking up early in the morning on Saturdays to go and wash the remaining pair of shorts and shirt at the nearby stream. I had to wait for them to dry while I wound myself with a towel at the waist. Suffering worsened when someone stole my underpants, hurting me even more.

I approached an older student, Rasugu Momanyi, who gave me a pair of his shoes, socks, shorts and shirt. I was tiny and when I wore them, it was clear that they were not mine. Some of the students laughed when they saw me in the oversize clothes but this never bothered me. My predicament was addressed a week later when all Form One students were given new uniforms. From Rasugu, I learnt that even in the midst of adversity, you will always find a shoulder to lean on.

I cannot forget the brotherly love Rasugu showed me and we have remained friends to the present day.

It is human nature to recall their low and high moments. To me, the low moments at Itibo Secondary School outweigh high ones. I cannot, for example, forget an incident where students in Form Three took us to an abandoned pit latrine within the compound. They ordered us to sniff the irritating smell emanating from therein. We were not allowed to hold our noses or spit but swallow the saliva. I have never understood why these guys wanted us to suffocate ourselves in the stench by restraining us from breathing in and out and inhaling clean air.

At times, during meal time, the older boys would tell us to stand in straight lines and sing to them, *"bwayire, n'eching'ende, ndindindi* (the morsel is ready alongside beans)", to their amusement and laughter which bordered on the ridiculous. As Form Ones we usually ate after the senior students and, occasionally, they emptied the food containers before we got our share. On lucky days, they unsparingly served themselves leaving too little food for us. No wonder most of the senior students especially prefects looked well-fed and too big for their clothes. This was unlike the Form Ones. We were silhouettes in our clothes for some months before we got used to the life in the school.

Notwithstanding my rather negative experience at Itibo, when I went home during the end of term holidays, many of my peers and their parents perceived me as a role model by virtue of having made it from the local primary school. Several of them were eager to seek my advice and/or help in their studies. I found this to be quite fulfilling and I tried as much as I could to give assistance, including coaching some of them in their class work. Indeed, some of these students ended up doing well in their examinations, even as I may not attribute their success wholly to my input.

Remarkable Achievement

Our Form One class of 1974 comprised of very brilliant boys despite the harsh environment we were in. We coached ourselves a number of times especially in the arts subjects but had challenges in sciences and mostly mathematics where we needed the assistance of teachers. This made most of us to shift our interest to the arts and languages.

If there was a teacher who loved his job most, then it was James Arisi who handled Christian Religious Education (CRE). He was one person who was very committed to his job and never skipped his lessons. In turn, this endeared him to students. In the long run, many of us ended up getting distinctions in the subject.

In the prevailing environment, there were frequent strikes over poor diet or absentee teachers at the school. During the riots, students destroyed property and were sent home for a number of days and were required to return while accompanied with their parents. They were then punished and fined to replace and repair what was vandalized during the riots.

I heaved a sigh of relief when education officers visited the school for a fact-finding mission one day. The officers resolved that for sanity to be restored in the school, nearly all teachers had to be transferred. New teachers were posted to the school. They included Mr. Amati who came in as the head teacher and resolved to revamp the school, to our excitement. Mr. Amati drove a Voxwagen, a classic car at the time. He did his part in revamping the school although cases of indiscipline were rooted to the core.

Of all people, I never knew that I could easily pick up bad behaviour from other students but I did. I was in Form Three when we decided that enough was enough and manhandled a teacher who was always absent as he spent time drinking in the neighbourhood. We chased him out of the compound one afternoon and warned him never to come back. We booed and heckled him, and it was by sheer luck that he fled to safety in one piece. The school was ungovernable that afternoon and police were called in before we were ordered to leave the compound in haste. We ended up staying at home for two weeks.

My father was not amused when he escorted me to school, but I was in for an even bigger shock when he was informed that I was among those who incited other students to go on rampage. When he was asked if it was true that I was among the ring leaders, out of fear I responded in the affirmative. 'How could I do that?' he must have wondered as I quavered, unsure of how he was going to handle my case.

"I'm perplexed that you can make such allegations against my son. I can tell you without fear or contradiction that I know my son in and out. He is a harmless youth who is well-behaved and devoted to his studies. My son has never given me any problem and I'm shocked that he has admitted the accusations labelled against him. Maybe he has gotten bad company here but kindly, don't expel him," my father pleaded with the teachers.

True to his request, I was spared expulsion. Some of us were given huge tree stumps to uproot while others were expelled. It took us several days to do the punishment but for me, it was better than being expelled.

The late Dr. Zachary Onyonka, who was the MP for Kitutu Chache Constituency where the school was situated, was a powerful Minister then, serving in President Jomo Kenyatta's administration in the Education docket. He was invited to the school to speak to us days later and he unsparingly gave us a dress down. I have never forgotten the strongly worded speech he gave us that day.

During those early days, there were very few people in the country who had studied to PhD level. Dr. Onyonka was one of them. To many, he was the epitome of academic success. That alone gave him prestige and bearing advantage over us students who had never seen a PhD holder.

"How can you even start imagining chasing a teacher who is a university graduate out of school? Do you even know what getting a degree entails? Do you know that there are very few people who are degree holders? How can useless Form Three boys go on strike against a highly qualified teacher?" Dr. Onyonka thundered.

He further challenged us that he was a global scholar and had an advantage of traversing the world and meeting equally learned personalities, including beautiful ladies. If we wanted to become successful and marry successful ladies from any part of the world, we had to work hard in our studies, he told us. This left me challenged and I am proud that I eventually rose through the education ladder to become a University Professor.

I was surprised when one morning, the headmaster came to our class after the strike issue was resolved looking for me. This was soon after we finished the punishment of uprooting the tree stumps. He announced that henceforth, I had been appointed to be the class prefect. I guess the decision must have been made on the basis of what my father said before him concerning my character as a young person. I held the position even up to Form Four, serving diligently and endeavouring never to let my colleagues down.

Being a class leader demanded that my behaviour stood apart. However, there were occasions when this threw me into confusion, especially when I strongly felt that the school administration was being unjust to students. Strikes were the easiest language the administration understood and responded to in fixing our problems. It was unheard of for a prefect to support a strike being engineered by students but one day I did exactly that.

The final Form Four examinations were around the corner when the pressure lamp in our class malfunctioned during our evening preps. The school did not have electricity and my colleagues demanded that we go to the Form Three class, acquire their lamp and leave them with the faulty one. I had been literally pushed into a tight corner. This was a litmus test for me. As the prefect, I was required to carry the faulty lamp and execute the plan.

The Form Three students, whom we thought would yield to our seniority status, did not take our mission kindly. No sooner had we taken their lamp than a fight ensued. They were going to win the fight had Form Ones and Form Twos not sided with us; we chased them out of the school compound.

With the head teacher away at that hour, the school became ungovernable once again. I knew the enormity of the mistake we had committed and, as the prefect, I was going to carry the highest responsibility. I ran to the teaching staff compound and informed the teacher on duty what had transpired. I have to admit that I twisted the story a little in favour of my class.

One of the lies I told him was that the Form Threes started the fight. I also told him that the faulty lamp belonged to the Form Threes who had attempted to replace it with the one belonging to Form Twos, occasioning the fight which Form Ones and Fours tried to contain it in vain.

Just then, the headmaster arrived and found the chaotic scene and was over the roof, baying for my blood. He had already been informed by the Form Threes who were by the roadside outside the school compound that I had started the fracas by forcefully taking away their pressure lamp. I remember he had a metal rod when we met and he hit me with it twice in the presence of the teacher on duty who tried to calm him down and defend me, saying I was innocent. The chaos continued the whole night, with some students like my friend Assa Nyakundi sustaining injuries. Nyakundi is now a prominent lawyer in Nairobi and as fate would have it, currently, he is the Chairman of the school's old boys' association and a member of the Board of Management of the school.

Education officials came in the following morning and partially closed the school by ordering that Form One to Two students to go home until we finished our national examinations. During their investigations, other issues arose which prompted the arrest of some students.

The fact that we sat for the national Form Four examinations in such an environment and most of us excelled was an act of God. It was luck, an accident or a combination of the three. Only humane cooks accepted to stay around and cook for us. Since there was no firewood, we destroyed a number of desks and the cooks used them to cook for us in what we called academic fires. We also organized ourselves and drew a roster indicating how each one of us had to take part in fetching water from down the cliff to be used for cooking and washing during free time.

As already mentioned, in the school in general, we lacked competent teachers in the sciences including mathematics. So, as the national examinations approached, most of us were not well prepared in the science subjects. Thus, there was a lot of anxiety and phobia in the days we were supposed to do the science related papers. The anxiety led to desperation and many of my student colleagues were prepared to do anything to reduce it. I recall that some boys in my class consumed marijuana in turns, believing that it would enable them do well in sciences and maths. I remember one of them got so inebriated and marked almost everything as being right in one of his answer sheets. The school was completely run down when we left it towards the end of 1977. It would later be reorganised and it continues to exist to this day.

In January 1978, I got wind that the national examinations results were out and I had scored Division 1, an equivalent to A plain in the current system of ranking. When I entered the school to collect my results slip, I was received with jubilation by the students. I had passed in all subjects, including the dreaded mathematics. That year, nearly all candidates in my class did well and the starring record we set stands to date.

Many of my 46 classmates at Itibo are now working locally and abroad as prominent lawyers, bankers, architects, teachers and public servants and have led successful lives. They include my friend Paul Oseko, John Ogeka, Joseph Ombogo, lawyer Assa Nyakundi, among others. However, in recent years, many have retired, especially those that were in public service.

When I look back at where most of us started, I conclude that if you have the capability and are determined to achieve success - be it in academics, sports or anything, no matter the hurdles - chances are that you will succeed. If you were born a star, even if the star is put under the table or bed, it will always shine brightest even in the darkest place.

Passing a national examination is a great achievement in Kenya. We instantly became heroes and to this day, our names are still celebrated as the people who excelled that year and left an indelible mark. In fact, I also surprised myself because I did not expect to score Division 1, however good I knew I was. This has been my trait throughout my academic journey; underestimating my capability.

In particular, excelling in examinations in Kenya brings happiness in the family. Although my mother was sickly, she was very happy, just as my father and siblings were.

However, with hindsight, I have to say that since I have spent most of my life in the academic environment and seen nearly all, we need to embrace a better education system. The Competence Based Curriculum (CBC) which is being rolled out has its pros and cons. We need to find a middle ground and ensure the rollout is a success for the present generation and posterity.

For instance, assessment is very central in any education system and examinations are there to assess the competence of students. However, an examination should not be an end in itself but a part of the education process. It should not be a matter of life and death as it has been perceived over the years.

Our education system lacks the aspect of character formation, way from primary school up to university. There is total laxity in inculcating moral values and good character in young people. This is one issue the new curriculum should urgently address.

Those who have been to school and succeeded in academics and co-curricular activities should be ready to be role models to others. It will serve to avert a situation where vices like violence, drug abuse, alcoholism and corruption thrive.

Secondly, I can testify that the unfortunate stories surrounding mismanagement of schools started a long time ago. Mismanagement includes embezzlement of funds, improper handling of the curriculum and failure to address students' grievances on time. The big question is why should such a situation prevail for such a long time? For example, mismanagement makes students, especially those in boarding schools, suffer because the environment and food they eat fails to favour their wellbeing.

I took my children for a tour of my former school a few years back. They wondered how I managed to come out of the place victorious. This is notwithstanding the fact that the school is now relatively improved, especially in terms of infrastructure compared to the 1970s. The institution now has permanent buildings and is connected to electricity and water. The teachers are now properly trained and are more committed. My children could not picture what it was like forty years ago. I took them to the cliff, which we scaled down and up to fetch water during my days there and they could not believe it.

However, despite the shortcomings, I am proud of the school and hold it in high regard. To a large extent, it contributed to making me who I am today. Gideon Bienda and James Arisi who are among those who taught me at the school are now retired. They used to occasionally visit me in my office at the university and I hold them in high esteem.

As an old boy of the school, I am a member of the old boys association. We are doing our part in assisting the school management improve the institution. In 2017, we raised money and built a library and stocked it with new books. We also recently sunk a borehole for the school. We endeavour to do more.

I remember that, as classmates, we were close knit and inspired one another to work hard in our studies. We did a lot of our class work together since we had embraced regular group discussions. This made us to freely share the available learning materials. Also, we had a lot of social interaction and participated together in various sporting activities. Indeed, our school was well known for excelling in some of the sporting competitions in the region. The school had, especially, over time cut itself a niche in cross-country and other long distance races.

At personal level, I was not left behind in sporting activities. Even so, I was not as athletic as some of my schoolmates who represented the school at the district, provincial and national competitions.

Through my unique experience at school, I learnt that in any form of academic endeavour one should at all times know the commonalities and point of convergence with colleagues and friends. Thus, in the academic journey, one should always walk with people of the same mindset in order to excel.

Biographer's Note: Nairobi-based lawyer Assa Nyakundi was Prof. Akama's deskmate at Itibo Secondary School. The city lawyer had this to say:

Prof. Akama was brilliant, but quiet and very effective. This may sound like an oxymoron but I can elaborate by saying that, back in the day, you could only ignore him at your own peril; he looked quiet but was very potent.

We were a very robust class that comprised of students who read ahead of most teachers. We could always answer questions, and accurately so, most of the time. This left our teachers challenged to give us more.

Let me add that we were a very radical bunch of boys. We went on strike twice in the four years we were at the school. In fact we were radical to the extent that, one time, the school ran for a whole year without a head boy. We had badly tormented the one who held that position (he is now a professor too) and no one else wanted to take that role.

Due to mischief, we once destroyed a water pump at the school! However, I am happy that, later in life, we have sunk a borehole at the school to alleviate water shortage; it is part of giving back to our alma mater. I am the chairman of the Board of Management (BoM) and Prof. Akama is among the old boys who are actively involved in giving the school a facelift. Students get encouraged when they see us; they believe that, if we excelled 40 or so years ago, they too can do even better.

Conquering Culture Shock

Kakamega High School was my first choice for A-levels which included Forms Five and Six education. With my exemplary performance in Form Four, I was certain that I would join the school. It was one of the best boys' high schools in the country at the time. The school admitted the top cream from across the country. I envisioned walking in its corridors for the next two years.

However, it is true that history has a way of repeating itself. Once again, I did not receive my letter of admission. Since the school is in the former Western Province, my father had to travel again. This time, he travelled all the way to Kakamega to find out what was amiss.

The names of students selected to join the school that year (1978) were written alphabetically and displayed on the notice board. Interestingly, my name Akama Sorana John was on top of the list yet I had not received my letter of admission. Overwhelmed with joy, my father nearly screamed. The Deputy Principal Assa Okoth who was also in charge of admissions gave him a copy of the letter. My father returned home, excited that his son had been admitted to the best high school in Western Kenya.

My parents took me for shopping. They bought for me extra clothes and a metallic box. Then on the material day of reporting in the month of May, we set off for the long journey from home to the school. It was yet another promising and adventurous journey.

We missed Getiro bus, which was the only vehicle plying through our home area at that time. We paid a hefty price for our lateness by walking a 15 kilometres distance to Metamanywa along the Kisii-Kericho road. My father was smartly dressed. I remember he wore a suit and well-polished shoes that day. Being a tidy man, he walked briskly, taking care not to dirt his trousers and shoes before we got to the vehicle.

The distance was tiring and unadventurous. My mother had packed about 20 kilograms of dry maize for us to deliver to my cousin who stayed in Kakamega. I carried the luggage while my father carried my items in the box.

I recall how we made several stops along the way to catch a breath. I heaved a sigh of relief when we got to Metamaywa and entered a vehicle which dropped us in Kisii Town. It was raining heavily and my father had to fold his long trousers to near knee level. We jumped pools of muddy water on our way to board another vehicle to take us to Kisumu. Roads in Kisii Town were muddy and full of gullies unlike today where most of them are paved.

It was as if it was raining all over Kenya. When we got to Kisumu at around 4 pm, it was pouring even more. We got drenched as we tried to find the next vehicle to Kakamega. Time was running fast and I got anxious as dusk struck before we got to our destination. We surprised the watchmen at Kakamega High School when we entered the compound at 8 pm, tired, drenched and hungry.

Peter Ofumbi who would days later teach me Geography showed me a place to sleep. My father found his way to his cousin's house in Kakamega Town where he spent the night. He joined me the following morning at the admissions office where he paid fees and left for home.

I quickly realised that my new and former schools were worlds apart. Kakamega had systems that worked from the onset. I was first taken to the school uniforms store where I was given time to select and fit myself with the clothes. It did not take long before I stepped out with two pairs of long trousers, shirts, a blazer, mattress, blankets and bed sheets.

My first impression of the school was that it had highly developed infrastructure. The walkways were paved and someone must have done a wonderful landscaping job. It's clearly manicured lawns and the ornamental and indigenous trees gave the school a scenic view.

The A-level students were allocated cubicles while those in O-level slept in open dormitories. Compared to the rest of the students, we were treated differently. For example, we could get out of school and come back without asking for permission. This was a privilege only A-level students enjoyed. We also wore long trousers just like the teachers.

I loved the diversity in our class. It was a galaxy of young, brilliant and promising young men. We had come together from various ethnic, religious and social backgrounds to sharpen our brains further in a collegial environment. Being in the school enabled me to get a wider view of life as I met and made new friends from various parts of Kenya.

In the school, academic and social lines were drawn from the onset. There was a subliminal struggle between students taking science subjects and those enrolled in arts-based courses. For instance, students taking History, Christian Religious Education (CRE) and Literature were looked down upon by those studying Maths, Physical Sciences (Physics and Chemistry) and Biology combinations. Those in the Maths, Physics and Chemistry (MPC) class proudly said that theirs was a Man Power Combination (MPC). To them, Maths, Physics and Chemistry combination was more prestigious than others and they were right. It gave them better career prospects at the time.

In particular, they were inspired that after high school, they would join universities to pursue 'superior' programmes such as medicine, architecture and engineering. Those in the arts section were seen to have limited and less prestigious career options ahead of them. Only law, public administration and perhaps a Bachelor's Degree in Anthropology or Bachelor of Education Arts were predominantly available to them. I was in the latter category.

As young people aspiring to be successful someday, some of us were worried that we were to be labelled inferior by virtue of the subjects we were studying. Our counterparts in the sciences section walked tall and appeared ever confident in the presence of girls from neighbouring schools. We had occasional pleasure to interact with them when they visited our school for educational and extra-curricular events. Students in the sciences track would walk with gaiety, while carrying huge science text books and files around the school.

At my level, I got somewhat disoriented. CRE was not well-regarded. I dropped it and went for History, Geography, English Literature and a General Paper (GP), which was compulsory for all students. I got depressed for some weeks before accepting the reality that I now faced. I had arrived with high expectations following my good performance in my O-level examinations. I had not imagined I was going to start my A-level studies this way.

Unlike Itibo, at Kakamega, we had some of the best teachers in Kenya. They included Assa Okoth who taught us History. Okoth was a famous name in the subject, having authored History textbooks that high school students used across the country. There was also Peter Ofumbi, the Geography teacher, and some expatriate teachers from the UK. Mr. Blackrock, a Mathematics teacher, was huge in size and an excellent teacher at that.

In the prevailing circumstances, we received the best teaching. I ended up liking Geography and History. The effectiveness of my teachers made me love the two subjects more and indeed, as it is, a teacher can influence a student's perception of a subject and eventual career choice.

We only assembled on Mondays and Fridays for school announcements and other pertinent matters. This was the time our teachers spoke to us and encouraged us to aim to be the best. Our Headmaster then was Gerald Avedi, a highly dignified and trained teacher. He would later become a Permanent Secretary in the Ministry of Education during President Moi's time. His trademark was Kaunda suits, well-trimmed hair and he had a gift of the gab. Mr. Gerald Avedi always left a lasting impression on everyone who met him.

Competition was very stiff in class and we were all proud of our school which we called the 'Alliance of Western Kenya'. Some of us were so proud that our pride made us walk in a peculiar style, especially when visiting Kakamega Town. We called it 'an angle of academic inclination', where you would stoop one of your shoulders as you walked. We were the academic and sports powerhouse of the region and were dreaded by neighbouring schools like Musingu, Lugulu and Kamusinga.

This, at times, made some boys arrogant. They thought that being in the school guaranteed them a place in the university. Many of them were wrong and ended up failing.

I loved outings to neighbouring schools, especially during sports events. This was especially so because, although I was not a good footballer or athlete, the school was inseparable with sporting, particularly football. We had a teacher who identified talent and coached the football team. This was unlike my former school where my dream of becoming an athlete was dimmed. Sports activities in Itibo boys were neither given much attention nor were there sports facilities to begin with.

Being in the school's football team dubbed 'The Green Commandos' had several benefits attached. Team members ate special meals and for the two years I was a student at the school, they were the national football champions. We walked with our heads held high for being the football powerhouse.

I recall an incident which occurred when we played and incidentally lost to neighbouring Musingu Boys' High School at Bukhungu Stadium. Our rivals enjoyed a strong fan base comprising of their neighbours, Mukumu Girls' School. This really infuriated us and, as the referee blew the last whistle, we got out of the stadium, waylaid the girls and attempted to stone their bus. Clearly, this was youthful mischief which can be dangerous sometimes. Luckily, although we smashed the windows of the bus, the girls were not injured. The girls were lucky as our headmaster, Mr. Avedi, appeared at the scene and made us flee before we could cause more damage. Strangely, none among us was punished.

Reflections on A-Level Education

My view is that the O-level and A-level system of education appeared to be effective in identifying the capabilities of students and ensuring that they brought out their best. After O-level training (Form 1 to Form 4), those who did not go to

A-level had an option of joining training colleges while others joined polytechnics where the main courses offered were agriculture, mechanics, carpentry, masonry, teaching and business. Those who proceeded to A-level did so by joining in either science or arts streams. This enabled the students to further test their professional inclinations. Those who did not join university could go to national polytechnics and colleges that offered training at diploma level.

Further, due to the admissions criteria, students from diverse backgrounds met and interacted. This bridged social and cultural gaps that are often perpetuated by ethnic tendencies that haunt our country to this day. This is true to the extent that Kakamega High School was a national school. Those schools that were either district or provincial schools still had the majority of students from local communities.

Personally, the system made me expand my horizon. It enriched my network and enabled me to make friends from different parts of the country. Further, I was able to understand and value our rich diversity as a country. This is a phenomenon I carry with me even today. I love, appreciate and enjoy making and keeping friends from different Kenyan communities.

This system of education was appropriate and relevant to the country's economic and socio-cultural environment. Those who went through it spent seven years in primary, four in O-level, two in A-level and three in universities if they qualified. They then left for the job market as mature people ready to serve the country. However, those pursuing medicine, pharmacy and engineering programmes stayed longer at campus. While the later took three and half years, medicine took five while pharmacy took four.

I also learnt that the company one keeps in school can either make or spoil you. Some students fell by the wayside when they followed others blindly. They ended up indulging in negative activities such as alcohol and drug abuse.

This reminds me of two of my friends who were staunch Seventh Day Adventists. It was their routine to suspend their studies at 6pm every Friday and resume on Saturday at the same time. According to the church's doctrines, the period between 6 pm Friday and 6 pm Saturday is regarded as holy and set aside for total rest. The Adventists spent the time praying, reading the Bible and singing church hymns.

Of the two young men, it appeared to me that one was misleading the other. One was a fast learner and when he eventually sat for national examinations, he did well in all papers while his prayer mate failed. It appeared to me that the one who failed was following his friend blindly. However, this should not be construed to mean that there was anything wrong with prayers and observance of the Sabbath. It is only the fact that the two friends did not appear sincere and helpful to one another, especially in academic matters.

I also remember one classmate who was a bookworm. I have never come across a person who reads day and night and all the time, the way the gentleman did. Unfortunately, he performed poorly in the final examinations.

One day, I jokingly asked him why he was spending all day and night on end reading if he was not improving his grades. This irked him and we fought physically like long-term enemies.

I discovered that bookworms hardly excel in their studies. In all my studies, I constantly have time gaps for relaxing. The interludes help me to refresh and grasp more information when I resume studying.

In this regard, educators recommend the same; the mind, like the body, needs a rest and it works best when it has fully rested and relaxed. But, the capacity of the mind to absorb things or act properly is substantially impaired if it is unduly extended and not given enough time to rest. I learned this principle early in life while interacting with diverse students. Equally, the advice I received from my experienced teachers as pertains to this matter was worthwhile.

Being a student at Kakamega High School enabled me to start thinking critically as encouraged by our teachers. In literature, we were encouraged to read between the lines to find hidden meanings of events and scenarios. In history, we went beyond stating facts and were required to be analytical and able to synthesize historical events in order to draw logical conclusions. This spirit of questioning and not taking things at face value has served me well up to the present time.

Towards the end of our A-level education, we were ready and mature to take on university education. Sometimes, our outings and adventure drove us into run-ins, some of which were crazy. I had this friend from Kisii by the name Charles Nyarunda whose mission was to get a girlfriend who also hailed from our community. One day, he told me to accompany him to meet the lady during a sporting activity in our school. We dressed in our best and confidently met the girl but she gave us a cold reception. This was against our expectations and my friend was extremely frustrated.

Hours later, we found the same girl with another young man who was our classmate. This annoyed my friend even more and we confronted the girl, throwing tantrums and insults. When we realized that the verbal exchange had drawn the attention of some teachers, we quickly vanished.

My friend was not done with her yet. He looked for the girl's school address and wrote her a terse letter in which he accused her of being arrogant and disrespectful to prospective and future husband material. What irritated him more is that she had audacity of dating someone from outside our community.

I never thought that our paths would ever cross again with the lady but as fate would have it, I met her in the university. We ended up becoming very good friends. It then occurred to me that while we stubbornly clung to our tribal biases in high school, she looked beyond it and dated a man of her choice.

Even if my friend Nyarunda did not win this girl's heart, he never gave up on finding one who would give him a softer landing. The two of us made several visits to a tea room in Amalemba Township, which is a stone throw away from Kakamega High School. The business was run by an elderly lady who had a stunningly beautiful daughter whose heart my friend yearned for. I remember we got caught one day by our headmaster outside the school compound during unauthorized hours and he gave us a stern warning never to repeat the offence.

Nevertheless, the girl finally accepted my friend's advances and he was untouchably over the moon. They arranged to meet in private and at that point nobody could tame his high expectations. They finally got to have their first intimate kiss but my friend fled and never went to see the girl again.

"That girl is a prostitute," he told me after that encounter.

"Why do you say that?" I asked?

"She stuck her tongue out and started kissing me intimately, then went ahead to demand a mouth to mouth kiss. I ran away," he said, frustrations evidently written all over his face.

That night my friend had a dream which scared him off his bed. He apparently saw the girl in the dream, kissing him. Perhaps Nyarunda's rowdy behaviour reflected his family upbringing. He used to tell us how his father would get easily annoyed and engage in physical confrontations with family members, including his mother and uncles. Sadly, when we were about to leave Kakamega High school, my friend received devastating news that his father had been murdered by unknown assailers. In this regard, one can say that probably the boy's parents, especially the father, were not good role models.

I have to finally note that were it not for my father's resilience, I would have missed the chance to study at Kakamega. This is why I credit my parents for their determination that saw us get education. They worked hard in the farm and ensured we never lacked food, clothing and school fees. My father's travel to the school to get the letter of admission showed his persistence. He also ensured that his son was well taken care of by paying fees, buying clothes and meeting my other needs.

I attribute this to my father's exposure during his stay in Kericho which enabled him to appreciate the value of education. His first cousin John Andrew Omanga, who later became a Member of Parliament for Nyaribari Constituency, had obtained an Economics Degree from Makerere University and returned home to serve as a Permanent Secretary during the time of Kenya's founding President, Jomo Kenyatta. He later became a Minister during President Moi's time. My father witnessed how Omanga became a trendsetter in the family and community due to his education.

Although my brother Dr. Mathew Kiriago Akama, a Maxillofacial Surgeon, and I got university education, my sisters never did. The environment then was not in favour of girls. They spent a lot of time running errands in the homes with their mothers while the boys got sufficient time to study. In this regard, most girls in the community dropped out of school earlier than those who continued with their studies. For example, my sister never went beyond Form 4. I am happy that the ground is changing and girls are catching up with the boys. Women are currently excelling in their education and are occupying remarkable ranks both in the public and private sector.

*****

Based on my academic journey and experience in the management of a learning institution, I have to admit that society has changed drastically. Indeed, as the saying goes, change is inevitable and I am yet to witness more of it. Technology and other social norms have changed the landscape and reversed the gender and workplace matrices. We no longer have a lot of the so called white collar jobs because a lot of work is done by machines like computers and robots.

This calls for change in the way we approach educational issues. Fundamentally, the role of education should be to better a person to become a critical thinker and/or a problem solver. Education should make one adaptive and able to manage situations as they arise right from personal, family and public level.

It is my hope that we will achieve a paradigm shift and have a curriculum that generates problem solvers, innovators and wealth creators. We need programmes that will instil patriotism in our young people to enable them think globally but act locally. This way, we can break the snares of tribalism and racism and be able to sustain ourselves, the country and the global community.

Here, it is important to note that, over the years, national education policies as captured in Commission reports such as the Gachathi Commission of 1979, Mackay Commission of 1982, Kamunge Commission of 1988, and the Koech Commission of 2000 basically tweaked the Kenyan education system at the margin. They have failed to fundamentally alter the philosophical and psychological disposition for educators and learners. There is a major gap between what our individual and national aspirations should be and what is taught in school. The value system required should focus on diversity and inclusion, ethical conduct and common aspirations. It should also focus on nurturing a population that is law abiding, selfless and focused on the prosperity of all. The actual stuff we do is quite different!

Rare Achievement

As candidates, we were apprehensive as A-level examinations drew nigh. The examinations came with a whirlwind of unpredictable thoughts, emotions, and anxiety. We had prepared well but still went through emotional turmoil. These final examinations determined those who would make it to university and who would not make the cut. I mulled if I overlooked any concepts, which could make it to the examination papers. I told myself secretly that if such a situation arose, I could try to carefully apply myself to the questions, the best way I possibly could.

In overall, the 1979 examination was tough. We sat for three examinable subjects which were graded from A at the top to F at the bottom. At the same time, students sat for a General Paper which examined general knowledge in politics, civic education, culture and other day to day issues.

In my view, the examinations were elitist in nature and were offered at a time when Kenya had only one university, the University of Nairobi. While extremely few students got admitted to the university, the majority joined middle level colleges, including the Kenya Science Teachers' College, Kagumo Training College, Kenya Polytechnic and Mombasa Polytechnic, among others. Still others got directly absorbed into the job market in the civil service and the private sector.

However, it is important to state that the 7-4-2-3 education system was properly structured. By the time the student went through high school, she or he had matured and could make informed decisions on career choices.

I was on cloud nine when the examinations results were released in February 1980. My prayers, hard work, discipline and determination had paid off. I had obtained three principal passes in my three disciplines; Geography, History and English Literature.

This was a sterling performance by all standards and it earned me a place at the University of Nairobi, Kenyatta Campus, to study for a Bachelor of Education degree with Geography and History as my teaching subjects. The campus, which was initially a military barrack, would later become a full-fledged university giving the mother university a run for its money in student enrolment and training programmes.

In the Kenyan context, passing a national examination, and particularly A-levels, elevated one to a higher social status. This is unlike today when graduates wallow in joblessness. Then, there was a time-lapse of nine months before one joined university. I instantly became a hot cake, being pursued by the management of secondary schools near my home. They all wanted to offer me a job as an Untrained Teacher (UT) as I waited to join university.

Our Parish priest, Father Aloyce Stuppner, a World-War II veteran, was a man always in a hurry. He usually drove very fast and appeared to have no time to waste. When he told me to be at his house in the newly-started Nyansiongo Catholic Parish by 6 am, I knew that I did not have any option other than doing exactly that.

He was up by the time I arrived. On his table were four boxes full of coins. I had never seen so many coins as I did that morning. I suspect it was tithe and offering collected the previous Sunday and brought to him from various churches within the parish.

"Help me carry these boxes to the pickup," Fr. Aloyce told me as he hastily walked out, carrying two of them. What surprised me was that even as some coins dropped from the boxes in his clear view, he never bothered.

He started the vehicle and accelerated fast once we got to the road. He seemed not to care that the road had huge gaping potholes that made driving uncomfortable and dangerous as the vehicle swerved from side to side.

There was a portable blackboard at the back of the car and as we cruised through the rough road, it was tossed from side to side. I was afraid that it would fall without him noticing it. I was also afraid that the mist that blurred the view did not befit the speed he was driving at. Nevertheless, we got to Sotik Town safely and he stopped the car at a bank.

I found it strange, once again, when we carried the money in the boxes to the cashier and left it with him. Before we left hurriedly, the Italian priest instructed the cashier to count the money and bank it.

Fr. Aloyce appeared to be more of a soldier than a priest, perhaps out of his experience in World War II. He barked orders even in church which the lay people seemed to obey without a second thought. Whoever failed to comply was chased out of the church.

I remember he chased one Mr. Ndege out of the church twice. In one of the occasions, Fr. Aloyce accused Ndege of making noise while the priest made announcements from the pulpit. To the amazement of the congregation, Ndege, who was known to be a very strict head teacher, left the church dramatically.

As we cruised on the murram road at life-threatening speed, Fr. Alloys' strict mien and no-nonsense approach to issues replayed in my mind. He was close to my father and had informed him that he was hiring me to teach at Nyagacho Secondary School, which the church had just established. I had never been to the school and could not fathom how far it was and what it looked like.

Our journey from Nyansiongo to Sotik and then to the school took us less than one hour. Once there, I noticed that the school did not have proper classrooms. However, what struck me most was the manner in which our arrival sent shivers down the spines of the teachers. The priest threw harsh words at the teachers and even went on to sack the head teacher on the spot by word of mouth. According to Fr. Aloyce the headmaster had failed to make sure that teaching started promptly on the opening day. As a young man, what I saw was completely shocking and unacceptable.

"Where do these teachers stay?" I asked him.

"Don't mind, you are going to know. You will teach in this school," he said.

He must have not have read my body language as we spoke and I had to give him my piece of mind immediately.

"I will not take the job," I said, with finality.

I saw him curl his face, bite his tongue, enter his pick-up, start it and zoom out of the compound. I thought of flagging him down but another thought crossed my mind that it was not necessary. It was better for me to trek the long distance from the school to my home than travel with him.

It was approaching 10 am and there was still restlessness among the teachers as I tightened my shoe laces to start my long walk home. A beam of light heated the left side of my face and I removed my cardigan to avoid sweating unnecessarily. When I raised my face, behold, there was a field of blue that stretched beyond where my eyes could track. Small birds cut across swooping, spinning, spiralling and diving making me have a feeling of gaiety.

I knew the sunny and cloudless day was perfect for a walk because if it were to rain, the journey would be much harder. Outside the school compound, the scent of some flowers by the wayside took me back in time a transitory evocation. Even as the sun's rays pierced on my forehead, I had to hasten my steps.

The weather in Kisii can change in the nick of time but that day it took me by surprise. I had covered about 10 km when I realized that thick clouds were quickly gathering. If I were at home, I would have spent the time admiring them as they gathered and let the rain fall right in our area. I hastened my steps but my haste was beaten by the fast approaching rain.

As the downpour commenced, I took shelter under a deserted makeshift house by the roadside. This was perhaps the best decision I made at that hour as the rain fell in torrents, accompanied with strong winds. When it subsided about two hours later, I stepped out and started walking in the showers, in the hope that I would get home before dusk.

My feet were racing against time and they lost. I only managed to arrive home at around 8 pm. My parents were very happy to see me, having been worried about my delay in getting back home. Their happiness was short-lived, though, once they realized that I had no enthusiasm in responding to their inquiry about my day.

My father got even more disappointed when I told him, with due respect, that I had turned down the priest's offer. "How dare you do that? How can you reject the honour bestowed upon this family by the priest?" he asked.

When my father spoke, we listened and quite often from a distance. It would be dishonourable to engage with one's father when he is annoyed. So, I let him talk for a while. When he was done, I apologized profusely, although I knew this did not come from deep in my heart.

"Count yourself lucky because you are now an adult. I would have punished you mercilessly for embarrassing us," he said. To my parents, my act was a clear show of disrespect for the church, and one they held in high esteem. How would I dare turn down a job offer from the Parish priest? "You are on your own," he said. It was unheard of for anyone to tell the priest off.

My father must have missed his sleep that night. The following morning, he woke up before sunrise and went to the parish to make an apology on behalf of the family.

Apart from his many negatives, in the overall, Fr. Aloyce did a tremendous and commendable job in our area. Apart from spiritually nourishing the followers, he converted the parish land into a demonstration farm. It thrived with pedigree cows and various crops. At the same time, he helped build several secondary schools including Raitigo, Nyagacho, and Riang'ombe. This is in addition to dispensaries like Nyansiongo, which is now a Level Four Hospital serving the community.

Time would finally come for Fr. Aloyce Stuppner to retire and return to his motherland, Italy, in May 2006. He was in his 70s and among the parishioners he invited to see him off was my father. Surprisingly when the parishioners got to his house, they found that he had a small box and his rosary. They could not believe that after working so hard and making the parish economically viable, the priest was going home almost empty handed, literally.

"*Bono inkogenda inde seito Rome. Bono aba'Keresito baminto motigare buya* (A time has come for me to return to Rome. My fellow Christians, may you remain in peace)." These were the last words that the priest, who had learnt Ekegusii, told the parishioners. He then entered the vehicle and was driven away.

Luck followed me after I turned down the priest's job offer. I was invited for an interview at Mecheo Secondary School which was near home. I passed the interview and was offered the job.

But I have to say that the interviewing panel comprised of members who were not very conversant with the teaching at secondary school level. Some of their questions were inappropriate and I considered them unfortunate. For instance, they asked me if I could teach Maths, Biology and Chemistry. This is despite the fact that they had my results slip indicating the subjects I had studied and passed.

Among the interviewees was a lady who applied to teach sciences but they hired her to handle English because, according to the panellists, she was very eloquent in the language. She turned the offer down.

Teaching was exciting and equally challenging. Here I was, handling students who were almost my age. In total, the school had about 250 students. This was not a small number considering its location and status. The teaching staff comprised of five members and the workload was heavy. The situation dictated that apart from teaching the subjects I was hired for (Geography, History and English Literature), I also handled Biology, which I had dropped in my O-levels.

A majority of the students came from my home area and we knew each other well. I realized that due to their background in schooling, many of them were not well-grounded in their studies but were doing their best. This encouraged me to offer them my best. Since most of us were untrained, we did not have pedagogical understanding. However, this did not stop the school administrators from asking us to handle subjects beyond our specialty. This perhaps compromised our teaching quality and effectiveness.

As I have mentioned, some students could not grasp simple concepts. I recall one day teaching the Form Four class the geographical concept of landlocked countries. I spent 45 minutes illustrating what landlocked countries were, and the advantages and disadvantages of being land locked. When I asked them questions at the end of the lesson, I discovered that some had not understood anything from the presentation. I went home a very disappointed person that evening and wondered if I was adding any value to the learners.

That evening I revised my mode of teaching. I decided to engage students by asking them focused questions and allowing them to ask me questions as well. Also, I encouraged them to have group discussions and assist one another. This is an approach that had worked for me some years earlier.

Biographer's Note: Prof. Washington Asembo Olima, a former Deputy Vice-Chancellor at Jaramogi Oginga Odinga University, was in Kakamega High School for A-Levels with Prof. Akama. He said thus:

> Prof. Akama was a very serious student; very focused and firm. We were very close, although we didn't know that we could become professors someday. I have been in contact with him over the years, especially during my tenure as Deputy Vice-Chancellor at Jaramogi Oginga Odinga University of Science and Technology.

Call to Duty

I did not know that my administrative skills, or otherwise, in an educational institution were to be tested in this school. The position of the principal fell vacant after Riang'a Maranga, who occupied the position, proceeded to university for studies. The Board of Management gave me a pleasant surprise by tasking me to hold the position on an acting capacity. I took the challenge in a positive stride.

My elevation to the position of headmaster of a secondary school put an enormous challenge on my shoulders. This was perhaps not commensurate to my administrative experience and exposure at the time. Before that, the only such position I had held was being a prefect at Itibo Secondary School.

The school was ill equipped and did not have the requisite financial resources for the smooth-running of its operations. Many students had huge fees balances too. Furthermore, not even parents, who were fairly financially stable, were willing to pay outstanding fees arrears because they believed the school was theirs anyway. It was a community school!

Due to my nature and character, I became very strict especially for those who were able but unwilling to support the school. I sent their children home severally and this put me on a collision course with them. Some even confronted me on the road side or came to our home to warn me never to send their children away due to non-payment of fees.

I found myself at loggerheads with the parents regularly but I never chose to soften my stand. I remember one parent who confronted me while I was on my way home. As soon as we shook hands he said, "you son of Akama! Who do you think you are, sending my children out of school? Do you know that we are the ones who started this school? You should know that I paid fees for my kids who are in Nyanchwa and Sameta and I don't have any money now to give you."

"You have many cows and goats. Kindly sell one or two and pay for your son and daughter in this school too," I calmly told him. My words appeared to prick him even more. He followed me to our home and complained to my father that I was running the school as my personal property. However, in such situations, my father who understood me well always sided with me.

However, despite the harassment and outright intimidation meted on me by some parents, I did not change my stand. Some yielded and started paying their outstanding fees balances in bits. This enabled the school to have some money to run a few activities. We could now pay the workers and acquire critical items such as learning materials.

Another memorable thing which would have grabbed news headlines today happened. The previous headmaster had taken school uniforms from an Indian trader in Kisii Town on credit and the debt was outstanding. One morning, auctioneers stormed the school accompanied by the police in a lorry. They carried away most movable assets including furniture, a photocopy machine and a typewriter.

This happened in the full glare of teachers and students. The school was paralyzed and everyone looked at me to salvage it from imminent collapse.

I travelled to Kisii Town and went straight to the office of the lawyer who gave the instructions on behalf of the trader. I was shocked with the lawyer's high-end arrogance and pride when he spoke to me. He was shouting at me and, at the back of my mind, I wondered if that was how he was trained to handle legal matters.

The lawyer disclosed to me that apart from the debt the school owed the trader, he had billed his fee to be paid once the items were auctioned.

I went back to my work station and convened a meeting with parents. Those who owed the school balances and others who were ashamed of the situation raised money. Workers agreed to go for two months without pay. This way, we got enough money with which we cleared the debt and recovered the items. This was a big relief. The school fraternity celebrated in song, dance and thanksgiving to God.

Days were quickly running into months. I was the custodian of the school's Post Office key. The office was situated in Keroka Town and I kept checking for any letters.

One day in June 1980, I opened the Post Office box and found a notably large brown envelope. My heart skipped a beat as my hands went for it. My instincts told me that this was my university admission letter. Indeed, my face radiated when I found that it was addressed to me. This was a pleasant surprise. In the past occasions, no letter had reached me. I neither received my O-level nor A-level letters of admission. This is why I suspect that perhaps someone who handled the Post Office key at that time ensured that I never got them.

Time had come for me to leave the school and I did without that month's salary, although it was sent to me much later. My letter showed that I was to join the University of Nairobi, Kenyatta Campus, now Kenyatta University, in September 1980. I spent the early days of August preparing myself for this, but a major misfortune struck my family and threw us into complete darkness.

My beloved mother who had been diabetic, succumbed to the illness! She died at the end of August, 1980. This was the time when her first-born son, and the one who bore the name of her late father, was about to join the university. Remember that qualifying for university at that time was no mean achievement. She had been looking forward, with anticipation, to celebrating with me when I would finally join the university.

I confronted the harsh reality of my mother's demise in a sea of tears of bereavement and sorrow as we buried her. It was a tough and life changing experience for me. It was bad timing as I was going to start a new life far from home. Her grave was still fresh when I left home one morning in September and travelled to commence my university studies.

It was one of the lowest moments of my life and, to date, it is etched in my memory, indelibly, as if it happened yesterday.

My Initial Lessons on Teaching and Administration

When I look back at my experience of teaching in a community school and coming from rural Gusii, it leaves me with a lot to wonder about. It is unfortunate that the problems the institution, which was my first station, faced are the same problems many schools face today. In fact, the situation is more complex, forty years later. I blame society as a whole for the lack of willingness and failure to take the bull by the horns and put an end to these bottlenecks in the education sector.

The situation has worsened because the people who succeed from the countryside proceed to cities and towns, and build their lives there. They hardly come home to help renovate the schools and other local institutions. As well, many schools face administrative and financial challenges due to non-payment of fees and embezzlement. This compromises growth in terms of establishing laboratories and libraries, and equipping them. Even back at Mecheo Secondary School, the infrastructure has not been expanded to the required standards. This is 40 years after I left the institution. It also lacks sufficient teaching materials and adequate personnel. Thus, to a large extent, the very problems that schools faced during my time are still festering today. And there seems to be no end in sight for these tribulations.

It is sad to say that, in most instances, teachers in most community schools are not motivated. Additionally, the schools face management challenges despite the policies and guidelines provided by the Ministry of Education. Some school management boards are chaired by the community's elites who work in far-flung areas. They never have time to be available for ongoing consultation with teachers and other stakeholders. This loses the essence of their acceptance to hold the positions as much as some try to use current technology such as mobile phones and e-mail to keep in touch.

It is high time education stakeholders, especially for the schools in the countryside, realized that the world is moving at a supersonic speed. Right now, information technology and the internet have revolutionized education. Teaching is no longer chalk and board as it was traditionally. The government needs to upscale internet and electricity connectivity to all schools and avail computers and manpower that is abreast with the use of modern technology to impart skills and knowledge to students.

I have also noticed that modern teaching methodologies are not applied in most upcountry schools. Students should be at the centre of learning through the use of pedagogical instruments like problem-based learning, exploratory studies or case study approaches. Students continue cramming facts, which they cannot apply in real life. This results in a situation where we raise a generation that cannot solve problems or critically analyze and manage situations.

The rate at which community schools are popping up in Gusii is also a worrying point. It appears that villages are in a competition to have a school of their own, while disregarding the basics including student catchment and prerequisite infrastructure. The mushrooming of schools is unhealthy and to a large extent wasteful. It encourages student nomadism and creates laxity, which dash the hopes of many for quality education.

Playing the clan card worked in the past but the idea is now archaic and unworkable. A situation where one is appointed to lead an institution on the strength of one's clan or tribe, and not based on one's ability to deliver, should be buried in the deepest grave. It is rather shameful that clansmen can perceive a teacher to be an outsider and chase him out of a school that it is run by their own 'son of the soil' who is incompetent. They fail to assess the implications their decision will have on their children's future.

My experience in the education sector has also taught me that drug abuse, premature sexual activities, incidents of arson in schools and other forms of indiscipline amongst students are on the rise. These issues are detrimental to the future of the youth as relates to their mental health and character. Thus, in many schools one can say that there is laxity in discipline due to poor leadership and administration.

Unemployment is a major challenge in the country, but the majority of those languishing in it are the youth in villages. They lack life skills and requisite competencies in a highly competitive local, national and international environment. We can do better to change this narrative.

And the narrative can change if elites from various areas occasionally retreat from their comfort zones in the local and global Diaspora to give back to the society. It is sad that people with the best academic credentials and training, skills and competencies have cut linkages with their motherland. This is brain drain and it negates the reasons as to why the community raised them. It is a cancer that is eating deep into the fabric of society, leading to increased marginalization, poverty and unemployment. These are the very problems that are particularly problematic to the majority of the youth in towns and rural environment of our country.

I have an example, which demonstrates how the villages we come from are currently at crossroads. I have a well learned friend who is an experienced medical doctor residing in the United States. His elderly mother back in his ancestral home is always sickly and the best he does is talk to her on the phone and prescribe drugs to her. Some of the drugs cannot be found locally even if he wired the money for their purchase.

My view is that the highly trained and successful Gusii people in the Diaspora should learn something from the Jews. As much as the Jews are domiciled in far off and diverse places in different parts of the world, they have committed themselves to sustenance of the State of Israel. They have done this in terms of skills and knowledge transfer, and remitting a proportion of their earnings to go to the country. There are opportunities in our communities and the elites can invest their skills in agriculture, education, health and industry among others to transform their villages. The tendency of wiring money from abroad to their relatives locally is not always a brilliant idea.

I say this because some recipients of the monies lack the capacity to invest and end up undertaking projects that are not worthwhile while some use the money for partying. Indeed, most of what is remitted is largely consumed and in many respects, perpetuate dependency.

There is another issue, which I refer to as the 'Kisii tragedy'. Even so, as I advance this, I wish not to be construed to be promoting tribalism. It is a fact that people with similar cultural and historical backgrounds tend to interact with one another more than they do with other communities. It is unfortunate that the Gusii community is highly fractured and the glue that once bound the community together appears to have melted away in recent years. We have acquired what I will call 'primitive individualism', where everyone is for themselves and God for us all.

In real sense, and to their credit, people with roots in Gusii work very hard as individuals to develop themselves but they lack a sense of belonging as a community. We have some Gusii people who are highly successful in education, business and other areas but have neither made nor cared to make any positive impact in areas where they come from. In fact, many of them hardly care to know what is happening in their home communities.

Nothing demonstrates this more than what I experienced in the United States sometimes back. I had a couple friends from Gusii who moved out of the country a while back. One time, when they invited me to their abode, I was indeed pleased. But when they received me at the airport and drove me home, I became more and more uneasy with what I observed. Their bungalow was located in a white sub-urban neighbourhood and as we approached it, I realized that they did not wave, let alone have any eye contact with their neighbours.

Even so, they told me that although their children were all grown up and married, they were comfortable in the US and will never want to be back to Kisii, let alone set foot in Kenya. They had spent more than twenty years in the US and were even asking me if there was a good road from Nairobi to Kisii. They talked very negatively about Kisii, calling it the land of insecurity, disease and extreme poverty, which they will never want to be associated with. This was indeed disheartening and surprising. If indeed Kisii was that backward, should it not have been their concern to contribute to improving their place of birth? Is this not similar to behaving like that person who knows that his/her mother walks naked and does nothing about it?

Light and Darkness

When my mother died in late August 1980, I saw darkness in a static world. Losing a parent is a catastrophe but it is even worse when it is one's loving mother. You feel like thunder has struck you and you are living on borrowed life.

That material day, I had accompanied my mother for routine treatment at the Kisii District Hospital currently the Kisii Teaching and Referral Hospital. We found it bursting at the seams with patients. There were as many patients sitting on the benches at the waiting bay as they were standing. Others lay under nearby trees. The general atmosphere was gloomy and awful. One wished to get out of there as soon as possible.

We did not have any option and had to stay up to until around 5 pm when she was attended to. Even as we walked out of the hospital and took the bus to go home, I noticed that she was getting weaker as time elapsed.

As we sat in the bus, she told me to buy her a bunch of ripe bananas. I signalled a hawker through the vehicle's window and bought her the bananas. This shocked me even more because of her health condition. I sensed that something was not adding up. I thought that, perhaps, her sugar levels had gone down because she had not had any meal since morning.

The vehicle dropped us in Keroka where we took another one to our home. No sooner had we arrived home than she collapsed, sending the entire family into panic. All my siblings who were present surrounded her and as we mulled over what to do, she told my father in a whisper, "please take care of my children!" These were the last words I heard from my dear mother. As much as the situation appeared to get desperate, my father maintained his cool and continued assuring us that all will be well. It appears that my father was making sure that we did not panic and let the situation get out of hand.

He dispatched me and our farm worker to get a vehicle from the neighbouring home to ferry my mother to hospital. At the home that owned the business vehicle, we found that the driver had parked it after the day's work and already left. Our frantic physical search for him took long since there were no mobile phones at the time. When we realized it was not going to bear fruits, we sought another alternative, which did not equally materialise fast. It took us over five hours to get a vehicle to get her to Kaplong Mission Hospital, in the current Bomet County. The facility was nearer home than Kisii but it was like it took us an eternity to get there.

Just when the medics lay her on the stretcher at 3 am, they announced to us that she had passed on. My heart sank and I felt an unforgettable weakness at the joints. It was confusion like no other I had experienced in my life.

The hospital did not have a morgue. In fact, I had not heard of a facility that had a mortuary at the time. We started our journey home with my mother's body strewn on a mattress on the floor of the pickup truck we had used. The journey was the longest I have ever had between Kaplong and my home. It ended at dawn.

There is a way death converts a lovable home into a strange world. My siblings, father and I were completely devastated when the body was evacuated from the vehicle and taken into the house. Some village elders prepared one corner of the house where the body was to lie in as funeral arrangements were underway.

I recall they made a mound using sawdust and fresh cypress tree branches before they sprinkled cold water. They then placed the body there. This was a rare science that I had not witnessed before. However rudimentary this method of body preservation was, it worked well.

Those days, a burial was just that. There were no sideshows as there are today. Arrangements took a day or two. It was not any different for my mother.

Some representatives of the family were sent to Kisii School where my younger brother Mathew Kiriago, was schooling. He was young, in Form One.

As I gathered, the messengers cooked a false story along the way which they used to get him out of school. They did this deliberately because they feared that breaking the sad news would be unbearable for the young man.

My brother's instincts must have been superb. However hard the messengers tried to conceal the sad news, their voices and eyes likely betrayed them. They arrived home with a teary and fragile young brother who confirmed his worst fears that he had lost his beloved mother.

When the day for my mother's burial came, which was two days after her passing, mourners thronged our home from all corners to condole us. It was a pure solemn ceremony. I cannot remember a single political word being uttered at the funeral. This is unlike today when politicians take advantage of the gathering of mourners. They see it as an opportunity to chest-thump. Most of the time they attempt to endear themselves to mourners or undermine their competitors and detractors, turning funerals into political duels.

Although we were ardent Catholics, I realized that some aspects of culture were observed. These are aspects of culture that have refused to go even to this day. Instead, they are blended with Christianity and are accepted.

For example, my mother's final resting place was dug at a specific place, to the left of our main house. When my father died much later, he was also buried at a specific place relative to the house, usually facing up the slope. Men's graves are situated at the right side of the main door. This happens even to this day.

I was appalled by the many pieces of advice the mourners gave us. When you try to synthesize what you are being told during your mother's burial, you realize that you are an orphan. Words of my aunts from my mother's side touched me even more.

I remember they told us that my father was going to marry now that my mother was dead. They added that they expected me, as the eldest son, to steer my brother and sisters into prosperity because I was already mature. These messages were confounding and painful. I had to take them in stride. As if they were prophetesses, my father indeed married, not long after my mother's passing.

ONTO HIGHER EDUCATION

Entering University

As it turned out, I joined university downtrodden, downcast, broken and in the lowest spirits. When I left home for university, reality was slowly sinking in that mother was in fact six feet under, never to be seen again. On the day of my departure, I was escorted by my elder sister and one of my cousins to board a bus at Keroka market at around 7.00am. I can recall that the bus was fairly rickety. The vehicle was packed with passengers and luggage, which made it stuffy and uncomfortable as it scaled on along the Keroka-Kericho-Nakuru-Nairobi highway. The tiring journey in the bus ended at around 3 pm when we arrived in the city.

I had never been to Nairobi and along the way, my mind wandered far and wide, not knowing what to expect. Once in the city, I was amazed by the sight of many vehicles, busy people and high-rise buildings, especially the iconic Kenyatta International Convention Centre (KICC), then known as the Kenyatta Conference Centre (KCC). It was assumed that one's trip to the city was never complete until one saw the landmark building.

In the city, everyone minds his or her business or pretends to be doing so.

This contrasts with the rural area where people exchange greetings even to strangers and ask for directions. In the city, you have to think twice before asking someone for directions. As it is now, so it was in the 1980s. The most reliable person to ask for directions in the city is a uniformed police officer or the uniformed guards.

The vehicle dropped me near the bus stage of vehicles that plied the Nairobi-Ruiru-Thika route. I found one officer who was very friendly from the moment we shook hands. He told me that I was not far from where I could take a bus to Kenyatta Campus. Not only that, he escorted me and ensured that I boarded the right vehicle.

I reported on a Monday. Registration at the university did not take long and, for the entire week, we underwent orientation. We were given students' handbooks and were addressed by various people who were well acquainted with University rules and regulations.

All in all, the nature of social and academic life in the environment was new to me. This ignited in me a burning desire to work smart in my studies for the next three years I was to be in the university.

Experiencing a New Environment

I had heard that there was total freedom in the university and here I was witnessing and confirming it firsthand. Unlike high school, there was no bell to mark the start, transitions or end of activities. We were all required to use common sense and reflect in our conscience, something that helped towards entrenching responsibility.

In the two years I was at Kakamega High School, I thought I saw the entire galaxy of students from all over the country. How wrong I was? A university offers the real face of the nation in terms of denomination, ethnicity and socio-economic status. It is the mosaic of the Kenyan society. However, I have to note that in general there were very few people from my community and I ended up making good friends from other communities. I am in touch with some of them to this day.

At that time, there were no privately sponsored students in public universities. Thus, all students who were admitted to the Kenyatta Campus were sponsored by the government. They were provided with quality and sufficient meals, accommodation, sanitary materials and cash, popularly known as 'boom'. The boom was offered in form of a concessionary loan, which the students serviced upon completion of university education and absorption into the ready job market.

The meals at the university were high class, especially for someone like me who had come from a rural village. Moreover, there was a lot of food as well. Quite often, at the mess, students served themselves with more food than they really needed. This to me was outright wastage. I knew that there were Kenyans out there struggling to have a meal.

The university environment offered the best life I had ever experienced, and for most students at that time. But I was aware that if I sat pretty to enjoy life, a time for gnashing teeth would not be far. I had to take my Bachelor of Education (Geography and History) studies seriously.

Attending lectures offered a unique experience. It entailed hovering from one lecture hall to the next. There were common units that were taken by up to 200 students at one go. The units were offered in common lecture halls where students were required to attend for their own good as far as the undergraduate training was concerned. Failure to attend lectures and comprehending what was being taught had serious consequences. It would lead to poor performance in examinations, and possible discontinuation of studies.

Some lecturers seemed not to care if they were effective or not. One could arrive in the lecture hall and instantly start the lecture without bothering to know if he was communicating. In situations where lecture rooms were not fitted with the public-address system, we jostled for space at the front of the class. This worked best for us when the lecturer dictated the notes fast.

The degree programme was wide and intense. I discovered that, to survive, I would not miss any lecture. I actually cannot remember missing any lecture at all, unless it was during extreme occasions such as when I was sick.

In most lectures, speed was everything. A lecturer could be teaching the East African Geography course and as he navigated through the ecological and climatic zones, he could use bombastic terminologies. It was common to hear terminologies like the inter-tropical convergence zones, the high and low pressure shells, convergence and divergence of air masses among others as relates to rainfall formations. You could easily be left behind and lost if you did not fully concentrate on what the lecturer was saying.

Students found solace in tutorials. These entailed going to smaller groups, interacting with the lecturer, doing group discussions, giving presentations and receiving feedback from both the students and the lecturer in charge. The tutorial system allowed us to dive deep into the subject in smaller groups. This approach made us have a clear grasp of the concepts and ideas that we had learned in the lectures.

I noticed that some lecturers were 'too much of themselves'. They exuded unmatched arrogance and threatened that we were going to fail flat in the Continuous Assessment Tests (CATS) and end of semester examinations. Some of their statements bordered on scaremongering but true to their word, the utterances came to haunt lax students. In a number of occasions, students never took the verbal bashing from the lecturers lying down. One day, a youthful lecturer entered our class for a history lesson. She had returned to the country from America where she furthered her studies and acquired an American accent. She appeared not to bother that she was 'twanging' in the lowest voice. When we discovered through our gentle murmurs that her volume was too low for us to grasp what she was saying we became unruly.

"You are idiots and I wonder how you made it to the university in the first place," she shouted. I am not sure if she really wanted to continue teaching us. If she ever did, then she must have regretted her statement. We physically ejected her from the lecture room and we never saw her again for the rest of our stay in campus.

Our view was that we needed lecturers who listened to our concerns and took necessary action. There was this senior history professor who bombarded us with big terminologies like historiography and histology, which made his lectures quite boring. At the end of his lecture, very few of us had understood anything, let alone written any notes.

"Before you start today's lecture, promise us that you are going to communicate," we confronted the professor one day when he came for the lesson.

"You boys and girls, do you know that I was a professor of history before you were born?" the lecturer asked, his face making furrows, which made him look older than he really was. He went on, "do you know that when I started teaching at the university, your mothers and fathers had not even met and were likely looking after their parents' cattle in the village? How dare you tell a professor who has taught hundreds of students before you that he is not communicating? You lack capacity and understanding, and don't deserve to be in a university."

We dragged our chairs on the floor, shot up and told him to get out of the class and he left in a huff. Our action did not amuse the Head of Department. He came to our class and warned against disrespecting lecturers.

The beauty of being a university student is that you can stand your ground when you believe that you are right. This was exactly what we did. We adamantly rejected the professor until he was replaced.

Generally, our class was competent and ready to learn. We were well grounded in training even if it was theoretical and elitist. There was no shortcut to graduation. Those who failed in end of semester examinations were given supplementary papers to do and if they failed again, they were discontinued.

Supplementary examinations were highly dreaded. As such, students worked hard to avoid them. When one failed in his examination, he came stealthily for the supplementary when his classmates were away, sat for it and disappeared. The shame as news spread that so and so sat for a supplementary paper was unbearable, especially for male students who never wanted to be humiliated before the ladies.

Also, it is important to highlight that during our time in the University, there was little sense of ethnic divide and other forms of parochial thinking. Thus, whenever students used to raise issues and sometimes organize demonstrations, they were mainly doing so on critical social, economic and political issues. Such issues especially revolved around poor governance, mismanagement of resources and corruption in the country.

Overall, the learning environment in the university was good. In most instances, the lecturers were prompt and we rarely missed lectures. Moreover, the University Library was well stocked with relevant books, journals, periodicals and newspapers. Thus, whenever we were given take-away assignments we had abundant sources of information to refer to.

Furthermore, public lectures from renowned public figures were common and they attracted huge audiences of students and lecturers. In addition, there were many active theatre groups (including Travelling Theatre) that challenged students' minds. Through organized seminars and workshops, professors could debate openly and differ on their ideological and philosophical underpinnings. This gave students the worldview of divergence in terms of academic ideas and values that are shared in a University setting.

Social Life at University

I remember my friend who often approached good looking girls in campus, claiming that he had a high affinity for them. He may have been right because he actually won quite a number of them in the process. He became so notorious that we nicknamed him 'Mr. High Affinity'.

His dream of conquering as many girls as he wished flopped when he failed in two papers. Consequently, he was forced to sit for supplementary papers. The university's gossip mills went into overdrive and, in a short time, whenever he passed comrades looked at him and cheekily giggled. This brought him down and he changed his amorous ways and resorted to concentrating in his studies.

One Barasa had a tendency of crossing over from Lukenya Hostel A, which accommodated male students and went hovering from room to room at Lukenya Hostel B, a ladies' hostel. He dressed in a funny manner and was often tipsy in the evening. This perhaps gave him some courage to randomly stop and hold the ladies, telling them how his body chemistry had an affinity for them.

But this amorous behaviour was not a reserve of a few male students. There were some lecturers who were equally immoral. Some of these male lecturers were too careless to the extent of not hiding their intentions to the girls. If they ever tried to conceal their intentions, then their remarks and body language betrayed them.

I remember one history lecturer whose huge appetite for relationships with female students was legendary. He once took us to the coast to study historical sites like Fort Jesus, ancient Mnarani and other ancient Arabic/Swahili settlements.

In the evening, he openly strolled with several girls at the beach. It was an open secret that he had sexual relationship with them and in return they got favourable grades. This was annoying to male students because the lecturer was old enough to be the girls' father.

A few of us hatched a plan and confronted the amorous lecturer. We told him to his face that what he was doing was wrong. Of course, some of us were eyeing the girls and he was offering an unfair competition to us. Sensing our fury, he excused himself and disappeared to the nearby building. We never saw him until the next day.

Our journey back to campus the following day was very tense. We travelled in the same bus and the lecturer sat next to the driver. He spent most of his time staring vacuously ahead, to the sides through the window, or slept. This contrasted sharply with his joyful nature during our journey to the coast. That time, he moved up and down in the bus interacting with us and whispering to the girls.

In his literary works, renowned novelist Chinua Achebe observes that amongst his people, 'the man who holds the knife and the yam will have the say.' Our lecturer fitted this description, given that he was going to administer and mark our examination. We were afraid that he could deliberately under-mark us due to the animosity between us and him occasioned by the manner in which we openly confronted him. True to our fears, although we did not fail, many of us scored poorly in his subject save for the girls who had been on his side during the confrontation at the coast.

From these experiences and many others which I have not captured in this narrative, I can deduce that over the years, some male lecturers have preyed on and bullied female students. The vice cuts across the school system, from primary school to university. The story was more devastating for male students who found themselves in secret relationships with their female lecturers. Particularly, if one wanted to leave such toxic relationships, one could be failed in the examinations. Failure in examinations had huge ramifications to an individual, including discontinuation of studies.

The good news is that reforms in education have, to a large extent, countered philandering teachers and lecturers who have clandestine relationships with their students. A lecturer who tosses marks in exchange of sexual favours from his students can easily find himself on the wrong side of the law and be disciplined. Additionally, the clamour for affirmative action has given women a voice and very few would choose to be intimidated and pinned down by their teachers and lecturers.

However, I have to state that on the whole, social life in the university was very interesting. We made a lot of discoveries of many things in life. It was in the university where some students tasted beer for the first time. Some became habitual drunkards and destroyed their lives while others drunk with utmost decorum.

There was none and there is nobody who controls a university student's choices in relationships, partying and studying. You are treated as an adult and expected to do what is right. A university creates an environment where people, especially the youth, interact freely and grow up in the process. Boys and girls go to the movies, theatre, church and other social gatherings freely.

During our time, the main pastime activity for male students was going to the female hostels at night to ignite relationships, some which never lasted a semester. In many instances, the male students got rowdy and verbally explicit if the girls locked them out or turned down their advances.

As naive as we were, those from the countryside were not cowards in matters of relationships. Unlike men from urban centres who were at ease to start relationships with any girl despite her background, those of us especially from Kisii were very selective. We found it easier talking to girls from our region than those from elsewhere.

Unfortunately, the girls were very few. You could find up to six men scrambling for the attention of one girl in her room. This worked against us. I sensed that the girls developed a negative attitude towards us and dated men from other communities, to our chagrin.

Strangely again, Kisii men had a tendency of cooking stories when their advances to the girls hit a dead end. They could start a rumour that the girl hailed from a family, which had a history of witchcraft. They then ensured that the rumour spread to every corner of the university.

I look back and see how unfair we were to our sisters. I remember one brilliant Kisii lady who turned down a kinsman's proposal for a relationship and lived to regret it. The gentleman had tried to forcefully embrace her and this did not go down well with the lady. She reported it to the university administration and the gentleman was nearly expelled.

He then served her with sweet revenge by spreading fake information that the girl's parents were notorious witches back in the village. I remember this stigmatized the girl and her social life totally changed. She hated Kisii men from then on and was finally married to someone from a different ethnic community. This reminds me that from time yonder, witchcraft has been an issue in both low and high places. Personally, I have never seen a witch and I will ever want to see one.

The Big Ideological Divide

At the height of the cold war involving the Soviet Union and the United States, there was a great ideological divide between those who believed in communism and those who supported capitalism. Interestingly, ideological conversations slowly crept into the nerves of university students and lecturers locally. Deliberately or otherwise, some of our history lecturers got divided into the two ideological underpinnings and inevitably dragged students into it.

I was mesmerized with the manner in which the conversations could ignite a clear academic divide even in teaching. Lecturers leaning towards communism pulled to one side with the works of Karl Marx and Vladimir Lenin while the capitalists opposed them. Students found themselves in between and it was upon them to decide which ideology to subscribe to.

I remember one lecturer, Maina wa Kinyatti, who was a sworn Marxist. Often, he walked into the lecture room and said, "I have come here to teach you about Marxism and class struggle." He dismissed the socio-economic and political on goings in the country, saying they were based on capitalism and exploitation, which turned Kenya into a 'man-eat man' society. He averred that everything Kenyans did was based on class struggle. The struggle, he said, involved those who owned the means of production, the rulers, and those who provided labour, the workers.

Kinyatti said that from the Marxist's point of view, there had to be a revolution to stop those who exploited the workers and eventually create a communist society where everything is owned by the state. Painting President Moi's leadership as capitalistic excited us. From where I sat, it appeared that most African leaders were puppets of the West and were being used in impoverishing our continent.

Kinyatti wrote extensively about the Mau Mau struggle. He said the struggle was particularly engineered by peasants who took up arms to overthrow colonialists and take the means of production, especially land, from the oppressors.

Occasionally, students took to the streets and engaged police in running battles. However, unlike today, our strikes were based on national issues. We also supported policies that we thought could change the country's economic and political narrative for the better.

Kenya was facing several challenges of national administration and governance. This included poverty, disease, poor administration, corruption and negative external influence. This did not excite revolutionaries who opined that these were the very challenges the struggle for independence from the colonial masters was supposed to address. Other lecturers like Prof. Ngugi wa Thiongo, Micere Mugo, Atieno Odhiambo, Anyang' Nyong'o and Shadrack Guto were put behind bars on accusations that they championed leftist ideologies. They were accused of being a danger to the state.

Some lecturers were banned by government from ever stepping in university premises. However, while we enjoyed unmatched freedom in the university, we knew very well that the narrative was the exact opposite outside the hallowed gates of the university, the Ivory Tower as some call it. This was at the height of single party rule. President Moi, who had assumed power in 1978 after the demise of the founding President Jomo Kenyatta, wielded unrivalled power. The situation evoked an intensive push for political freedom and association.

It was within this socio-political environment that there was an attempted military coup in 1982. It was alleged that the attempt to topple Moi was staged by some disgruntled junior members of the Kenya Air Force.

However, our forefathers may have been right when they said, *'tiyana gokwa etaberegeti getondo* (The cause of each death has an explanation, whether real or imagined).' The saying simply means that when an incident occurs, it involves real or imagined underlying causes. True to this, apart from the military and their godfathers in the political arena, university students were also accused of having been party to the attempted coup to oust President Moi.

It is worth noting that even before the attempt to overthrow the government happened, several leftist leaning scholars and politicians had been arrested and put in detention without trial. There were also outright assassinations that targeted anti-government politicians. Some of the killings especially after the coup were blood-wrenching and remain a mystery to date. The key trigger of the failed coup was an attempt to register a new Party by a political maverick of the time by the name George Anyona Moseti. Anyona was detained as he planned to announce the formation of the party alongside Jaramogi Oginga Odinga who was termed the *doyen of opposition politics* in Kenya. This led to the enactment of Section 2A of the Constitution that made Kenya a *de jure* one party state with KANU as the sole party.

The state policy of detentions without trial painted a picture of outright human rights abuse. Since independence many politicians, who had differed with the establishment, were locked away without being heard. With the constitutional change, detention without trial was back in full force and Jaramogi is one of the leaders who were apprehended and put under house arrest. Jaramogi, the father of former Prime Minister Raila Odinga, had served as Jomo Kenyatta's Vice-President at independence before the two broke ranks.'

Sleuths did not spare university students who were perceived to be radicalized. They rounded students up while others were expelled from the university, igniting student demonstrations that paralyzed the academic calendar for months.

When students rioted, I have to admit that I also took part in as much as I was not outspoken. Some 'comrades' got out of the university and used stones and other crude items to barricade roads. They also lit fires, stoned motorists and looted shops and literary robbed travellers. Police arrived with teargas, clubs and other weapons and clobbered them. The students' running battles with the police could last several hours. During the confrontations, several students would be arrested and taken behind bars. When they were taken to court, comrades turned up in solidarity and there was always a likelihood of the strikes starting all over again.

The university management decided to mitigate the crisis by suspending the ringleaders and closing the institutions for a number of weeks. When we came back, we were usually given some forms to fill and commit ourselves not to take part in any unruly behaviour again.

I noticed that on a number of occasions, students who got a run into the wrong side of the law were innocent. The ring leaders often disappeared into thin air way before the police arrived. The officers then pounced on innocent students who were perhaps getting out of the library or hostels.

In the early 1980s, many students who were initially apolitical found their voice in the university. However, I can say that participation of students in national politics dates back to the 1970s. At the time, it pertained to the mass failing of students by expatriate teaching staff in faculties such as engineering and architecture and the introduction of student loans. This was vehemently resisted by students who were then led by James Orengo. The 1975 assassination of JM Kariuki, a popular politician in the 1960s and 1970s, equally paralyzed normal University operations as students protested the killing. The 1980s demonstrations were a continuum of the foregoing. Indeed, there were demonstrations that occurred as early as in the beginning of Moi regime, such as in 1979 just before national elections when he failed to clear former detainees to contest. This led to the extended closure of the University; it was Moi's first taste of 'student power'.

Campaigns for student body's leadership were highly charged. We could meet in highly charged *kamukunjis* (informal student meetings) where we invoked clauses like; Comrade Power! Power to the People!

As much as I may have had personally thought of running to lead students, I chose not to because a lot of student leaders usually ended up in trouble. Some got expelled. Expulsion marked the end of one's academic life and studies at the university. It reduced a student into a laughing stock in the village. This is largely why most students from humble backgrounds, and to whom families looked up to lay low to ensure that they did not cause undue duress for their families.

Living through a Coup Attempt

What happened on August 1st 1982 remains ingrained in the memories of many Kenyans. I am not an exception. This is the day the failed coup attempt happened. It was a dark day, just as it was when the founding President Jomo Kenyatta died.

The events which unfolded showed the failure and dysfunctionality of the country's social-economic and political institutional framework. It showed lack of clear foundations of African state formations where tribalism, ethnicity and personification of leadership is deeply rooted.

The night before the coup, I was woken up at around midnight by my friend, who was also my classmate, by the name Pius Kakai. Kakai, who is now a lecturer, banged my door with urgency. I rubbed off the remainder of sleep from the eyes and woke up. For a second, I thought my life was under threat. As a man, I assured myself that if I was in danger I was not going to die like a fly. So, I quickly went for a broom that leaned against the wall in my room and swiftly opened the door ready to counter the enemy.

My friend Kakai was shouting, "power to the people! Power to the people!" This got me even more confused. I got out and found students in jubilation, dancing and beating drums. Some had hijacked the university buses and were speedily driving around campus. A number of them hang precariously on the vehicles and I was afraid the worst could happen to them.

At around 9 am, student leaders addressed us. There was evident excitement that a majority of the students were happy that the government had been toppled. When a situation like this prevails, mob psychology sets in. It was spontaneously agreed that we drive to Nairobi to congratulate the coup plotters and executers.

God works in miraculous was as it happened that day. It so occurred that the two university gates had been locked by the guards who took off upon sensing the commotion. For starters, the campus was well secured since it used to be a military barrack.

With the two gates closed, there was no other motorable exit from the university. We were frustrated that it was now impossible to travel in our university buses to town to stand in solidarity with our comrades from the main campus who were already in the streets. As it turned out, the guards unknowingly saved our lives.

We did not know that a battalion of the Kenya Army, now the Kenya Defence Forces, which is based in Kahawa Barracks along Thika Road, had been deployed to contain the situation. The forces confronted the mutinous soldiers and Kenyans who were celebrating the illegitimate takeover of the government. Hundreds of them were on Thika Road, which connected Kenyatta Campus and Nairobi. More of them had been deployed to secure government installations like the Voice of Kenya – VoK, now called the Kenya Broadcasting Cooperation (KBC). I bet if we had managed to get out of the university, we could have easily fallen into the hands of the ruthless army officers.

We were at limbo during much of the day. The broadcast centre VOK, which was the only broadcasting station at the time, only played Lingala music until the 'wayward' soldiers were ferreted out of the station. There were no mobile phones to enable us find out what was happening in town. Anxiety loomed supreme.

The coup actors had hijacked celebrated radio personality Leonard Mambo Mbotela and taken him to the studio. He was forced to announce that the government had been toppled and Moi had ceased to be the president.

The same continuity announcer announced at around midday that the coup had been neutralized and the government had reverted into the able hands of President Moi. Even as he made the announcement, we could hear gunshots in the background.

As I learnt later, several loyal and rebel soldiers died in the combat between loyalists and the coup plotters. The majority of those who died were the rebels who had poured into the streets of the city.

In general, the attempt to oust Moi was poorly organized and disjointed. It had been planned by a section of disgruntled non-commissioned soldiers at the Eastleigh Airbase. Following the failed attempted coup, witnesses recounted that the plotters were in a drunken stupor when they took guns from the armoury and marched to the national broadcaster where they took Mbotela captive and forced him to make their illegitimate announcement. It later emerged that aircraft from Nanyuki Air Base that were sent to bomb major government installations in Nairobi were deliberrately misdirected and 'missed' the targets. For instance, State House survived the bombing because the aircrafts missed and bombed the nearby Karura forest.

During the crisis, looters among them students from the Main Campus of the University of Nairobi stormed the city streets. They looted jewellery, clothes, and electronics, among other items. They were joined by rebel soldiers and civilians in a looting spree. Nairobi, famously described as the 'City in the Sun' and the nerve centre of peace and tranquillity in a troubled continent, was suddenly transformed into a battlefield. It was a dark day for the country and never again should there be a coup in this country.

As the attempted coup happened, President Moi was missing in action! Like most citizens, we got anxious of his whereabouts and looked forward to hear his voice over the radio. This was the only way we could be sure that he was safe wherever he was. When Mbotela announced that Moi was back in power, our anxiety to hear his voice and be sure that he was alive and in control of our country intensified.

It was not until 4 pm that a tensed President Moi was heard from the national broadcaster assuring Kenyans that he was in charge of the country. I may not recall the exact words in Kiswahili but an abridged version of an article in The New York Times newspaper archive available in the newspaper's website quoted Moi, "The uprising by the air force has been crushed by our army and police..... This action by the Air Force which took it upon itself to destroy all that we stand for has been defeated, and, therefore, be calm wherever you are."

The government was not done with the situation and its civilians yet. A twenty-four-hour curfew was declared throughout the country. Anybody who would be found loitering or gathering aimlessly, especially in town, would be dealt with ruthlessly.

Soldiers were deployed in the streets in their numbers. In particular, they arrived in their hundreds and cordoned off the university. Others took vantage positions around the fence and stood vigil, in full military fatigue, their guns ready. This made us more apprehensive, not sure what was going to happen next.

An open-ended Land Rover vehicle carrying menacingly looking soldiers who were heavily armed with guns went around campus, with a blaring public address system. The person behind the microphone announced that no student should be seen outside the hostels. Whoever disobeyed the directive would be smashed or shot dead, he reiterated. Our otherwise calm campus, which had been full of life and vibrancy, was now not any different from a war zone.

It is believed that it is only a fool who can engage a soldier who is armed to the teeth once a curfew has been imposed. There were no fools in the university that hour. We all obeyed the orders and locked ourselves in our rooms, in anticipation of the situation ending soon.

The soldiers then went around, searched one room after another and grilled the occupants. They inquired where we were when the coup happened and what we were doing. Further, whoever was found with Marxist literature and

Mwakenya, a syndicated underground publication, was arrested at gunpoint. By the end of the swoop, many students were arrested and taken to detention.

I clearly recall how the officers entered my room, their eyes and body language declaring that they were in for serious business. They ordered me to stand up and asked me to narrate where I was when news of the coup broke and what I knew about it. I gave my part of the story and they seemed convinced as they got out and ordered me to lock the door and sleep.

What has not been told by those who have told this story before is that the soldiers ruthlessly manhandled female students. The ladies hostel, Lukenya B, stood next to Lukenya A where we stayed. We could hear the ladies screaming and when it got too much, we approached their hostel and from a safe distance, we could see the ordeal they were going through.

When the officers spotted us, they rounded us up for a thrashing. They then frog matched us to our rooms, our hands lifted up in submission. That night was one of the longest nights I ever had in my life, comparable only to the night when I lost my mother.

When morning arrived, it was announced that the university had been closed indefinitely and we were supposed to vacate the premises as soon as possible. Further, we were instructed to head straight to our homes. And, upon reaching home, we were required to report to our local chiefs.

I was aware that a stitch in time saved nine. That is why I quickly picked some money and got out of the university within minutes. I wanted to take public transport to town and immediately connect to Kisii.

To my surprise, there were several roadblocks. We were repeatedly ordered to disembark and show our identification documents. The police mainly frisked university students. On a number of cases, other travellers were left to proceed with their journey while we remained with the paramilitary police, kneeling down by the roadside.

Ordinarily, it takes less than 30 minutes to get to Nairobi from the university by bus. That day, it took me a record three hours. My decision to travel straight to the city was not a good one. My comrades who went through Thika and connected to various parts of the country from there found it much easier.

I was afraid my journey to Kisii was going to get more cumbersome and I opted to take a vehicle to Pumwani Estate on the outskirts of the city. My uncle stayed there and I thought it could be easier getting out of the mess that the city was.

More trouble lay ahead of me. There were bodies strewn on the roads and I could smell fear and blood in the air. It must have taken me another three hours to reach the estate, a journey that can ordinarily take one less than twenty minutes when there is no vehicular traffic congestion.

I spent that night at my uncle's abode and proceeded to Kisii through Nakuru the following morning. The journey took me two days due to the several road blocks that were mounted by the police who unashamedly frisked travellers and took their time to interrogate the passengers. I spent the first night in Nakuru Town whose streets were deserted when I got there. I proceeded home the following morning.

My face beamed with a smile when I alighted at Metamwaya junction along the Kericho-Kisii road from whence I walked to my home. Several members of the community had gathered at our homestead and, as I learnt, a rumour had circulated that most university students had been shot dead by the soldiers. Some were shedding painful tears. Upon seeing me, they broke into jubilation and prayers. I had come home safe and in one piece.

I was traumatized and tired but I thanked God that I had made it home. My father was overjoyed and a goat was slaughtered for the gathering to feast on and celebrate my return. As instructed, I went to the Chief's Office the following morning and reported to him that I had come home as was ordered by the government.

At the office, I met another student George Nyagwachi from the university and the chief gave both of us a verbal bashing. He then told us to hoist the national flag and sing the national anthem. I learnt that some students who had reported to their chiefs were arrested and taken back to Nairobi where they were detained.

Reporting to the chief, hoisting the flag, singing the national anthem and being assigned menial work like clearing bushes and sweeping the chief's compound would be our punishment for the period we were home. We did this twice every week, on Monday and Friday.

It was sad that word went around the country that university students were part and parcel of the attempted coup. The rumour mills went overdrive that students had planned to kill the Head of State but they were outsmarted by the military. In the village, we became marked people. We could be passing and then someone stops us for a verbal bashing, calling us criminals who should have been killed for staging a coup against a legitimate government.

I remember one old man who, one day, stopped me on the road and retorted, *"ekero okonyora engoge ekoria eng'uko, tari okonyetaburia"* (when you see a leopard eating a mole, you don't attempt to snatch the mole)." Interpreted, metaphorically, it meant that by virtue of the President's position, we students were too junior to question him.

Another man whose son was a casualty of the failed coup made a more hurting remark. The son had been dismissed from the military and put in detention, just as many soldiers were, on suspicion that he took part in the attempted coup. The man retorted, *"ekebago ekio giachiete korwania Moi nonya kiare goitwa tinare gokumia* (I would not have missed sleep if that criminal who went to fight Moi were killed)." I could not believe that I was now being called a criminal right in my own community.

Away from the hostility that confronted us as university students in the village, there were a few in the area who understood what had happened and were sympathetic.

On the whole, I will say that the events of August 1st 1982 that spilled to many days, months and even years ahead were the lowest moments for the country's history. For us in the university then, we saw death with our naked eyes. There is nothing as bad as the military men coming out of the barracks to manage and control civilians. By nature of their training, they are like killing machines. Military men should stay in the barracks unless the country is facing an external threat.

It is obvious that a lot of billions went up in smoke during that moment of national shame. The event also dented our national image globally and affected the Kenyan economy for many years.

It is an open secret that the majority of the military officers who were accused of being behind the coup attempt and their godfathers from the political wing came from a particular region of Kenya. If students were involved too, then they were very few and the blanket condemnation of all of us was unpalatable and unacceptable. The majority of us did not even see the insurrection coming; it took us by surprise and affected us just as much. Maybe, just maybe, some student leaders from the main campus were involved or privy to the plans from the initial stages.

When I read former Kitui Senator David Musila's memoir, *Seasons of Hope*, I learnt that according to him, the government had got wind of the impending take-over prior to the day it happened. However, Musila who was then the Central Kenya Provincial Commissioner stationed in Nyeri, reveals that although the government was on a high alert, it did not know exactly when the coup d'état would be staged. This, to me, should exonerate innocent Kenyans especially university students who were caught up in the confusion. They did not deserve to be harassed, beaten and unfairly arrested and detained without trial.

It pains me when I remember that some of my comrades died due to torture while in detention. One of them was Titus Adungosi who was a leader in the Students Union Nairobi University (SONU). Adungosi did issue hard hitting statements in support of the coup. When it was quashed, he was arrested, arraigned in court and sentenced to 6 years in prison. Later, perhaps after being convinced by someone that he could be granted mercy by the courts, he confessed to having known about the plans for the coup in advance. Whether he did this under duress is not known. However, following the 'confession', his sentence was enhanced to 10 years by the magistrate who indicated that Adungosi had been given a lighter sentence. He served time in jail and was reported dead at the cusp of his release. The cause of the sudden death of the student leader was never revealed.

I sadly learnt that his father never recovered from the shock of losing a son he had taken to the university and banked hopes on to transform his household. The old man followed his son to dance with the angels soon after. No Kenyan parent should go through such harrowing and heart wrenching experience again.

Back on Campus

The university environment looked new and strange altogether when we reported back to resume our studies. The aborted coup had occurred when we were about to sit for the end of semester examinations. Just like that, it disrupted our academic calendar.

As a consequence, before we started attending lectures for the new semester, we were required to sit for examinations of the previous period. The timetable which indicated that the examinations would start a couple of days after reporting greeted us from the notice boards and threw us into a spin. It was a chaotic start of that semester for us. The long duration we had stayed at home did not help at all. The uncertain environment had made what we had learnt the previous semester to evaporate.

I went through my notes and they were not proving meaningful in allowing or empowering me sit for the examinations. It required tenacity and spending sleepless nights, reading, holding group discussions and making references to various academic sources to get ready for the impending examinations.

Because of the pressure and anxiety, some students suffered mental breakdown. I remember a lady who was found walking from one end of the campus to the other end aimlessly. She was eventually hospitalized to receive psychiatric treatment. A male student was also taken to a psychiatrist after he was found standing in the rain like a statue. Others sought solace in excessive drinking. This worsened matters for them. If they knew that the examinations were not going to be postponed anyway, they would have spent the little time in reading instead of emptying bottle after bottle of brew in the nearby pubs.

This underlines the system's brutality. At the time, universities did not have counseling services. Those that created the pressure-cooker environment knew no better about human beings' capacity to withstand stress and the breaking points thereof. Perhaps they would have been more considerate had they known. For some students, drinking was their coping mechanism. But this underlines a major problem in society beyond the education system. There is little consideration for mental health issues of people in a particular environment. No wonder suicide, crimes of passion and other forms of murder have been on the rise over the years.

It was indeed a sad week when the lecturers released the results shortly after. Many students failed and would have to take supplementary examinations. In fact, some even failed the supplementary examinations!

I heaved a sigh of relief because I was among those who skipped the embarrassing and agonizing eventuality of retaking any of my papers due to failure. This alone made me leave behind a number of my classmates who were made to repeat the year as I started my third and final year of study.

There were broader impacts of the sad events that preceded August 1st, 1982 coup. One, some lecturers and students were incarcerated for allegedly being in cahoots with the coup plotters. Furthermore, the vibrancy with which students and lecturers expressed themselves prior to the coup attempt seemed to have gone down tremendously. In a way, we sobered up and learnt that being in the university was one thing and completing your studies was another.

It can be argued that the coup attempt had long term effects not only on the broader social, political and economic sectors of the country but also university education. More undercover agents and intelligence gathering personnel were planted at the institutions and, in many instances, students had to look behind their shoulders whenever they discussed critical issues affecting the university and the country in general. In other words, the democratic space and freedom of expression at university level was trampled upon as was the case in the broader Kenyan society.

In terms of political governance, it appeared President Moi woke up to the reality that it was possible to lose the grip of the country. Previously known as a soft-spoken populist leader, Moi became tougher, spoke with finality and without leaving any doubt that he was at the helm and he was not going anywhere. As it turned out, he held the country's Number One position for a cool uninterrupted 24 years. Moi also became autocratic, ruling by decree. He crushed opposition, detaining some and jailing many. Nyayo torture chambers became a symbol of this authoritarian power. It is due to entrenched impunity that he could run the 1988 elections under a farce called *mlolongo* without much ado. By then, Moi had absolute control over all government machinery, and tools of political and economic governance.

In the university, those of us who were spared expulsion became eager to work harder, graduate and move on. The saying that, "everyone for himself and God for us all," appeared to apply well to the prevailing situation. The reality further dawned on us that, although we were students, we came from different backgrounds and each one of us had his or her personal targets to achieve. Time was not waiting for anyone and it did not have favourites.

However, joining university for undergraduate studies offers a period of experimentation and discovery of oneself and society. In particular, there were too many things to adjust oneself to. It thus took a while to understand that the freedom one enjoyed in the university could lead to diverse consequences. The freedom could also be curtailed any time and you will be left gnashing your teeth.

It is sad to note that life is harder now for university students. It was relatively easier for us because the government offered us almost everything on top of the subsidized loans that we later repaid with ease. The repayment of the loans was quite possible since the job market was open and ready for us after our studies. Employment systems worked and getting a job after campus was guaranteed.

Currently, the money given to students as concessionary loan is not commensurate with the rising cost of living. Further, in many instances, students are not provided with accommodation and meals as happened during our time. Worse yet, after completion of their studies, the graduates find it difficult to secure employment. As a consequence, unemployment is piling up even as universities continue to graduate thousands of young people from time to time.

It did not take us long to put the aftermath of the aborted coup behind us. Save for a tone-down of political rhetoric, our social and academic life got back on track.

As part of the package, sexual adventure, was part and parcel of most university students' lives. However, this was before the world was thrown into panic following widespread reportage of the HIV/Aids outbreak. Over-indulgence in unprotected sexual activities would have had students dying like flies.

In this regard, this happened shortly before the pandemic hit the nation, sending many Kenyans early to their graves. Undeniably, the reports on HIV/Aids were marred with misinformation, distortion, exaggeration and scaremongering. Thanks to science, we now have life prolonging drugs for those infected. Additionally, there has been insurmountable sensitization of the society on the devastating effects of the HIV/AIDS scourge and stigma.

The Karumaindo Experience

My personal account will not be complete if I fail to disclose that, just as many of my comrades during my university days in the 1980s, I frequented Karumaindo in downtown Nairobi. This was a favourite drinking joint for students from both the University of Nairobi Main Campus and its Kenyatta campus. The club was also frequented by commercial sex workers mainly targeting male university students. Since it takes two to tango, I will be right to say that the male students engaged in amorous behaviour too.

At Karumaindo, the women joined the students in drinking, smoking and merrymaking. When everyone got drunk, it was possible for anything to take place. I recall one time walking to the ablutions, only to find one of my friend engrossed in a deep kiss with a woman. He was fondling the lady who I thought was elderly and ugly. In fact, she could easily have been the age of his mother. It can be said that most of the students who kept off the Karumaindo women were ones of particular upbringing. They could see or feel what was right or wrong while others remained carefree, especially when they had had one drink too many. Although I had already imbibed a few bottles, on that day, the incident made me sober up. "Comrade, what are you doing? Stop it?" I shouted to draw my friend's attention. He dropped his hold and the lady staggered towards me. We hurriedly walked out of the joint as the woman hurled all kinds of insults at me.

I had another friend whose policy was, once he got the boom, he drunk to the last penny during the first one or two weeks of the semester. After he finished his money, he never stepped out of the university until the end of the semester.

The password at Karumaindo was 'Comrades'. I remember my friend Kakai and myself lost each other on our way out of the club one evening after having one too many. I cannot tell how I found myself in my room that night. He told me that he too lost direction to his room but was finally assisted to locate it.

It is good to remember that, as I said, I was born and brought up in a home where *chang'aa* and *busaa* were consumed by adults. Despite the influence in campus, I knew the shortcomings, which befell some of my relatives due to over-indulgence in drinking. This cautioned me to drink in moderation even as I sailed in a students' mob psychology environment, characterised by overindulgence in drinking and merrymaking on end.

Whoever said that education is the best equalizer must have had someone like me in mind. At the university, I carried myself modestly. Nobody among my comrades ever imagined that back home I lived in a grass thatched, earthen house built for me by my parents. Using savings from the students' loan, I replaced the hut with a corrugated iron sheet roofed one. The house monumentally stands on our land to this day. I also used some of the monies to pay fees for my younger brother Kiriago Akama who was studying at Kisii School.

In the long run, I did well in my studies. In the final results, I scored a strong Upper Second Honours Degree with an average mark of 68 per cent and graduated from the University in 1984. I had laid a strong foundation and was given powers to read and do all that appertained to the degree.

Power to Read

In Kenya, a university graduation ceremony is a community affair. My father, brother and sisters, cousins, uncles, aunties and neighbours travelled the whole night to be in time for the ceremony at the University of Nairobi's Graduation Square, popularly known as the 'Great Court'. President Moi was the Chancellor of all universities. By virtue of the position, he was to grace the ceremony. By the time he arrived, graduands, academic staff and Kenyans from all walks of life were seated as protocol demanded.

Names of the granduands were announced and each time a group heard the name of their son or daughter, they ululated and whistled. My heart melted with joy when mine was mentioned, prompting my group to ululate and whistle loudest, to the bemusement of the congregation. Being in graduation regalia exemplified one's academic accomplishments. I looked forward to another stage of career advancement in my area of training.

Tracing my relatives, friends and home mates after the graduation ceremony was a herculean task at that time. This was compounded by the fact that there were no mobile phones. Interestingly, people were relatively well disciplined. They kept time and ensured they assembled at a particular spot as agreed earlier on. This is how my team and I met after the graduation ceremony. We left the university for a party in the evening at an eatery on the outskirts of Nairobi City.

Walking into the eating joint while clad in the graduation regalia and in the company of a group of people appeared to confuse some onlookers. I remember eavesdropping on someone who told other onlookers that I was a Legio Maria (a local religious sect) priest being escorted by members of the church.

I restrained my laughter with the understanding that, in those early days (1980s), a graduation ceremony was not a familiar event for most Kenyans. The few people who understood the event saw it as a ceremony for the academic elites who were far removed from the realities of daily life. I was surprised to find that even some of my relatives never understood why they travelled to the city. Some knew that I got a certificate from the university and I had invited them because I was the first one from my family lineage and village to do so.

Unlike now, the employability rate of graduates was very high. All students who graduated with me that day were immediately absorbed into the job market in both the private and public sector. In many instances, one got the letter of employment during the last semester in the university. Since

I had obtained a Bachelor of Education Degree, I got a letter from the Teachers' Service Commission (TSC) posting me to Mariera High School in the current Siaya County. Indeed, time had come for me to reap the fruits of my academic investment.

> **Biographr's Note:** Prof. Bosire Monari Mwebi studied with Prof. Akama at the University of Nairobi's Kenyatta Campus. Prof. Mwebi is presently an Education Consultant and Associate Professor at St. Francis Xaxier University, Nova Scotia, Canada. He said the following about his comrade:
>
> *"Prof. Akama is a very visionary person who is ever committed in whatever he sets his eyes on. I can bet that he is a great educator and resource in academia."*

My First Posting as a Graduate Teacher

It is often said that beggars should not be selective but I was not one. However, in June 1984 when the TSC posted me to Mariera, I was not happy with their decision. This was a surprise that left me without words. Through what I heard people say and what I knew from my basic Geography lessons, the school was situated in the interior of Siaya District (current Siaya County), near Lake Victoria. This is a region, which has extremely high incidences of malaria. At the time, malaria was among the top killer diseases in the country.

I approached the TSC and humbly requested that the posting be revoked in favour of a better working environment. However, I did not succeed in my quest. With the realisation that I had no any other alternative, I reluctantly reported to Mariera.

When I reported for work, Henry Anyim, the Principal of the school, was overjoyed to receive me. He disclosed to me that I was the first graduate teacher to be posted to the school. He excitedly addressed me as *Japuonji Maber* (a very good teacher). The majority of the staff were either Secondary One (S1) certificate or diploma holders. They were all happy that I had joined them to steer the school forward.

Despite all this, I was not excited. The environment appeared strange to me. In the evening, some teachers took me to a pub in the nearby market where we indulged in drinking till very late. From where we sat on the long stools at the counter, I could see female prostitutes prancing around. Unlike me, the teachers were used to such scenes.

Overall, I was concerned about my stay and wellbeing at the place. The grapevine had it that young men in the area never took it kindly when they learnt that an outsider was in a sexual relationship with their women. Mr. Anyim disclosed to me that the boys were over protective of their women and could easily clobber one without warning. I got to know that not long ago they had killed a man from Ukambani, Eastern Kenya who had a relationship with a local girl.

Starting life at the school, I discovered that my stay at the university had not prepared me well for the harsh realities of the outside world. I was not ready to settle down. Although the house I was allocated was well furnished, I did not have simple items like utensils.

Ugali made of corn flour is the staple food of most Kenyans and I wanted to prepare some for myself that evening. Just when the water boiled and I added some flour, I discovered that I did not have a cooking stick. I also remembered that I did not have salt. This compelled me to remove the *sufuria* (cooking pan) from the fire and throw the contents away. Need I say that I slept on an empty stomach that night.

I have to state that I did not have a good sleep on my first night in Mariera. There was a funeral in the neighbourhood and people screamed and danced while howling amid loud music throughout the night. These unwelcoming incidents made me think and rethink of how I was going to cope with the reality that I was to be there for many days, if not years, to come.

I did not finish a week at Mariera before a bout of malaria attacked me. I underwent a feverish experience. The sickness was coupled with vomiting, which made me noticeably lose weight. My health deteriorated faster than I anticipated. It appeared that I was becoming too thin for my long trousers.

When I looked at myself in the mirror, I realised that the sickness had really affected me and I was emaciated.

When my college mate, Nyaribo Mosioma, knocked at my door one evening, I thought I was daydreaming.

"What brings you here?" I asked him as we shook hands, firmly. I knew he had been posted to a school in the Rusinga Islands off Lake Victoria and he also did not like it. Yet here he was at my doorstep, broadly smiling.

"*Omogaka oyo, imoka togende seito* (dear brother, let's go home)," he said. This confused me more. I also got more anxious to know what he was driving at.

He pulled an envelope out of his handbag and passed it to me. My fingers shook like tendrils in a windy evening. As I opened it, my eyes fell on the writings, to the excitement of the heart. It was a transfer letter from the TSC moving me to Nyamagwa High School in Kisii. He too had been moved to the same school and we were to be together once again. I came to learn that the Headmaster of Nyamagwa, Alex Osiemo, who was aggressively looking for newly qualified teachers, had managed to secure my transfer to his school through the then Nyanza Provincial TSC Office. I promptly and excitedly alerted Mr. Anyim that I would not stay any longer at the school following the transfer.

My Transfer to Nyamagwa Boys' School

When the sun rose the following morning, it did not find us in Mariera Secondary School. We had taken a bus to Kisumu from whence we connected to our home District, Kisii. I had not stayed for long at Mariera and the Principal, Mr. Anyim, was not amused by my transfer. He made several attempts to counter it; including visiting the TSC Headquarters in Nairobi. However, in the long run, he did not succeed in having me recalled to his school.

Mr. Osiemo, the Principal of Nyamagwa Boys' High School, gladly received us. He was a generous man who allowed us to stay in his house within the school compound for a number of days before we got allocated separate abodes. Apart from Nyaribo and me, the school had received another young energetic, freshly qualified, graduate teacher, James Ongaki. Mr. Osiemo was also new to the school. The three of us were more than willing to stay in one furnished house in the school compound. At the time, we were youthful and unmarried. Thus, it was not a big issue sharing a house. In fact, our fellow colleagues became fond of jokingly referring to us as 'Abasae Bosa' a Kisii phrase meaning 'unmarried youthful males.'

At that time, the school had two streams for each class from Form One to Form Four, with a student population of slightly over 400. It was a provincial school, having been started by the Catholic Church in the 1960s. As much as it later became a public school, it remained under the Catholic Church sponsorship.

In the early 1980s, the school was run down and indiscipline was rife among students. However, when Mr. Osiemo was transferred to the school as Principal, he worked hard to improve the institution. One of the things he did was looking for well trained and qualified teachers. It was under those efforts that he managed to have me transferred from Mariera to his school.

The starting salary for secondary school teachers at the time was Kshs. 3,000. With inflation and depreciation of the shilling, the money we earned that time could be equivalent to Kshs. 30,000 today.

As we settled down, it dawned on us that many students were badly behaved. Some sneaked out of school to indulge in drinking illicit brew while others befriended widows and married women in the neighbourhood. The school was posting poor grades in the national examinations. It was in utter mess. Under the tutelage of the new Principal, we embarked on instilling discipline to restore sanity.

We put measures in place such as suspending truants and expelling the notorious ones. We also subjected others to corporal punishment or manual labour. I remember one boy was caned until he became unconscious and had to be rushed to hospital. Luckily, when he recovered, he changed his crooked ways and started excelling in his studies. He is now a Principal of a secondary school. However, as things stand now, I do not support corporal punishment.

I had a burning desire to offer my best as a young, energetic and well trained teacher. This is exactly what I did as I took the Form Three and Four students in Geography and History lessons. My students did very well, producing excellent results in the national examinations.

I left the school on a high note in February 1986 when all my Form Four candidates passed my course with flying colours. However, the results did not excite some teachers. They wondered and questioned, in low tones, how some candidates did well in my subject and failed in others if I did not give them an examination leakage. This did not scare me. I knew the results were a reflection of the efforts I put into preparing the candidates well for the examinations.

It gladdens my heart when I find my former students from Nyamagwa High School working in various offices locally and abroad. I usually meet several of them who are successful lawyers. Others are doctors and high school teachers. It gives me satisfaction to know that I took part in shaping their lives.

I have to credit Mr. Osiemo for taking the school from going to the dogs and lifting it to good standing. I learnt from him that, in any institution of learning, leadership is what makes the difference. It was under his leadership that the school was refurbished, new books and other learning items purchased, and teachers got motivated to offer their best. Parents also saw the value of the financial resources they spent on their sons to be in the school.

I shuddered when I later learnt that Mr. Osiemo was unceremoniously demoted from headship under unclear circumstances. Some claimed the demotion was occasioned by the rivalry from the sponsor of the school. However, I later learnt that clan factors caused his removal from the school. As the institution continued to grow, local elites and politicians of the Bobasi Clan, where the school is situated, felt that their own should be the Principal. Mr. Osiemo was from the neighbouring Nyaribari clan. However, since that time, a lot of water has gone under the bridge. I will therefore not duel on the issue further.

That said, the issue of clannism and nepotism has over the years affected the proper management of schools in Gusii. It is sad to note that, often, some people vouch for clansman or woman to be in charge of a school even when the person is out rightly incompetent. This negates the spirit of building solid traditions for schools as centres of academic and co-curricular excellence.

Even so, my view is that had Mr. Osiemo not stayed for too long at the school, perhaps he would not have received such an embarrassing turn in his robust career.

I have noticed a worrying trend, especially in the management of learning institutions. When one stays in an institution for long, however good one may be, there is a likelihood of one making a misstep at some stage. That misstep can dent one's image and one may never be able to redeem it again. This is why there has to be clear policy guidelines on how long a teacher should teach in a school.

Poor management of schools is also occasioned by lack of proper training of the head teachers on management of finances, administration and institutional ethics in general. Many heads of schools learn this on the job and are likely to make mistakes. These missteps could be avoided if head teachers got related training before they assumed the daunting responsibilities of management and administration of schools. Alternatively, they could be given frequent professional courses on leadership and school administration. Since these schools are dominated by students who are adolescents, proper guidance and counselling is essential in managing them.

There is more. Poor financial management coupled with acts of corruption stagnate school development. When the head lacks the prerequisite financial management skills, he leaves it to the cashiers and bursars to run the show. This may allow corruption to creep in, affecting the viability of the whole institution.

Further, the nature of curricula and the forms of pedagogy in most schools are wanting. Over time, our education system has been examination oriented to the extent that if you prepare the students to cram facts, they will do well in the examinations. But logically, an examination should not be viewed as an end in itself. Institutions of learning should be avenues for students to develop proper character and enable them discover and explore their capabilities, apart from acquiring problem solving and cognitive skills.

As I have said elsewhere, it is my hope that if Kenya gets it right, the Competence Based Curriculum (CBC), which is replacing the 8-4-4 system of education, will fix many of the existing gaps. If it does, the level of unemployment and underemployment will go down and learners will exploit their full potential. This includes venturing into business development, industrialisation and other forms of wealth creation initiatives. Implemented properly, the CBC will confirm to us all that Thomas Dewar was right when he said, "Our minds are parachutes…they only function when open!"

2. THE AMERICAN DREAM

My USA Scholarship

I had neither known nor planned to undertake my Masters' studies in the United States of America. It was a pleasant surprise that God had it in store for me. I learnt the plans after I received a letter of regret from the University of Nairobi where I had applied for a Masters' scholarship to study history.

At first, the regret surprised me, to say the least. I had performed well in my undergraduate studies. On paper, I qualified and this was the yardstick the university used to award the scholarships. It never happened. When I travelled to the city and visited the university, I was dumbfounded. I found that my former classmates, who had not performed as well as I had, were the ones who were awarded scholarships.

I analyzed the list of the successful applicants and realized that it comprised of students who had social connections in the institution. There was every indication that nepotism had taken dominance over meritocracy in the selection process. Some people whose names appeared in the list were relatives of some lecturers and it did not need one to be a rocket scientist to read foul play.

I came face to face with the reality that I was expecting fairness from a corrupt system. Clearly, there was no transparency and accountability in the manner the selection was done. For a long time, meritocracy was rarely appreciated in professional advancement, especially at postgraduate level in the country's universities. It is no wonder that sometimes there used to be mass failure of post-graduate students.

I digested the sad news and, as it came to pass, the situation offered another turning point for my life. I reflected on the options at hand and resolved to pursue my dream abroad. I then made applications for scholarships to several universities overseas. Some of the communication went unanswered but Howard University in the United States of America (USA) offered me the chance to go there for my Masters' degree studies.

This excited me but I opted to do further due diligence with my mentor Prof. Celia Nyamweru. A Briton married to a Kenyan, she was the Geography Head of Department at Kenyatta University College. She introduced me to an American Professor, Dr. Ted Bernard who was in the university on sabbatical leave. Dr. Bernard was to guide me on how to make applications to prestigious universities in the US.

"How come you were not admitted to this University (UoN) for your Masters," Dr. Bernard asked me when he looked at my credentials. I was looking for the best answer when he went on to encourage me to apply for admission to Ohio University where he taught in the Department of Geography. I did and was excited to receive the letter of admission to the university soon after to undertake MA studies in Geography.

The fact that I was not able to get admission in my *alma mater* turned out to be a blessing in disguise. Due to my undergraduate performance, Ohio University offered me a full scholarship which required that I work as a teaching assistant in the same university. All my tuition fees and other expenses (approximately US$30,000 annually) were covered in the two-year period of study. Above this, I would receive a stipend of about US$1,000 per month during the study period.

Biographer's Note: Prof. Celia Nyamweru, one of Prof. Akama's lecturers at Kenyatta University College, had this to say:

John was one of the first of several students from Kisii whom I taught in the Department of Geography at Kenyatta University College (later Kenyatta University) in the 1970s and 1980s. I soon recognized his ability and energy; he was a clear candidate for graduate studies. During those years, there were very few such opportunities in Kenya, so John had to face the challenges of life in the USA where he completed his PhD studies in 1993. His research on 'A Political-Ecological Analysis of Wildlife Conservation in Kenya' drew on interviews with people living on the borders of Nairobi and Tsavo National Parks. Many of them demonstrated negative attitudes towards state policies of wildlife conservation. His research, presented in several important co-authored papers, formed the foundation for a productive academic career after his return to Kenya.

Celia Nyamweru
Professor Emeritus of Anthropology
St. Lawrence University
Canton, New York, USA

Aborted Fundraising Initiative

Now that I had the admission letter and a scholarship, my next hurdle was to prepare to fly out of Kenya to the United States of America. The United States only existed in my wildest imagination from the books I had read, movies I watched and news I heard. Preparing for such a journey was a test of its own kind. It came at a time when I had not made any reasonable savings to cater for the huge travel expenses which included a paid return ticket and a student visa. I was also required to demonstrate that I had some money which would enable me settle down in the country.

I did not have the money to do all this. So, I decided to organize for a fundraiser. The idea of fundraising popularly known as *harambee* has helped many people in Kenya, but it has also frustrated others. Organizing for the event itself is not doable unless you have a starting budget to enable you undertake various planning and organisational activities for the event.

I believed that I enjoyed a lot of goodwill from my friends and relatives who knew that I had excelled in my undergraduate studies. I thought they were also happy that I was lucky to get the admission to study in the United States. How wrong I was!

As a start, I formed an organizing committee to assist me get in touch with people I thought would help me. The committee promised to make the noble venture a success and I gave it my trust. They agreed that I print funds collection booklets that contained fundraising receipts, and I did so. The committee also planned to have two fundraising events in the capital, Nairobi. One was to be held at the Kenya National

Union of Teachers (KNUT) premises in Nairobi and another at Kariobangi Social Hall, on the outskirts of the city.

However, I realized that even as we were planning, the plans were not working. I discovered that some people in the committee were rocking the boat from the inside. Several others who were not in the committee but were privy of the plans were equally sabotaging the forthcoming events. Many of the people were privately arguing that since I had already had my degree, I did not need further training. To them, therefore, I was being overly ambitious since many of my peers had not gone as far as I had. Indeed, most of my age mates did not go beyond Form 4. Furthermore, without shame, even some of my relatives were going around saying that I was troubling them.

"What does he want? He has a degree and a job," one of my uncles said when not within my earshot but the information reached me later. According to him, I was troubling them to give me money with which I would fly to the sky and never return. "He is the one who should be assisting us," my uncle reportedly claimed.

The manner in which issues unfolded as the fundraising date approached indicated to me that some people, including some of my very close relatives, were wolves camouflaged in sheepskin. They were doing a good job at sabotaging my plans. When the day came, I went to the venue at the KNUT Headquarters and waited for my guests to turn up. Despite the rumours I had heard, I still had hope that people will turn up and help me raise a descent amount. My eyes reddened when I came to the realisation that not many people will show up. A lot of my relatives gave the function a wide berth. When the day ended, I counted the money collected and it was barely the amount I used to pay for the hall.

One of my uncles did not wait for the sad news to sink in. He quickly saw it as an opportunity to add fuel to the fire. He told me that the fundraising flopped because I walked with 'my nose in the air.' He said I had humiliated them even when I was well educated. It is why they chose to teach me a memorable lesson, he said. This was shocking news to me because I had all along believed that I was down to earth and held them in high esteem.

Plans for the second fundraiser at Kariobangi also collapsed. But unlike the first event, this one was too embarrassing. What happened evidently made me understand that I had given my trust to the wrong people in my fundraising plans.

This is what happened. Apart from booking the hall, I had tasked my uncles and they had agreed to mobilize people and invite Super Mazembe Band to entertain the guests. During this period in the 1980s, the music band was very popular in the country and wherever they played, people turned up in large numbers.

As fate would have it, the fans and other invited guests arrived in large numbers but as the clock ticked away, there were no signs that the band was going to show up. I frantically got in touch with the band leader and I was petrified to learn that they were out of town for another function. He went ahead to tell me that they were neither invited nor aware of my function. At that moment, I wished the ground on which I stood would flip open and swallow me alive.

The hall had been paid for. I had also bought a lot of drinks for my guests. When they realized that they had been duped, they grabbed the drinks, emptied the bottles and left the venue.

I travelled back home a disappointed person. In Kisii, I started following the fundraising booklets I had given to individuals. Unfortunately, again, those I approached on the first day had not collected any money. This prompted me to drop this other embarrassing route.

But I have to appreciate three people; my mentor Prof. Celia Nyamweru managed to raise Kshs. 10,000, a good amount of money for that time! The fundraising organizing committee chairman also managed to get Kshs. 5000. My late father had also earned Kshs. 40,000 in the year's tea bonus. He gave me the whole amount! Furthermore, as a young man, I had managed to make some savings. Additionally, I had harvested maize which I managed to sell at Kshs. 6,000. I also sold a plot I had bought in Kisii Town at Kshs. 25,000. Cumulatively, the money was now sufficient to bankroll all my travel plans. I was happy.

There was yet another hurdle! The American Embassy in Nairobi was not going to approve my Visa unless I produced a qualified bank statement indicating that I had enough money for my travel and initial upkeep in the USA. I was lucky as James Nyakundi, a businessman cum banker, understood my predicament and agreed to be my sponsor. This gentleman went out of his way to transfer money, which I later returned, to my bank account. Indeed, this was an act of rare generosity. I remember it to date.

In the long run, with all the hurdles I faced now behind me, the devil was ashamed when I went for my interview at the American Embassy and was issued with Student Visa. I felt like I had acquired artificial wings when I walked out of the embassy precincts. As per the dates in the Visa, I had to depart for the USA in seven days' time. Time flew fast between that day and when I flew out of the country. But before I left, I thought of making it absolutely clear to my relatives that even without their support, my dreams were not going to be quashed.

"We are saddened that you will not travel to America," my uncle said when I got to his house that evening.

"You know people failed to support our fundraising initiatives because we come from a poor family. Had it been we were rich, they would have all come. Others mocked us that, 'even if we wear smart suits', we do not have money to assist you," another one said.

I listened to them as they shed crocodile tears. When they thought that I was convinced beyond doubt that they wished me well, I dropped the bombshell! "Thank you for your concern. I have the Visa with me and I will take the flight at the Jomo Kenyatta International Airport to the USA tomorrow in the evening," I told them as I flashed the document.

You should have been there to see the shock with which they received the news! They never uttered a word on the subject until we slept and I left their house the following day. This clearly shows that the very people whom you owe a lot of trust as relatives, friends and even colleagues, may not necessarily come to your aid at your time of need. At the worst, they can even sabotage your plans and even make matters worse possibly due to envy and petty jealousy.

Since I had limited time to allow me start processing a study leave through TSC, which could have taken me over two months, I decided to tender my immediate resignation from my teaching job. This decision was risky but I knew that my earlier attempts to apply for study leave with pay had been turned down. Thus, resignation was the only route left for me. I had to take it.

In the skies

Days were flying fast. Within no time, I was supposed to take off for the USA. This was towards the end of January, 1986. Time to start my journey to the United States of America had finally come! My heart throbbed as I shook my dad and sister's hands at the Jomo Kenyatta International Airport. I had never been airborne before, let alone come so close to a giant plane at an airport. The hour had come and for several hours, I was going to be up in the skies to a faraway destination I had never been to.

It was around 7 pm but the airport was not dark for me to see my sister Florence Obaga's face. I saw something which looked like a tear at the corners of her eyes. Then, as I embraced my father with an assurance that I would come back, the tears fell on my sister's cheeks. It was an emotional departure but I did not want to betray myself by shedding tears too.

Right there, I spotted my friend Aaron Ombaso. Coincidentally, Ombaso, who had been at university with me, was headed to Ohio University to study African History. Nothing binds people more than having known each other before, especially when faced by circumstances we were in at the time, and flying in the same airplane to a foreign land. Ombaso was definitely going to be very close to me.

The plane's take off offered a frightening experience to me. I remember Ombaso asking me, *"omogaka oyo, imechando ki eye* (elder, are we in trouble?). It should be noted that although *omogaka* is a word used to address an elderly person, it is common practice for men peers amongst Abagusii people to address each other using the term.

I was momentarily lost in a whirlwind of thoughts. In part, this was due to the anxiety of flying to a foreign country for the first time. Were it not that Ombaso was seated next to me, I would have even forgotten to wave to my relatives as the plane hit the runway and took to the skies. Those days, there was a waving bay atop the departure area. It would later be closed due to threats of terrorism.

It did not take long before the air hostesses announced that they were serving us with various foods and drinks. The food looked quite strange to the two of us who were used to the common Kenyan diet. We were served with macaroni, cheese, mashed potatoes and bread. There was no beef, vegetable or *ugali*, which are our staple food. As the journey progressed, I looked outside but was not able to see anything. It was pitch dark. What excited my friend and I was that the airline served free beer. As strange as it may appear, we happily jumped into the idea of partaking whisky to kill the boredom and anxiety that we were in.

Our Arrival in America

We had been drinking but were not so high when the plane made a stopover in Brussels. From there, we took the next flight to Columbus Airport in Ohio State. No sooner had the plane touched down than we discovered that we were relatively inebriated. Even so, my senses were still with me and I could tell that I was in a highly cosmopolitan airport. People of different colours and backgrounds were moving here and there, each minding their business and bypassing one another as if without noticing them. This threw Ombaso and me in a cultural shock. It was around midnight and we chose to occupy some seats that were nearby.

"How far is Athens, Ohio from this place?" Ombaso asked me.

"About 300km," I replied.

"How do we get there?"

"Maybe we wait until dawn."

Ombaso had telephone contacts of an American friend who had been to Kenya. But when Ombaso called his number from a landline boot, the person on the other end dropped the call. Ombaso called again and the call went unanswered.

"What do we do now? It seems there's a communication breakdown with the person I thought could assist us," Ombaso said as he dropped the phone in its place. In retrospect, getting out of the airport would have been easier if we had mobile phones then. In recent times, communication has been made easier so long as one has a cellular phone.

As we were consulting on our next action, we spotted a group of black people and we decided to approach them. Yes, they were black, but they were black Americans. It was difficult for us to communicate because of the language accent.

We eventually decided to take a taxi to the university but we had to break the bank first. We paid a whopping US$200 dollars! This cost was way above what we had spent for any form of road transport back in Kenya.

On Kenyan roads, it is common for motorists to drive in a disorderly manner against oncoming traffic. Moreover, you may come across a dilapidated jalopy that would be a disgrace even at the junkyard, let alone on a road. Then, it comes to a sudden shuddering stop and blocks lanes on a busy highway. In such a situation, your mood may change and your sugar levels may go high.

As soon as we set foot in the United States, we experienced culture shock in the name of order. Vehicular traffic flow in the cities was systematic. On the sides, there were skyscrapers that were as tall as our eyes could see from the cab. I was mesmerized to spot people cleaning the roads in the night. This was winter season, and the roadsides were covered with thick snow. As we cruised to Athens, I realized that we were getting into the countryside. There were trees, which looked haggard because they did not have leaves and I could not figure out what had happened. Our cab driver must have sensed that this question was necessary to be answered without it being asked. "The leaves fall before the winter," he said with a feel of confidence.

We got to the university's guest house about two hours later and paid to spend the remaining part of the night there. The fee of US$ 250 per night was prohibitive to a foreign student. We had started to feel the pinch of America's capitalistic economy. In America, there is nothing for free.

I loved the aesthetic beauty of the town. The area is built in the unique American architecture of the 19th century. We had arrived a week to the start of the semester. We needed to be busy so that we could not feel out of place. Our love for the African food made us miss home on the first day and we sought to find a joint that served it.

What we ate was strange. The hotels never served ugali, which we were really yearning for. Instead, they served us with cheese, bread, cooked potatoes and broiler chicken cooked the American way. This worried us. We wondered if we were ever going to get used to that type of diet.

Whoever said that two heads are better than one was right. Had it been that I were alone, I would have been overwhelmed in making a number of decisions. Or, maybe, just maybe, I would have made better decisions.

Take the example of accommodation. Ombaso and I quickly learnt that being accommodated in the University was more expensive than outside the institution. The two of us thought of finding a fellow African, possibly from East Africa, to assist us understand the alien environment we were in. It did not take long for us to find where students from Africa stayed. We luckily bumped into Rodgers Chimela, a student from Uganda who soon became our best friend.

Rodgers exuded a lot of friendship and excitement on finding fellow East Africans. He cut an image of a nice guy. He took us to his room and cooked *ugali* and beef for us. A born again Christian, Rodgers carried himself with humility and understanding. We were happy to meet such a person in a foreign country. He was Godsend!

"There are a few vacant rooms in this apartment. You better hurry up and get your rooms," said Rodgers.

We knew that time never waited for any man and we hastened to get ourselves a bigger room. It had two beds, some chairs and tables. Until we reported to the university the following Monday, the Ugandan was very helpful to us. He oriented us to the American way of life and he urged us to adjust ourselves accordingly.

"This is a capitalistic country. Nothing is given for free," Rodgers said. He was almost our age but he seemed wiser, perhaps due to the fact that he had been in the country for a while.

"I have a fully sponsored scholarship," I revealed to Rodgers after some time.

"You are very lucky! Full scholarships in America are given to American students and exceedingly brilliant foreigners. For you to keep the scholarship, you must be an A grade student all through," he said.

Unlike me, Ombaso had a partial scholarship that only catered for tuition. Rodgers was on a United States Agency for International Development (USAID) scholarship, pursuing a degree in International Affairs. His course was very popular in the university, especially with foreign students.

It was through Rodgers that we were able to meet and mingle with two Kenyan students undertaking PhD studies. One of them was Abdalla Maloba, a very talkative Kenyan. Within no time, he told us that he was married to a British woman. He also informed us that he was about to complete his PhD course and was planning to fly back to Kenya to contest for the Sabatia parliamentary seat in Western Kenya. I could not take him seriously though. The seat was in the firm grip of Moses Mudamba Mudavadi, Musalia Mudavadi's father. Moses was a key political figure in Luhyia land at that time and was also very close to President Moi. It could be a very hard sell to dethrone the seasoned politician.

Even as we tried to settle down, we had mixed feelings. The culture was different from what we were accustomed to back in our motherland. Then, we remembered that when one goes to Rome, one has the options of doing as the Romans do or continue suffering in a delirium of non-conformities and home sickness.

We realized that African students socialized mainly amongst themselves. They also shopped at particular business premises like the Super Dupa Supermarket where prices were pocket friendly. This is the same supermarket from where we purchased items like corn flour, chicken, eggs and vegetables. What worried us, and it did concern my friend Ombaso more, was that the items were very expensive. Being on a partial scholarship, he wondered how he was going to sustain himself. And when the economic pressure became too much for him to bear, he moved to a different city and university where the cost of living was more affordable. It was also easier to get a temporary job to assist him in paying his tuition and maintenance.

The American Shocks

Monday morning. "Welcome to Ohio University," Dr. Wilhelm told me as he firmly shook my hand and ushered me to a chair in his well-furnished and expansive office at the Geography Building. He was the Head of Department (HoD).

I easily got along with him like a long-time acquaintance. He inquired from me about Kenyan issues. Our conversation centred on the Maasai Mara wildlife, famine in parts of the country and the then prevailing political environment. When I walked beside him to the office of post-graduate students, I felt that the rapport between us had existed for decades.

I was happy to be allocated an office in the post-graduate students wing where I was also briefed of the duties I was required to do as a teaching assistant. I was to work under a Ghanaian Professor; Dr. Michael Darkoh. The professor, was on a sabbatical leave attached to the university where he taught African Geography. The same day, I was also introduced to some post graduate students and professors in the Department. They were glad to have me join them. I was most elated to have such a warm welcome, miles and miles away from my motherland.

I sat at my office desk picturing the fact that I was starting my career once again in a faraway foreign country with a different culture whose foundation is based on the values of capitalism and liberalism. To me, and this is what I learnt during my studies there, America is indeed the land of the free and the brave. I had to be free and brave to face life and ensure I completed my studies within the stipulated time frame of my scholarship.

In America, it seems that everyone is chasing the American dream. However, this dream can be along mirage. Indeed, many Americans have never achieved the so called cherished dream. It can be even more challenging for a foreigner to achieve this elusive dream.

Over time, I learnt that many black Americans appeared to be alienated from the American dream for factors I may not be able to explain fully. Some are political while others are based on racial and historical injustices. For instance, the issue of race in America is a big and emotive topic of its own. It may require another expose beyond the limits of this book.

The beauty of America is that it has strong institutions that have kept the country together for more than two hundred years. It is built on socio-economic and political institutions alongside a strong legal system, which is well developed and effective. These institutions can be attributed to making America a prosperous and stable country. I can bet that were it not for these well-established institutions, America could be wallowing in racial, political and economic trenches. It could be doing more poorly than most other developing countries.

Another shock greeted me in America. In the country, adults are encouraged to support themselves in all matters and not depend on others. When a young person in America reaches the age of 18 years, he/she is supposed to leave his/her parents' abode. He/she should find a job, go stay in his rented apartment and start paying the bills while pursuing his or her studies. This is ideally the true sense of being an adult as per the capitalistic principles.

Furthermore, it appears that young Americans succeed because they have not centred their career advancement on white collar jobs as is the case of their counterparts in other parts of the world. You will find a youth from a wealthy family wiping tables at a restaurant, working in university hostels, kitchen or the library doing manual work. In Kenya, such jobs are presumed to be for those who come from poor family backgrounds or have not had a good education.

When students in America work in the universities, there is a win-win situation. They are able to pay their bills and fees, and enable the university cut on operating costs. Americans do not discriminate on jobs and I found them to be relatively well grounded and functional people. They do things beyond their areas of expertise. Surely, this is the way a country like Kenya, with very high levels of unemployment, should ideally go.

It is my view that many of the frustrations that young Kenyans confront after college would not arise if parents prepared their children well for the challenging world. It is good to emulate good practices. One of these is encouraging young people to do any job that comes or may come their way while they pursue their life dreams, provided it does not involve crime. Young Americans are even encouraged to join the military. In such environment, they are able to learn personal discipline and protective skills even as they broaden their experience and worldview. In a sense, one is taught to be an independent person from an early age.

Understanding Capitalism

In America, nothing is for free. In fact, they say in America 'there is no free lunch'. I learnt this the hard way and I cannot forget the experience.

One afternoon, a professor invited my friend Ombaso and me to join him for lunch at a cafeteria on campus. We did and thought he was going to buy the lunch for us just as it happens in our country. So, we all served ourselves, took our seats at the table and had an enjoyable conversation as we ate. When time to pay came, the good professor picked his receipt and paid his bill. This behaviour shocked us very much because in Kenya, if someone invites you for lunch, it means he is going to pay for it.

I was lucky because I had some money on me. I paid our bill with ease and we left. But when we animatedly shared our experience with other African students, they laughed and said this was the real American experience.

If some American invites you for lunch and he intends to pay, he will make it clear from the onset. So, you need to be keen and know the terms in which you are going for a meal together. Obviously, it can be very embarrassing if you ate a meal in a restaurant and then it dawns on you that your companion who asked you to join him or her is not going to pay and you do not have money on you. American people are not fond of free things and can turn down an offer for the same.

Around that time again, Ombaso and I managed to make acquaintances of some American ladies. One day, we invited them to join us for a drink in the evening. The girls gladly accepted and we had a good time together. However, we realized that each time they ordered for a drink they paid for themselves. This was new to us. Our thinking was that since we had invited them, we were going to pay for their drinks.

It took a while for them to reluctantly accept our line of thought. We swallowed drinks worth a few dollars and my friend thought this was an excuse for him to make advances to one of the ladies who looked pretty as they danced together. How wrong he was!

"No! I have my boyfriend!" exclaimed the lady.

"Yes, but we have bought you drinks," said my friend.

"That's not an issue. My boyfriend is coming to pick me up," she said with a sense of finality.

And for sure, it did not take long before her boyfriend came. They walked out holding hands, to Ombaso's chagrin. It was our first day to find a way of dating an American lady and it flopped badly. We went to the house disappointed.

However, through these unique experiences, we were being inculcated gradually into the American way of life. We learnt that giving an American something for free can be annoying and unacceptable. They find it outrageous and abnormal and do not countenance the culture of free things. It is taken that one must work hard to be able to live their desire, their American dream.

Another thing I appreciated concerning America is their functional social-welfare system. It is a system that helps those who, for one reason or another, are unable to support themselves. The vetting process for the welfare benefits is very clear and transparent unlike in other countries where non-deserving citizens make it to the list, to the disadvantage and disquiet of the deserving beneficiaries. I found it funny that still some Americans were too proud, feeling that their dignity would be hurt, if they enlisted themselves to get welfare support. Instead, they chose to be homeless.

I also learnt that in the university, some students were sons and daughters of senior government officers and business people. But this did not make them any different; their social status never featured in what they did. I was prodding friends during a social event when I learnt that one student was a son of a high level medical doctor who was also the director of the university's medical school. Despite this, the young man worked at the university library to fund his studies.

"My father is an international businessman but all the wealth he has belongs to him," another student who worked at the university cafeteria told me.

He went ahead to say that his parents drove him out of their home after he joined bad company. He further told me that his grandfather was a wealthy man who died and left millions of dollars in the bank as well as several estates.

"All those riches will be donated to charitable organizations at some stage," he said.

The American dream is there to be pursued by each person in America. It dawned on me that everybody contributes to wealth creation, although some are super rich. The likes of the owners of Microsoft, Apple and other blue chip companies control the economy. However, everyone in America is contributing to the country's economy, however small that contribution may be.

The Kenyan youths should draw lessons from what happens in America. Even when they come from wealthy families, they should not feel entitled to be supported by their parents even when they become adults. Africa needs to go this way so that the continent reduces the many dependents and hangers-on that exist in our society. The culture of hangers-on, people who cannot support themselves but expect handouts from others, should be discouraged.

Further, it is my view that parents should stop pampering their children. It is ironical that parents that grew up working in *shambas* (agricultural farms) cannot allow their children to do chores at home, let alone soil their hands. Parents should allow their sons and daughters to do any kind of work at home and outside. According to published data in Kenya, less than 30% of the population is in gainful work while the rest are dependents. Wealth cannot be created when most of the populace is dependent on such a small number of producers.

Consequently, in Kenya, as is the case with many African countries, those who generate income are unable to invest it. When you give handouts freely, this is taken as a social investment. However, it should be noted that social support systems of this kind worked in the past, especially in the face of hardships such as famine, cattle disease, drought or some other calamities. They were more of community welfare systems that supported individuals to weather the worst and enable them have a chance to do better. Even then, lazy and unproductive people were not condoned and were shunned. People lived by the principle of reciprocity (that is, today it is my turn to be helped bearing in mind that, when time comes, I will reciprocate in kind). It was a social safety valve which worked quite well at the times of need. Today, people take other people's charity for granted and the values that traditionally guarded this philosophy have since faded.

This is a concept which is not tenable in the highly competitive and globalized economic system. No wonder African societies continue being poor and cannot compete on the global stage.

I suggest that we practice responsible capitalism, which entails all of us working for ourselves to earn sustainable livelihoods. This is doable by us becoming investors, industrialists and entrepreneurs (wealth creators). This way, our country's Gross Domestic Product (GDP) and the overall welfare will rise for the betterment of the entire population.

However, over the years, in most African societies, people practise what can be termed as 'African socialism' where creating wealth is frowned upon. In Africa, not being willing to share what you have, however little, can be seen as an act of selfishness and you can become an outcast. This makes some to use unorthodox means like taking state resources to support their kinsmen and hangers-on. No wonder corruption is a major menace in most African countries including our country Kenya.

In Class at Ohio

If there are people who understand that time waits for no man then it is the Americans. This is particularly reflected in American universities. At Ohio University, the first semester started in earnest as the university calendar indicated. I did not see any student who reported late for the commencement of the semester.

From the onset, I also realized that the lecturers strictly kept time. I had to up my game by ensuring that I also trained myself to live up to the dictates of the environment I was in. This, to a large extent, has helped me to this day.

It did not take me long to adjust to the new system however different it was from the one in my home country. In particular, the lecturers were very interactive, thus making lectures to be enjoyable. Lecturers in the university had concepts at their fingertips, or so I thought, due to their clarity in expression and academic exposure. In particular, lecturers also engaged in continuous research that allowed them to continually absorb and generate more knowledge, new ideas and skills.

Furthermore, their forms of pedagogy stood apart from what I experienced at the University of Nairobi. They mostly guided us to prepare for specific topics. This paved way for interactive learning experiences. It made us students very active in the learning discourse, well aware that we were also being graded, based on our level of participation and contribution to the understanding of academic issues. We were also given regular tests and end of semester examinations.

However, I was not amused when some lecturers said that my command of English language was rather poor. To them, they believed that foreign students had difficulty in comprehending the complexity of the English language. Perhaps they had come across several of such cases. They therefore expected the students to attend a language lab. They believed that this could lift the students' understanding and abilities to engage in proper English.

"No, I'm not a fan of the American twanging," I answered the lecturers. The American accent never impressed me. Americans from various parts of the America twang differently. Further, to my ears, their words and intonations at times sounded vulgar. I thought it would be better for me to hear them speaking and understand what they were saying than aping them and acquiring an accent that would sound strange to me and my contemporaries back home.

When I stood my ground, and said that I was comfortable with my language abilities, they were astonished at first, and then they came to respect me as a principled person. Initially, they had viewed me as a weak and misplaced student from Africa. Soon, I would prove them wrong.

I enjoyed Geography practical lessons in Climatology, Physical Geography and Cartography. However, I realized that American students were quicker in practical lessons than in the theories and grasp of concepts. Their upbringing makes them to be quick in handling practical lessons that required demonstration of specific skills. For foreigners, we struggled in the first few days to catch up with them.

I took my studies seriously from the start. My seriousness bore results in the first examination where I scored 'As' in all the courses. This surprised the Americans who took note that there was an African in their midst who was topping in class. Gradually, I won respect and was also handled with a lot of decorum. This motivated me to be even more focused as I acclimatized myself with the American academic system.

The goodness of the American system is that it is based on meritocracy and nobody can short change one from getting rewarded for one's academic performance. All along, I had held a wrong notion that certain races and countries were superior to others particularly in the areas of skills development and academic performance. I proved the contrary while in Ohio University.

After finishing course work, I decided to pick a topic on 'the dexterity of pastoralism in Kenya' as my research topic for my Master's thesis. I chose this topic due to the fact that I was going to deal with what I thought was an existing problem that was affecting pastoral communities in Kenya, particularly as relates to environmental degradation. However, when I shared it with my supervisor, I discovered that he was not interested in the topic. He was frank to tell me that he wanted me to undertake research on wildlife conservation issues and I had no option but to embrace the idea. As much as I was disappointed as a student, I knew very well that standing to oppose my academic advisor was not to be a wise thing to do.

It did not take long before I discovered that he had discussed the issue with the other faculty members. That was how I changed my research topic to *The Deterioration of Wildlife Conservation in Kenya; a Case Study of Nairobi and Amboseli National Parks.*

At the onset, I combed the library shelves for relevant materials but to no avail. I started thinking that this was going to give me a headache. But upon doing a catalogue search, I came across a book titled, *Planning Human Activities on Protected National Ecosystems in Kenya*, by Walter Lusigi, 1978. The efficiency of the America system was once again revealed when the chief librarian placed an order for the book through the inter-library book exchange. It took just three days for the book to be delivered from the Library of Congress.

This book set me off and enabled me to undertake my research. I gradually developed keen interest in wildlife conservation and I have over the years written and published extensively on the topic. During my research undertakings, I ploughed through a lot of literature as required. This entailed searching for information from academic journals and archives. With the guidance of my academic supervisors, Dr. Ted Bernard and Dr. Bob Walter, I was able to finish my Masters' research assignment in good time. I was over the moon when I presented the thesis, defended it successfully and passed in mid-1988.

I have to state that, throughout my studies in American universities (Ohio and Southern Illinois), I worked as a Teaching or Research Assistant. This work entailed assisting an assigned professor in making preparations for teaching. I was also required to stand in for the professor in teaching, advising students and administering examinations. It was also within my mandate to keep students' academic records and submit their marks and grades to the Central Examinations Processing Office for final tabulation before the results were released to the students. The money that

I was paid as a teaching assistant covered my tuition fees. I also got a stipend of about US$ 1,500, which I used for my maintenance. For a student, this amount of money was enough to meet all my basic needs.

Having completed my Masters in Geography degree, I found that I had almost one year before my scholarship funding elapsed. I had learnt to make maximum use of any opportunity that came my way and that is exactly what I did. I enrolled for another Master's degree in Curriculum and Instruction, which I finished within one year. This was achievable because the university exempted me from some units like Research and Statistics, which I had already covered under the initial programme.

Nothing made me happier than the fact that I had obtained two Masters Degrees (in Geography and in Curriculum and Instruction) in a record two and half year's period. Above all, I finished the training as a distinguished 'A' student. This was no mean feat. I had killed two birds with one stone, in the literal sense of the meaning of this expression.

As I noted earlier, in the American education system, nobody can deny you what you rightly deserve. It therefore goes without saying that it was my good performance in the Masters programmes that earned me another scholarship to pursue PhD studies at the Southern Illinois University.

The Southern Illinois University is situated to the extreme south of the State of Illinois. The State is in the American heartland famed for agricultural production. In the region, farming is done using high level scientific skills and technological understanding. Farmers there are the leading producers of wheat, soya beans, corn and livestock. Simply said, I was moving to the food basket of America.

Social Life in Ohio

I was born and brought up in an area whose dwellers went to bed soon after the sun dipped in the horizon. It was in college where I learnt that some people in other parts of the world remained active through the night. In urban centres, people especially the youth, hop from one entertainment spot to the other, partying, socializing and drinking through the night particularly during weekends. Interestingly, you will find them in their workplace in the morning.

As much as I worked hard in my studies, I had a relatively active social life. My friends from Kenya, South Africa and Botswana and me developed a habit for us to party on Fridays through Saturdays. We made consumption of American beer our pastime social activity. It was government policy that beer should have lower alcohol content. However, one obviously got inebriated after consuming several bottles.

Being in Ohio provided me with a unique privilege that I never fathomed in my wildest imagination. The university provided an international environment with students from all over the world. It offered a mosaic of diverse cultures that co-existed in the understanding that they belonged to one human race.

We had International Cultural Week every Semester. In the events, several unique cultural performances were showcased. The activities included the African Night, the Chinese Night, and the Arabian Night, among others. This contributed to cultural exchanges, which implanted indelible memories in us.

Unfortunately, what I also noted during my stay in America is the tendency of students from Africa to sometimes over-indulge in alcohol. This particularly got more noticeable during weekends. It could have been caused by the feeling of being homesick and bored when one is away from class. Alcohol in America, being fairly cheap, did not make it any easier. Its affordability tempted a good number of students to indulge in drinking. This was particularly common during pay time at the end of the month or during weekends when one was free from work or studies.

In our case, we had a social group made up of students from Eastern and Southern Africa. During weekends, we could flock bars during the Happy Hours (4-8 pm) when prices of beer got reduced to almost half. As we continued drinking, we could be heard uttering statements such as, "get us more beer from the reservoir!"; "hit me again!"; and "the day is still young!"

American students enjoyed their beer too. Over the weekends, there could be several house parties with open invitations. All you needed to do was buy a bottle of whisky or a pack of six beers and pop into the party.

Surprisingly, I discovered that, at the crescendo, some of the party venues turned into *marijuana* smoking dens. The drug was taken freely, amid proclamations, "I want to get high!" "I want to be stoned!" Then past midnight, the floodgates of promiscuity flew ajar.

The HIV/AIDS scourge was highly-dreaded when I landed in the United States in the mid-1980s. In such an environment, anything could happen. However, the students were so keen to the extent that they could not indulge in unprotected sex, whatever the circumstances. It was common for men to have condoms in their pocket waiting to get 'lucky'.

Despite its advancement in technology, research and healthcare, for a long time, America grappled with the pandemic. It did not discriminate against people's social status. It affected all people all the same. The worst part is that it did not have a cure.

The beauty of America, though, is that, there is widespread and quick flow of information through many and varied channels of communication. Particularly, the government invested heavily on widespread creation of awareness using print and electronic media, seminars, symposia and conferences. Researchers, meanwhile, spent days on end in the laboratories in search of a cure or prevention.

The sensitization efforts bore fruits, going by the rapid behavioural change, which both men and women exhibited especially in matters of sex. Whenever students attended house parties, they invariably carried condoms in their pockets, just in case they got 'lucky', as some put it. It slowly became a habit that one could not engage in casual sex without protection. This perhaps saved many young men and women who would have either transmitted or contracted the dreaded HIV/AIDS virus. Also, it must have saved many young men who would have landed into trouble for putting their female colleagues in the family way at the wrong time apart from contracting the virus. This is what it meant to live in the most advanced country in the world where there is always efficient flow of information and creation of awareness.

A social gathering could be dangerous. A small disagreement between two people could degenerate into a brawl where one could be injured. At times I imagined that if anything bad happened to me in such social gatherings, I would find it difficult to explain why I was there in the first place.

I find it interesting that, as much as we partied, no major ugly incident happened. What appeared close to an ugly incident occurred one night at a bar when one old American woman walked towards our table, her eyes looking straight at me. She then embraced me and forcefully started to kiss me even as I protested the unbecoming behaviour. Noticing her unbecoming behaviour, on-looking patrons chased her away. However, as she exited she fell into the hands of an Arabian male student who appeared to have been on wait for such a lady and they disappeared together into the night.

On the overall, my social life experience made me understand that I was in a free society with a lot of socializing and networking. It, however, needed one to be cautious and not indulge in any extremity as it could destroy one's life. I also found that Americans are quite social and outgoing.

I discovered that it was not easy to comprehend American students' viewpoints on sensitive social issues of race, religious, social and economic development. Most of them could do very well in Public Relations. They cut an image of very friendly people and you could not discover the underlying racial tendencies. In fact, we did not discuss religion and racial issues at all. Instead, we focused on broader issues like politics and socialization.

As a young man then, I had a relatively good experience at Ohio. Unlike me, my long term friend Ombaso who was not on full scholarship, had to move to the East Coast where he joined the Sacred Heart College in Connecticut. I appreciate the fact that he was an extremely enterprising young man. He got jobs and raised money to pay for his fees. He gladly graduated with a Masters in Religious Studies from Sacred Heart University College. He promptly flew back to Kenya and immediately got a job at Kenyatta University where he was hired to teach in his area of specialization.

My Special American Mentors

My life story at Ohio will not be complete underscoring that Ted Bernard turned out to be a very nice person to me. He could invite me to his house where he prepared American dishes. We then dined together and he could give me a maximum of two bottles of beer. In the back of his mind, he detested seeing an inebriated person who is unable to control himself.

I hold Dr. Bernard in high regard. I will say that I have never met such a good hearted, friendly, highly contentious and wise person anywhere else. He was my mentor and I have fond memories of him.

My other great friend in the university was Dr. Gifford Doxsee. He was the Director of International Affairs Studies during my time at Ohio. A staunch protestant, he was married to Mary Doxsee, although they never had children. Nevertheless, they lived according to their marriage vows until the wife died after suffering from dementia.

Dr. Doxsee continued doing voluntary work after retirement. While at Ohio University, he became quite fond of me. We kept in touch even after I left the university. I was saddened to learn of his demise that happened in 2017.

While I was in the university, Dr. Doxsee visited Kenya and took several photos. Upon return to the United States, he made slides and invited his friends to come and have a look. I was in their midst and could see their mixed reactions.

I, however, realized that his photography dwelt on wildlife in Maasai Mara, the Maasai culture and physical features he saw in the countryside. He did not have any images of

Nairobi or any other Kenyan cities or the hotels where he had stayed. Perhaps this is the same approach many visitors, especially from the Western world, have when they visit Africa. No wonder those of them who have never been to Kenya think we live in forests with wild animals surrounding us.

Dr. Doxsee addressed me as a young Kenyan with athletic features. "I hear you are doing very well in your studies," he often told me. This informed me that the American lecturers were sharing information about me during their interactions, appreciating my academic performance.

Perhaps the fact that he fought in the Second World War, where he was a prisoner of war and survived, made him have the human face he exhibited. He told me that it pained him whenever he saw people, especially women and children, suffering due to wars that they neither started nor knew anything about. His cherished wish was to see a peaceful world free of bloodshed and abuse of human rights.

I noted earlier that you will not get anything for free in America. That is why I found it interesting that Dr. Doxsee occasionally gave me money which I neither worked for nor requested.

The last time I was in Ohio in August 1988, he took me for lunch in a restaurant then gave me US$ 400 for my upkeep. When we parted ways, I felt like I was leaving my father behind in Ohio.

Other Take-Home Encounters

One may wonder whether I ever stepped in church while in America, given that I was born and brought up by Catholic parents. Yes, I did go to church a couple of times. However, I found that their approach to Christianity was very different from the way I understood it from Kenya. Particularly, the modes and manner of interaction was quite different from the one I was used to. For instance, the Sunday Mass used to be quite formal to the level of being mechanical and there was not much exchange of pleasantries after the church service. I also noticed that in the church, everyone else was White. This made me uncomfortable because I appeared to be the centre of interest and found it hard to concentrate on worshipping.

Importantly again, I noted that in America there are churches for African-Americans and others for white Americans. The ones for the African-Americans were not near where we stayed. Again, the divide along racial lines, yet we were worshiping the same God, discouraged me from attending church in America.

It was sad that a good number of Americans were relatively ignorant on international issues. I discovered that some knew very little about Africa. Most of them, including black Americans, viewed Africa as one country and a dark continent. They saw Africa as the epicentre of war, famine, poverty, ignorance, disease and uncivilized people.

It irritated me when I found out that some of my American classmates never knew that there existed a country called Kenya. They had heard of Africa and Nigeria and could not differentiate that one was a continent and the other was a country in the continent. Also, many of them held the notion that Africans never wore clothes and lived with wild animals in forests and on the African Savannah.

Some could say that I was very lucky to be in America but wondered if I came in while in clothes or I was dressed at the airport. It was more annoying when some asked if I was interested in returning home. But I simply told them that you can traverse the world but you will never find a place which is better than your home.

My face would light up when I met some Americans who understood Africa well. They had widely travelled and when they spoke about the good things they saw in Africa, and particularly in Kenya, they lifted my spirit. They talked about the friendliness of the Kenyan people, the beautiful and unique Kenyan landscape, and the iconic wildlife in our national parks and game reserves.

I will not shy away from saying that America, once touted as the Super Power is indeed a super power. It is blessed with a diversity of people, natural resources and covers miles and miles of land. It interests me that America has more forest cover now than it did a hundred years ago. Additionally, the country is highly cosmopolitan and industrialized. It is the hub of global commerce.

There are several take-home lessons Kenya could draw from America. The lessons apply particularly to food production and conservation of the environment. Because their agriculture is highly mechanized, a mere 2% of the population does farming to feed the remaining 98% and have a surplus for export. In Kenya, more than half the population is engaged in agriculture, in one way or the other, yet we face challenges in feeding ourselves as a nation.

Let me add that America is highly urbanized and advanced in terms of industry and commerce. The industrial and commercial investments are the foundation of employment, providng many jobs for the urban population. Furthermore, for proper urbanization to occur, there is the need to be able to provide essential services such as housing, security and education efficiently. In particular, given the change of seasons, such as harsh winter weather conditions, urbanization is essential for survival. This is especially in the extreme global north and the extreme global south of the planet Earth where weather conditions tend to be very harsh.

Similarly in recent years, Kenya has experienced an upsurge of rural to urban migration. Young people are now going to towns such as Nairobi, Mombasa, Nakuru and Kisumu in search of employment after finishing school. However, this urban surge has led to the emergence of slums in the cities. Most people end up working in the informal sector as labourers, hawkers, cleaners and security guards where they get very low pay. Furthermore, unlike in the USA and other parts of the Western world, South and East Asia, in Kenya, as is the case with most of Africa, the majority of people are not permanent urbanites. Instead, they have dual-residence; they live in the cities yet they invest in their rural homes where they deem they belong. Most of them even travel upcountry to vote during elections such that they end up with no say on who governs them in the urban centres where they spend most of their lives.

Another USA Scholarship

I left Ohio mature and with more experience in American life that when I first came into the country. I flew to Illinois to embark on my doctoral studies in Geography, specializing in Natural Resources Planning and Management. I was not as confused when I got to the university in Carbondale City as happened when I first landed in America. Then, I was only a country lad with little to no experience with life in a first world nation. Then, everything came to me as a rude culture shock. Now, here I was, conquering the United States one city at a time.

I had contacted some Kenyan students in Carbondale. They happily welcomed me and within no time, I was able to find a place to stay. My abode was in the Southern Hills Apartments, situated to the south of the University's Main Campus. The apartments exclusively hosted post-graduate students. Some were married and stayed with their families. My two-bedroom apartment offered more space than I needed but I loved it.

I had never owned a vehicle before and navigating the breadth of Carbondale on foot or using public transport was proving cumbersome and time consuming. With the little savings I had made, I decided to buy a used Buick car which was maroon in colour. This was the first ever automobile I owned. It drew me back US$2,000 dollars. However, I knew it was a worthwhile investment and it indeed served me well.

I did not look out of place on my first day in the University's Geography Department. As was the norm, I was shown the office I would occupy and introduced to two professors. I was going to work under Dr. Chris Lant and Dr. Horsley as their teaching assistant.

Pursuing a PhD in America is a rigorous venture. It entails spending two years doing course work amid comprehensive examinations that knock many to the wayside. After the examinations, you are allowed to defend your research proposal then get admitted into the PhD candidacy. Getting to this stage takes sweat and commitment.

Professors in America do not respect persons based on social networks. They will tell you point-blank from the onset that PhD training was not meant for everybody. "With your Masters, you have already obtained sufficient competence in your area of specialization," they would tell you. They added that the PhD training only made you a high-level researcher and contributor of knowledge, in your area of expertise.

One would have mistaken the professors for scaremongers but they meant what they said. The dropout rate in doctoral training could go up to 70 percent in some schools or programmes. One started the PhD programme on the understanding that one was being tested to be proven that one was indeed PhD material.

The University appeared to send a strong signal when it lumped masters and doctoral students together in a number of courses but expected the latter to get A grades. For a doctoral student, anything below B+ was seen as failure that could lead to disqualification. True to the set standards, a number of students I started the course with never completed the programme. Some did but after taking a much longer duration than they ever thought when they joined the programme. This happened because they had to make several attempts to pass their comprehensive examinations, research proposal defence or final defence of dissertation.

What amazed me was the fact that our professors treated us as colleagues. They engaged us in high-level discussions and made us appreciate that we were supposed to understand issues well and challenge them accordingly. The professors looked forward to and enjoyed being challenged by their students. They got satisfied that in the students before them were potential professors when we challenged the theories and concepts they put across.

In such an environment, I realized that, to succeed, I was not going to combine studying and drinking. One of the two had to go. I did not go to America to drink. Therefore, it was not hard to decide what to sacrifice between drinking and studying. That is how I arrived at the decision of quitting drinking to concentrate on my studies. It was a good decision and I have never looked back. I have stayed sober since.

Some students in my class were very close to our professors to the extent of going to social places together. This made me fear that the professors would favour them during examinations. Far from it! American professors will give you the grade you deserve after evaluating your work objectively. They have drawn and known the line between friendship and academics.

I further discovered that Americans never bought excuses. To them, looking for excuses is akin to whining. You must do what is expected of you and do it right.

I was the only African student in our class. There was one student from Brazil, three from China, one from Puerto Rico and four Americans.

Nothing confirmed that I was in an environment with cut-throat competition than the fact that when we finished course work and sat for final comprehensive examinations, the three Chinese and two American students failed but were given a window to re-take the examinations. The rest of us proceeded to defend our PhD proposals but, again, only two were admitted to PhD candidacy.

I heaved a sigh of relief when our professors confirmed that I had been fully accepted into PhD candidacy system. I was happier when they said that I was an exceptional student. Dr. Chris opined, openly, that I was not giving them difficulties and that if I maintained the tempo, nothing would stop me from obtaining my PhD within the stipulated time.

Through Dr. Chris' guidance, I submitted two proposals for funding and they were successful. The National Science Foundation (NSF) funded me with US$ 50,000, while the Biodiversity Society of America availed US$ 10,000.

My PhD topic was *The Political Ecology of Wildlife Conservation in Kenya.* The study was based in Nairobi, Amboseli and Tsavo National Parks. It entailed rigorous research that applied the theory of political ecology to analyse diverse issues of wildlife conservation in Kenya. Basically, the main point of departure in the study was that wildlife conservation is more than a biological activity and it transits into a political contestation where diverse groups attempted to advance their interests.

I will further simplify the study findings by saying that whenever conservationists or governments start conservation programmes, the process may be perceived purely as a conservation issue but it eventually becomes a political matter where there are winners and losers. This happens because various stakeholders in the conservation process do not wield equal power. Whereas governments, bureaucrats, international conservationists and local elites may hold relatively more power, the local communities, where conservation takes place are in most cases powerless and become losers. For example, the revenue generated out of conservation and tourism development hardly trickles down to local communities and this makes them resist conservation projects however good they may appear to be.

This is why the local people usually engage in destruction of vegetation, poisoning of wild animals and poaching. The situation is compounded when conservationists look at the issue partially, without examining the socio-economic and political issues surrounding the matter.

The research took me nearly a year to finalize. I interrogated issues in the three parks using various methodologies like administering questionnaires to various respondents and in-depth interviews that provided abundant information and data.

Before undertaking the research, I had to apply for a research permit from the Ministry of Education in Nairobi. This took me over one month. Also, for me to go to the field to collect data, I had to hire a research assistant. This was a critical person in the research. He assisted me in administering my research questionnaire and helped me insert data in the spread sheet. Collecting data in the field was challenging. It needed patience since I had to take time to explain to the local people and other interviewees about myself and why I was interviewing them. This was to clear any suspicion and create an enabling environment to allow the interviews to take place in a congenial manner.

In many instances, I needed a local interpreter to assist in communicating to some of my interviewees. Due to these constraints, it took me an average of thirty minutes to interview one person. At the same time, since we were in unfamiliar territory, in remote areas, especially adjacent to Amboseli and Tsavo West National Park, we were always cautious and made sure that we were in safe hands at all times. This sometimes included enlisting the assistance of local government administrators like chiefs, sub-chiefs and village headmen.

Back in America, with the assistance of Dr. Lant and Dr. Wes Burnett, I managed to analyse the data using various data analysis tools. I then systematically compiled my research dissertation and qualified to graduate in record time. My heart does throb in pride because my research became one of the pioneer works concerning the political-ecology of wildlife conservation in Kenya and Africa.

My research work has been cited by researchers from all over the world. From it, I have also published more than five articles in high impact peer reviewed international journals especially in the United States and Europe. It goes without saying that I qualify to be cited as an expert in wildlife conservation issues in the African context.

However, just like many Kenyan academicians, I am rarely consulted be it by the government or other stakeholders in my area of expertise as relates to pertinent issues of conservation. Nevertheless, this has not stopped me from extending my research to incorporate aspects of tourism management and development in Kenya and Africa. From these research platforms, I have published more than fifty articles in high impact peer reviewed journals. The research on tourism and hospitality issues has also been quoted by academicians with interests in similar studies globally. It can indeed be asserted that African scholars are rarely appreciated in their home countries. Expatriate consultants are hired at exorbitant prices to undertake assignments that can be done adequately and satisfactorily by local experts.

Thus, sadly, over the years, there seems to be an apparent disconnect between government and the academic fraternity. The relationship between the two can even be antagonistic. This is one of the major dilemmas confronting many African countries, including Kenya. It so happens that politicians who control the government machinery are made to believe that local academicians are a threat to their power. Thus, they marginalise academicians and refuse to engage them in specialised issues. Worse yet, many African governments appear not to value the role of research in policy making and economic development. Thus, academicians do not play any central role in policy making and leadership.

However, as much as I may appear to present a rosy picture of America, I have to admit that while in the US, there were instances where I encountered elements of racism and prejudice. This was noticeable even among some lecturers who had a negative attitude towards blacks. To a certain extent, though, existing mature institutions of governance and socio-economic development tended to mellow down the impact of racism, at least during the time I was living in the US.

Biographer's Note: Prof. Christopher Lant, who supervised Prof. Akama's PhD studies, wrote the following:

John Akama was my first PhD advisee when I was a faculty member at Southern Illinois University. He wrote his dissertation in Geography on 'The Political Ecology of Wildlife Conservation in Kenya' in 1993. I, along with Dr. G. Wesley Burnett of Clemson University, also co-authored two peer-reviewed journal, articles with Dr. Akama. The first, 'A political ecology approach to wildlife conservation in Kenya' was published in the academic journal Environmental Values and has received 38 citations. The other, titled 'Conflicting Attitudes of Local People and Conservation Officials in Kenya' appeared in Natural Resources and Society, and has received 110 citations. Over the years, John and I have stayed in touch on academic issues, the roller-coaster of politics in both countries, challenges like the current pandemic and the welfare of our respective families. I remember John fondly and have been thrilled at the success he has achieved in his academic career in Kenya, for which I claim little to no credit. "Good luck with your biographical work about Dr. Akama.

Christopher Lant,
Professor & Head Department of Environment and Society
Quinney College of Natural Resources
Utah State University

Special Thanks to America

For America to get where it is today, its forefathers sacrificed their self-interests and put their country first. They laid in place systems, which have stood the test of time, that work for most Americans. These are the very systems that attract many nationals from different parts of the world to move to America to pursue the American dream. This observation should not appear to wipe out my earlier assertion that as much as America was envisioned to offer opportunity for all, there is systemic racism in the country against the black and other people of colour.

There is a school of thought that contends that the rapid development of the USA was due to cheap slave labour. Black people who had been captured from the African continent in the 19th century toiled under inhuman conditions while under the control of their white masters. That arguments goes o suggest that it is this toil and sweat by the black people in plantations in the southern part of the USA that jumpstarted the country's rapid development. However, as much as there are these diverse opinions, America is now an economic and political super-power.

Of particular mention are the various scholarship programmes that attract many Kenyans and others from developing countries to pursue higher education in America. A number of Kenyans who have left a mark in Kenya's political, social and economic landscape were beneficiaries of such scholarships. They include Nobel Prize laureate the late Wangari Maathai who rose from a lowly socio-economic background to become a global icon.

It is a fact that many Kenyans may not know or appreciate the fact that the scholarships are funded by the American tax payers. I was among the many fortunate Kenyans because the Americans funded my Masters and PhD studies in two of their well-established universities. Indeed, I can say that without this funding, I could not have been able to raise the requisite financial resources for my post-graduate studies.

Furthermore, Kenya and Africa in general can draw a critical lesson from America. America offers an example of a country where systems are based on meritocracy. In America, as long as you are competent and hardworking, the doors will be opened for you. This is unlike many countries in our continent where those in authority use inappropriate criteria, social networks like ethnicity, nepotism and political ganging to reward their kin and deny the deserving ones a chance.

Truly, these inappropriate reward systems destroy developments such as education advancement and other aspects of socio-economic development. Existing systems end up bringing out and supporting people who very often are unfit to hold offices both in the public and private sector. In turn, the government and other organizations they serve fail to achieve the set national goals and development targets. Their inefficiency boils down to a clogged country where much does not seem to work. In many spheres of development, Kenya is either dancing on a spot or sliding backwards.

*****

In particular, my stay in America gave me a clear understanding of many global issues. It made me understand pertinent matters such as racism and underdevelopment, among others. It also made me take a keen interest in African issues. In fact, due to my training background, I do not have problems interacting with people from any corner of the world. I can therefore say that I always have a global perspective in my approach to life.

Were it that I never lived in America, I would never have understood the workings of a capitalistic system as manifested in the American society and most of the Western world. I was also able to understand the working of Western democracy and became a faithful follower of international news channels such as CNN, Al-Jazeera and BBC.

To a great extent, this exposure has made me understand how unfair the world is. I understand that in this world there are no free things, people only reap what they sow. And, it is true that countries are always pushing their national interests even through their charitable and volunteer work. I will say that in the international geo-politics, every country is fighting for itself even as we entertain globalization and global village narrative.

In recent years, a horrible trend of nationalism has emerged where people in many countries have turned inwards. An example is America's former President Donald Trump who built walls ostensibly to deter immigrants from stepping in his country. In Britain, they have moved out of the European Union and chart their own nationalistic socio-economic and political agenda. It can be argued that the Brexit movement could be aimed at eventually barring immigrants from other parts of Europe, Africa and the rest of the world from ever setting their feet in the UK.

This is why I am of the opinion that Kenya must search for home grown solutions to home-grown problems. As a nation, we need to reflect on our cultures and histories. This will then help us strive to come up with home-grown models of economic development and political governance. We should never allow ourselves to wholeheartedly embrace Western ideologies, values and philosophical underpinnings. In fact, quite often, I wonder whether there can be real democracy in a country where there is extreme poverty, ignorance and negative ethnicity.

Governance challenges confronting Kenya include multiparty democracy or lack of it and constitution implementation processes. These need a critical understanding and evaluation of our ingrained social, cultural, political and economic systems. Kenyans must ask themselves who they are, where they are, and where they are going. Is it by accident that countries where people have retained their cultural identity, for instance Japan, South Korea and China, consistently register rapid economic development? If Kenya's GDP per capita was at par with Singapore in the 1970s when and where did the rain start beating us?

I strongly think that African people can do themselves justice if they shun blindly aping Westernization. We have taken European names. We want to transform our tongues as we struggle to speak like them. We want to eat their food and, while at it, we are increasingly impoverishing ourselves. This is why I agree with the Kiswahili saying, *mwacha mila ni mtumwa* (he who shuns one's culture is a slave). If we continue aping the Western culture, we will continue being slaves of other people and we will continue wallowing in poverty.

Kenya, and indeed Africa, is at crossroads. We need to fix the African tragedy where Africans look outward to the United States, Europe and Asia for support and economic development. It is unfortunate that our colonial masters succeeded in fragmenting us into non-viable entities in the name of states. We now have more than fifty African states and most of them are not viable politically, socially and economically.

This fragmentation goes further to affect communities and ethnicities. This, to me, is the worst form of social and cultural fragmentation. Time has come for us to think beyond our ethnic and tribal cocoons. We need to look at the bigger picture of nationhood and Africanhood.

Biographer's Note: Prof. Ted Bernard taught Prof. Akama at Ohio University. He wrote the following:

Yes, indeed, I did know, worked with and highly respected John Akama during his MA and PhD work in the USA. As a graduate student at Ohio University, John took a couple of my classes and then we linked up as he worked on and defended his MA thesis. Because our interests were similar (conservation, resource management, sustainability, wildlife and tourism), I found great simpatico in our emerging friendship and intellectual companionship. More specifically, John was such a hard worker and thorough and thoughtful scholar that I, and his committee, urged him on to completion with no significant delays. After leaving Ohio University, John went on for PhD studies at Southern Illinois and I had the great pleasure of staying in touch with him and serving as an outside member of his PhD dissertation committee. Again, John excelled. And, at last, he returned to Kenya to Moi University and a has had very productive, internationally recognized research career in wildlife and tourism.

We do still stay in touch via email and Christmas cards. I'm very pleased that a biography is in the works. I look forward to reading it.

Ted Bernard
Professor Emeritus of Geography and Environmental Studies,
Ohio University, Athens Ohio USA

3. MY TURBULENT TIMES

The Aborted Dream

In the 1990s, negative stories from Kenya spread like rapid fire across the world. This was at the height of the ruling party KANU's reign. There were reports of dissenters in the name of opposition leaders, receiving brutal retaliation from the government. Dissidents went through indescribable torture, violent attacks and incarcerations. Corruption was also at its peak. However well one was qualified, it was not easy to land a job that one deserved without oiling someone's fingers. One could have been excused to believe that the country was on its knees.

It was against this backdrop that I successfully completed my PhD studies from Southern Illinois University in March 1993. I wanted to fly back home and serve my country but my friends and relatives had a contrary opinion. They averred that due to the fact that the system was rotten, it could be difficult to get an appropriate job commensurate to my level of training. Indeed, they were right to discourage me from going home and I was smart to heed their advice.

Towards the end of 1993, I came across a job advertisement in the American newspapers. There was a vacant position of a Programme Officer at a quasi-governmental organization called the World Wildlife Fund of America (WWF-A). I did a background check and established that the organization had its headquarters at the centre of Washington, DC, along the Pennsylvania Avenue, not far from the White House.

I submitted my application and was interviewed. Luckily enough, I passed the interview and was offered the job. America's system of meritocracy was clearly manifested once again. I was upbeat to land such a plum job with a monthly salary tag of a whopping US$ 7,000. This amount was way above what I was earning as a teaching assistant.

I made appropriate plans to shift base from Illinois to Washington, DC, to take up the position. My worry, however, was that being the capital of the USA, DC was one of the most expensive cities in the world to live in. So, my immediate worry was finding an affordable house in which to stay. To ease my relocation to DC, I sold my car to a fellow student and gave away other items like utensils to my African friends. The Kenyan Embassy in Washington DC appeared helpful from the onset. However, as you will find out later, their efforts advertently or inadvertently shuttered my dream. Someone I spoke to at the embassy requested me to call him after a week in the hope that he would have scouted around and found a place for me.

A week later, I made the call. The gentleman was happy to inform me that he had contacted a Kenyan couple that stayed in Maryland which is just outside of DC. He added that the couple was willing to host me for some time. I was excited when he said that he had taken their physical address and that all I needed was to take a flight from Illinois to Baltimore-Maryland and connect to the house via taxi.

On the material day, I took a flight and later used a taxi to the place where I was supposed to stay. I arrived at the home at around 7 pm and was warmly received by a lady and as we conversed, I realized that the couple was from Kisii.

All was going well and I was at ease due to the lady's hospitality. She showed me a room where she placed my luggage. My luggage had my most valued possessions, including my clothing in a briefcase and some of my treasured books, a laptop and other personal documents that were in a box.

Soon, her husband arrived and we started the introductions all over again. As we had dinner, I learnt that the man knew me very well and could take me down my family lineage easily.

But something was not adding up in the home. The couple looked friendly, but it was either the food they were serving me that was laced with unpalatable substances or I was unwell.

I slept in discomfort and woke up the following morning feeling exhausted. Even so, I was able to report to work at my new station where the CEO and the entire staff were waiting for me. I received a warm welcome and was taken around for formal introductions and familiarisation of my new work environment. But even as they showed me my office and the staff who were to work under me, they kept asking me if I was okay. I kept responding in the affirmative.

However, as the day wore on, I realized that I was not coordinating myself properly. I was exhausted and decided to take a taxi to the house. I was very weak in the joints. Generally, I was in a haze and appeared hypnotized.

The following morning came and I contacted my former academic supervisor Dr. Lant and others who knew me in Illinois. Each one of them said that I was not myself the very moment they heard my voice on the phone. This got me even more worried that I was going to die in a foreign country in a short while, yet I had enjoyed good health for several years.

"John, I don't know what the problem is but please, I will advise that you take a flight to Kenya," Dr. Lant told me. I received similar advice from a few other friends. Their reasoning was that I was very sick in a totally strange city, which I knew little about. They argued that it would be better if I immediately got to my family in Kenya before the sickness took a toll on me.

I telephoned my brother Dr. Kiriago, who was then working as a dentist at Kenyatta National Hospital. However hard I explained that I was taking a flight to Nairobi, he was not about to understand. Just a few days earlier, I had happily told him that I had landed a good job in Washington, DC, and had reported to start work.

My flight from DC to Nairobi offered me the most harrowing experience in my life. Truly, it was by God's grace that I made it to Nairobi where my brother picked me from the airport and took me to his house.

"A few days ago, dad had called me saying he had a very bad dream some nights back," Kiriago said.

"What was it all about?" I inquired.

"Dad saw you sickly and in a very bad state," he answered, but added that he had explained to our father that we had talked on the phone and I was doing fine.

We travelled to our Kisii home a few days after. When my father saw me, he jumped as if he had been sitting on fire.

"What brings you here my son in this state?" my father asked. Tears welled at the corners of my eyes but I managed to restrain myself. We sat down and I chronologically explained what had happened to me. When I mentioned the name of the man who hosted me in Washington, he jumped once again and retorted, *"omwana one! Egwasoete amaboko amabe. Abwo nigo bakobayanetie* (my son, you fell in evil hands. They messed you up)." You are lucky to be alive. I'm lucky to see you alive. Those people were capable of killing you. You got off the jaws of crocodiles. I was not going to see you again, were it not for the grace of God," my father tearfully said as we listened. He went down on his knees, lifted his hands up and said a prayer, thanking God for bringing me home safely. He told God that he did not mind that I returned home empty-handed. His joy was that I was alive.

After the prayers and a meal, my father opened up. He poured secrets he had kept in his inner heart. He disclosed that the man who was about to destroy my life in the United States was a well-known witch and his family line was notorious of witchcraft. My father also organized a ceremony, called in community members, slaughtered a bull and celebrated my return and gave thanks to God.

Many people who know me have never understood why I left my job in Washington and decided to return to Kenya. Even so, the decision I made was the best at that time, however unwise it may seem to people who may not understand what I went through in the hands of my fellow kinsmen who I met in the far off land. Only my father could explain how I survived the dark side of our culture.

At this juncture, I cannot accurately narrate the kind of nightmare I went through. But, for sure, I can state that the drinks and the food that the couple served me with must have been laced with substances that disoriented my control and sense of understanding. Indeed, after the meals, I lost myself and was not in control of my senses. I became a zombie. This situation lasted for several days, prompting me to return to Kenya for I could not manage myself in a foreign country in the status I was in. It is through God's grace that I made it home safely.

Personally, I have never brought myself to the fact that I took myself to people who were going to harm me. My guess is that they were unhappy of my academic accomplishments. They could not imagine that someone from our family tree could occupy an office in the capital city of the most powerful country. They perhaps thought that after they made it to Washington, the doors were closed for any other person from our village to ever step in the American city.

I am alive to the fact that one may conclude that what I am narrating here is mere speculation without any evidence. I have to state that these are the intricacies of black magic or witchcraft. But people who have understanding how these dark forces work can agree with me that some experiences, which appear to be mere fantasies do happen. These strange events and experiences end up destroying individuals as it could have happened to me.

I have said before and I will repeat it again, in my whole life, I have never seen a witch in action. I have also said before, and I will repeat it, I will never want to see one. But if it is true that my sickness was an act of witchcraft, it shows that this is the most evil activity done by wicked and destructive human beings. Maybe this evil is spread in many parts of the world and is one of the factors that have hindered development in many parts of Africa.

My research tells me that wherever such incidents of witchcraft are prevalent, people are least developed and are backward. Apart from Kenya, such stories abound in African countries such as Cameroon, Zambia and Nigeria among others.

"It is unfortunate that the man crossed several countries and seas with his witchery and settled amongst the civilized people of America," my father said.

Picking the Pieces

The scary experience of abandoning a high paying job in the United States, only days after getting it, dealt me a hard blow physically, socially and mentally. As I regained my health and sanity, I felt like I was waking up from a terrible dream. All this time, I had been in a nightmarish slumber. When I pieced together my memory, I discovered that trouble started when I entered the strange home. For two months after that, I was not my real self.

Soon, truth gradually sank in that I had abandoned a plum job in America. I was now in the village with my PhD, doing nothing and unable to support myself. It was a traumatizing experience. Rumour mills went overdrive in the community. The mongers claimed that I had come from America to burden my widowed father after I wasted money and time drinking myself silly and taking drugs. They painted an image of first-hand witnesses of what they said.

I was lucky to recover within the next few weeks. Since I understood the Kenyan environment well, all I needed was a slight financial push for me to leave home and go for a job hunting mission. God and our ancestors were on my side. After my friends in America sent my belongings that I had left behind, it did not take long before I landed a teaching position at the Department of Tourism and Hospitality Management at Moi University in April 1994.

My starting salary was Kshs.27,000. This amount was way below what I earned as a teaching assistant in America. I have to admit that I was again in another reverse culture shock. I had left a well-paying job and private transport in a developed country and here I was, using public transport to work where I earned peanuts at the end of the month.

It took me about one year to fully put myself together. However, due to my sad experience in the United States, I decided never to go back there.

The same year, 1994 was bad in Kisii too. This was the time when several people especially the elderly, were being lynched on claims that they were witches. It has been claimed that in some cases stories were fabricated that the victims were witches due to land disputes. I will however not want to go there. The story will probably be told in another forum outside this book.

When I share my story with friends, especially those who are educated, they dismiss it as fantasy. I have kept most of these details close to my chest and I found this book to be the ideal platform to share it, albeit briefly. This book is telling the highs and lows of my life. I have dedicated this section to capture one of my lowest moments in my life.

I know people may wonder why a highly-learned person can give a story of this kind. However, remember that it is my story. Each and every one of us has a story to tell, whether good or bad. We are all at liberty to either tell our stories or go to the graves with them. I have chosen the first option.

I will not want anybody, not even my worst enemy to go through what I experienced during those trying times. The good that came out of it is that it made me stronger in both character and faith. It made me understand that this world is full of trials, temptations, tribulations, low moments and joy. Many things happen mysteriously that you are not able to comprehend why they did.

Most importantly, the experience made me choose to serve humanity with dedication throughout my life. I believe that it all happened according to God's plans. Perhaps as much as it was very unfortunate, the incident in DC was meant to make me return home. Indeed, I believe that I have been and continue to be of more value here than I was or I would have become in the United States.

In Search of a Spouse

Had I married in 1979, my grandchildren could be milling around me as I write this story. This never came to pass. Although I was not too young to marry, I was not ready to. But my father's friend had something else in his mind.

"Would you allow your son to be betrothed to my daughter?" my father's friend asked him one day.

"Which son?"

"Sorana."

My father was dumbfounded! He found the proposal outrageous and shocking. As I learnt from him that evening, he never knew that he had a son who was ripe for marriage. I was proceeding to university and was not ready to start a family of my own.

Secondly, his friend had gone against the traditional and customary contestation as far as marriage proposals were concerned. Amongst Abagusii people, especially in times long gone, it was the family of the aspiring bridegroom that approached that of the would-be bride with a marriage proposal. This was done through *esigani* (a go-between).

My father must have read mischief in his friend's proposal. Maybe, just maybe, the man wanted to have me drift from my academic journey. For, what else would make anyone imagine that I could mix my studies with marital responsibilities, particularly at that tender age? This act alone scarred the two old men's friendship forever.

Additionally, as I mentioned elsewhere in my story, the death of my mother in 1980 offered me a transformational experience. It came days before I joined university and made me change my understanding of and outlook to life.

Similar to my father's thinking, in my mind, marriage was at the backburner. When I joined high school, my focus was on studies. I passed my A-level examinations that provided a gateway to join university. With that, I wanted to study to the pinnacle of learning, that is, to university. My dreams were premised on the understanding that I had an ample opportunity to do so. I did not want anything to make me digress and squander the chance.

My mother's death re-energized me. It reminded me that I should strive even harder to quench my thirst for knowledge. This, I knew, would enable me be able to shoulder the huge responsibilities of taking care of my siblings. I wanted to be the pillar that my family could lean and cling on in the near future.

I knew that since I had lost my mother, I had to reorganize my life and be more focused on doing the right things, and doing them right. In fact, for the whole period I was at Kenyatta University College, the issue of marriage was the least of my priorities. Even so, as a young man, I would have relationships with girls. However, I never gave any of these a chance to blossom into marriage. I was focused on other priorities in life and, at that stage of life, it is better to experiment and discover critical things that mattered in life.

I recall a funny incident that happened shortly after I completed my studies from Kakamega High School. I was walking with a girl by my side in my home area when an elderly woman spotted us and ran to our home to report it to my mother. This was the period shortly before my mum passed away.

The woman told my mother to warn me never to be seen again with the girl. She claimed that the girl's parents were notorious witches and I should not take the risk of marrying her. I could not ascertain the claims about witchcraft but I did not have any plans of marrying the girl anyway.

However, I will be quick to note that such claims often emerged whenever people in the community suspected that a lasting relationship was in the works. This often shattered some relationships or challenged one to do more due diligence before making any long-term commitments.

I noted earlier that when I completed my undergraduate studies, I got my first job almost immediately. It excited my relatives, including my father who thought that I was ripe and ready for marriage since I now had a reliable salary. They looked forward to seeing me have a family of my own to perpetuate the family lineage. However, it did not take long before they found out the truth; they were in for another disappointment!

Issues of my marriage increasingly became a big concern among members of my family. I remember my elder sister coming all the way to my work place at Nyamagwa Boys' High School to introduce to me a pretty lady who was her friend. Although it was her first time to meet me, the lady was ready for us to get married. This shocked me. I wondered whether my marriage was such a major issue of concern to my elder sister to the extent that she could attempt to introduce me to a suitable girl with whom to start a family.

However, before I could fully digest my sister's idea, I got a scholarship to join Ohio University in the USA to pursue my Master's degree. I was excited and as the adage goes 'out of sight, out of mind' worked well for me. I forgot about the marriage proposal all together and, as I flew out of Kenya, the understanding was that I was still single.

Once again, I would repeat the adage: America is the land of the free. I found that young adults have a lot of freedom from society, parents and the church. Thus, youths in the United States enjoy lots of freedom unlike in our Kenyan society. This has its pros and cons but I may not dwell on them in this book.

Interestingly, I noticed that girls in the United States appeared to be more outgoing than their male counterparts who portrayed restraint. You could enter a pub and find it flooded with more ladies than gentlemen. Even more interesting, the girls could approach the men for a dance, something which can be seen as an abomination in Africa.

Hence, in the USA, there is a lot of interactive socialization. This can shock the uninitiated coming from outside the country. But it is better you get surprised than live to regret the plunders that could cost your life if you avoided them.

However, and this is unfortunate, living in the United States has messed several African students who went there in pursuit of perceived greener pastures. Those who got immersed into the American life on the first lane dropped out of college to look for low-level paying blue collar jobs to sustain themselves and support their lifestyles. I did not want to form part of these sad statistics.

****

I will be departing from the truth if I paint a picture of myself confining my life to studies, work and resting in my room while studying in the USA. The truth is that I also indulged in partying. I had friends from South Africa, Botswana, Zambia, Cameroon and Kenya who became my drinking buddies. We joined our fellow American students in socializing and partying. Even as I did this, I was very careful not to mess myself through negative social behaviour. I worked hard to ensure that my studies, the main reason for going to America, did not suffer.

In that kind of environment, most of us became extremely careful in indulging in casual relationships. Such relationships did not last long and had their own serious consequences.

When I flew out of Ohio for my PhD studies at Southern Illinois University, I was relatively mature. I had a clear understanding of what life in the United States meant, be it social, economic and otherwise. Again, it was around this time when it dawned on me that I was almost winding up my studies and I should start thinking of getting married. And this time, it was because I wanted to do so rather than due to family and community pressures. I, however, told myself that I would do due diligence before I settled on the lady to marry.

In 1991, when I arrived in Nairobi, I had two serious issues in my mind; one was undertaking my field work to collect data for my PhD research, and second to identify a suitable lady to whom I would propose when the opportune time arose. I was introduced to Mallion Kwamboka, a tall beautiful lady who was then a final year student at my *alma mater* Kenyatta University College (now Kenyatta University). At a glance, I knew that, if God answered my inner prayers, Mallion would be my life partner.

Mallion and I met severally during my stay in Kenya. When time came for me to return to the United States to prepare, submit and defend my research project, we agreed that in principle, we would become man and wife. Keeping in touch at that time was not as easy as it is today. The most convenient way then was writing letters to each other. True to our word, we kept writing to each other and this kept our bond intact despite the fact that we were separated by tens of thousands of miles.

If you have ever been in a relationship, then you know that nothing can be more disruptive and disturbing than a communication breakdown. This is exactly what happened between Mallion and me when I suffered the misfortune of abrupt sickness just after I landed and abruptly left a plum job in Washington DC. The lady I had gotten acquainted to could not understand why she was not receiving letters from me.

I actually came to learn that she had sent several letters to me that went unanswered during the communication lapse that lasted almost three months. This of course portended untold disturbance to her.

When I returned to Kenya and got well, the first assignment alongside getting a job was to link up with Mallion. I did not want it to appear that I had bamboozled her. At this time, she had graduated and taken a teaching job at Friends School, Kiamokama in Kisii. You can imagine how happy it was for us when we reconnected once again!

When I took a job at Moi University's Chepkoilel Campus (now University of Eldoret), I organized for her transfer. As luck would have it, she was transferred to Uasin Gishu High School. It is where we started our family in 1995.

Formalizing my Marriage

To formalize my marriage with Mallion, we had to get members of both our families to get acquainted with each other. As tradition demanded, there were several visitations by representatives of the two families to Mallion's home at Riokindo in Bomachoge Borabu of the present-day Kisii County and to my place in Borabu Settlement Scheme in the current Nyamira County.

In line with the demands of tradition, I was the first one to visit her family. I was accompanied by a few of my close age mates. This was a landmark visit in our relationship. If the visitation were not well received by our would be in-laws, or if they told us point-blank that they did not support the tender relationship, the news would have poured cold water in our life plans and shuttered our dream of spending the remaining part of our lives together. For us to move forward smoothly, we needed the blessings of Mallion's family and I hoped that all would end well.

True to my wish, we were happily received and well feted. The warm reception, and the deliberations that followed, opened the door for other visitations. For instance, my father accompanied by a few selected elders visited Mallion's family soon after. Equally, her people reciprocated by making visits to our home.

Towards the end of these initial visitations, there were negotiations for dowry payment at Mallion's home. The deliberations were serious business that lasted almost the whole day as both sides haggled on the number of livestock and amount of money I was to pay. For the uninitiated, in such negations, it would appear likely that things would hit a dead end given the tone of discussions. However, in most times, the two parties reach a compromise on the critical matter at hand.

Therefore, on this material day, it was agreed that I pay Ksh260, 000 plus four heads of cattle and two he-goats. I then started making plans on how to raise the dowry payment. With the support of my family, we were able to raise a half of the money plus the required goats.

As per Gusii tradition concerning dowry payment, it was not absolute that one should pay the whole dowry at once. To the people, partial payment was an indication of commitment to honour the sanctity of marriage and the creation of long-term family relationships. Thus, the available dowry was delivered to the in-laws.

Furthermore, in the Gusii culture, once dowry has been paid it signalled in principle that you are man and wife. Thus, to cut the long story short, due to existing circumstances, we did not have extra money to spend to prepare for a grand wedding. I managed to convince Mallion that we should start our family without much funfair. This is exactly what we did. It was only recently in 2018 that we managed to solemnize our marriage through the church in the Catholic Cathedral in Kisii Town.

In a nutshell, God has been good to us. He has blessed us with two sons and a daughter. My eldest son Bruce Orang'o is a finalist Business Information Technology (IT) student at Strathmore University in 2020. His sibling, Larry Otwori is also in the same university, doing the same course, now in his first year. My daughter Teresia Nyakoinani graduated in 2019 with a Bachelor of Law degree from the Catholic University of Eastern Africa.

I thank God because I am now a settled family man. Moreover, the Almighty has given me children who are doing well academically. I am also thankful to God for giving me Mallion to be my life companion. She too is an academician in her own right and has been very supportive to me. We share my social and academic matters. In terms of academics we have co-authored a book entitled, *Gusii Soapstone Industry: Critical Issues, Opportunities, Challenges & Future Alternatives*, which is a testimony that we walk together both academically and socially.

Currently, Mallion is a lecturer of History at Kisii University, Eldoret Campus. She is finalising her PhD research in History.

Starting Work as a Lecturer

When I abruptly returned home from the United States, it appeared like the world had caved in on me. There was a lot of uncertainty. My mind was overloaded with thoughts of what really lay ahead of me and how I was going to get it right once more. I got more prayerful than ever before. I also looked up for every chance to pick up the pieces and restructure things in my life, which had been fractured when I least expected.

God was not about to abandon me. One of my professors from the United States linked me to his friend who was the Head of Department (HoD) of Tourism and Hospitality Management at Moi University, Eldoret. The Department was just starting and the university was on a lecturers' recruitment drive.

I seized the opportunity and submitted my application. Fortune struck once again, in my favour. I was hired to teach in the Department, which was based at the Chepkoilel Campus (now University of Eldoret).

The appointment letter was followed by yet another one, in May 1994, which directed me to report and start teaching. I had even been allocated three courses; Anthropology and Tourism, Tourism Planning and Management, and Tourism Development in Africa.

Although I desperately needed a job, the two letters evoked in me a number of questions. I wondered who between the department and I needed the other more. This threw me at crossroads. I was at a temporary loss because my area of specialization was Geography and I had been hired to handle students in an area which I had minimal expertise in.

I dismissed this line of thought and told myself that my training background in Geography will be handy. I got confident since I knew that Geography as a discipline is multi-disciplinary in all aspects of teaching and research. Further, due to my training up to PhD level and the subject of my PhD thesis, I was not going to get into much difficulty interacting with majorly undergraduate students.

It was from this underlying perspective that I approached the courses I was allocated. My starting salary of Kshs. 27,000 was just a drop in the ocean compared to what I was to be paid in the job that I had gotten in Washington. However, I understood that it was better to get a small loaf of bread than nothing.

When I reported at Moi University, I was received by the Head of Tourism and Hospitality Management Department, the late Prof. Isaac Sindiga who immediately introduced me to members of the Department and assigned me office space. The following day, he took me for an extensive tour of the university, including Chepkoilel Campus where our Department was domiciled. In the tour, Prof. Sindiga introduced me to the Central University Administration Office where I presented my personal details. I also availed my acceptance letter, updated CV and copies of my higher education certificates. They used these documents to open my personal employment file at the University's Main Registry.

The first hurdle I encountered once I reported at Chepkoilel Campus was lack of teaching and reference materials in the area of Tourism and Hospitality. Particularly, I learnt that the Department did not have any textbooks in the subject. I was facilitated by the Head of Department to travel to Nairobi to search for teaching materials. The trip took me to the University of Nairobi, Utalii College and the United Nations Library in Gigiri where I combed through books, research documents and journals in search of relevant teaching materials.

My efforts were not in vain. I was able to get substantial teaching materials at the University of Nairobi Main Library and Utalii College. This enabled me to start having a systematic understanding of tourism especially as relates to the courses I was allocated to teach.

Loaded with sufficient material to start me off, I returned to Eldoret, with satisfaction that I was ready to start my teaching job. But more confusion awaited me at the University. The Department, then comprised of four lecturers including myself, did not have a clear administrative structure. This made it difficult whenever there was need for in-house consultations on diverse administrative and academic issues.

I did not want to use this as an excuse. I embarked on teaching, giving it the best I could. But at the back of my mind, I gradually realized that the curriculum was not as relevant and as exhaustive for Tourism and Hospitality Management training as would be desirable. I realized that it needed refocusing to align it with tourism as an area of study. In particular, the curriculum was too general in nature. It also looked at tourism majorly from the wildlife perspective. This was to the extent that one would be made to believe that tourism and wildlife conservation were one and the same thing.

When I dissected the curriculum further, I realised that it had many courses on Human Ecology and Geography that were not relevant in tourism training. However, this challenge as regards to curriculum development was not confined to Moi University. Many universities face a similar challenge when they introduce new academic programmes. This particularly affects new applied fields of study such as Tourism, Actuarial Science, Sales and Procurement, among others.

For Moi University, training in Tourism and Hospitality Management started due to a directive by the Head of State and Chancellor of the University, Daniel Arap Moi, during a previous graduation ceremony. For the institution to start a new degree in Tourism and Hospitality Management, one can presuppose that the main rationale for the president's directive was because the tourism industry in Kenya was and still is a key economic pillar. It earns the country much needed foreign exchange and employs thousands of Kenyans. As such, the industry needed highly skilled manpower trained at university level to manage the industry, both in the public and private sector. Such requisite human resource would propel the fledgling industry to greater heights of prosperity and enhance sustainable development in the country.

In Kenya, as is the case with many developing countries, a President's word was always final. Since he had made the directive, it had to be implemented at all costs. It is worth noting that, for political expedience, the university was named after President Moi who was its initiator.

However, in most contemporary university settings including Moi University, the Senate is in charge of all academic issues. This includes curriculum development and examination processing. Consequently, it is the mandate of the Senate to ensure that curricula are developed and implemented as per set regulations and guidelines. I learnt that when the issue of developing the Department's curriculum came before the Senate, members equated tourism to wildlife conservation since they did not have much understanding of the various facets of tourism training.

Notwithstanding the aforementioned, in order to implement the Presidential directive, the Moi University Senate appointed an *ad hoc* committee to develop the curriculum. The committee was made up of senior lecturers from the Departments of Wildlife Management and Geography. It is against this university context that the pioneer tourism curriculum was developed, mainly by non-tourism experts. It clearly explains why the curriculum was more of a wildlife and natural resources management course than tourism studies.

However, it did not take long for the Department to realize the problems with the curriculum. This then generated a conversation that resulted in the need for a systematic review of the curriculum. It is how I ended up being appointed Chairman of the Department's Curriculum Review Committee.

The process of overhauling the curriculum required conducting broad background research on Tourism and Hospitality training. It also entailed talking to various stakeholders and visiting various institutions of higher learning, particularly in Europe and North America that offered tourism training to get information on the type of human resource that the industry needed.

A new development took place around that time. Our Head of Department (HoD), the late Prof. Isaac Sindiga, was promoted to become the Principal of Kisii University Campus of Egerton University. Prof. Sindiga was a prominent and brilliant scholar who, like me, had studied at Ohio University and later at Syracuse University in the United States.

With Prof. Sindiga's exit, the position of HoD fell vacant. It was resolved that I fill the position. This came as a surprise to me. I was still a young academician without much experience in university administration but here I was, being appointed as Head of Department. It was a critical time for the nascent Department but I committed myself to give it my best.

No sooner had I settled in the position of HoD than the rain started beating us in the Department. Top honchos in the University Management started to push for the recruitment of more lecturers. This was not a bad idea at face value. Indeed, we were few and we needed more hands to ease the workload on us and to grow the programme. The only problem I had was the approach taken in the recruitment.

The Chief Administrative Officer at the university wielded immense power at the institution. He could forward applications and Curriculum Vitae (CVs) of prospective applicants to me, with a note that I look at them and recommend their hiring in the department. I became really saddened and embarrassingly underwhelmed while interrogating the testimonials forwarded to me. Most of them had post-graduate degree qualifications from universities in India. This in itself was not a problem. The moral problem was that these applicants had performed dismally in their Kenya Certificate of Secondary Education (KCSE) examinations. This left me wondering how they managed to pursue university training with such dismal performance.

Some of these individuals had scored as low as D+ in their Form Four examinations and had taken a very short time to complete their undergraduate and post-graduate training in India. They then flew back to Kenya, armed with these post-graduate degrees and applied to teach at the university. Some had obtained PhD in a record six years from the time they sat for their KCSE. These were the people I was told to hire and entrust them with the responsibility of teaching the children of unsuspecting Kenyans. I obstinately refused.

"Is it fair to hire somebody with D+ to teach an undergraduate student who got direct admission to the university after scoring not less than a B+ grade in the KCSE?" I asked myself. I thought it was morally and academically wrong; it was unacceptable.

Obviously with such lowly grades at secondary school level, in most instances, it is rare for a person to end up excelling in higher education training. Ideally, higher education is a build-up of the educational foundation created at the critical primary and secondary school levels. Moreover, these applicants who were presented for university employment appeared to have obtained their undergraduate and post-graduate certification within a very short timeframe. Some had received both their undergraduate and master's degrees training in less than four years.

Faced with such a scenario, I vowed to maintain the integrity and standards of the Department of Tourism, come rain or shine.

Removal from Departmental Headship

The quote, "success will not lower its standards to accommodate us," attributed to Rev. Randal McBride got me energised. Additionally, in my life, I have never allowed myself to do anything against my conscience. Further, I realised that my academic and moral values were being put to test. I was sure I was right and the originator of the directives was ill advised. Having attained post-graduate training myself, I knew what it took to qualify. In addition, having taught both in Kenya and the USA, I knew what it took to be a good university lecturer. I could not imagine people with mediocre academic credentials handling bright students of the kind that we had, some that could even be brighter than their would-be lecturers. Inevitably, the department would end up with lower standards and mis-training for the students.

Soon, rumour mills started doing the rounds in the institution. I received signals from the University Management that I was a difficult person to work with. According to the University Management, I was dancing to my own music and a plan had been hatched to trim me to size.

A university is expected to be the centre of academic excellence and the heartbeat of teaching, research and innovation. This was never the case at the university. My disagreements with the management were fast taking a tribal and ethnic dimension. There were allegations that I had taken the cue from my predecessor, Prof. Sindiga, who also hailed from Gusii. He too was a man of unwavering principles. Prof. Sindiga was known as an accomplished academician, and never budged in favour of academic and management malpractices.

It did not take long for my nemesis to find an excuse to kick me out of the HoD portfolio. It happened that Prof. Sindiga had surrendered a vehicle to the university, on condition that it would be attached to the Department of Tourism. The vehicle had been brought for the university to facilitate the implementation of a research project funded by an international body, Deutscher Akademischer Austauschdienst (DAAD). Prof. Sindiga had won the grant.

One morning, I arrived in the office and found a memo directing me to surrender the vehicle from the Department of Tourism. The memo further instructed me to ensure that the vehicle was returned to the university's Central Transport Department. In my naive thinking, I downplayed the matter, oblivious of the fact that these were part of the intricacies hatched by the Management to axe me out. "I will follow up the matter," I said to myself.

The following morning, I was welcomed with unusual commotion at my office. I arrived to find the Transport Manager and Head of Security who were under express instructions from the Chief Administration Officer to take the vehicle. I could not understand why the Management was employing such ruthless and high-handed tactics, causing an ugly scene in the process. Nevertheless, I surrendered the vehicle.

The Management was not done with me yet. Two days later, I received another letter, this time directing me to show-cause why disciplinary action would not be taken against me for disobeying a directive from my seniors. This trend was now set and it was indeed shocking to me.

The following day, I went straight to the Main Campus to see the Chief Administration Officer. I was not sure what his reaction would be once I got to his office. Nevertheless, I was prepared for anything, but not the verbal dressing down that I got that morning in his office.

"Who do you think you are in the Moi University hierarchy? Do you know what it means to disobey an order of the university' appointing authority?" he thundered, his body shaking as if he was restraining himself from slapping me.

I could not take it any longer. "If I were in your position, I would not be talking to an officer below me like that. From what you are saying, it means that you can as well sack me," I said to him.

This made him angrier and I was afraid he was going to jump through the roof. "Young man, do you know that when senior professors come here, they kneel before me, and here you are, a junior lecturer, talking to me in this manner?" he fumed and added, "get out of my office!"

I closed the door behind me, afraid that the worst was about to happen to me. I desperately needed the job that I was holding and I did not have a plan B. I had this bird, however small it was, but it was worth more than any two in the bush. I was afraid that I would be sacked but prayed that it doesn't happen.

I was extremely stressed and worried at the turn of events. So, I headed straight to my Department at Chepkoilel Campus. I could not believe it when I reached there at around 3 pm and found that a letter vacating me from the position of HoD had been delivered and a colleague in the Department had been assigned the job.

I came to learn that whenever bad things happen, we should not give up, curse and gnash our teeth. I believe that every cloud has a silver lining. To me, my sacking from the position of HoD was a blessing in disguise. I now had ample time to work as a lecturer and researcher, the core responsibilities bestowed upon me as per the terms of employment. I decided to focus on fleshing my academic title. It did not take long before I started submitting papers to several peer reviewed international journals. Most of these papers were accepted for publication. This was alongside going to lecture halls to impart knowledge to my students as required, something I enjoyed doing.

I suspect that another reason why I was sacked from the HoD position relates to the usage of available funds for the Department. In particular, there was a Dutch-funded government project under the Organisation for Internationalisation in Education through the Dutch Ministry of Education that was started during the beginning of my tenure as the HoD. It was to assist academic departments in capacity building and initial uplifting of the teaching and research infrastructure. My Department alone was allocated over Kshs. 100 million.

I came to learn later that some top echelons of University Management were persuaded to believe that I could not be convinced to engage in underhand deals. Indeed, just around the time I was removed from office, a scandal was unearthed on orchestrated efforts to squander the money. This led to the sacking of some junior officers who became sacrificial lambs. In reality, the scandal involved senior university officers who were untouchable and had the ability to shift blame to the junior staff.

Defining my Own Niche

I am a firm believer of the saying that 'if God has allowed your star to shine, no one can dim it'. As much as I was being sabotaged and frustrated by some of my bosses at Moi University, I chose not to lose focus on the bigger picture. I let bygones be bygones as I concentrated on doing research and teaching.

The Dutch funding required that lecturers in the user departments be linked with similar academic divisions in universities in the Netherlands. This was aimed at creating grounds for capacity building, skills transfer and staff training. It also promoted professional association and supply of relevant teaching materials.

Our Department was linked to the Department of Sociology, Environment and Tourism Studies in Wagenhegen University. Through the project support, we managed to go for short, yet invaluable, staff exchange initiatives in the Netherlands. In this exchange programme, one of the main objectives was to develop a new and relevant curriculum for our Department.

I have to credit these interactions between the academic staff of the two universities for helping us overhaul the curriculum of the Department of Tourism at Moi University. It was during these academic interactions that we realised that tourism training encompassed several facets and areas of study. In particular, there were three distinct areas yet interrelated fields of tourism training. These were tourism management, hospitality management, and travel and tour operations management.

These consultations and interactions enabled us to refocus the curriculum to encompass the three specific areas of training. In our understanding, these three programmes would help impart the necessary and specific skills, knowledge and competencies to the students.

I do not mean to toot my own horn but I played a critical role in laying a strong foundation for the new Faculty design and development of new curricula of Tourism and Hospitality and Events Management at Moi University.

Notwithstanding these academic milestones, there were still several hurdles before us. These deliberate barriers affected the overall competence of the new Faculty with respect to specific areas of training.

One, all the prospective lecturers whose applications I had rejected on the basis of their suspect educational and professional backgrounds were immediately hired after my removal from the position of HoD. This was to my utter disbelief. I knew that they lacked the basic competencies and academic grounding needed for effective teaching at university level. They were actually academically challenged and prone to using unorthodox means to hoodwink students to accept them.

It was not a hidden secret that these unqualified lecturers would promise students good grades despite their inability to deliver in their teaching assignments. This made students to take it easy with the understanding that they would get good grades even if they did not work hard for them. This was indeed sad! It was a complete disservice to the innocent students, the university and the country.

The demerits of taking such undeserving elements on board as lecturers became evident shortly after. I noticed that students were gradually becoming stunted academically. In their third and fourth years of study they could not grasp basic concepts such as Principles of Tourism Planning and Management, Destination Management, Ecotourism and Sustainable Tourism Development. Clearly, this was due to the poor training they received in the first two years. This was the time when they sailed through the hands of incompetent lecturers whose strength was dishing out undeserved grades.

As a lecturer, and one committed to requisite academic and teaching standards, this was very frustrating. It required extra effort and commitment to bring the students to the level they could understand the basic concepts and theories of tourism. The extra work could not have been necessary had they been properly trained in their formative years in the university.

It was sad that a culture of non-performance and casualness had crept into our Department despite our efforts to make it stand out as a centre of excellence in tourism training. This scenario divided the teaching staff down the middle. Those of us who strove to live as per the dictates of a university as centre of academic excellence were marked and monitored.

Soon, things worsened and, sadly, the rifts started to take a tribal dimension. This happened because the majority of those lecturers who had been hired using less than stellar credentials hailed from a particular ethnic community which had a bigger say in the management of the university. They would say, "our University has been taken over by *madoadoa* (foreigners) and we must reclaim it."

It was a coded reference to those who were perceived to be outsiders in the ethnic context. I must admit that these were dark times as far as university training is concerned. I was worried that if university education never liberated people to look beyond their tribal cocoons, then nothing would. Nevertheless, I did my level best, as far as it was humanly possible, to satisfy my conscience that what I was doing was the right thing in my teaching and research endeavours. This also justified the pay I received as a lecturer and researcher in the university.

It did not take too long before I rose the ranks from Lecturer in 1994 to Associate Professor in the year 2000. This came, despite the impediments I encountered, courtesy of my indisputable competencies in teaching, research and publishing.

It should be noted that in the Kenyan public university setting, as is the case in most universities in the world, promotion from one academic cadre to another, say from Lecturer to Senior Lecturer, all the way to Professorship is a very rigorous academic process. It requires meeting specified criteria such as having done several publications and attendance of both local and international conferences, university administration experience, and participation in community service as well as comprehensive review reports from senior colleagues, among others.

I have to state that I had indeed become a tourism scholar and attended international conferences in many parts of the world including Africa, Europe and the United States. It is within this academic context that we held a well-publicized International Conference whose proceedings I co-edited to produce a book titled; Cultural Tourism In Africa: *Proceedings of the ATLAS Africa International Conference, December 2000, Mombasa, Kenya,* edited by John Akama and Dr. Patricia Sterry. Indeed, the conference itself was well attended. It had delegates from Africa, Europe, North America, Asia and Australia.

I may have been dropped from the HoD post earlier. However, as fate would have it, I was reappointed later. By this time, the original Department had been divided into three fields of study as I indicated earlier. At the start of 2003, I was appointed to serve as the new HoD in the Department of Travel and Tour Operations Management. This was of course against my wish due to my previous experience and prevailing environment in the University. I knew I was not in good books of some of my seniors, and probably this could be another trap laid to frustrate and humiliate me.

Thus, if I say that I was at ease, I would be lying. I witnessed a lot of petty gossip and competition such as being accused of not being a good team player (read sycophant in the prevailing context) and not following orders from higher office (read standing on principle). My interests in research and publication were in complete variance with the prevailing situation. When some lecturers learnt that I was doing extensive research, they wondered what I was up to. Some of the lecturers thought that public transport business and land purchases as well as political connections were more important than academic pursuits. This made the atmosphere in the Department very frustrating, only that I did not have any other place to run to.

Academic Activism

Coincidentally, around the time I was re-appointed as the HOD in 2003, the Universities' Academic Staff Union (UASU) called for a nationwide strike. As a result, activities in public universities were totally paralysed for several weeks. The union used the strike to push the government to provide better working conditions and enhanced remuneration for its members.

Although I did not hold any position in the union, I thought this was the right time for me to address the grievances that bedevilled lecturers. I aired my views freely each time the academic staff gathered for deliberations on the strike. Little did I know that I would once more irritate the University Management for articulating obvious issues concerning the plight of lecturers.

When you are a member of staff at university and the Vice Chancellor calls you at an unexpected hour, your heart can skip a beat. When I saw my boss calling, my heart skipped several beats. Instinctively, I knew that I was in trouble.

"Is this Prof. Akama," he asked.

"Yes sir," I answered in the affirmative.

"Prof. Akama, do you know that by virtue of you being the HoD, you are part and parcel of the University Management and as such you are not supposed to participate in any industrial action?" he stated and asked at the same time.

I quickly found my words and right tone and told the VC that we were fighting for a justified cause and were not attacking the university administration, *per se*. "We are only airing our views on critical issues affecting the overall welfare of the academic staff. The issues affect the whole university community including members of management."

The VC laughed sarcastically and hung up the phone. I knew this reaction would be followed by sanctions. True to my fears, I received a letter the following morning, stripping me of the position of HoD of the Department of Travel and Tour Operations Management.

When news of my sacking went out, it did not sink in well with officials of the UASU Chapter at Moi University. They contemplated to raise the matter during the ongoing strike. However, I objected and told them that such an individual matter was not central at the time when we were having a national strike.

Once again, I had more time in my hands to conduct research, publish and submit research proposals for possible funding. It was within this context that my research proposal for funding from the African American Institute (AAI), a Non-Governmental Organization based in Washington DC, was accepted for funding.

The AAI funding was within the framework of the Claude Ake Fellowship Programme. It was developed by the AAI in honour of a famous Nigerian scholar, Claude Ake. Its objective was to support emerging African scholars to travel to the United States and be attached to a well-established university for one month to conduct research in their area of interest. The scholars would engage with relevant faculty in the universities on various scholarly pursuits, especially on issues of governance and socio-economic development in Africa.

The fellowship also required that the nominated budding scholars attend and participate in a one-week African Studies Association (ASA) Conference. This was a good highlight in my academic career and its timing could not be more perfect. It filled the gaps presented by drawbacks at my workplace.

I was attached to Boston University in Massachusetts and also attended the one week ASA Conference in Washington, DC. The two activities provided me with a platform to interact with highly experienced scholars and researchers from across the globe. They included Ali Mazrui, Robert Maxon, Celia Nyamweru and my mentor at Ohio University, Ted Bernard.

Of all the panel presentations, two excited me the most and I am able to recall their details to date. I will present the first one in the next few paragraphs and the second one in the subsequent subheading.

Dr. Robert Maxon's paper on *risaga* (communal work) amongst the Gusii people of Western Kenya evoked utmost interest in me. Dr. Maxon was a Senior Professor of History at the West Virginia University. His subject pertained to my home area, Gusii. When I was young, I participated in activities in my village where women and occasionally young men joined hands to undertake work that required a lot of labour within a short period. This included tilling land, weeding for crops, clearing bushes and constructing houses. Here was an American scholar tackling a socio-economic activity I had been involved in with members of my kinship and was presenting it in a very scholarly manner; I wondered.

I was mesmerised by Dr. Maxon's presentation. The Professor explained the concept of *risaga* as someone who had participated in it. He clearly articulated that this activity was anchored on the Gusii social and cultural orientation. Further, his presentation showed that *risaga* was a unique bonding activity where the Gusii people came together to tackle common causes as they arose. The process, he said, redefined their existence as families and communities that formed the Gusii society.

Here I'm a scholar of Gusii origin and I have not written anything about my community, notwithstanding the fact that I have done research and published widely in other fields, I pondered as Dr. Maxon's presentation drew to a close. Here is an American who could not even pronounce the word *risaga* properly but has done extensive research on the same.

This really piqued my conscience and generated my interest in researching on cultural, historical, social and economic issues concerning the Gusii community.

In society, we believe that when you interact with brilliant people, you will learn and there is a likelihood that you will follow in their footsteps; and indeed that some of their brilliance would rub off on one. This tells you why I followed Dr. Maxon at the side-lines of the Conference for a one-on-one engagement. We struck a rapport and agreed that we would bring together a number of Kenyan scholars to write an extensive book on the history and culture of the Gusii It is within this context that we co-edited a book titled, *The Ethnography of the Gusii of Western Kenya: A vanishing Cultural Heritage*. It was published in 2006 by the Edwin Mellen Press, a popular academic publishing company based in New York. It was no mean feat for our book to make it to the Edwin Mellen Press.

The book remains widely read and cited by many scholars in diverse fields, globally.

Washing Dirty Linen in Public

"*Il fault laver son linge sale enfamille* (we should wash our dirty linen in private)," so said Napoleon on return from the Island of Elba in 1815. This French idiom is now commonly used as, "we should not wash our dirty linen in public."

The saying struck my mind during that Conference in Washington, DC in 2002. It happened when an African scholar took to the podium to present a paper under the heading, *"Have African Universities Become Glorified High Schools: A case Study of Makerere University."*

The title aroused my interest, one because I taught at a university and two because it pertained to the oldest and perhaps most famous university in East Africa. I followed the presentation keenly. However, as he developed his thesis, it turned out that he was out rightly ridiculing African universities at a global stage. To him, African universities were no longer universities worth of mention. His stand was that Africa's centres of knowledge had degenerated into glorified high schools.

His point of departure was that, in the of case Makerere, education had reached a level of extreme massification and commercialization. He averred that the oldest University in Africa was admitting thousands of students in various departments beyond the institution's teaching capacity. This was supported by the fact that the university's lecture rooms were bursting at the seams with youthful students, he said. Further, the university had insufficient teaching materials such as books, labs, periodicals and journals and could not offer comprehensive and exhaustive training to students.

The professor claimed that Makerere University lecturers were moonlighting in other 'jobs' because of poor pay. They hopped from one lecture room to the other and one university to the other in Kampala, running late in a bid to handle as many classes as possible. They had an understanding that the more courses they taught, the more money they would receive at the end of the month.

He further accused lecturers in African universities, saying that they majorly relied on the so-called 'yellow notes' that were rarely updated. To him, the lecturers were too busy chasing money and did not have an iota of time to do research and update their teaching notes. "They regurgitate the same material to students from year to year and this is why African universities are churning out half-baked graduates," he asserted.

The presentation showcased the sorry state of African universities. He advanced his sentiments that the universities had gone to the dogs and were not in any way different from high schools. "The once famed universities like Makerere are no longer institutions of higher learning due to years of mismanagement, neglect and poor governance," he argued.

Further, the presenter insinuated that most professors in universities in Africa, that could be worth mentioning, had run away from the continent and were now domiciled in universities in the West. "As such, African universities lack relevant and high quality academic staff who are central to proper training and research in any university," he added. It did not escape one noticing that the professor, a Ugandan, was condescendingly attacking African Universities at an international forum.

I got disturbed. Here I was, a professor born in Africa and domiciled in an African university, listening to a presentation in the Western world ridiculing my continent and my vocation. I felt the presentation was an affront, not only to African universities but the African people in general.

Yes, I have mentioned the case of inefficiencies and administrative gaps at Moi University in my story. I also have to admit that there were aspects of the presentation that reflected the challenges facing universities in Africa. However, to state that all African universities had gone to the dogs was unacceptable and could not go unchallenged. The professor was plainly washing our dirty linen on a global stage.

Africa is a diverse continent with several universities spread across fifty-two countries. These countries got their independence at different times and have their strengths and weaknesses. Within these countries, we have excellent institutions of higher learning that are ranked highly in the global ranking of universities.

We also have to admit that there are several universities in Africa that are not doing well. Due to this, they are ranked poorly not only in their countries but globally. This is why I felt challenged by the discourse at the Conference and chose to respond.

All eyes were riveted on me when I took the microphone to dissect the professor's school of thought. I informed the academicians that to start with, the professor's presentation was too generalized.

"It is scientifically and logically wrong to use one university in one country to be a representation of what happens in the institutions of higher learning in the entire continent," I said. I added that it was ironical that the presenter was an African, trained in an African university before he proceeded for further training abroad. How, I wondered, would he have become who he was without his training in an African university? He had tasted greener pastures and was now taking advantage of the available academic platforms to degrade Africa and paint African universities as dysfunctional cases that were beyond redemption.

The discussion at the Conference got heated following my criticism. Some scholars supported the professor while several others were on my side. A good number of the delegates were professors from African universities and had their own memories and understanding of the institutions.

In the rare sense, the behaviour of the African professor falls within the ambient of what I refer to as the 'African tragedy'. Brain drain has impoverished the African continent.

Worse yet, instead of revitalizing home countries through research and skills transfer, some African scholars are busy perpetuating and reinforcing negative stereotypes and biased images of Africa as a doomed continent. Thank goodness that this is not true. All over Africa, even in the least developed parts of the continent, one can find many positive things to 'write home' about. There are many positive things happening in the broader spectrum of socio-economic and political development. These are the stories we should be telling the world.

As Africans, if we are indeed patriotic, we should share our success stories with pride. We may wash our dirty linen but let us do it when outsiders are not watching. Indeed, even then, let's balance and present facts as they are: the good, the bad and the ugly. This is what scholars from other parts of the world, including America, do.

For instance, America has negative social issues such as racism and the socio-economic divide. We saw and heard their President Donald Trump call Africans names. At one time, he was busy building a wall to ring Mexico out of America. Further, drugs and substance abuse are deeply entrenched amongst some of the American youths. So are violent crime and homicides due to easy access to guns.

In this regard, some parts of New York and Chicago for instance, are no-go zones due to crime. However, you will not hear all these negative issues being given prominence in the American media and scholarly fora. Moreover, the American people including professors are busy working day and night to find solutions to their problems.

Scholars from the 'Asian Tiger Countries' - China, South Korea, Japan, India, Singapore and the likes - are busy importing high level scientific and technological skills and knowledge to their home countries. This is making major positive impacts. Thus, currently, Asian scholars in universities in the West have managed to contribute immensely to the current socio-economic and technological advancements of their home countries.

In this regard, one may ask: What is happening with us Africans?

The answer is simple. Many of us have been brainwashed to think that Africa is a dark continent and that it is doomed. Far from it! We have some of the best brains, many of who are domiciled in foreign universities and industries. If you visit Silicon Valley, the American hub of technological innovation and enterprise, you will be surprised to find many Africans including people from my own community working there. Sadly, the Africans have made little or no impact in their home countries.

****

The foregoing account reminds me of an engineer originally from the Gusii community who is based in the United States. The Medical Technologist works for a well-established manufacturing company, which makes equipment such as Computerized Tomography (CT) scans, mammograms, and chemotherapy as well as dialysis machines.

In one of my trips to the USA, the engineer invited me to his house. While in the house, the first thing he told me was that he was lucky to have come to America. He said that he was fully settled in America alongside his wife, children, brothers and sisters. He was a little worried of his aging parents whom he claimed were ignorant and had refused to join their son in America.

"We make high quality equipment in our factory. But due to competition in America, some get obsolete quickly and are lying in the stores," he told me.

When I inquired why he was not using his position to convince the company to donate some of the items to Kenya, he told me that our country is not regarded highly. Above that, he did not see the need of assisting Kenya to get the machines.

"We usually donate to Asian countries and South America. I don't see the need for donating the machines to Kenya because they will definitely fall in the wrong hands. They will be taken to private hospitals where poor Kenyans will not afford their services, let alone know that they are available," the engineer told me.

I found his sentiments degrading. I will say without fear of contradiction that Africans need a change of mindset. We need to change our perspective and start thinking positively of who we are as a people. We need to ask ourselves what is our ultimate goal and, while at it, unlearn our misplaced attitude about the continent.

It is utterly wrong to always think that Africa is the epicentre of famine, wars and diseases. We can change this narrative. All we need to do is to change the way we do things and stop suffering from high level inferiority complex. In the long run, we should stop whining and talking derogatively about our mother-land once we get to the Western world. People see themselves lucky to be away from the miseries of Africa, whether real or imagined.

Let me state it once again: the manner in which many African scholars present themselves out there depicts Africa in an unpleasant manner.

Here is another example of what I gathered during my brief stay in Boston when I had won the AAI fellowship.

To my surprise, I was booked in the Hyatt Group of Hotels in Boston. The five-star establishment is touted to be one of the most expensive and prestigious hospitality facilities in the world. As a Claude-Ake scholar from an African university, I did not understand why my hosts, Boston University, booked me in such an expensive hotel whose daily full board charge was a cool US$ 600. This amount was almost equivalent to my monthly pay at Moi University.

When I entered my room in the hotel, I felt out of place. It was a high class executive room with a mini-bar, a sofa set, tables and a luxury bed. The high-end hotel was definitely beyond the class of a humble lecturer who is used to living in a simply furnished house.

I enquired why the organisers chose to have me accommodated in the hotel and their response astonished me. They said that a visiting Kenyan scholar was once accommodated in the Boston University guest house and ranted that it was not up to his class. From then on, the university assumed that all Kenyan scholars wanted to stay in high-end, luxurious hotels. That was how I ended up being accommodated in the expensive five-star hotel.

At the Boston University's African Studies library section, I found a lot of literature on the Gusii community. Surprisingly, some of it dated back to the 1930s. Some of the literature was written by pioneer anthropologists and historians. I was gratified to lay my hands on the unique literature.

I made copies of most of it and carried a huge consignment of material when the fellowship period elapsed. The material came in handy during my research and compiling the aforementioned book. Some of the material was quite seminal and it forms part of my library to date.

More Academic Publications

It was in the year 2004, and the Department of Tourism and Hospitality Management was growing fast. The three distinct programmes - Tourism Management, Travel and Tour Operations, and Hotel and Hospitality Management - became hot cake courses for students from all over Kenya. This prompted us to start developing a curriculum for Masters and PhD studies.

Once again, I played a central role in the development of both programmes. This involved undertaking initial research and examining tourism and hospitality curricula from selected universities. It also entailed visiting tourism and hospitality stakeholders both in the public and private sector. I was also in charge of co-ordinating and organising stakeholder meetings to discuss the draft curricula.

The Department was also working on a project dubbed, *Responsible Tourism* supported by the University of Greenwich in the United Kingdom. The Department of Sustainable Tourism and Hospitality Management in the University of Greenwich was the project coordinator. It involved staff exchange, undertaking joint research, publication and organising conferences to promote the concept of responsible tourism. In a nutshell, responsible tourism entails forms of tourism development that are cognisant of the needs of local people in tourism destinations. It also promotes sustainable utilization of existing tourism resources such as wildlife, beaches and cultural attractions, among others.

Once again, I had an opportunity to make several visits to the UK for consultations and learning from the experience of others. This enabled me to expand my networks. I linked up with prominent scholars and professors in the Department of Sustainable Tourism and Hospitality Management at the University of Greenwich, some whose contacts I keep to this day.

In one of my visits to the UK, I was accompanied with Prof. Bob Weshitemi who later rose to become the Deputy Vice Chancellor (DVC) in charge of Academic and Research at Moi University. He was at that time the HoD of Tourism and Hospitality Management. The teaching resources at Greenwich enabled us to fully develop the Masters and PhD curricula. Our counterparts at Greenwich were amazed with the results and requested us to allow them to use the same curricula in their university.

I proudly say that I played a critical role in the development and expansion of tourism training at Moi University. The fact that core curricula in the School of Tourism, Travel, Hospitality and Events Management were developed under my guidance as the person in charge of curriculum development justifies my assertion.

I believe that I utilized my time at Moi University well. My ability to have more than fifty publications in peer-reviewed international journals is a testimony to this. The publications continue to be widely cited in the tourism and hospitality literature. Others have formed seminal literature used by many universities in Kenya and beyond.

It is gratifying when I attend international conferences in other parts of the world and find academicians who already know my work. I attribute this to my many publications in tourism and wildlife management that they have come across. This is why I can proudly say that I have played a critical role in the enhancement of the tourism and wildlife research frontier in Kenya and across Africa.

My interest in the study of the Gusii people is also worth mentioning. In the recent past, I have undertaken research on the history and culture of the Gusii, which has culminated in the publication of four books. I have also written book chapters and article publications on the same.

Here are the four titles on Gusii I have either authored or co-authored (a) *Ethnography of the Gusii of Western Kenya: A Vanishing Cultural Heritage,* co-edited with Robert Maxon, Edwin Mellen Press, 2006; *(b) The Gusii of Kenya: Social, Economic, Cultural, Political & Judicial Perspectives,* Nsemia Inc., 2017; *(c) Gusii Soapstone Industry: Critical Issues, Opportunities, Challenges & Future Alternatives,* co-authored with Mallion Onyambu, Nsemia Inc., 2018; *and (d) The Untold Story of the Gusii of Kenya: Survival Techniques and Resistance to the Establishment of British Colonial Rule,* Nsemia Inc., 2019.

In later years at Moi University, I was also engaged in the teaching and supervision of post-graduate students. In recent years, I have managed and supervised more than 30 Masters and twelve PhD candidates.

I have to mention that one thing I did not like during my tenure as HoD was attending University Senate meetings. This was due to the high-level sycophancy and blind allegiance to the Management. During the Senate meetings, some professors fought to outshine each other in showering praises and compliments to Senior University Management. They did this even on issues that appeared to be promoting personal interests to the detriment of the institution.

I remember the over-use of the phrase: "I concur with what the VC or DVC has said." In the Senate boardroom, whenever members of the Senate stood to react to the viewpoint of Senior Management some members always sided with the Management. They did this even on grave matters such as opposing lecturers' push for better pay and working conditions. I got amused one time when a senior professor rose to speak in support of Management, wondering where the institution would get money to increase staff salaries. It should be noted that the payment of salaries to Public University staff is the obligation of the National Government and not the university.

Regardless of the daunting challenges I faced there, I am thankful because it was within the Moi University system that I was able to rise through the academic ranks. I had joined the university as a Lecturer and rose to Senior Lecturer, Associate Professor and eventually Full Professor in a period of less than ten years. This was no mean feat.

I thank God for giving me the strength to be proficient and committed to conducting research, teaching, writing and publishing. I have managed to walk the talk in academia where you have a clear choice to either publish or perish. I grew to become a Professor of Moi University in a timely manner because I was able to publish widely in my area of expertise.

Of course, I was not a very popular person at Moi University particularly with Management. This was due to the principled stand I took on many issues. I always advocated for and articulated issues some of which were not favourable to the Management. A good example is when I declined to hire unqualified staff to teach and when I championed for better pay and working conditions for academic staff.

In a way, due to these endeavours involving fighting for the rights of lecturers, I became a marked man by the Management of Moi University. This is perhaps why I was not able to rise through the ranks in the administration hierarchy. However, I have never regretted anything or any decision I made while at Moi. I am a firm believer in my principles and I have never supported sycophancy. It is not in my nature to stay silent when injustices are happening. I would rather raise my voice and stand to be counted than play court poet.

The downside of speaking one's mind in some environments is that one's seniors will not shy away from 'cutting one to size'. Ironically, not being entangled in some management and administrative activities came as a relief. I always had ample time to engage in my academic endeavours. It was due to these accomplishments that some disgruntled and envious elements in the Management hierarchy were unable to curtail my professional progression in a relatively short time.

Biographer's Note: Dr. Shem Maingi undertook PhD studies under the guidance of Prof. Akama. He wrote the following:

> Prof. John Akama is an ardent and one of the top professors in the subject of Tourism in the African region. I first met him as a young post-graduate student in Moi University in October, 2015. He was an amazing teacher, scholar and mentor to me. I attribute what I am today to his mentorship.

Prof. Akama's academic leadership, research publications, books and mentorship of upcoming academicians are a testimony to his exemplary career and contributions to academia. My impression of these exceptional qualities were amplified when I had an opportunity to jointly write a research paper titled 'Wildlife Conservation, Safari Tourism and the Role of Tourism Certification in Kenya: A Post-Colonial Critique' which was published in Tourism Recreation Research Journal. It was voted the winner of the 2011 Article of the Year Award by editors of the journal (see citation among the pictures).

I am greatly honoured and proud to have been Prof. Akama's student and mentee. Forever, I will cherish the great training and mentorship. Thank you Sir.

Shem Wambugu Maingi, PhD
Lecturer, School of Hospitality, Tourism and Leisure studies,
Kenyatta University, Kenya

Interview for Professorship

Dave Willis may have been right when he said that, "show respect even to people that don't deserve it; not as a reflection of their character but as a reflection of yours."

This is exactly what I did while I worked at Moi University. One of my bosses never appeared happy with my sustained professional rise. I was rising fast and all was based on the work I was doing. I never went to his office on bended knees to pledge my loyalty to him. It appeared that being a sycophant was an unwritten criterion for one to get some favours. My conscience refused to let me dance to that tune.

In this regard, when the time came for my interview for Professorship, my Dean deliberately absented himself on the day of the interview. Instead of attending and pushing my case, he sent a Senior Professor to represent him. From the start of the interview, it appeared that the Professor was under instructions to make sure that I flopped in the endeavour. I think that was why the Dean kept away. I knew I was not in his good books and maybe, he thought, it would appear awkward if he revealed his bias during the interview.

My independent mindedness and principled stand sometimes ended up painting me in bad light with the powers that were. For instance, when I resisted attempts to recruit academic staff who did not meet the laid down criteria due to nepotism and tribalism, many in the Management hierarchy were not happy. However, I was not sure if this past would resurface during the interview but I prepared for the worst and hoped for the best. Despite the issue with my Faculty boss, I still prepared well. I arranged my academic testimonials accordingly and came up with competent responses for the interviewing panel.

These included providing a clear profile of my academic, professional and administrative experiences, and the nature of research activities and publications that I had engaged in over the years. I also assessed my position-vis-a vis the criteria for promotion and everything checked out. I was beaming with confidence. I knew that, as long as I thoroughly prepared and made sure I met the requirements; I was going to dismantle any hurdle placed before me. I was not going to allow anyone to get in the way of my hard work of many years. It was unlikely that anyone could; at least not with my impeccable CV.

During the interview, the Senior Professor started interrogating me from a very negative note. He asked me if I had attained the required years for promotion and I answered in the affirmative. He also asked me if I was sure of my competency in teaching. His undertones insinuated that I was more of a researcher than a lecturer.

The designated Professor continued to intimidate me with overbearing questions that were close to irrelevant. He asked, "have you had problems as a teacher, and other exogenous issues that were not central in the promotion process?" Coincidentally, this negative approach worked in my favour. By the time he was done, the other panellists had seen that he was unashamedly hostile to me. They then asked me very specific questions on my area of expertise in Tourism and Wildlife Management, and I calmly and convincingly answered them to the best of my knowledge.

Save for the Professor in question, the other twelve panellists thanked me for my research and publishing work as well as supervising PhD and Masters students. This must have embarrassed the Professor who obviously had ill intentions of failing and dishonouring me.

Interestingly, the same Professor went against odds to send me a congratulatory letter the following day for passing the interview. This was uncharacteristic in such a situation because members of the interview panel are not required to directly communicate the outcome of the interview to a candidate. I believe that he felt guilty because of his unorthodox behaviour whose objective was to derail me during the interview.

Based on my experience in Moi University, if you remain disciplined and focused, you will always achieve your long-term objectives, no matter how hostile the environment may be. As much as they may try, your detractors cannot manage to dim your star. Were it not for my focus and hard work, I would not have survived the hostile academic environment during my call of duty at Moi University.

To this day, I have kept asking myself, "why should senior managers of a university, which is supposed to be a centre of excellence, get tempted to promote academics on the basis of social networks, tribe and ethnic background?" This made a university, which was quite promising to end up compromising standards due to the hiring and promotion of unqualified/undeserving lecturers. This perpetuated negative exogenous factors such as clannism, ethnicity and corruption in the management and governance of institutions of higher learning.

To a certain extent, negative ethnicity and corruption does not affect Kenyan universities only. Other African Universities probably face the same challenges. This is similar to what is happening in other social, economic and political institutions across the continent.

Over the years, my interaction with colleagues from different African countries and reports in various media and research documents have shown examples of widespread social and economic vices that afflict the continent. As much as one can say that these issues can be found anywhere in the world, their negative impact on Africa is a major concern.

Hence, the three vices- nepotism, negative ethnicity and corruption -are major challenges confronting most African countries' institutions including universities that are supposed to be centres of excellence.

The African people need concerted efforts and focus to overcome the mess troubling institutions occasioned by, among others, these retrogressive factors. This statement may appear overly general but it is the truth. This analytical breakdown is based on my understanding and 30 years of work experience in the African continent.

Biographer's Note: Prof. Bob Wishitemi, a colleague of Prof. Akama at Moi Univeristy, had the following to say:

I have interacted with Prof. John Sorana Akama in most of my professional life. For over twenty five years, he has been a colleague and friend in the industry. He has made a tremendous contribution to academia and industrial practice in Kenya (and East Africa), particularly at Moi University's School of Tourism, Hospitality and Events Management. John's wide exposure and experience has been instrumental to the development and implementation of our tourism curriculum for both undergraduate and postgraduate programmes.

John is a prolific writer, conducting ground-breaking research and contributing to scholarly publications in many refereed journals. He has been phenomenal in steering the discourse of pedagogy and research in Tourism Policy and Planning, Wildlife and Protected Area Management and Sustainability in the region. He is a renowned scholar contributing to numerous reference materials including books, book chapters, and research articles, among others, used widely in University level teaching. Other than academia, he has served several universities, university colleges, schools and departments, in various administrative capacities culminating to his current position as Vice Chancellor of Kisii University, Kenya. John's career, spanning over 30 (thirty) years, is an epitome of dedication, commitment, and selflessness. I celebrate him!

Bob E. L. Wishitemi,
Professor of Tourism and Wildlife Studies,
Department of Tourism and Travel Operations Management
Moi University, Kenya.

This could be my first ever photo. I am in my mother's hands; standing at the back to the left is my father. The rest are my parents' friends.

Myself in 1977.

My elder sister, Florence Obaga with my younger sister Prisca Mogoi in 1981.

Standing to the right, I posed for a photo with friends at Kakamega High School.

Myself, second from right with school mates Anasi, Nyarunda and Auka

Myself to the extreme right with school mates Nyarunda, Onchwati, Auka and Getugi (standing), and Nyaundi and Anasi (in bent position) at Kakamega High School in 1979.

My friend Getugi (left) and myself at Kakamega High School in 1979. Mr Getugi was my room mate.

With my friend Pius Kakai (left) at the main entrance to Kenyatta Campus (now Kenyatta University) in 1984.

Myself at the main entrance to Ohio University

With my friend Tabo Muda during the African Week celebrations at Ohio University in 1987.

Myself at the entracnce of Southern Illinois University in 1991

With my Academic Advisor and Mentor, Prof. Chris Lant during my graduation at Southern Illinois University in 1993

My Academic Advisor and Mentor, Prof. Chris Lant (right), Head of Geography Department Prof. David Sharpe (middle) & a classmate outside the Auditorium at Southern Illinois University in 1993

I am on the right with my friend, Esami, in a wooded area at Southern Illinois University in 1993.

Myself outside the White House (Washington DC-USA) when I was a visiting Clande Ike Scholar in 2002.

Part of Kisii. The photo shows how land has been subdivided due to rising population.

My wife Mallion Kwamboka (left) with a colleague at Uasin Gishu High School.

My wife Mallion Kwamboka carrying our daughter Teresia Nyakoinani, followed by our first born son Bruce Orang'o and myself in our home in Eldoret in 1996.

Myself carrying my son Larry Otwori, with my daughter Teresia Nyakoinani to the right and my son Bruce Orang'o to the left outside Eldoret Municipal Building in 2000.

Myself with my daughter Teresia Nyakoinani (left) and my son Larry Otwori (right) during a graduation ceremony at Moi University.

My first born child, Bruce Orang'o.

My daughter Teresia Nyakoinani clad in her Alliance High School uniform.

My last born son Larry Otwori outside the Alliance High School Chapel.

I am with my father (left) at our home in Eldoret in 2004.

Myself, my father and my son Bruce Orang'o at our home in Eldoret in 2010.

My father, myself in the middle holding my last born son Larry Otwori and my late uncle Obabi in our rural home at Borabu in 2002.

With my colleagues from the Department of Tourism Management outside the Adminstration Block of Chepkoilel Campus, Moi University in 2003. I am standing fourth from the right.

Myself with Prof. Gudu (middle) and Prof. Ole Karei (right) during one of the graduation ceremonies at Moi University.

4. NURTURING KISII UNIVERSITY

Another Academic Move

Kisii University has a unique history. It started as a primary teachers' training college in 1964. It was later upgraded to offer S1 or diploma teachers' training. In 1994, it was made a Campus of Egerton University, which is located in Njoro, Nakuru County. It eventually obtained its current status through an award of Charter on February 6th, 2013.

In mid-2008, the Egerton University Council placed an advertisement in the print media. The Council wanted to fill the vacancy of Principal for the newly created Kisii Constituent College. I was satisfied that I met the job requirements and submitted my application. I felt that time was ripe for me to advance my career, preferably in a different environment.

I was elated when I got shortlisted. I received a letter inviting me for an interview at Egerton University's Main Campus at Njoro. As expected of an interviewee, I prepared myself and got relevant documents, certificates and other testimonials ready. At the university, I learnt that five other applicants had been invited for the same interview.

The interview resonated around issues of leadership and governance in a higher educational institution setup as well as my academic expertise. I answered the questions to the best of my knowledge during the intensive and elaborate session, which lasted for about two hours. When it drew to a close, the panellists thanked me for turning up for the interview and informed me that the outcome would be communicated to me later. I knew I had stood my ground well and left the room optimistic that I would get the job.

This world is full of surprises and that day had one for me. Before I left the university, a senior administrator took me aside and whispered to my ear not to tell anybody about the interview. I did not understand what this meant and he did not give me time to ask for an elaboration. To this day, I have wondered about the person's intention.

Back in Moi University, I continued with the routine work of teaching and research. One, two, three weeks elapsed. Then one month, two months passed. There was no communication forthcoming from Egerton University. Around that time, rumours started going round concerning the results of the interview, which made me anxious.

I received a call from a member of staff at Egerton University one morning.

"Are you Professor Akama?"

"Yes sir."

"Did you do any interview at Egerton University?"

"Yes."

The caller confided in me that I took position one. As per university regulations, being ranked position one is not a guarantee that you will get the job. The Council has discretion to pick any of the top three candidates to take the slot.

The caller informed me that although there was a consensus that I was the best suited for the job, there was an underground initiative hatched to deny me the opportunity. He further divulged to me in confidence that the number three ranked candidate was going to be appointed to the position. Once again, it ran through my mind that someone's tribe and connections were paying off to the disadvantage of the most qualified candidate in the interview.

This made me confirm the rumours that had been doing the rounds that tribalism was at play in the appointment process. True to my voluntary informer and the rumours, it did not take long to be known to all and sundry that the job had been given to a candidate who emerged third in the interview. It was annoying that the university did not have the audacity to inform me through a letter how I had faired on in the interview. It soon became a public fact that I was unfairly denied the job.

No one ever chooses where to be born. However, on this fateful day being born in Kisii worked in my favour. It so happened that the Constituent College, now Kisii University, is situated within the Kisii region.

There was immediate uproar, which reverberated in the land of Kisii following reports that I had been short-changed from becoming the pioneer principal of an institution located in my homeland. Politicians, members of the clergy and opinion leaders and the Gusii Council of Elders came together and started to mount pressure on the Council of Egerton University. They wanted the Management to rescind its decision and offer the job to me because I had topped in the interview.

One may see this as tribal and criticise me for condoning tribalism when it favours me. However, I believe the dissenters were fighting for a worthy cause. Some leaders including the then mayor of Kisii Municipality Samuel Nyangeso called me to Kisii. In those days, councillors who were led by the mayor were powerful and vocal at the grassroots. The councillors' positions were disbanded when a new constitution was passed in 2010 and promulgated three years later. Positions of mayors and municipal heads were taken by governors in the new constitutional dispensation.

It is important to state that I had support from various quarters. For instance, many of my colleagues at Moi University and the University of Nairobi and other places were in support of my case. I would have never known that I was the leading candidate for the coveted position of principal, except for someone who pricked by his conscience. The information was leaked by some colleagues in Egerton University who were privy of the matter and the intricacies at play.

Members of Parliament from the Gusii region also joined the fray and invited me to Parliament. They wanted to have an understanding of what had transpired before, during and after the interview at Egerton University.

They agreed to carry the burden of fighting for what I merited. This they did by raising questions and making pronouncements in Parliament concerning my case. Some led delegations to the Ministry of Education headquarters where they lodged a complaint, while others held ground shaking demonstrations in Kisii Town. The peaceful demonstrations were widely covered in both print and electronic media by correspondents working for various media outlets.

What started as a personal problem quickly metamorphosed into a community issue. It eventually escalated to the highest office of the land, the Office of President Emilio Mwai Kibaki. The pressure must have been heavy and unrelenting too. In the long run, the authorities gave in.

It did not take long before I received a letter informing me that I had been appointed to be the pioneer Principal of Kisii Constituent College of Egerton University. The letter was duly signed by the Minister for Education, Dr. Sally Kosgey. It directed me to report to my new work station on January 5th, 2009.

This confirmed to me once again that if an opportunity was meant for you, you will get it, be it through providence or God's wish. I was about to be sacrificed at the altar of ethnicity, which afflicts Kenya. We had not met before with the many people who stood with and by me, but through their struggle, I got the appointment. I was extremely elated.

The letter was hand delivered to me. When I got it, I knew it marked another landmark in my life. Ironically, one can say, I got the job when I had lost it. Left on my own, it is most unlikely that I would have gotten the appointment.

In the Kenyan environment, positions of high level leadership (and this perhaps happens elsewhere), have intricate and complex exogenous factors that always come into play. Powerful forces can derail even the most competent Kenyan from getting these coveted appointments. Plainly, I got to know and understand that one's academic and professional credentials may not be enough for one to be given some of those positions perceived to be plum.

Actually, networks are the key determinants of many outcomes across the world. It is the reason people join clubs, go to professional organization events, conferences and all. In networks, information flows about critical happenings. Such information is usually out of reach to many outside the networks. The difference is that, in Kenya, our networks revolve around ethnic and corrupt interests rather than on the best practices that could best help a company or institution thrive. For instance, if one got a job because of their tribe and other parochial reasons, their interest would be to serve the tribe rather than excel at it.

On top of academic credentials and competencies, there are networks of stakeholders who are crucial determinants of one's success. These stakeholders occupy positions at the national, regional and grassroots levels. They include politicians, businessmen, opinion leaders and shapers, and even the clergy.

Perhaps, there are many people who disagree with my assertion. However, in many instances especially in the African settings, meritocracy may not be entirely relied on when determining who should be given what in terms of appointments and resource allocation.

For my case, centrifugal forces came together to rescue me against powerful centripetal forces that wanted to derail my advancement. Fate was with me and they were defeated!

Biographer's Note: Dr. Matunda Nyanchama is the proprietor of Nsemia Inc. Publishers. He recounted the sentiments expressed by the Late Simeon Nyachae regarding the apparent controversy surrounding Prof. Akama's appointment as the founding Principal of Kisii University Constituent College:

I was staying abroad at the time the issue regarding the appointment of a Principal for the newly established Kisii Constituent College of Egerton University came up in the news. I followed the developments keenly, as did many of my friends from within and outside the community. Specifically, as the leadership of Gusii Education & Advancement Resource (GEAR; an NGO dealing with educational and development matters in Kenya), we were keen on the kind of person who would become Principal and how receptive the person would be to work with us on matters pertaining to education and socio-economic development in the community. Unfortunately, some of the reporting regarding this initial appointment, and subsequent protests, painted the matter as being driven by ethnic interests.

However, Prof. Akama was finally appointed and the matter settled down but, to some extent, the original storyline remained ingrained in certain people's minds.

A few years later, together with a few friends, we visited Mzee Simeon Nyachae at his Riverside Road offices in Nairobi. We had gone to consult on community development initiatives that would be important with the coming of devolution as enunciated in the 2010 Constitution. Inevitably, the matter of education came up and the need to have Kisii Constituent College of Egerton University become a full-fledged university arose. Predictably its leadership and the previous perceived controversy came up in the discussion.

Mzee Nyachae was quite candid and categorical that it was unfair to have wanted to short-change Prof. Akama on the appointment. The sage argued that Prof. Akama's ethnicity, like for all of us, was an accident of birth. Prof. Akama was not simply qualified for the job, but he was the most qualified of those who were competing for the position. Mzee Nyachae said frankly that, along with other leaders from Gusii and beyond, they had to do what was necessary to support a fair process. It was good not just for the community but for the country at large, he reaffirmed. He went on to urge us to be more engaged in promoting education in Gusii, and especially the strategically placed budding institution that is now Kisii University.

Coincidentally, a few years later, Prof. Akama allowed GEAR to hold a daylong conference on education in Gusii at the institution. Opened by the then Kisii University Council Chairman, the late Prof. Joseph Nyasani, this landmark conference crystalized the problems, the challenges and proposed a number of ways to tackle the monumental challenge of ensuring qualify education for all.

Postscript: I write this as the community and Kenya as a whole are mourning the passing of Hon. Simeon Nyachae. Eulogized by many as a great leader, elder-statesman, administrator, manager and businessman, Nyachae leaves a rich legacy that reverberates across Kenya and beyond.

Managing Kisii University Constituent College

I did not expect to be received in Kisii Town with jubilation when I arrived there in the morning of January 5th, 2009. To my pleasant surprise, there were several excited residents of diverse ages waiting to welcome me. Some were students of the college, while others were traders in the town. Others had come, specifically, to see me take over the leadership of the institution, which they held dear. Probably, this was by virtue of it being the only institution of higher learning in the region. Others may have been there because of the controversy preceding this formal take over.

Soon after, I was ushered into the college and the handing over process started in earnest. During the weeklong exercise, I was taken through handover reports as relates to movable and immovable assets, the human resource status, liabilities, students' data and other outstanding matters. This exercise culminated in a meeting of the Council to discuss and adopt the handover report. I then officially took over as the first Principal of the Kisii Constituent College. This day went down in history as a noteworthy moment.

I was surprised to learn that the institution had been declared a Constituent College by President Mwai Kibaki way back in 2007. Kibaki signed declaration letters the same year but there was a lacuna up to 2009, in terms of institutional administration and governance. For the three years, the institution had been administered by three acting principals who came in and left in quick succession.

Moreover, as much as the elevation was done in 2007, it was not until 2008 that the Council of the Constituent College was appointed. In this regard, the college had inadvertently or otherwise been left in limbo. The institution could not run as expected since the top organs of governance, including the Council and Management, were not in place. Furthermore, it was after three years that I was posted as the substantive Principal of the institution.

Without a Principal and a Council, which are key organs of governance, activities of the college, including incurring of expenditure and promulgation of policies, were at a standstill. In short, the institution had stagnated for those three years. As much as the college received funding directly from the exchequer, it could not incur any expenditure without the approval of the Council, which was also non-existent. This particularly affected the development initiatives since the funds that were meant for infrastructural expansion and physical facelift were not utilised.

It was very unfortunate that, as much as the institution needed the funds for infrastructural development, the money which had been allocated to it in the two consecutive years was not expended. Instead, part of it was returned to treasury as unutilized funds while some was re-routed to other universities and constituent colleges. This was how the college lost a staggering Kshs. 300 million of the development budget in its nascent stage.

I also discovered that there had been neither hiring of new staff nor the establishment of new academic programmes during that period as much as it was a major requirement for any new Constituent College.

The more I got into understanding the institution, the more I discovered many shortfalls. It appeared that as much as it had been declared a Constituent College, it was probably not going to rise within the stipulated time to become a full-fledged university. It should be understood that in the Kenyan scenario, a Constituent College is ideally a mini-university which is expected to transit into a Chartered University within, ideally, a period of three years.

By any description, the situation on the ground in terms of infrastructure, student enrolment and rollout of new academic programmes was totally inadequate for the growth of the institution. I even wondered the criteria the government used to promote the campus into a constituent college in the first place. However, as already indicated, this was not surprising in the Kenyan situation where many exogenous factors come into play whenever any critical policy matter is decided.

Surely, with only two degree programmes (Bachelor of Commerce, and Bachelor of Library Information Science) the institution was far from meeting the academic requirements of a constituent college. Further, the institution had about three hundred students, seven academic staff members and fifty non-teaching staff. Clearly, my job of getting the institution on its feet and running, as expected, was well cut out.

It should therefore be stated that Kisii University of today has indeed metamorphosed during the recent past. When the institution became a constituent college, most of its infrastructure was from its formative stages when it was a primary teachers training college. Thus, the institution lacked basic facilities of a university. It did not have lecture rooms, staff offices, a library or ablution blocks. I remember one morning, as I was strolling in the compound, I spotted female students bathing in the open near their hostels. I was taken aback! It reinforced the fact that the responsibility before me was humongous.

At the time I took the reins of the institution, renowned scholar, the late Prof. Joseph Nyasani, had been appointed Chairman of the College Council. With the support of Prof. Nyasani as the head of the Council, the Management embarked on a vigorous journey of developing the institution to achieve its requisite status. Fortunately, the Council understood well and was up to the task at hand. The immediate task of the Council was to ensure that the college did not lose its financial allocation for infrastructure development for the 2008/09 Financial Year. The allocated amount of Kshs. 117 million was sufficient to cover initial planned projects.

The Financial Management Act stipulated that without having properly tendered projects as per the Procurement and Disposal Act, it was illegal to start any development project in a government institution. With this realization, the Council developed the Physical Master Plan using available experts from the Ministry of Public Works. In the Master Plan, we identified priority projects that included a library, lecture rooms, hostel complex and ICT Centre.

This was arrived at after identification of the most pressing needs and also the understanding that we were supposed to transit the Constituent College to a Chartered University within a three-year period. The initial Strategic Plan provided for the implementation of the identified projects in three phases, spanning a timeframe of six years.

There was no time to waste. We advertised the tenders and went through the tendering process, which entailed pre-qualification, receiving quotations, and evaluation of the quotations. We undertook due diligence before awarding the projects to the winning contractors.

I was in for surprise yet again! A process which I thought was straight forward and transparent faced bottlenecks along the way. I discovered that there were many interested parties, including powerful politicians who wanted to get the tenders through hook and crook.

The Council stuck to the procurement law and several companies that did not meet the requirements were locked out. I recall being approached by influence seekers who wanted the projects to be awarded to their briefcase companies. However, I stood my ground and made sure that due process was followed in the tendering process. My firm stand led to the award of the tenders to the best qualified contractors, most of them from Nairobi.

This transparent process kicked a storm. I was accused of having awarded Kisii projects to 'foreigners' shortly after I was assisted by the community to become the Principal. "How can money come from Nairobi and you return it there?" the busybodies wondered. This was in reference to the Council's decision to award the tenders to the most qualified contracting companies that happened to be based in the capital city.

These meddlers were ruthless and had connections in higher offices. True to their threats, I was summoned to Nairobi by a section of politicians. When I got there, the political leaders gave me a dressing down, and did not hide their misgivings that I was not living up to their expectations.

By the time I left the meeting, it had sunk in me that I was a man on the radar and whatever I did was being closely watched by diverse interest groups.

The Vice Chancellor of Egerton University, who was a Council member by virtue of his position as the CEO of the Main University as per the Universities regulations, also took that opportunity to attack the budding institution. In my reading, this was payback time because he was unhappy that he had failed to install the man he wanted to be the Principal.

The Vice Chancellor secretly wrote a letter to the Ministry of Education and copied the same to the National Treasury and the Inspectorate of State Corporations, making allegations against the Council. He accused the Council and me of over committing the government by starting projects without a line budget for them. According to his argument, which was obviously false, we had overcommitted the budget because the project sum was way beyond what the government had allocated the institution for development during that Financial Year.

For sure, at face value, that accusation was a heinous offense with punitive sanctions as per the law which stipulates that any government official who commits the government beyond the available funds can face dire consequences. The punishment includes summary dismissal and/or prosecution to face charges of financial mismanagement.

However, truth be told, the Vice Chancellor was being economical with the truth. He knew that according to our Strategic Plan, the projects were staggered to run for three phases covering a period of six years and not one year as he claimed in the letter. Having been in University Management for a longer period than myself and as a member of the College Council, he knew this very well, but was feigning ignorance to fix us.

The Council was immediately summoned by the Ministry of Education to report at the Headquarters in Nairobi with express instructions that we avail a comprehensive explanation on these procurement anomalies. As the CEO of the college, I prepared a comprehensive report, which we presented to the Ministry as instructed.

At the same time, auditors from the National Treasury and the Inspectorate of State Corporations were dispatched to the college. They pitched tent for several days, auditing books of accounts as relates to the award of the tenders. During the time, they thoroughly scrutinised the tender documents and interviewed various staff members. They hoped to get answers to the concerns raised and if indeed we had overcommitted the government. I knew the accounts and the procedures we had followed were watertight but I kept my fingers crossed. I was well aware that if the witch hunters got their way, we could be in a lot of trouble.

The team from the National Treasury concluded its investigations within a week and I heaved a sigh of relief when its report exonerated the Council and me of any wrong doing. They found that the projects were in line with the College Strategic Plan and were supposed to be implemented in six years, and not one year as the detractors claimed. Hence, they reached a conclusion that there was no over commitment of the budget for the tendered projects.

The other squad of investigators from the Inspectorate of State Corporations took a longer time to finish their job. They were more thorough and did not want to leave any stone unturned in their investigations.

When the team returned to Nairobi, they summoned the Council Chairman, his Deputy and myself to appear before them. We went to their offices at the Kenyatta International Convention Centre (KICC). For several hours, they thoroughly grilled us on the legality of the projects. They were trying to find out if our responses rhymed with the documents in their possession and if indeed we had committed any financial irregularities. The team too exonerated us of flouting any government rules and regulations.

As Council, we were relieved when the library, ICT Centre, Laboratory Complex and lecture halls, that were major capital projects captured in the Strategic Plan, were given a clean bill of health. We would soon hit the ground running. Or so we thought.

Unknown to us, the perceived enemies and detractors wanted us to stay in the woods longer. One of the contractors who had missed out lodged a complaint with the Public Procurement Oversight Authority (PPOA). He claimed that he was unfairly treated in the award of tender for the Laboratory Complex.

Once again, we were compelled to provide more information to this oversight body. The issue dragged on for over two years before we were exonerated. Due to the delays, the project never took off. It died at its inception. In this regard, I have to state that conceptualizing projects and implementing them has been my most challenging undertaking. And it has spanned the period since I was appointed as the Principal to date when I am serving as Vice Chancellor.

There have been similar concerns expressed by many regarding the PPOA law and the way it has become a hindrance especially on the implementation of development projects in the public sector. While the law was well-intended as a means of ensuring fairness and accountability, it has been used to torpedo many a project, especially where a lot of money is involved. As per the law, PPOA must pay attention to every complaint and investigate the same prior to passing judgement. As things stand, the authority has not developed rapid response mechanisms with which to resolve such matters, and, hence, the unwarranted delays and, in many cases, the 'death' of many development projects.

Despite everything, it gives me immense joy when I walk around the institution and see the projects that we have completed and are serving their purpose. These include the library, which we had prioritised in the understanding that it is the engine of any learning institution. This ultra-modern library was constructed to completion in a record time of one and a half years. It is a four-storied building with a sitting capacity of four thousand users. It is arguably one of the ultra-modern structures in our university physical setting.

Also, by the time the institution received its Charter, we had completed ten lecture halls with a capacity of a hundred students each. All these critical projects were funded by the exchequer. Although fairly nascent, we also managed to generate internal revenue. Out of these funds, we managed to construct a four hundred bed capacity students' hostel. We named the facility Nyasani Hostels in honour of the founding Council Chairman. A huge chunk of the funds that went to the project were pooled from the fees payments by privately sponsored students.

Other new infrastructure, which has been put in place include the office building now being used by the Finance Department. We have also managed to use internally generated revenues to construct a science complex, which has chemistry, biology and physics labs, among others.

The pioneer Council also focused on the development of the academic and administrative structure for the university. With clear guidance from the members of the Council and the Management, we strategically came up with seven new Faculties and Schools as captured in the Strategic Plan. These led to the promulgation of several schools including the School of Education and Human Resources Development, School of Law, School of Agriculture and Natural Resources Management, School of Information and Communication Technology, School of Arts and Social Sciences, School of Pure and Applied Sciences and School of Health Sciences. These new schools added unto the existing School of Commerce, which we later renamed the School of Business and Economics.

In Search of Lecturers

Any educationist will tell you that establishing an institution of higher learning is one thing; offering quality training and research is another. After developing the new schools, our next daunting assignment was finding relevant high-level academic staff, preferably PhD holders.

We needed academic staff at the various ranks including professors, associate professors, senior lecturers, lecturers and tutorial fellows. These were the people who would strategically drive our Vision and Mission of making Kisii University College gear up to providing high quality teaching, research and innovation.

We placed an advertisement in the mainstream newspapers in October 2009. In it, we declared more than sixty vacancies in the various faculties and schools. The response from few applicants was very poor. I recall that nobody applied for full or associate professor positions. Very few applied for senior lecturer and lecturer positions and majority did apply for tutorial fellow positions.

However, our interest was to recruit staff at senior academic levels who would lay firm foundations for the new schools. To our great disappointment, we did not get a good number of applicants who met our requirements when we scanned through the applications. We then short-listed the applicants who met the stated criteria before we took them through a competitive interview. We then hired a number of them at lecturer and tutorial fellow positions.

The challenge of getting the requisite senior academic staff to develop curricula and lay the academic foundation continued being a big challenge to all of us as Council and Management due to the urgent need at the institution. We placed another advertisement but, similar to the earlier one, the response was equally poor.

This compelled the Council to go back to the drawing board to find an alternative strategy that would unravel the task that was confronting us. This is how the head-hunting policy for the hiring of academic staff was born. The strategy entailed systematically scouting around in Kenyan universities and abroad, to identify and convince the identified staff to come and join Kisii University College. We came up with procedures and guidelines on how the University Management and existing senior staff would conduct the head-hunting process.

Those involved were assigned specific targets in a bid to approach specific senior lecturers in the identified disciplines. We used various networks to approach, talk and persuade those lecturers to join our institution. This process was systematically executed.

Whenever we identified someone who showed interest to join us, we requested for his updated Curriculum Vitae (CV) and relevant academic credentials. The testimonials then underwent careful scrutiny by a standing *ad-hoc* committee for eventual approval or otherwise. This rigorous procedure paid off in the long-run.

We managed to lure well-trained academicians who became pioneer lecturers in the new faculties and schools. The head-hunting strategy enabled us to recruit various cadres of academic staff some of whom eventually got appointed as Deans and Directors of the newly created schools, faculties and directorates.

Thus, by 2010, we had managed to hire basic academic staff for each and every academic field, which was on offer at the institution. The staff's first assignment was to develop new curricula for the schools and faculties. The supportive Council did not hesitate to approve funds for this noble venture.

I greatly admired the way the newly recruited staff worked with determination. They vigorously engaged various stakeholders in the development of the new curricula. On schedule, the College Academic Board had them validated as was the requirement. The end result was 35 curricula that were approved by the College Academic Board at the start of 2010. We then forwarded them to the Egerton University Senate for approval as required by university regulations and rules.

However, it was saddening to note that while we tried to run, Egerton University Management was hell-bent to pull us backwards as was the case with other activities. We faced hurdles in having the curricula approved by the University Senate. Worse yet, the Senate delayed in giving us official response on the fate of the curricula. It should be noted that these documents were submitted to Egerton and we did not get a response over a period of seven months. This got us really worried. We had raced to beat the deadline so that the Joint Admissions Board (JAB) -now the Kenya Universities and Colleges Central Placement Services (KUCCPS)-would allocate us students for the new academic programmes. It was saddening that Egerton University was not willing to assist us achieve that noble initiative.

The outright lack of willingness by Egerton University to approve our academic programmes was becoming an insurmountable obstacle. Days were moving fast and JAB was not going to allocate us students to be taught by the many lecturers we had recruited. This could put us in a real mess. We were going to be accused of having several lecturers on the payroll that had no work to do to justify their payment.

It is usually not in my nature to swim against the current, unless the situation begs me to. It was now a do or die situation for us. As the Kisii University College Academic Board, we made a bold step and declared to JAB our student capacity. We presented the thirty five degree programmes and requested to be given students. We made it clear that our programmes were yet to be approved by the Egerton University Senate.

We were overwhelmed with joy when our college was allocated about five hundred students for the various academic programmes. Even before they reported, we were very much aware that this decision had enabled our student population to shoot up from about three hundred to over eight hundred. This was going to be a major boost to our plans of becoming a fully chartered university.

You may think that this was now the end of our tribulations; far from it! In a JAB meeting held at Maseno University, our senior, the Vice Chancellor of Egerton University openly accused our institution of having unprocedurally declared capacity in programmes that had not been approved by the University Senate as enshrined in the universities' rules and regulations.

At its face value, this assertion could be seen as valid. It meant that students were admitted to academic programmes that did not exist as they had not been approved by the Senate and this anomaly would be met with sanctions. One of the consequences would be the withdrawal of students allocated to our college and censoring the Principal.

I pensively listened as the accusations against our college were being levelled. Then, I thought it was proper for me to take the bull by the horns and give our side of the story. I lifted my hand to be allowed by the Chairman of the JAB at that time, Prof. Fredrick Onyango, who was also the Vice Chancellor of Maseno University to give me a chance to give a rebuttal to the assertions of the Egerton University Vice Chancellor.

I clearly stated that the College Academic Board had submitted the new curricula for approval several months earlier and as far as we were concerned, the Egerton University Senate was sitting on the report. I went on to elaborate that, as a college, we were at a loss on what to do when we found ourselves in a situation where time was fast running out, yet we were being derailed from mounting new academic programmes for unclear reasons.

"We urgently need the new students because we have already recruited over sixty lecturers. The college now has seventy academic staff. It would be completely irregular to be paying the seventy members of the academic staff who would not have work to do," I added.

My sentiments seemed to stir the room as the situation became tense. I finished my remarks by throwing the ball squarely in the doorstep of the Egerton University Senate. This was to the annoyance and chagrin of the Vice Chancellor. "The Senate is not assisting us as required to develop and mount new programmes and instead it appears to be hell-bent stifling the growth of the young college," I said as I took my seat.

As expected, my remarks raised fireworks in the meeting. Some Vice Chancellors sided with their colleague while many others stood with me. I vividly remember what the then Vice Chancellor of Masinde Muliro University of Science and

Technology (MMUST) the late Prof. Barasa Wangira said. Prof. Wangira argued candidly that what Kisii University College was undergoing was not new.

He averred that in several instances in the past, JAB had allowed constituent colleges to admit students to new programmes that were not yet approved by the Senate on condition that the programmes would be availed for the Senate approval as soon as possible. My victory in this critical conversation appeared to be a bitter pill which the Vice Chancellor of Egerton University had to swallow.

Prof. Onyango ordered that the students who had been selected to join Kisii University College be allowed to remain in the institution. He also directed that the Egerton University Senate assess the academic programmes with the aim of approving them for eventual implementation.

It was another milestone for the nascent college and me as the Principal.

However, as would be expected, the Egerton University Vice Chancellor was not happy with what had transpired. But I knew that we had made a major accomplishment for the fledgling institution; with the directive of JAB he had no option but have our programmes approved.

Out of this unfortunate incident, I learnt that a mother University can do everything within its power to strangle the progress of its constituent colleges. Sometimes, the Vice Chancellor may tend to be condescending. Since he or she is your boss, he may expect that you should always supplicate to his or her whims.

Put in another way, if for one reason or another, some disagreement emerges between the two institutions, the leadership at the Main University may try to frustrate the constituent college as it happened in our case.

As I look back, I trace where this injustice meted on our college by its Main University started. The undermining and blackmail of the institution goes back to the time it was a Campus of Egerton University.

For reasons beyond my understanding, Egerton University perceived Kisii Campus as an unworthy appendage that deserved little or no attention. Indeed, before the institution became a constituent college, there were concerted attempts to close it on flimsy grounds. Those pushing for its closure were top honchos at the Main University who claimed that the Campus was not viable since it was located in a remote 'village' far away from the Main University.

There were other falsehoods that were peddled at the time concerning the Campus. One of them was that the institution stood on land which was too small for a Campus. This was false. The true story is that the institution sits on 63 acres of land. In my wildest imagination, I would not understand why someone would lie to the government and the general public that the institution had less than ten acres of land.

Worse yet, I am informed that in the late 1990s and early 2000, Egerton University periodically dismantled facilities at the Campus. During this vandalism, all movable facilities in the science labs were vandalized. They were carted away to the Main Campus in the pretext that science courses were unpopular with most students at Kisii Campus. It was not true! With their equipment taken away, the science students were compelled to transfer to the Main University at Njoro to complete their studies.

Furthermore, between 1994 and when the institution became a Constituent College, there was no single project which was undertaken at the institution. With most projects at the institution paralysed, the Kisii campus came to the brink of closure. I was made to understand that it was through the intervention of Gusii leaders, led by Senior Politician, Mzee Simeon Nyachae, that the government was prevailed upon not to close the campus. The Egerton University Council's recommendation to have us discontinued failed once again. Nyachae, who passed on recently, was an influential administrator, politician and businessman who hails from the Kisii region.

This narrative provides the historical and political context in which I found myself in when I took over as the substantive Principal of Kisii University College. This is the institution which would eventually become a full-fledged University. I took over the leadership of the institution when it was at its knees and led by absentee acting principals. I am happy because the institution has now taken off, and there is no looking back. Our ultimate desire is to make Kisii University a centre of excellence in learning, research, innovation and community outreach.

Biographer's Note:

KANU owned Kenya Times *newspaper, which has since folded, reported on June 16, 2003 that there were deliberate plans by Egerton University Management to block Kisii Campus from becoming a Constituent College as it was becoming a burden to the mother institution. This sad development was countered by a section of leaders and the story was prominently covered in the media. For instance, the* Daily Nation *report of March 31, 2003 on the subject blamed the University leadership for failing to prepare a development budget for the Campus. However, the Management had previously denied such reports. Further, the* Daily Nation *reported on April 1, 2003 that reports of the University's lack of commitment to the development of Kisii Campus were untrue and misleading. Due to this perceived bad blood between the university leadership and students, the then Vice Chancellor Ezra Maritim received a rude reception at Kisii Campus, as was reported on March 29, 2003 by the* Daily Nation. *The VC had made good his plans to visit the Campus after postponing the journey, as reported on March 26, 2003 by* Daily Nation.*

Furthermore, on September 23, 2003, the Daily Nation *reported that plans to move Egerton University's Kisii Campus had been shelved after the Government issued the institution with the title deed for the contentious land it occupied. "The University Council had twice threatened to close the college and move students to the Njoro Main Campus because of the land row," the paper reported. One of such threats had been reported by the same paper on July 30, 2003.*

Developing the University Strategic Plan

I will not belabour to say that it has been an up-hill battle to get Kisii University where it is today. As the person who has been in the thick of things, since the University was a constituent college of Egerton University, I can attest that we have walked a long journey. This journey has not ended. We are yet to transform the institution fully for it to take its rightful place as one of the top institutions of higher learning in Kenya and the world.

One may argue that I am being overly ambitious but that is far from the truth. Although fairly nascent, Kisii University has made major strides in recent years. As the proverbial boy who washed his hands and was allowed to dine with the kings, our university has won the right to occupy its rightful space at the national and regional universities' podia.

This journey would have taken longer had we yielded to the pressures and negativities that came at us from diverse corners. As already indicated, I went through fire to become the founding Principal and later the Vice Chancellor of the institution.

I recall that as much as those opposed to my work at the Constituent College placed hurdles along my way, it did not cross my mind that I become a cry-baby. My wife Mallion became a strong pillar when the world was caving in on me. She is a prayerful woman. She always encouraged me that the battle before me was not mine and God was always in charge.

I therefore resolved to swim in the turbulent waters with the realization that history would judge me harshly if I left the institution worse than I found it. In reality, I always pitied the opposing forces. They seemed not to understand that while fighting me, they were undermining an embryonic institution, which needed their support for the sake of posterity.

It is clear that the people who were waging war against the fledgling institution were driven by greed and self-centredness. It blurred their vision and clogged their minds.

They chose to fabricate lies in their attempt to paint me as an incompetent manager who should be kicked out of the institution.

When I look back, I wonder how evil people can be. Issues like seeing the Council getting accused of over committing the government by tendering projects beyond the available budget were unfounded and malicious. These are people who probably wanted that I not only lose my job but also end up in prison. Thank God, they were not the judge, jury and executioner.

It is Mark Twain who said that *a lie gets halfway around the world before truth has a chance to get its pants on*. These lies are often amplified by the media for various reasons. Sometimes, I found it extremely difficult to respond to the kind of accusations levelled against me. It appeared that in many instances, my detractors wanted me to be convicted without being heard.

The governance and management of Kenyan universities, as is the case of institutions of higher education worldwide, are guided by defined policies that are recognised by the government and other relevant agencies. In the Kenyan context, these policies and guidelines include the 2012 Universities' Act as reviewed in 2016. It stipulates that establishing a constituent college is a transitional arrangement, which is supposed to enable an institution transit to a full-fledged institution in, ideally, a three-year period.

So, from the very beginning the Council and Management of Kisii Constituent College understood that they had an onerous responsibility to expand and transition the institution into a full-fledged university. Come what may, this mission was unstoppable. We prioritized strategic and visionary leadership.

To achieve this mission, we were required to put in place various administrative and academic structures, apart from the development of physical infrastructure. This included the development of policies, rules and regulations to govern the institution.

As a guiding framework for the development of the institution, we formulated a ten-year Strategic Plan. The plan would guide the overall development of the Constituent College into a full-fledged university. The Strategic Plan contained the Vision, Mission and core values of the college. It encapsulated how the college objectives would be implemented and the specific resources needed for the implementation.

Specifically, the Strategic Plan was based on the core mandate of the university, including teaching, research, innovation and community extension. One critical highlight of the Strategic Plan was the provision of hierarchical leadership and governance structure. In the teaching and research section, we developed a clear academic organogram, which encompassed the Deputy Principal in charge of Academic and Students Affairs (DPASA). As a policy, the occupant of this position is required to report to the Principal.

Below the DPASA were two registrars, one in charge of Student Affairs and the second one responsible for Research and Extension. Just below the registrars were Deans and Directors of Schools, who were followed by the Heads of Departments (HoDs). In the arrangement, the HoDs were basically the immediate implementers of academic policies on teaching, research and extension.

In addition, the Strategic Plan encapsulated the Administrative and Human Resources system of the college. This section was to be headed by the Deputy Principal in charge of Administration, Planning and Finance (DPAPF). He too reported to the Principal as per the laid down regulations.

Below the DPAPF was the Registrar in charge of Administration and the Finance Officer. This was followed by various administrative units including Human Resource, Central services and Halls. These administrative units were headed by Senior Administrative Officers. Below the administrative heads of sections were HoDs in charge of specific administrative units such as Transport, Halls, Maintenance, Human Resource and Security.

Guided by the Strategic Plan, we came up with priority areas that required to be implemented as soon as possible. These included academics, research, human resource, financial management and infrastructural development.

In this regard, the Strategic Plan provided specific activities and initiatives that were to be implemented in order for the college to eventually transit to a fully-fledged University. More importantly, guided by the document, we developed various faculties and schools that formed the bedrock of academic programmes.

Concerning human resource development, we looked into various cadres of personnel that were required for the college to take off. This provided a window for the recruitment of new staff, and capacity building and training of the available teaching staff.

The development of human resource further entailed identifying existing gaps in the area of non-teaching staff. Hiring of new staff was necessary in ensuring proper and efficient delivery of services.

By 2012, we had succeeded in establishing the requisite academic and administrative arrangements for the smooth running of the institution. This was critical for creating a strong foundation of the Constituent College in terms of human resource development, programme implementation and infrastructural development.

Infrastructural Facelift

Someone who was in Kisii University before the year 2000 would bear witness that the institution has metamorphosed in terms of infrastructural development. I joined the institution when it had run-down and limited physical infrastructure as a result of many years of neglect by its mother institution. For example, what was passed as a library was a storeroom measuring fifty square metres. It had dusty old and out-dated books on the shelves. The makeshift library had limited and rickety furniture.

This is why we placed emphasis in the infrastructural development and starting with strategic projects including the library, lecture halls and lecture theatres, hostels and the ICT centre. Although we have made significant strides in this front, I have to admit that development of physical infrastructure has been one daunting challenge.

As is the case with most projects in public institutions, the projects at Kisii University were supposed to be implemented depending on funding from the National Government as per the approved Annual Printed Estimates. In the case of our projects, after awarding the tenders and receiving approval, the contractors moved to the site to start the construction.

However, the catch was that the contractors required regular payments as per the payment certificates, which they submitted to us from time to time. The certificates are usually drawn based on the amount of work done as per project milestones. These certificates started piling because the rate at which the government was releasing project funds to us was not in tandem with the speed at which our projects were progressing. This made some of the contractors to start slowing down their work. It caused delays in the realization of our cherished vision of developing state of the art physical infrastructure.

This challenge is not confined to Kisii University. Many public projects that are funded by the Exchequer are hardly finished on time. The worst case scenario is that many of the projects completely stall. This often compels the intended users, individuals and other stakeholders to speculate that there is laxity either being perpetuated by the contractor or the management of the institution or both.

Struggling to pay our contractors and/or asking them not to abandon the projects since there is anticipated payment of the owed arrears is one of the major challenge that we have faced over the years. In this connection, in the recent past, I have made several visits to the Ministry of Education and Treasury to request for the release of the project funds. These visits do yield fruits, albeit slowly. The worst effect of delayed payments is the likelihood of the cost of the project going up over time due to accruing interest and compensation claims.

However, we did not reduce ourselves to cry-babies. With this frustrating and yet enlightening understanding that government resources will never be enough, we have sought to find financial solutions to some of the challenges confronting the institution.

The university has continued to focus on implementing the stipulated projects as captured in the Strategic Plan. In particular, we opted to give priority to projects that directly affect our core mandate, including the Library Complex and lecture halls. So, we in a way gave bias for the two critical projects. We ensured that we paid the contractors promptly for the priority projects so that they do not abandon the site.

This is how we managed to complete the ultra-modern library and ten lecture theatres in time. The facilities were ready before the end of 2012 when the contractors handed them over to the University. The completion of these priority projects was a major milestone for the University in terms of infrastructural development.

It appeared that we were right when we prioritized the library and the lecture halls. It did not take long for us to realize that private investors in the neighbourhood had spotted an opportunity to invest in the construction of hostels to house students and staff. High-rise buildings and flats fit for students' and staff accommodation came up in Nyamage and Mwembe area adjacent to the University faster than anticipated.

Soon, it turned out that the University policy dictated only First Year students would be accommodated in the university hostels while the rest sought private accommodation. Clearly, it dawned on us that the official hostels we were constructing were not going to be occupied to capacity.

In a pragmatic way and with the approval of the Council, the building which was intended to be a hostel complex was turned into a tuition block. Thus, when the first phase of the project was completed, we converted it into lecture halls and offices for lecturers and professors.

The Sakagwa Tuition Complex, named after an acclaimed Gusii traditional prophet, is now a landmark building in the

University. I am happy to state that with our Strategic Plan being followed, we do not have any stalled project in our institution. In fact, the construction of the second phase of the tuition complex is at an advanced stage and should be ready for use before the end of 2020.

The university has in recent times accelerated the implementation of the remaining projects. This happened after the government heeded to our humble request and increased our share of the development budget in the 2018/2019 Financial Year. Our request was based on the perceived urgent need to complete the projects so that they benefit our students and staff.

The fruits of the government's benevolent gesture can already be seen. The ICT centre has taken shape and it catches one's eye from as far as the Kisii-Kilgoris Road. This is despite the fact that the university is situated in fairly low ground and is sandwiched by tall indigenous and exotic trees and high rise privately-owned buildings. Construction of the amphitheatre is also in its final stages.

Of all the implemented projects, the ICT complex is a major flagship project, and the most ambitious one according to our strategic thinking. Envisioned to be a Vision 2030 Flagship Project, the ICT centre will house Information Technology offices as well as Entrepreneurship and Business Incubation offices, and Innovation Centre facilities.

Thus, upon completion, the ICT Complex will be the ICT hub of Kisii University. It will be the nerve centre of learning, research, business incubation and innovation. Thanks to the enhanced financial allocation from the National Treasury, the central structure, which is 70% of the project, will be ready for use in the course of 2021. The remaining 30% of the project will consist of two extended wings that will house administrative offices.

Away from the government funded projects, the university also managed to use its internally generated revenue to construct and complete some small and medium scale projects. These include the science complex, office space, the Nyasani Hostel, the Chancellor's Pavilion, the main university gate and several fish ponds. Our fisheries students use the ponds for their practical studies. The university also generates revenue from the project.

With hindsight, it can be said that Kisii University would not have been started if those opposed to it from the onset got their way. It is the National Government education policy that for an institution to be elevated to a full-fledged University, it needs to have at least fifty acres of land. Contrary to the falsehoods that were peddled, Kisii University Main Campus sits on 63 acres of land. Consequently, the available land is more than adequate to meet the policy requirements with respect to the size of land.

Additionally, working with communities in the broader Gusii region and with the support of the now defunct Gusii County Council, we managed to acquire seventy acres of land in Nyosia area in Nyaribari Chache Constituency. The land is about 13 km from the Main Campus. The piece of land was originally donated by former Senior Chief Musa Nyandusi to the now defunct Gusii County Council. And as good fortune would have it, Nyandusi's renowned son Simon Nyachae, supported the university in acquiring the land, which is a stone throw away from his rural residence.

The Nyosia land has turned out to be a major benchmarking site for students and farmers. This is where the university practices modern agriculture in terms of maize cultivation, dairy farming and horticulture. At the same time, we use the farm to provide hands on training to our students in the School of Agriculture and Natural Resource Management. We also provide free short-term training in agriculture to local farmers as part of the university's Corporate Social Responsibility (CSR) initiatives.

Kisii University also acquired 67 acres of land in Nyangweta area of South Mugirango Constituency. This happened after a fruitful engagement and dialogue with residents of the area. Also, in the current Nyamira County, the university obtained 15 acres of land in Kiamogake area in North Mugirango

Constituency. In total therefore, currently the university has over 200 acres of land.

It is envisaged that the land at Nyangweta will be used to establish the School of Environment and Natural Resource Management. Most of the land, which is now covered with exotic cypress trees will be reclaimed and planted with indigenous trees and flora. Also, there are plans to start a botanical garden on the land where indigenous plants with medicinal value will be planted while existing ones will be conserved. This will aid in conducting scientific research and testing the plants for their probable medical efficacy.

As Chief Executive Officer (CEO) of the University, I have to admit that due to scarcity of resources, we may take a longer time to develop these additional parcels of land. However, it is the vision of the university that the parcels will, in the long-run, benefit future generations. Literally speaking, we have acquired the parcels of land for posterity.

It is important to note that currently, in Gusii, most of the land has been subdivided to small portions. This does not only compromise the land's agricultural productivity but it also curtails space available for the development of public institutions and other facilities. It is envisioned that the parcels of land that are in the custody of Kisii University will eventually be used for the expansion of the institution in future.

Curriculum Relevant to the Times

While good physical infrastructure in an institution creates a congenial environment for learning, teaching, and research, academic success is also pegged on the type of curriculum that is implemented. The quality of the academic staff is fundamental too. So, we particularly placed emphasis in the establishment of appropriate academic systems in the institution. As mentioned earlier, when we were unable to recruit staff through advertisement, we turned to head-hunting to get requisite teaching personnel who were going to play a central role in the academic advancement of the institution.

In the head-hunting process, our preference was placed on PhD holders in various academic fields and specialities. This strategy entailed approaching senior academic staff already working in universities locally and abroad. Our main bait was promotions and elevation of the head-hunted staff to be Heads of Departments (HoDs) and Directors of institutes as well as giving them enhanced allowances. We also brought to the attention of the staff the fact that the university is situated in a highly productive agricultural area where food items and other living expenses were relatively low compared to other parts of Kenya. This strategy eventually worked very well and we were able to recruit many academic staff.

As we continued recruiting new academic staff, memories of what I witnessed at Moi University never escaped me. Thus, I treaded carefully, lest we plunge our young institution into a similar mess as happened at Moi. Our hiring approach had to be above board and free of ethnic and other exigencies not related to academics. This would guard against the potential impact on the quality of education. In this regard, I promised that I would not allow anything untoward to happen to a nascent institution of higher learning under my watch.

I had witnessed, in the 1990s and early 2000s, the serious negative impacts caused by the hiring of lecturers while disregarding their competencies. This greatly compromised quality education in the institution. Within a very short timeframe, this unprofessional recruitment made Moi University's standards of teaching and research plummet badly. This flip-flop in training standards has affected the university to date. At Kisii, we ensured that the process of hiring was as transparent as possible and was not shrouded in ethnic considerations and other forms of corruption.

It should be noted that during the head-hunting process, the University Management Board systematically scrutinised the academic credentials of the prospective staff. This included examining their certificates right from high school to university level. It was after the thorough scrutiny of one's academic and professional profile that a conclusion was reached whether to hire or not to hire the applicant.

The rigorous process paid off. We boast of some of the best academic staff in the country. These are the very academicians who are currently empowering our students with relevant knowledge, skills and competencies.

In this regard, since the award of Charter, the university has continued to utilize the expertise of the academic staff and other related stakeholders to offer the best training to our students. These stakeholders include regulatory agencies such as the Commission for University Education (CUE), the Council for Legal Education (CLE) and the Kenya Medical Practitioners and Dentists Board (KMPDB). With the support of these stakeholders, we have managed to develop and implement some of the most up-to-date market-suitable academic programmes, and other support facilities and services.

These programmes are rich in pedagogy, course content including relevant practical professional skills and competencies. In particular, most of our courses have looped in components of industrial attachment, internships and professional mentorship.

But we are not resting pretty yet. Our curricula are continuously reviewed and revised as the need arises. This is guided by feedback from academia, students and other stakeholders.

The University Management also allows the academic staff to benchmark with other institutions of higher learning in Kenya and other countries. Some of the institutions we are in collaboration with on our benchmark programme include University of Minnesota, East Tennessee State University, Arkansas Medical School, and University of Nanjing in China, University of Finland and University of Busan in South Korea. Locally, we collaborate with the Primate Research Institute, the Kenya Medical Research Institute (KEMRI), and the Kenya Forestry Research Institute (KEFRI), among others.

These collaborations have assisted staff and students exchange up-to-date skills and knowledge. In these arrangements, Kisii University students and staff visit the respective institutions to learn new ideas, skills and innovations. Students and staff from these collaborating institutions also visit our university from time to time for the same.

Furthermore, through the Fulbright programmes (an American Government supported project), various scholars visit our university to undertake research and teaching. Through other organisations such as Computer Aid (UK) and Books for Africa (USA), Kisii University has managed to receive and continues to receive a lot of teaching and research materials. The latest consignment from Books for Africa to our university contained over 40,000 books. This enriched our library even further. The organization has promised to deliver even more volumes.

Through these sources, we have stocked our library with some of the best teaching and reference materials. Additionally, our laboratories now have computers and other ICT facilities including smart boards. The ICT resources have seen us slowly, but steadily; embark on a journey of replacing white boards with smart boards. This modernization of our teaching facilities is a correct step in the right direction. We have also established the e-learning platform, which our lecturers use to deliver their teaching in an up-to-date and modernistic manner.

I have to confess that one of the biggest challenges universities in Africa face is in research and innovation. There is inadequate research funding and limited exposure to relevant research organisations and industry. In many instances, scholars in African universities are highly constrained in undertaking research and innovation activities, which form part of the core mandate of universities.

Even so, all is not lost. The National Government through the Ministry of Educations (MoE), the Commission for University Education (CUE) and other stakeholders is encouraging people in academic and research institutions to engage in research and innovation. Research and innovation is critical in assisting our country reach higher levels of socio-economic development as projected in Vision 2030 and the United Nations' Sustainable Development Goals (SDGs). In particular, research in diverse areas will assist our country find solutions to problems facing various sectors of the economy.

Within this broad context, Kisii University Management and Council encourage its members of academia to engage in research, publication and innovation. We have created the Division of Research and Extension to assist our nascent scholars to pursue knowledge creation and its application. Staff at tutorial and lecturer level are regularly trained and mentored. We focus on research skills such as development of research proposals for funding and presentation of research findings in conferences, seminars and symposia, locally and globally.

Furthermore, staff and students are encouraged to conduct innovative activities in their fields of study. This is done mainly through the provision of mentorship programmes and provision of seed funding to emerging researchers and innovators. This has borne fruits in recent years. For example, it has enabled our students to make patentable landmark innovations especially in the areas of ICT and innovation, smart farming and business incubation. Through these initiatives, many of our lecturers are actively involved in research and have succeeded in having their research work published in high impact, peer-reviewed international journals and books.

The University Council has come up with a research kitty, which allows the academic staff to be funded internally. This is done through submission of research proposals that are competitively evaluated by a team of reviewers. Those that meet the stipulated criteria are eventually funded by the university.

The university is undertaking all these endeavours in order to motivate and impact our individual students and staff in their academic and scholarly initiatives. Overall, this will improve the institution's academic ranking globally. For instance, in the recent Web-Metric Ranking, our university took position 21 out of 73 Kenyan universities. I am certain that with the many research initiatives that we have put in place, this is going to improve in the coming years.

Furthermore, the University Senate identifies academic and research champions of the year that are recognised by the Management and given special awards. Through these diverse programmes, Kisii University has seen great improvements in teaching, research and innovation in recent years.

From Constituent College to University

We owned up to the responsibility to transition the institution to a full-fledged university. We focused on the formulation of regulations and policies that would govern the institution once it got elevated to the coveted status. This was a major requirement without which the institution would not get a Charter. The governance and administrative structures included the development of the university statutes, and rules and regulations to run the institution. This enormous and critical task was executed conclusively in 2012, a year before the award of Charter.

The process of developing the university administrative and governance structures was tedious and thorough. It involved team work and creating rapport amongst the teaching and non-academic staff, students, the Council and other stakeholders. The other stakeholders included religious and political leaders, various non-governmental organisations and other external interest groups.

With the support of existing internal and external stakeholders, we formed various committees to handle different tasks. One would handle the development of the Charter as another initiated the development of the statutes. Other committees tackled the promulgation of the students' handbook and examinations policy, streamlining of academic programmes as approved by the Egerton University Senate and the Commission of Higher Education (CHE), now the Commission for University Education (CUE).

It took us several months to develop these critical documents. We also had to continue improving other areas of the college. We developed and reorganized existing programmes and existing physical infrastructure among other projects.

These critical activities proceeded concurrently with the recruitment and development of both academic and non-academic staff of the institution. Along this was the promulgation of several policy documents that would guide the strategic implementation of various activities in the institution. These included human resource policy, staff establishment policy, and the anti-corruption policy, the code of conduct policy, library operations policy and the IT policy, among others.

Becoming the Founding Vice Chancellor

We were pleased to receive a letter from the Commission for University Education (CHE) in 2012. In the communiqué, the Commission expressed intent to inspect our institution for the purpose of award of Charter. This was another milestone that the constituent college was expected to surmount before it would acquire the much sought-after status of a chartered university.

As procedure demands, the Commission first sent us a self-assessment document, which we were supposed to use for self-evaluation. This would also act as a springboard for getting the institution ready for the eventual assessment by the Commission. This inevitably made us to work even harder. We burnt the midnight oil to avoid any unfortunate situation that might arise during the inspection.

The Commission kept its word and visited the institution toward the end of 2012 for thorough inspection. The intensive inspection was in line with the Commission's standards and guidelines. It was the role of the inspectors to ensure that there were no lapses as far as the preparedness of the institution to become a full-fledged university was concerned.

The Commission particularly examined the newly developed University Charter document, Strategic Plan, policies and regulations. It also took into account whether we had requisite human resource including teaching and non-teaching staff. In addition, they examined existing infrastructure and other academic and extra-curricular facilities.

After the rigorous evaluation processes and procedures that lasted for five days, the Commission went back to Nairobi to compile a report and eventually communicated to us that the Constituent College had met the requisite criteria for the award of Charter. The CUE report was an indicator that our college was on the homestretch to becoming a full-fledged university. The next step was to prepare for the award of charter.

I will be far from the truth if I fail to confess here that I was filled with zeal and anxiety on the days leading to the award of charter. The fact that we were going to play host to the Head of State did not make it any easier for me. According to the Constitution and the 2012 Universities' Act as reviewed in 2016, it is the prerogative of the Head of State to award charter to all Kenyan universities.

We therefore committed ourselves in finalizing the various activities that would lead to that milestone in our journey. This entailed preparing the entire college community and other stakeholders to be ready for the big day. As I later found out, this process can create anxiety amongst the entire University Management and the Council. This is rightly so because the award of charter is both a historical and landmark event for the university, and indeed the whole country.

On the material day of the award of charter, a university is given various instruments of governance. These include the appointment of Chancellor, Members of Council, and installation of the University maze, among other things.

Eventually, with a lot of excitement, the institution was awarded Charter in February 6th, 2013 by President Mwai Kibaki.

It is interesting to note that in the days preceding the award of Charter, there were high level intrigues. There was burning curiosity on who would occupy the strategic positions when the institution becomes the new kid in the block of public universities in the country.

As expounded earlier, our country is quite interesting when it comes to appointment and installation of personnel to key positions. The process can evoke intense excitement, anxiety, overdrive lobbying and even backstabbing. Unfortunately, universities are not exempted from such intrigues.

It was against this backdrop that I came to learn from various sources that there was massive campaign aimed at bringing my career as the CEO of the institution to an abrupt end. Plans had been hatched to ensure that I would be edged out of the appointment. This was to happen notwithstanding my academic, professional, management skills and leadership experience in higher education. And all this despite the fact that I had led the institution from a constituent college to getting a charter!

The ugly side of Kenyan politics sprung up and was very much in play, with some Members of Parliament openly saying that as much as I had worked hard to develop the institution, time had come for me to leave. I further learnt that a number of senior professors who originate from the larger Gusii were lobbying for the position of Vice Chancellor. It was rather ironical that these very professors had never set foot in the institution, notwithstanding the fact that it was situated at the doorstep of their rural homes. Ironically, this was the first time they were pretentiously creating an impression of having the institution so close to their hearts.

I further learnt that this lobbying involved lengthy meetings in top hotels, sometimes extending to the wee hours of the night. Other people went an extra mile by approaching the highest office in the land, the Presidency, to lobby for their cronies. According to them, compared to myself, there were other professors who were 'better qualified' for the position.

To this day, I recall this narrative and keep wondering the criteria the lobbyists were using to rank the seniority or capabilities of the people they had in mind. However, it should be noted that in the world of academia, seniority is majorly gauged through teaching, research, publishing, and administration and governance experience. The more I examined the credentials of those who were being touted to be the better suited candidates for the position against the stipulated yardsticks, the more I realized that most of them were not in any way superior to me.

Apart from serving as the founding Principal of the institution, I had worked for several years as a lecturer and later as a professor. I had taught at Moi University where I rose from the position of lecturer to a full professor. In the area of research, I had published extensively in high impact peer-reviewed international journals. I had also authored books and made chapter contributions in many other books.

In academic administration, I served twice as HoD, and had been assigned various critical assignments. For example, I was in charge of curriculum development. I had been director of post-graduate studies and a member of the University Senate. I had also served in several *ad hoc* committees of the institution. These included the Senate *ad hoc* committee on the creation of the School of Business and Economics, and the *ad hoc* committee on the restructuring of the School of Post-Graduate Studies.

By any chance, these credentials positioned me as a formidable candidate for the position of Vice Chancellor. I had experience and academic grounding capable of steering the young university to greater heights.

I came to a sad realization that to be seen as a professor in the Kenyan situation, probably what I had achieved in the United States, Moi University and Kisii College, was inconsequential to other people. To them, a professor was someone with lots of political connections. It was someone who attended various social forums, schmoozed with the powerful and licked their boots. I have to admit that these are the very things I have never been good at.

I was made to understand that those who were against me had reached a stage where they were very sure that they were going to get their way. They knew that they had knocked the doors of the right offices. To them, they had touched the right buttons. They knew that, in the end, the government was going to install their preferred candidate as the Vice Chancellor and they were going to have the last laugh. Thus, obviously, it must have caught them flatfooted when I was appointed as the acting Vice Chancellor of Kisii University, a position into which I later got confirmed.

In this regard, President Kibaki was not a man you could bully or manipulate for narrow personal or political interests. He is a scholar in his own right. Through his state machinery, he knew he was right when he entrusted the university leadership in my hands.

At this point, I wish to thank the church for living to its righteous calling and standing with me during the turbulent period. The church leaders led by the long-serving Kisii Catholic Diocese Bishop Joseph Mairura Okemwa, supported by Father Mandere and Father Obanyi, currently the Bishop of Kakamega Catholic Diocese, among other members of the clergy were of great support. These leaders played a critical role in countering the malevolent forces that were hell-bent in making sure that I was not appointed as the founding Vice Chancellor of Kisii University.

One of the reasons why the church stood with me is because most of them had closely interacted with me and understood the kind of work I had done in developing the institution. Additionally, as a practicing Christian, I had cultivated a cordial working relationship with the church.

It is also important to note that these church leaders are also well-educated and understand matters of academics very well. Some went through some of the best universities in Rome and other parts of the world. They had exposure to the best leadership practices, devoid of political manipulation. These leaders appreciated my work in turning the institution around and getting it to the status of qualifying for the award of a charter. I also believe that the church leaders prayed and their prayers worked. They also used the local and national church network to reach the executive and argue my case.

Even so, as we approached the day of the award of charter, I witnessed more intrigues from even the very people who were supposed to assist us in organizing for the event. Indeed, some of these misguided individuals were plotting to wreck the boat from within.

As preparations got underway, one of the top officials from CUE, the body that was responsible for guiding us to draw the programme for the award of charter was sabotaging us. Very late into the preparation for the event, the official asked us to make unwarranted changes to the programme. Some of these changes appeared not to add value to the forthcoming function. They included changing the venue where the function was to be held and adding new names to the list of speakers. He was also trying to push for the change of the content on the official speeches that had already been dexterously developed by the university staff. This official continued taking us in circles and when I realised that he was up to no good, I told members of the University Council to strategically ignore him and never budge to his uninformed orders.

"I think the days of Nyayo era when you were a very powerful figure in a university where your word was the law are way behind us. Wake up and understand that this is a new order," I told this official who during President Moi's time had served as a Vice Chancellor in one of the Kenyan public universities.

Material Day for Award of Charter

The day for the award of charter, February 6th, 2013, was fast approaching. Although, together with the Council, we had ensured that everything was in place, I did not know what lay ahead of me that day. It was a rather awkward situation to be in. I had not known my fate on the issue of being appointed acting Vice Chancellor.

I am an early riser and by 7.30 am, I was already in the office on that day. However, I was not prepared for the shock that awaited me. To say the least, I was petrified when I entered the office and saw two elderly professors who were already dressed in academic regalia, comfortably seated there.

It appears that through political lobbying, they had been promised the new position of acting Vice Chancellor. At this juncture, even I was not very sure that I would get the appointment because I had not received any communication until the last minute (on the very day of award of charter).

"What's the matter? How do you enter someone's office in his absence and even go ahead to occupy his seat?" I asked them. They were dumbfounded.

It quickly crossed my mind that these were individuals with sinister motives. It later turned out that they were expecting to be appointed to head the institution. Think about it, these are people who had never stepped in the institution to offer any advice on how to develop it or even for purposes of paying courtesy. Here they were now trying to take over the institution's leadership through the backdoor. I must have gathered some rare courage and ordered them to get out and let me prepare for the long programme that lay ahead. They reluctantly obliged.

No sooner had I settled down than the Minister of Education, Prof. Margaret Kamar, was ushered into my office by my orderlies. "Here is your appointment letter and congratulations," she announced as she passed an envelope to me after exchanging greetings and other pleasantries.

I was especially excited when I opened the envelope and took out the letter. My eyes radiated with joy as I read the official document appointing me to the position of Vice Chancellor, although in acting capacity. I knew that God had enabled me overcome a major hurdle in my academic leadership progression.

Meanwhile, the two professors whom I had ejected out of my office were not done yet with their unfortunate theatrics. When I stepped out of the office, I saw them moving up and down the corridor of the administration building. One of them started arranging the Academic Procession for the award of charter. The venue used for the event would later become known as the Graduation Square, which houses a magnificent Chancellor's Pavilion building whose picturesque and architectural design is a marvel. I ignored the two professors as they continued with their sideshows, which for me were an unfortunate embarrassment to them.

The behaviour of these two professors was, to say the least, completely out of tune with the stipulated procedure of such an important and historical function. An event of that magnitude requires that when guests arrive, they should sign visitors' book and wait to be taken for an official tour of the institution. It is only after this tour that the Academic Procession heads to the official ground for the ceremony, having also restated the protocols of the ceremony.

Soon President Kibaki, his entourage, invited guests, the university fraternity and members of the public took their sitting arrangement at the stipulated venue. I discovered another hitch that would have been a total embarrassment. I did not have my maiden speech and my personal assistant who had carried it for me was nowhere to be seen! This was a relatively well articulated academic speech, which would not have been easy to paraphrase. Definitely, this was another covert sabotage but I had to be smarter.

I cannot recall how I quickly vanished out of the VIP stand without being noticed and returned to my office, which is about 200 metres away. I opened my computer and reprinted the speech and made it back to my seat before my absence was noticed. The melodious musical entertainments that were being showcased carried away the attention of most of the dignitaries and members of the public to the extent that they were unable to notice my absence.

However, my wife who sat not far from the VIP area later told me that she had noticed my absence and known that something was amiss. Nonetheless, she could not tell what was amiss and as protocol dictated, she could not get out and lend me support, if any at all. She would tell me later that she said a special prayer for the Lord's assistance to overcome whatever obstacle was standing on my way during this historic moment.

As things will go, another lapse occurred soon after. We were under strict instructions to offer short and thematic speeches that were relevant to the historic occasion. In particular, the Chairman of the Council, the late Prof. Joseph Nyasani, was supposed to give a brief speech centred on welcoming the guests. He was then required to make another brief statement concerning the progress of the university. Of course, we had prepared a speech for him, which was tailored to those requirements.

To the surprise of many, Prof. Nyasani rejected the official speech. He said it was too shallow and did not capture his understanding and viewpoint of Kisii University and higher education in general. He then pulled out a 15-page speech from his pocket, written in a colourful language. Since he was a gifted philosopher and a linguist to match, he went through it amid reaction from the audience. He took over thirty minutes to deliver his speech to the bemusement of the dignitaries and other guests. Obviously, the speech was off the mark and not appropriate for the occasion. It also took an inordinate long time and the contents neither reflected nor enhanced the key objective of the historical occasion at hand.

At the end of the ceremony, one of the officials in charge of protocol from CUE confronted him. He told the professor to his face that he had gone astray by giving an irrelevant speech that did not meet the expectations of the occasion. Prof. Nyasani was very infuriated.

"Give me the physical address of that officer. I will send him all my philosophy books and publications to show him how much I have accomplished as a scholar," Prof. Nyasani whispered to me later. But he never made good his promise.

Apart from these hitches, the ceremony went on smoothly. You will tell that the President really enjoyed the pieces of entertainment from students and invited artists. The climax was when President Kibaki enthroned the founding Chancellor of the University Prof. Godfrey Muriuki as was required.

Prof. Muriuki is a long serving History Professor who has now retired. He had spent most of his academic career life, spanning over fifty years, teaching History at the University of Nairobi. Prof. Muriuki was one time the HoD and Dean of the School of Arts in Kenya's oldest University. He taught and provided academic leadership to many, leaving behind a rich legacy as an accomplished scholar.

In addition, Prof. Muriuki is one of the pioneer history professors in Kenya. Many of his age mates are either retired or hold emeritus professorships. Several of these distinguished Kenyan academicians, including Prof. Nyasani, have since passed on.

For Prof. Nyasani, it appears that he had a premonition of his death. I remember he once publicly said that his goal as the founding Chairman of the Council was to guide Kisii to become a full-fledged university. And once this happened, he was free to retire. For sure, he relinquished the Council Chair position in 2013 immediately after the university received its charter, leading to the reconstitution of the Council. Sadly, Nyasani passed away in 2016.

I remember after taking President Kibaki around the university to see and inaugurate some finished projects such as the ultra-modern library, he was quite impressed and congratulated us for work well done. He promised to continue supporting the institution in terms of funding. At the end of the ceremony, he stayed in the institution until late, which was uncommon for a Head of State.

Something interesting happened that evening away from the institution. Kisii University, being the first institution of higher learning in Kisii, many local residents did not have a clear understanding of the university's administrative and governance structure. So, when they heard that I had not been enthroned as the Chancellor of the university, they felt cheated. "How can our son be made to be Vice Chancellor after steering the institution to its current status?" they wondered.

To them, they thought that this was a demotion. They did not understand that a Chancellor is basically a ceremonial head of the institution whose main function was that of a titular head mainly presiding over the award of degrees during graduation ceremonies. They did not know that the Vice Chancellor is the CEO of the university in charge of the day to day operations. So, they wanted to organize protestations until the government reversed its decision of not appointing me to the Chancellor position.

It took the attention and intervention of a few people who understood the universities' administrative system to convince the masses who had gathered not to demonstrate. But by the time they were convinced, people had gathered in large numbers, made placards and rehearsed the *'Haki Yetu'* song, which is popular during protests in Kenya. People were just about to match to the university when they were eventually convinced that the right thing had been done and they dispersed.

That night, I went to bed well satisfied that Kisii University had marked a new chapter for further advancement. On the whole, we continued to apply the existing Strategic Plan, and, also, ensured that we operationalized the statutes and policies that had been developed to guide the growth of the institution to become a world class university of the 21st century.

It is important to note, as stated elsewhere, that Kisii University is guided by a clear Vision, Mission, and Core Values. The vision of the university is: *'To be a world class university in the advancement of social welfare, research and academic excellence.'* while the mission is; *'To train high level human resource that meets the development needs of the country and international labour market, and to sustain production of high quality research and consultancy, and dissemination of knowledge, skills and competencies for the advancement of humanity.'*

So far, the Mission and Vision of the university have continued to guide development and expansion of the institution to date.

Campuses Phase One

It is worth noting that one of the key highlights of President Mwai Kibaki's leadership is what could be termed as the 'demystification of university education in Kenya'. For many years, higher education was perceived to be a preserve for a few top achievers as determined by national examinations. This, coupled with the limited number of vacancies in the then existing universities, denied a large number of eligible students a chance to join the institutions of higher learning.

President Kibaki, who once served as President Daniel Moi's deputy, showed qualities of a great leader. He identified a gaping discrepancy and solved it by implementing a policy of awarding charters to a number of existing educational institutions. Perhaps Kisii University would not have become a full-fledged University were it not for the Kibaki presidency and his foresight.

Following the initiative of the national government, Kisii University developed a plan to take university education closer to the people. This saw the establishment of a number of satellite campuses in strategic towns. This was a welcome move that would see many Kenyans access university education, which was, for many years, a preserve of a few elites.

Opening the campuses needed proper planning. It included conducting surveys, viability analysis, examining staff requirements and availability of appropriate infrastructure to house the planned campuses. It also needed a business plan. The plans for the start of the campuses entailed getting endorsement by the Senate and the University Council. Before such approvals, the University Management had to demonstrate to the Council that the proposed new campuses would be academically and financially viable. Viability was measured by among other things, infrastructure available, human resource (teaching and non-teaching), student enrolment and financial status.

It should be clear that a few of the Council members expressed misgivings on the proposed plan to open campuses. These members of Council felt that the process was being done in a hurried manner, hence could compromise the quality of education. They were particularly concerned with matters of existing facilities, teaching resources and available staff. However, in the long run, we managed to convince the Council and it allowed us to open these new campuses.

During the first phase (2011-2013), Kisii University opened campuses in Nyamira and Keroka Towns in Nyamira County and Ogembo Town in Kisii County. We also started campuses in Isebania and Kehancha in Migori County.

From the beginning, these campuses became very popular with students who saw it as a good opportunity for them to acquire university education at affordable rates. This was due to the fact that most of the students who enrolled in these campuses came from areas adjacent to the institutions. As such, they could be able to save on some costs. Most of them operated from their homes thus saving on accommodation and other maintenance expenses.

By the year 2013, we had a total enrolment of 2000 students in these campuses. At the Main Campus, we had 3,200 students. In the long-run, the campuses became a major source of our revenues, generating over 50% of the equivalent of our recurrent budget. For instance, in 2013, the University generated about Ksh500 million from these campuses.

At the same time, we experienced an influx of privately sponsored students in the Main Campus in Kisii Town. This was to a large extent due to strategic planning, which made the campuses become very competitive. For instance, as a policy, we only allowed academic staff, with requisite academic credentials and people who had graduated from recognized universities locally and globally as stipulated by CUE standards and guidelines, to teach our students as part-time lecturers.

Also, as University Management, we made sure that we supplied adequate teaching resources including computer labs, lecture rooms and office space. As I stated, it was our noble intention that by creating these campuses, we were practically taking the much-cherished university education closer to the Kenyan citizenry.

We came to learn over time that a majority of the students who joined the campuses were mainly from poor family backgrounds. They were students who would not have managed to receive university education in far off places due to financial difficulties. In this regard, it was quite gratifying to find that our campuses were meeting the needs of a specific niche, people who wanted a university education but would not afford it as traditionally offered.

It was indeed convenient for the students who would not have afforded high financial requirements in far off places to commute from home. Their parents and guardians were happy that university education for their children was affordable. In the first place, they would not have afforded to pay high fees and other maintenance and transport expenses that had to be incurred if the students were attending college far from home.

Furthermore, with the realization that most of the students came from poor backgrounds, we restructured modes of paying fees. We could come to an agreement with individual parents on the best way to stagger their payments. We encouraged them to pay in instalments so that their children would continue attending classes as they incrementally offset the balances.

This strategy of empathizing with parents made our campuses very popular in the areas where they were located. The local communities saw the campuses as theirs. They also regarded them as a game changer that had eluded them for decades with respect to access to university education. They particularly saw the campuses as instruments that could empower their children and enable them secure a better future. To the parents and their kids, this was a dream come true and they embraced it with a lot of commitment.

Also, within the Main Campus, we continued working. We continued expanding our academic programmes, guided by existing market demand. In a span of four years, the expansion saw our academic programmes rise from a paltry 34 to slightly over two hundred courses, all of them fully accredited by the Commission for University Education. Professional courses such as Law, Veterinary and Health Sciences were also accredited by the relevant professional bodies.

The curricula were systematically developed with the input of relevant stakeholders including students, lecturers, professional bodies and industry, among others. We have always made sure that our curricula match the existing market needs. For instance, in Business and Management programmes, we made sure that new developments such as in-building of information technology and computer skills in their training was done as required.

One of the niche programmes at Kisii University is training in law. With the assistance of the Council of Legal Education, the Kenya School of Law, the Judiciary and other legal practitioners, we have managed to develop a state of the art undergraduate law curriculum. It covers critical facets and emerging trends in the field of law and the legal profession. Further, we have also identified key areas where our law students have shone.

The arrangement is that in the final two years of study, the students are directed to choose the areas of Law where they would want to specialize in. These critical areas of specialization include Research and Report Writing, Conservation Law, Security, International Law and Conveyance among others.

Within the School of Law, we have established a state of the art Moot Court where students practice their jurisprudence skills. The students are also supposed to go for extended industrial attachment in courts, private legal practice offices and other areas of jurisprudence. It is always gratifying when we get feedback that our law students are ranked highly during their industrial attachment period.

To make the law students hone their skills, they are

encouraged to attend national and international mooting competitions. These are high level competitions where the students battle it out with their counterparts from other universities. One such competition is the Nelson Mandela Law Award, which is held annually in Geneva, Switzerland. Here, our selected students compete with students from the best law schools such as the Yale School of Law and the Harvard Law School. Despite the fact that our law school is nascent, our students have stood their ground and done very well over the last few years. In fact, they were once ranked the runners up in the competition, which is no mean feat.

Locally, Kisii University's Law School has managed to outsmart law students from other universities in the Council of Legal Education examinations. For instance, in the 2019 CLE examinations, our Law students took position one, beating law schools from pioneer universities such as Strathmore, Moi, Kenyatta and Nairobi.

The Law School has definitely set the right pace, which is being emulated by other schools in the university. As Management, we are continually striving to improve all academic programmes with the aim of meeting expectations of the local and international labour market. I always advice our students and staff that, "when you are pursuing a degree in any university worth its salt, that degree should be universal. It should measure with other degrees from other universities globally."

In this regard, with the commitment and specialized training, it is my conviction that we are equipping our students with the best skills, knowledge and competencies. Our graduates are now working in various sectors of the economy, locally and abroad. Some of our former students are now working or undertaking further studies in countries such as the United States, Canada, Australia and the United Kingdom.

In particular, Kisii University seeks to remain competitive by engaging and collaborating with other universities in Kenya and other parts of the world. One method that we have embraced is signing Memoranda of Understanding (MoUs) with several renowned universities from different parts of the world. These pave way for student and faculty exchanges, enhance shared experience and knowledge exchange. Our overall aim as enunciated in our Vision is to make our institution a world class university in the advancement of academic excellence and social welfare.

My many years of experience have shown me that the calibre of students in Kenyan public universities is competent and always aspiring to achieve the best in their academic endeavours. These are students who always demand the best services from the universities in training, research and engagement in extracurricular activities. Anything below this may compel students to seek alternative ways to voice their concerns. They can sometimes turn rowdy, and at times confrontational.

At Kisii University, we have always tried as much as possible to provide our students the best services that we can afford. This is, however, dependent on available resources. To attend to existing challenges, we have institutionalized open-door policy. Students and staff interact with Management and engage in dialogue to find solutions to the problems confronting them, and the institution in general.

Good governance in universities cannot be attained without actively engaging the students, academic and administrative staff. We always strive to encourage our students to be part of the solutions and not part of the problems confronting them as individuals and as the Kisii University family. We encourage our students to espouse the life philosophy as once articulated by former American President John F. Kennedy, which can be paraphrased, "ask yourself not what your university can do for you but what you can do for your university."

Another pragmatic message that has served us well is emphasizing the fact that Kisii University is one big family. We strive to love and care for one another, notwithstanding our individual and collective shortcomings that may not be due to our making.

*****

All work and no play makes Tom and Mary dull is a message that has been ingrained in our institution. In this connection, we always encourage our students to engage in extra-curricular activities to promote their varied talents and exploit their full potential. These activities include participating in the University Scouts Movement, religious clubs, the Kenya Revenue Authority (KRA) Association, the St. Johns' Ambulance Club and several sporting activities. In these associations, the students engage in various extracurricular activities and undertake various Corporate Social Responsibility (CSR) initiatives.

For instance, the Kisii University Scouting Association has been voted the best Scouting Movement in Africa thrice. This is due to its engagement in environmental conservation activities. They have participated in tree planting and promotion of peace initiatives in different parts of the country. They loop in the youth from other institutions to engage in these voluntary activities. They have also been to different parts of the country promoting their voluntary initiatives.

The university has also done well in various indoor and outdoor sporting activities such as table tennis, badminton, rugby, tennis, football, and athletics, among others. This illustrates that apart from academic pursuits, Kisii University students take part in diverse extra-curricular activities. They also serve humanity in different capacities. In the long run, they leave Kisii University as all rounded individuals who are critical thinkers and problem solvers, ready to serve and impact the world positively.

Kisii University also has a well-established entrepreneurship and incubation centre. Students are encouraged to become wealth creators and not job seekers through business and entrepreneurial skills training. This way, we are gradually changing the concept of university training as a place where people acquire theories and abstract knowledge that are far removed from the realities, but as a place where people are training to be critical thinkers and solvers of complex problems and challenges confronting the modern society.

Thus, through entrepreneurial skills training, we challenge our students to look at existing opportunities to start Small and Medium Enterprises (SMEs). We encourage them to promote a culture of entrepreneurship development and be able to produce specific products and services. This will go a long way in improving the living and the social welfare of the Kenyan people as encapsulated in the country's Vision 2030 and other Sustainable Development Goals.

Campuses Phase Two

The proven success of Kisii University's first set of satellite campuses triggered demand for the creation of additional campuses across the country. We responded to the demand and opened new campus locations in Eldoret, Kericho, Kabarnet, Nairobi, Eldama Ravine, Kitale and Kapenguria. There was a criterion for choosing these places for establishment of the campuses. We particularly based our selection of the locations on foreseeable student catchment area and the strategic location of the towns in the country.

As was the case with the first set of campuses, these ones too became very popular in the regions where they were situated. There was a notable influx of students who enrolled for certificate, diploma and degree courses. This response proved that these campuses were availing relevant education to the youth who embraced them wholeheartedly.

Some of the courses offered in the campuses included Business Management, Supply Chain and Purchase Management, Criminology, Public Administration, Education, Information Technology, among others. To enhance quality, we ensured that the campuses were manned by competent directors, considering our commitment to quality education. Each of the academic programmes in the campuses was headed by an academic leader who was at Senior Lecturer level as stipulated by CUE.

Additionally, in each campus, we hired the requisite academic and administrative staff. We also developed a data base of well qualified part-time lecturers whom we hired to teach in the campuses as the need arose.

Furthermore, we made sure that the campuses were closely linked to the Main Campus. Students from both the satellite campuses and the Main Campus would for instance sit for the same Continuous Assessment Tests (CATs) and end of semester examinations.

We did not stop there. The Main Campus Deans of Schools made regular visits to the campuses to supervise and give advice on academic and administrative issues. In other words, the programmes that were offered in the campuses were under the control and supervision of the respective Deans who were domiciled at the Main Campus. It is a requirement that the Deans make regular visits to the satellite campuses to check out and supervise teaching there.

In this regard, all students at the campuses got value for their money similar to those in the Main Campus. Through all these initiatives, the outcome was there to be seen. By 2016, the campuses were generating over 60% of the university's revenues that ran to hundreds of millions of shillings. The money was efficiently managed by the Management and was used in the core mandate of the university namely, teaching, research, innovation and community outreach. For instance, we used some of the revenue to equip our laboratories and avail state of the art equipment, and other training and research facilities.

Sadly, it did not take long before the rains started beating us. Our rising popularity became our Achilles heel. It appears that some people in higher education offices were unhappy with our success and hatched a plan to bring us down in a thud by ensuring that all our campuses were closed.

Thus, some people started tarnishing the names of Kisii University and the campuses. These evil schemes came into full gear in January 2016 when it was reported in the press that the Commission for University Education (CUE) had ordered closure of ten out of our thirteen campuses. The news hit us like thunder. We least expected a high level government body like CUE to release its findings through the press before officially communicating to us.

I recall that towards the end of 2015, CUE had made a routine inspection of all our campuses. During these inspections, the University Management and the Deans of Schools had availed themselves and provided the requisite documents. These documents related to campus policies, business plans, academic programmes on offer, physical infrastructure, staff establishment, library materials and other auxiliary resources. To us, it appeared that the inspection exercise had gone on well. Our thinking was based on the exit reports that the inspection team shared with us.

Of course, such information was confidential and should have been guarded jealously by the inspection team. As procedure demands, we should not have gotten wind of the report from other sources before it got released to us officially. More importantly, CUE should not have allowed any third party, including the media, to see the report before we did. Thus, ideally, the Commission should have first communicated its final official findings to the Kisii University Management Board and Council at the opportune time, before availing the same to other parties.

I was taken aback when the Daily Nation of January 19, 2016 quoted the report compiled by the CUE Chief Executive Officer, David Some, and his team, as saying that Kisii University had been given 90 days to close its satellite campuses. The news article listed the affected campuses namely, Eldoret, Eldama Ravine, Nyamira, Kabarnet, Migori, Ogembo, Keroka, Kehancha, Kapenguria and Isebania.

The news, coming at the start of the New Year, was extremely terrifying and unbearable. Panic gripped stakeholders, especially students and their parents in the affected campuses. They conveyed their frustrations to my office at the Main Campus. They all wanted immediate answers as to what had transpired and what the news meant to the students and their future.

As a short term measure, I issued a rebuttal through the press and dismissed the report. My right of reply was adequately highlighted in both print and electronic media. For instance, the Daily Nation quoted Management's statement issued by the Deputy Vice-Chancellor in charge of Academic and Students Affairs Prof. Maurice Amutabi to the effect that, "Information has been going round that some university campuses may be facing closure. This information is disturbing and has caused anxiety among Kisii University stakeholders." However, the damage had already been done and we had to do more to arrest the evolving unfortunate situation.

Worse yet, it appeared that CUE was releasing segments of its findings through the press in piecemeal. Indeed, barely 24 hours after the first story, the Daily Nation carried yet again another article touching on Kisii University. The article was about five students who had been conferred PhD degrees in 2014. Headlined *'CUE revokes degrees awarded to five students by Kisii University'*, the paper went further to say that *"students admissions were highly irregular based on a postgraduate credit transfer policy that is not provided for either in the Kisii University Statutes or the Universities Standards and Guidelines, 2014."* This statement was attributed to the Commission Chairman, Henry Thairu.

My conscience was clear that during that graduation ceremony, we conferred 5 PhD degrees to students who had met all the Senate and university academic requirements for the conferment of the respective degrees. Even so, we received a terse communication from CUE soon after the graduation ceremony, which to our surprise, claimed that the PhD degrees were conferred unprocedurally. Further, a top CUE official was heard saying openly that Kisii University did not have the capacity to train and confer PhD degrees. This was notwithstanding the fact that, at that time, Kisii was a full-fledged University with competent senior faculty to train and supervise PhD candidates in various post-graduate programmes.

Specifically, therefore, we were accused of having gone against the laid down CUE standards and guidelines on post-graduate training. Soon after, I was summoned to the Ministry of Education Headquarters in Nairobi to explain this alleged unfortunate scenario. At the same time, I was ordered to compile and submit a comprehensive report on the same. This was equally covered by the Daily Nation of January 23, 2016.

After submitting the required report, I appeared before the ministry officials to explain in detail the circumstances that precipitated the award of the five PhD degrees. These post-graduate students had met all the requirements of the Kisii University Senate for conferment of PhD degrees. Specifically, they had completed the requisite course work as stipulated in the Kisii University statutes and other policy documents and regulations. The candidates had also successfully defended their PhD dissertations as a major requirement for the conferment of the degrees.

In my explanation, I told the officials that the degrees were validly conferred based on merit. Perhaps, I further informed the officials, the only anomaly was procedural in nature since the students had transferred from other universities where they were undertaking their training. To my further surprise, CUE officials who were part of the team at the ministry interrogating me clung on the issue of procedure as a major anomaly.

Against my expectations, this was taken as a major loophole. I was immediately reprimanded particularly since Kisii University did not have a post-graduate credit transfer policy upon which we could have pegged the admission of the five PhD students. Thus, the admission and award of the PhD degrees to the five candidates was declared null and void.

I squirmed in my chair when this verdict was made. I knew that this was a major set-back to the fledgling institution, the helm of which I held.

However, I must note that it was one top official who hailed from a region where our campuses had blossomed who was the power behind this unfortunate move. In fact, during my interrogation session at the Ministry Headquarters, he had stated that if the PhD awards were legitimised, he was ready to step down from his position in protest. "After all, how many Kenyans have had their degrees revoked by CUE?" he retorted, rage evidently displayed in his face.

This official went further to make derogatory and demeaning remarks about Kisii University to the extent of portraying his personal ill-motive that he must have harboured against the institution. However, notwithstanding the official's protestations, the meeting made a resolution that all the five students be allowed to re-do certain core courses before they could be allowed to graduate. Interestingly, these were courses that they had already successfully pursued in their previous universities before they transferred to Kisii University.

Of course, this was not very pleasant news to share especially to the affected students. However, I had to find a way around it and I eventually communicated this sad reality to them. Notwithstanding the situation, the affected students eventually went through the courses and re-sat the examinations, which they passed. They were awarded their PhD degrees a year later.

This incident shows the unfortunate situation on how powerful external forces interfere with academic autonomy of universities in Kenya. It should be observed that, all over the world, when a university receives charter, it has the power through its Senate, which is the highest academic organ of the institution, to examine and award degrees, including post-graduate degrees, on condition that the students meet all the academic requirements as set by the University Senate.

Ideally, the Senate's decision is final and is not supposed to be challenged by any other internal or external entity. This is mainly because the Senate is made up of senior academic staff, including PhD holders and professors. Their opinion stands because they are qualified and understand what it takes to achieve high academic awards such as Masters and PhD degrees.

I agree that in recent years, some of our universities have been facing challenges in producing graduates at PhD level. They are especially faced with question about the standards of the training. However, these challenges are more intricate and complex than procedural issues such as credit transfer, which Kisii University was being accused of not following.

Particularly, as institutions of higher learning, we need to examine the quality and ability of the students who get admitted into PhD training. To undertake doctoral studies requires somebody with high level academic and research potential. Further, it takes sacrifice and commitment to go through PhD training. This process is supposed to train and empower the candidate to transition and become a researcher and/or producer of knowledge in his/her area of specialisation.

In a country such as the USA, where I did my doctoral studies, the situation is different from what is happening in our country. During orientation, you are openly informed that PhD training is not for everybody. In the American academic environment, PhD training is a special academic arrangement, which requires people with capacity, focus, commitment, tenacity and sacrifice to achieve excellence in academia.

In most American Universities, therefore, to enter into PhD training, you should be an A-grade student. To these institutions of higher learning, grades that are below B+ (Plus) will lead to you being advised that you are not benefitting from the academic resources at your disposal. In some instances you may be advised to seek other alternative ventures elsewhere. This is usually a polite way of saying that you have been discontinued.

Indeed, when I enrolled for my doctoral studies in Southern Illinois University, I was not alone. We started the academic journey with nine other students; three Chinese, four Americans, a Brazilian and another student from Puerto Rico. However, at the end of the programme over the five-year period, I was the only candidate who managed to graduate.

The other students were either discontinued during course work while some failed comprehensive examinations. Still others were unable to pass their PhD proposal defences and were required to repeat their defences before they could be allowed to proceed to the next stage of conducting research and compiling their dissertations for defence. Here, you were also required to pass your dissertation defence before you were awarded the PhD qualification.

In the first case, in most American Universities, one does not become a PhD candidate until one has excelled in course work, comprehensive examinations and PhD proposal defence. It is after going through these stages that one is eventually allowed to embark on research work then compile and defend one's dissertation. It is an extremely demanding academic journey and I find it proper.

It is presumed that in the academic journey, a person who eventually attains Master's Degree has high knowledge, competence and skills in his or her field of expertise. Thus, going past Master's Degree training entails rigorous academic work and being taken through various demanding academic and research initiatives. This journey is supposed to eventually transform one from a person who uses knowledge to one who does knowledge production. It goes without saying that, if you hold PhD in any field of study and you are not engaged in research and publication, then you are not worth to be a PhD holder.

Unlike the other levels of academia, once one gets to doctoral level, one is academically empowered to conduct research and interrogate critical theories and concepts in one's discipline and beyond. Thus, upon acquisition of PhD qualification, one is expected to contribute to the production of knowledge and new ideas and concepts in ones' area of speciality and beyond. Nothing less is expected of one, other than enhancing knowledge.

Consequently, a PhD holder should be part and parcel of that specialized group of scholars who are engaged in regular research and dissemination of skills and knowledge. This is achieved through research, innovation, attending and presenting research findings in conferences, seminars, workshops and symposia, locally and internationally.

However, it should be stated that most of us are not playing an active role in the production, dissemination and transfer of knowledge and skills in our areas of expertise.

This scenario is very unfortunate, to say the least. One of the noble mandates of a university is to conduct research, share knowledge and innovations that help solve societal problems and challenges. Perhaps, to a limited extent, as one professor contends, African universities have slowly become "glorified high schools". It is a notion I disagree with and one that is obviously too generalized. It does not present an accurate picture of the academic situation of African Universities.

Here, it is important to note that Africa is a large and diverse continent with hundreds of universities that are relatively good as reflected in the Webometric ranking of universities. However, we have to admit that, similar to what happens in other parts of the world, there are also some universities in Africa that are performing dismally. This is particularly in regards to research and dissemination of knowledge, new ideas and discoveries.

In the Kenyan situation, to a larger extent, our university education is highly centralized. The scenario is so because the national education policies provide that, save for early childhood education and vocational training, which is under the county governments, university education is under the prerogative of the National Government. In particular, rules and regulations, including the 2012 Universities Act as reviewed in 2016, and CUE standards and regulations give a lot of powers to the Ministry of Education. In this situation, the Cabinet Secretary and the Principal Secretary in the Ministry wield a lot of power over universities. The risk is that university education can be substantially hampered if the leadership at this level is wanting.

A more interesting development in the recent past is the decision to remove the powers of appointment office chancellors, deputy vice chancellors and principals of universities and colleges from the institutions' councils and place it on the Public Service Commission (PSC). In my view, the rationale for this policy change has not been clearly articulated. One can argue that the underlying reason is the fact that it is presumed that the PSC is more neutral and may face minimal conflict of interest compared to councils. However, this is not necessarily true. Moreover, in a corrupt environment, even the PSC can be influenced by negative external forces that would want the preferred candidate appointed to the coveted positions. In this critical matter, this scenario is unfortunate as PSC may not do a good job. In the Kenyan situation, most members who sit in PSC have minimal understanding of university governance and administration.

The practice all over the world is that a vice chancellor is appointed by the University Council and/or Board of Trustees. This is as stipulated in the respective university charters and statutes. Thus, by bringing in an exogenous body such as the PSC to be responsible for the appointment of vice chancellors may lead to the politicisation and external interference in the important process of recruitment of university CEOs. As a consequence, vice chancellors and principals may be appointed under the influence of extraneous factors, away from the academic and administrative criteria relevant in the appointment of top University Management personnel.

Restructuring the Campuses

At this juncture, it is important for me to revisit the story of Kisii University campuses. As I noted, there were powerful external malevolent forces that wanted to have all our campuses closed, regardless of what the impact it would have on the students, staff (teaching and support) and the institution. Towards the end of 2015, CUE officially wrote to us, indicating their intention of undertaking inspection of all the campuses. To us, this appeared to be a normal and routine procedure, which we had to abide by.

As per CUE standards and guidelines, the Commission is required to make periodic visits to inspect institutions of higher learning to make sure that the institutions meet the requisite academic standards for accreditation. As the University Management, we fully yielded ourselves for the inspection exercise which took slightly over a fortnight. CUE team inspected various components of the campuses as stipulated in the regulations. In particular, they looked at the existing physical infrastructure, architectural design compliance, staff establishment, governance structure, academic programmes, library resources and the overall ambience of the campuses, among other aspects.

But as an administrator, I noted that probably CUE officers did not have sufficient time for the immense task. Given that we had several campuses situated in many parts of the country, two weeks were not enough to allow for a comprehensive inspection.

In particular, I noticed that the officials were hurriedly going through campus profiles, information on building structures and occupation, human resource establishment and status of the campus libraries. They were also placing an inordinate amount of time on issues that were not central to the university core mandate of teaching, research and innovation. For instance, they expected to find doors that opened outwards. They were also counting the number of toilets, the size of staff offices, presence and viability of fire extinguishers and the nature of ceiling boards and painting.

As much as these issues are important, I expected the team to spend more time in interrogating our various curricula, existing teaching materials and available IT services, among others. However, what they were looking at were, to a large extent, peripheral issues that are not core to the University mandate, and which could be fixed easily.

Nevertheless, we cooperated with CUE inspectors and availed information as was sought. However, to our surprise and dismay, when they gave us their exit reports, it appeared that they indeed concentrated on details that did not cover the core mandate of university, that is teaching and research. Ideally, they should have focused on the availability and relevance of the various curricular that were being implemented in the campuses and the quality of the teaching staff.

At the end of the inspection, it seemed that there was a lull before a real storm. After one month, worrying rumours started milling around and made things worrisome. There were claims that the commission was going to close down all our campuses because they were situated in noisy and dingy places. We also received claims that, as much as most of our campuses had passed the inspection, some senior members of CUE had overturned the findings of the original inspection report and instead recommended that all our campuses close shop.

As already shown, the rumours came to pass when one morning I woke up to see a news splash in a national newspaper saying that CUE had closed all campuses of Kisii University for non-compliance to set standards. The screaming Kisii University headline hit me like a thunderbolt. This was a dark day which can only be compared to that time when I became suddenly sick and had to return home, losing a promising job I had secured in Washington, DC.

To me, the decision to release the inspection report through the media before communicating the information to the concerned party was a clear indication that the process was, to say the least, ill-intentioned, malicious and impartial. Its purpose must have been to malign and reverse all the gains we had achieved and bring Kisii University to its knees. As a University, we issued terse rebuttals to these allegations that we believed were ill-intended.

The news spread like bushfire within a very short timeframe. The whole country was aware that Kisii University was crumpling as all its fourteen campuses had been closed.

Several questions crossed my mind without answers. What would happen to our students in the campuses? What about the massive investments that we had put in these campuses?

Indeed, in the making, was a catastrophe of unprecedented proportions. The entire university was shaken to the core.

If there is any situation where one can get drained and lose it out, then this was it. It was an existential crisis! For the first time, the whole university was faced with looming probable collapse and total alienation under my watch.

The situation was worsened by summons we received from the Ministry of Education. They directed the University Council to avail itself at the Ministry Headquarters at Jogoo House, Nairobi, to respond to the presumed 'mess' that had been allegedly unearthed in our campuses and the whole university system in general.

We travelled the same day to spend the night in the city so as to rise up and be on time for the summons. That night, sleep eluded me. It must have been one of the longest nights that I ever had over a long time.

At the Ministry Headquarters, we were ushered into the main boardroom on the 10th floor of Jogoo House. I could feel extreme tension in the air, although the Minister and other senior Ministry officials had not taken their seats. Something in my conscience told me that the day was going to be messy; very messy. Nevertheless, we were here; we would face it as it came.

When the Minister, the Principal Secretary and the CEO of CUE came in, I knew from their body language that they had prepared to deal with us mercilessly. Indeed, no sooner had they taken their seats at the front than they started giving us a harsh reprimand and dress down. They accused us of opening campuses haphazardly on top of bars and supermarkets, without any regard.

"In some campuses, the bar is a floor away from the lecture rooms," one of the officials said in a rather ridiculing manner. "Students have the option of entering the bar first, and then join the lecture when they are already inebriated. Kisii Campuses are in a total mess," he concluded.

We were further accused of recklessly opening campuses in village markets such as Nyamache (in Kisii), yet we did not have a campus there. I was also accused of admitting people who were not qualified for studies at the university. This really surprised and irked me, but I had to contain myself as much as possible.

In particular, to the officials, it was ironical and unacceptable that we had admitted retired civil servants who were members of Abagusii Council of Elders to undertake a degree in Peace and Conflict Studies. Of course, we had started to offer that degree programme at the university. The course targeted highly experienced senior retirees from the Gusii region and beyond for training. This would particularly assist them in addressing societal conflicts and help offer practical solutions, and put to use their lengthy practical experience. This is exactly what most of our graduates in the programme are currently doing all over the country.

Interestingly, one beneficiary of this programme is ex-Senior Chief Araka Matundura who is currently the Chairman of the Gusii Council of Elders. Due to his extensive administrative experience as a former senior chief, combined with the training he had received from Kisii University, he was later appointed by President Uhuru Kenyatta to be a member of the Building Bridges Initiative (BBI).

The BBI was formed after the now famous handshake between the two protagonists, President Uhuru and opposition leader Raila Odinga. The two leaders would not see each other eye to eye after the opposition disputed the Presidential poll in October 2017. Although the poll results were over-turned by the Supreme Court, the opposition boycotted the repeat poll, saying that the playing field was tilted in favour of President Kenyatta.

The disagreement led to intensified acrimony between the two leaders and their supporters. The economy was hard hit as tourists and investors avoided Kenya, and the international community had warned that Kenya was hurtling towards a precipice.

Consequently, Kenyans were happy and pleasantly surprised when Kenyatta and Odinga publicly said that

Kenya was bigger than any one of them and they were going to work together for the sake of the country. This retreat from near anarchy earned the two leaders national, regional and international acclaim. They then tasked BBI task force to seek views from Kenyans on how to build and develop all-inclusive nation that promotes democratic governance and economic inclusivity. It is in this magnanimous and historical national committee which one of the graduates of the maligned degree programme was appointed to serve, and with all likelihood has done so with distinction.

In the meeting at Jogoo House, we were ordered to come up with a detailed roadmap on the way forward. In spite of the heartbreaking dress down we were served, several of our campuses such as Nairobi, Kabarnet, Kericho, Eldoret, Kapenguria, Kisumu and Migori were allowed to survive while the rest were to be closed.

I must confess that the verbal bashing we got that day left us dumbfounded. Once we got out of the boardroom, we scampered in various directions. My wife was in Nairobi and she offered a shoulder for me to lean on since I was totally beaten down, disturbed and agonising. As we returned to Kisii with her, my mind oscillated like a pendulum. I wondered where the rain started beating us and how we were going to wriggle ourselves out of this major quagmire.

To our pleasant surprise, as the campuses were being closed, the local people around them rose spontaneously to resist the move. During the protests, politicians, religious leaders and members of the public piled pressure on the government to rescind the decision. The situation was particularly tense in the North Rift region due to the fact that our campuses had become very popular there. The closure of the campuses was going to affect thousands of students and staff.

In Eldoret, the Campus Director and members of the Campus Management Board had to step in fast to stop a huge demonstration. Many people were matching towards an adjacent campus of another university, which had survived

CUE assessment. In Pokot, the local people were so angry especially bearing in mind that the Campus in Kapenguria Town was the only institution of higher learning in the region. The people of Pokot could not understand why the imposing and modernistic building in Makutano, where the Campus was domiciled, was being termed as substandard.

To the people of this region, the move to close the West Pokot Campus was a mockery in itself and a slap in the face of the local community. They wondered aloud why the same government that allowed pupils to study in extremely dilapidated classrooms, without even basic facilities such as chairs and desks, was closing down a campus, which was occupying a relatively well developed training facility. There were demonstrations that lasted for several days and looped in Pokot warriors as they marched to the governor's office and demanded him to address the situation.

Interestingly, our Kapenguria Campus was located in the town where the founding fathers of Kenya, 'the Kapenguria Six', were incarcerated by the colonial government. The Kapenguria Six were Jomo Kenyatta (the first President of Kenya), Paul Ngei, Achieng' Oneko, Bildad Kaggia, Fred Kubai and Kung'u Karumba.

Generally, there were major contestations and demonstrations in all places where our campuses were situated. Several church leaders and politicians joined the bandwagon. Perhaps even more importantly, the students in all the campuses stood with the Management and contested the move. Through their leaders, the students said that the decision to close down their campuses was ill-timed, malicious and discriminatory. These protests were widely covered in the media in the better part of January. For instance, on January 27, 2016 the *Daily Nation* carried a stand-alone photo in its front page showing hundreds of Kisii University's Eldoret Campus students in a protest match in Eldoret Town. In some places, residents went a step further to hire lawyers to take the battle of closure of the campuses to the courts.

The prevailing sad situation remained on the lips of many Kenyans for days, with some turning to media platforms to air their views. For instance, the Standard published a page lead in its Reader's Digest on January 26, 2016 where Solomon Njenga said that CUE needed to do more than just close universities. In his view, Njenga said, "it is undeniably true that CUE has been entrusted with keeping and checking the quality in higher education, but it is also imperative for it to observe rules and procedures before its delivery of the imminent closure of any institution."

It was within this socio-political environment that the Cabinet Secretary for Education, Dr. Fred Matiang'i, appointed a Committee of Eminent Persons to look into the matter with sobriety. They included Prof. George Magoha who later assumed the Education ministerial docket, former Permanent Secretary, Crispus Kiamba and Prof. Jane Mbote who was at the time the Dean School of Law at the University of Nairobi.

The committee was inaugurated by the Education Cabinet Secretary with clear instructions to visit all our campuses with the aim of recommending the way forward and report to the CS, which ones would be spared the axe. The team was also to recommend, which campuses needed to be given some grace period to work and meet CUE requirements. This was another phase of inspection of the campuses, an assignment which started at the Main Campus.

As they conducted the inspection, most of the members of the Committee did not mince words when they saw what was happening in our campuses. They undeniably got shocked to see the opposite of what they expected based on the hullabaloo that had been created concerning our campuses. They confessed that the status of the campuses surpassed their expectations and I remember one of the committee members asking me, "it looks like the Main University is doing very well; what was indeed happening in the campuses?"

The committee took several days to complete their assignment. They visited all the campuses and went through the earlier inspection reports that had been prepared by CUE. They also engaged the University Council and Management in discussions concerning the development of the Campuses Roadmap. This way, they sought to understand what we had in mind as far as the continuity and future of the campuses were concerned.

In particular, the committee recommended that Nyamira, Kehancha and Eldama Ravine Campuses be closed forthwith and students be moved to the Main University or any other close-by campus that had survived the closure. The outcome of the Committee of Eminent Persons report, therefore, meant that we were not out of the woods yet. We therefore started this painful process of restructuring the campuses and re-organizing the remaining ones as directed.

This nerve-wrenching experience triggered the emergence of divisions in the University Council. Some members of the Council started pulling in different directions. As Management, we had developed a detailed technical report to guide a systematic closure of the identified campuses as recommended by the Committee of Eminent Persons. But it appeared that some members of Council were not in agreement with some of the recommendations on the way forward. Nevertheless, as recommended in the report, we started closing down the identified campuses. This process involved dispatching Deans to the earmarked Campuses to talk to and counsel the students, staff and lecturers to, as much as possible, bear with the situation and accept the inevitable.

As could be expected, the people in the campuses were not amused when the Deans visited them. They did not want to hear that as the University Management, we had yielded to the demands to relocate students and staff to other places, and close shop in their locations. In many instances, the people became hostile and rebellious as the reality of what was happening sunk in.

Furthermore, as Management, we also appointed a technical committee in charge of the implementation of the Campuses

Roadmap as recommended by the Eminent Persons. Indeed, through systematic engagements, we managed to transfer students from the closed campuses to those of their choices that had survived the painful onslaught. This was followed by the dismantling and evacuating all movable assets to the Main Campus. This process was overseen by the Internal Audit Department and involved stock-taking and supervising the transfer of the assets.

This process took the better part of 2016. Luckily, we were able to restructure and re- organise the remaining campuses as guided by the Committee of Eminent Persons. From fourteen campuses, we eventually remained with eight, namely: Kabarnet, Eldoret, Kapenguria, Kitale, Kisumu, Migori, Kericho and Nairobi.

Further, in 2017, based on internal self-assessment, the Council decided to close Kitale, Kabarnet and Kisumu campuses. This decision was mainly informed by their financial viability and student enrolment. Thus, we now have five remaining campuses, namely, Kapenguria, Eldoret, Migori, Kericho and Nairobi. The five campuses are currently viable, with several students and vibrant teaching and training initiatives.

We also decided to restructure the number of courses offered in the campuses and eliminated some in order to make the remaining courses more effective. We particularly remained with those programmes that were viable based on student enrolment. In addition, we relocated most of the remaining campuses to better premises. An example is the Eldoret Campus, which is now housed in the expansive Kapsoya Complex. Kericho Campus is now situated in Imarisha Plaza, while Migori Campus is situated at Musomi Complex. Finally, Nairobi Campus is located at Corner House in the city's Central Business District.

Nevertheless, notwithstanding the daunting experience we went through, our remaining campuses are now vibrant and better organized. Thus, all in all, as a university, the tough experience of 2015-2017 made us come out even stronger.

We are now more focused and ready to take the university to a higher level. Consequently, as we are developing the University, we are also learning from past mistakes as we look into the future.

Creating a Medical School

It can be argued that starting a highly specialized professional degree such as Medicine and Surgery, is an indication that the university is maturing in teaching and training. The same can also be said of the Law degree programme as presented earlier. It is worth noting, therefore, that of all universities that received Charter in 2013, very few have launched training in the fields of Medicine and Law.

Kisii University received its first batch of Bachelor of Medicine and Surgery students in September 2019. Even so, getting accreditation was not a walk in the park. The university went through a rigorous and watertight procedure to get the necessary accreditation for the programme. Prior to that, the university had been offering courses in Nursing and Clinical Medicine that are also fully accredited by the relevant professional bodies.

In early 2019, our new curriculum in Medicine and Surgery was subjected to rigorous scrutiny by the Kenya Medical Practitioners and Dentists Board (KMPDB). This is the professional board, which is responsible of supervision and provision of accreditation to schools that offer degree in Medicine and Surgery, among other assignments. The Board also inspected existing physical infrastructure and available human resources to ascertain our readiness and efficacy in offering the medical programme. The two exercises culminated in the issuance of the accreditation certificate in May 2019 for the university to start training doctors.

A Memorandum of Understanding with the Government of Kisii County allows us to use the Kisii Teaching and Referral Hospital (KTRH) as our practical training facility. Students studying Medicine and Surgery and other health-related courses are regularly granted access to the health facility as needed. At the time of accreditation of our programme, the hospital was also accredited by the KMPDB as a training centre for the degree of Medicine and Surgery.

To allow for up to date practical training, we have developed a state of the art anatomy, histology and physiology laboratories in the Teaching and Referral Hospital. These facilities are equipped with modern medical facilities and equipment that are required for the training of medical and health personnel of the 21st Century.

As part of boosting our training and research initiatives, the university also hired over forty medical experts who are now training our students. With this kind of specialised personnel at hand and the high quality facilities in place, we have no doubt that we will train some of the best doctors and other health professionals in Kenya, and indeed in the East African region. Furthermore, the university envisions that stakeholders will continue supporting the institution in transforming the provision of medical services in the Kisii region and beyond.

In this regard, the highly qualified doctors who have been hired as lecturers also offer services at KTRH. Some have also opened private clinics in Kisii Town and nearby townships. This is really good news to people from the local community who can access specialised medical services near home at subsidised costs. Previously, specialized medical services such as urology, cardio-vascular treatment, neurology and oncology were not available in Kisii. People had to travel to far flung places like Eldoret and Nairobi for treatment.

It is our envisioned goal that, through the advancement of medical services offered by the hospital and the university, we will transform Kisii Town into a medical hub cum health tourist destination in Western Kenya. We will be able to provide specialised and referral services to patients from the region and beyond. These medical facilities will also serve our neighbours in Western Kenya and parts of North-Western Tanzania. These are major milestones for Kisii University that we plan to bring into fruition in due course.

Furthermore, using the doctors, nurses and medical students, our university conducts regular medical camps in the region. In the camps, we offer free medical services to Kenyans who could otherwise not afford them.

Through our Strategic Plan, we want to enhance the multiplier effect of healthcare training by providing the best medical services in the region. Our aspiration is that diseases like malaria, typhoid and amoeba should not kill Kenyans. In particular, we have a special role to play in taming the rising number of deaths in the region.

This is one way in which our university is assisting the National Government achieve aspects of the Big Four Agenda, as relates to the goal of Universal Health Care for all Kenyans.

On the whole, through all these strategic initiatives, Kisii University is well positioned to move forward with its plans of becoming a world class university in the provision of academic excellence, research, and innovation in the advancement of social welfare. The university will also continue to be highly competitive in attracting both government and self-sponsored students through the provision of high quality market-driven academic programmes.

As already stated, the National Government has also come up with a strategic policy called the Big Four Agenda. Free and quality healthcare is one of the pillars. The collaboration between the two levels of government and institutions that are training high level personnel for the health sector like Kisii University will highly improve the delivery of efficient and quality healthcare services to Kenyans from all walks of life. We particularly want to make the lives of our children and grandchildren better than ours. My mother worked to make my life better. It is my aspiration to make that of the current and the next generation even better.

I believe that we are on the right trajectory with respect to the stipulated plans. For instance, in the 2019/2020 Academic Year, the university received over 3,000 government sponsored students. We were among the top ten universities in terms of government sponsored student enrolment. The

2020/2021 Academic Year saw this number jump to 6,000 government sponsored students, placing us in position three of universities that received most students. On our part, we have committed to offer the best education possible to these students.

As the CEO of the institution, I am always gratified each time I hear that our students are regarded highly in the job market. It has not taken a miracle to get here. Rather, it is due to painstaking hard work, commitment and determination exhibited by all stakeholders including the staff (teaching and administrative staff), students, Management, government and the community.

Biographer's Note

In a candid one on one interview, Prof. Akama was quoted on September 12, 2019 by Hashtag Magazine, *which is published by the* Standard *saying, "one of the unique features of our University (is that) it is the only 'young' university in Kenya offering professional degrees in medicine and law."*

Further, according to Dr. Wycliff N. Mogoa (the Dean, School of Health Sciences), in a 2019 advertorial appearing in the Daily Nation, *highlighted the value of the collaboration between the university and KTRH, saying "The collaboration has seen Kisii Teaching and Referral Hospital benefit from Kisii University staff members who are specialists in various fields of medicine and health sciences in general. Equally, Kisii University has used the facility to train students in various fields of medicine."*

Enhancing Research and Innovation

In academia, the mantra is that you *either publish or perish*. This is a statement we take seriously as an institution of higher learning. It is through research and publication of research findings that we can find solutions to complex problems facing humanity, be they be social, economic, health, culture or engineering issues, As highlighted in a story carried by *The East African* in October 2015: we have an established Department of Research and Extension at Kisii University. This is a Department that is charged with research, innovation and community outreach initiatives of the university. In particular, it assists emerging researchers and students in proposal writing, conducting research and publishing research findings in reputable international publications.

However, I must admit that the Department of Research and Extension is at its inception stage and has teething challenges. More so, as a young university, we have not fully entrenched the culture of research and publishing among our academic staff. Furthermore, we have a shortfall of high-level manpower in overall research administration and management. At the same time, there is need for adequate mentors in the name of highly experienced professors, with clear research ethos, to guide and nurture the upcoming academicians.

While it should not be seen that I am blowing my own trumpet, I believe that I have led from the front in this frontier. In that respect, I have indeed done my bit in research and authorship and I am not about to hang my boots in the space yet. Thus, over the years, I have managed to do research and made my work published in several high impact peer-reviewed international journals. I have also published several books and contributed to book chapters in my area of academic expertise.

My research work covers broad areas of knowledge, including natural resource planning and management, socio-economic development, tourism planning and management, culture and ethnography. The over-reaching theme in my research work has been on issues of sustainable use of resources. I have also explored ideas on sustainable development of tourism, poverty reduction and preservation of our cultural values. I noted earlier that my initial research was on political ecology of wildlife conservation in Kenya. I am happy because the research has guided policy formulations that mitigate existing human-wildlife conflict. It has empowered local people through resource conservation and sustainable tourism development.

My research in tourism is assisting in the reflection and initiation of policies to mitigate the negative social, economic and environmental impacts of tourism development. The research has also contributed in the development of sustainable tourism beneficial to the local people, such as the Maasai. It has also proved fundamental to the coastal region communities adjacent to existing centres for wildlife conservation, beaches and cultural tourism.

Consequently, being at the helm of university leadership makes one to be the fulcrum of many critical issues. The top most one is offering direction and always informing others that research, innovation and community out-reach initiatives are core mandates of a university and are a central part of their terms of employment. These are critical issues that we cannot run away from despite the fact that universities continually face a myriad of challenges such as lack of funds needed for the full comport of academic activities.

However, it is important to state that the challenges confronting research and innovation are not unique to Kisii University. Indeed, many universities in Kenya, across Africa and the world also have similar challenges.

Even so, as much as these challenges exist, academic staff should always conduct research in their fields of specialization. This is rightly so since, ideally, what differentiates a university from other institutions of learning is the research and innovations it carries out. In fact, it is a cardinal responsibility that university faculty should continually engage in research in order to find solutions to complex problems and challenges confronting society.

Thus, within their diverse areas of academic specialization, university academics are required to contribute knowledge and skills that are aimed at extending the academic frontier and filling the existing knowledge gaps. Apart from being consumers of existing knowledge, university dons are also expected to produce knowledge in their own right.

The Constitution of Kenya provides various rights and freedoms. One of such provisions is academic freedom and scientific research *(Section 33, Clause 1c of Chapter Four of the Bill of Rights)*. In this regard, university dons should endeavour to disseminate and share their research work in conferences, symposia and workshops. Without this, one cannot sincerely claim to be a university academic if one is not involved in research initiatives in one's area of specialization.

With this realization of the importance of research and innovation, Kisii University provides seed money which lecturers access competitively for research and publication. The university also assists lecturers in writing research proposals for funding by providing training and availing to them facilities for proposal writing. In addition, the university links them to probable funders in Kenya and overseas.

Furthermore, in order to enhance our research capacity, the university has established collaboration with many universities and other institutions of higher learning in Kenya and other parts of the world. These collaborations and linkages allow our staff and students to participate in exchange programmes for training and undertaking joint research activities and publication, and organizing joint conferences and symposia.

At this juncture, I am glad to note that in the recent past, our lecturers have managed to visit various foreign universities on joint research initiatives. An interesting example is Evans Onyancha, a lecturer in Biochemistry, who undertook specialized research on herbal medicine using high level and sophisticated laboratory equipment at the University of Minnesota. The lecturer, in collaboration with colleagues at the University of Minnesota, has been able to extract and test the efficacy of indigenous herb extracts in the treatment of certain types of cancer.

Further, Kisii University is working with the Institute of Primate Studies in Nairobi. Here, our lecturers engage in joint research in areas of Biochemistry, Biology and Ecology. Also, over the years, many of our lecturers have travelled for academic engagements in China, South Korea, South Africa, UK and USA, among others.

In the overall, the Government should do more in supporting research initiatives in our universities. This is what happens in countries in the West, Asia and other parts of the world. It is why I agree in part to an article authored by Dr. Bob Wekesa of University of Witwatersrand, South Africa and published in the *Sunday Nation* on March 11, 2018. In the article, Dr. Wekesa said, "while South African lecturers who publish in accredited peer-reviewed journals can expect a subsidy from the Ministry of Higher Education, Kenyan academics are virtually on their own, removing an incentive that would have encouraged research."

There is a gap between the stipulated national policies and regulations in research. For instance, it has been articulated that ideally, the country should spend at least 2% of the National Budget in research. However, the reality is that only an insignificant amount of the budget is allocated for research. As a result, the country's research agenda is lagging far behind where it should be. In such a scenario, many of the critical national and regional policy decisions are made without incorporating critical research findings on socio-economic and political perspectives in the country.

Celebrating University Cultural Week

On September 12, 2019, I was featured in the Hashtag, a pull-out magazine published by *The Standard* Newspaper. The full-page article quoted me on various issues concerning Kisii University. In my parting shot, I said, "Kenya is a great country and I encourage all of us, especially the youth, to be proud of our motherland. Let us always strive to understand where we have come from, who we are, and where we are going as a people."

Every March, we dedicate a whole week in the University Calendar for cultural activities. The initiation of Annual Cultural Festival in 2009 was informed by the fact that Kisii University is a public institution and, by virtue of this, its students and staff come from diverse ethnic communities. The broader university family comprises of people from diverse cultural and economic backgrounds, and various social and religious origins. In terms of religion, some are Christians who subscribe to different denominations like Protestant and Catholic. We also have Muslims and traditionalists. This makes Kisii University a mosaic of diverse cultures.

As such, each year, the one week cultural festival allows for out of class close-knit cultural interactions. During this period, the students and staff share and appreciate Kenya's diverse cultures. In part, the intention is to let them learn to co-exist as one Kenyan family with an understanding that we belong to one big family called Kenya. When students from diverse Kenyan communities mingle and showcase each other's cultural identities, they come into an agreement that by standing united we form a beautiful and cohesive rainbow nation called Kenya. It is these diverse cultures that make Kenya a unique nation-state, and make her stand out in the global family of nations.

Furthermore, the students also learn that from their respective cultures, there are many cultural commonalties and values. Examples of common aspects include respect for one another, ethical and moral values, the sanctity of human life, respect of elders and sharing with others, especially the less fortunate. Indeed, these values of African humanism cut across almost all African ethnic communities.

Specifically, during the latest 2020 cultural week, which was held before the outbreak of COVID-19 pandemic, I emphasized to our students that, as Kenyans, we should use these unique cross-cutting values as a middle ground to appreciate our oneness. Even among the various religions, we should encourage the spirit of ecumenism, tolerance and acceptance of the diverse religions in the world. In this regard, I also aver that our diverse religions have commonalities, including the belief in one God and religious values that emphasize on love the equality of life, and happiness to all.

Furthermore, during the cultural week, students are encouraged and are also supported to showcase various cultural performances such as tug–of–war, indigenous fire lighting, music, traditional attires, dances, poetry and storytelling. They also display indigenous cuisines, food storage techniques and traditional farming implements.

They proudly exhibit various weapons such as traditional spears, shields, bows, arrows, swords and knives that our forefathers used to protect themselves against their internal and external enemies.

At a broader level, I believe that as a nation, we need to encourage inter-ethnic courtship and marriages in the spirit of nationhood and togetherness. Young Kenyans should be encouraged to befriend and marry spouses from other communities.

Kenya will be poorer as a nation if we lose a single positive element of Kenyan culture through mindless aping and assimilation of other people's cultural attributes. As a nation, we need to find practical ways of preserving the threatened indigenous cultures of smaller ethnic groups such as the Ndorobo, Suba and Elmoro. The trio have been noted to be highly endangered with their languages and cultures at the verge of extinction. Before they go extinct, we should set up a Supreme National Cultural Council made of diverse stakeholders drawn from all over the country. Once formed, the national outfit should be in charge of the development (including formal documentation) and preservation of our diverse Kenyan cultures.

Last but not least, let me qualify my understanding with the following observation; before the advent and slow, but steady, takeover by modernity and Western medicine, indigenous communities had abundant knowledge of herbs, traditional farming techniques and soil management systems, among others. They also knew various indigenous crops and vegetables that were well adapted to the existing climatic and ecological conditions. Many of these crops were of great nutritional value. This indigenous knowledge is gradually disappearing as the practitioners such as herbalists leave the stage. We must endeavour to protect and conserve these indigenous resources and knowledge and enhance them as part of our national heritage; a heritage that we must keep for posterity.

Myself, in academic regalia, greeting President Mwai Kibaki during the award of charter

Former President Mwai Kibaki (6th from left) and other dignitaries during the award of charter.

Former President Mwai Kibaki plants a tree outside the University's main library on the day of award of charter.

Nurturing Kisii University

Myself (right), next to President Mwai Kibaki as he gets ready to cut the tape during the opening of the University Main Library on the day of award of charter.

A group photo with President Mwai Kibaki after the award of the university charter ceremony.

President Uhuru Kenyatta (left) hands over a trophy on behalf of the Kenya Revenue Authority in recognition of the exemplary CSR work done by the Kisii University Tax Association

With students at State House, Nairobi.

The newly finished Sakagwa Academic Blocks. The completion of the two blocks has given the University a complete new look.

The University's main library is a one stop reference and study destination for students and staff.

The ICT centre

The rear view of the ICT Complex. It is a marvel at the University.

The Chancelor's Pavilion is a conspicuous structure that welcomes one to Kisii University

The School of Law building at Kisii University. The Law programme has been ranked highly, nationally, due to the quality of training offered

An aerial view of the Law School complex at Kisii University.

With guests including University Counciil chair Dr. Mildred Mudany and CUE chairman Prof. Chacha Nyaigoti Chacha during the launch of the University Strategic Plan.

Standing second left is myself with senior Ministry of Education officials who made a courtesy call to the University, led by Ambassador Simon Nabukwesa, Ps *second left*

Standing fourth from left is myself with members of the University Council and University Management.

When I received the accreditation certificate for the Medical School. Looking on President Uhuru Kenyatta (seated), ODM leader Raila Odinga (right) and Education CS Prof. George Magoha (left).

Members of the University band.

A jig with students.

Putting the best foot forward during the University Cultural week.

With students during a Cultural Week at the University.

Awarding students at the close of the University Cultural week.

Receiving an award from officials of the Cohesion and Integration Commission in Nairobi in 2018

A section of youths following political speeches at a rally in Gusii Stadium. The country should create an enabling environment for its youth to thrive.

A walk during a Road Safety sensitization exercise in Kisii.

During a World Leaders' Forum in 2019. I am standing right below the date indicated in the banner.

Memories from my visit to South Korea.

During my visit to Seoul, South Korea.

Having good time in South Korea.

Visiting recreational sites in South Korea. This was organized by the host family, under the auspices of the God Mission Church in 2019.

Standing third right is myself with officials from the Ministry of Education who toured Kisii University to assess our preparedness for re-opening following closure of institutions due to the COVID-19 outbreak.

A team from the university distributes masks in Nyamira County.

An awareness creation meeting observing social distancing due to COVID 19 disease

With students during a tree planting exercise in Nyamira County.

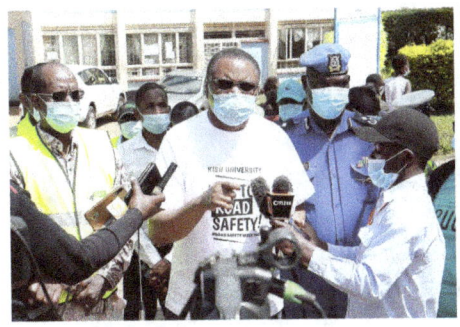

Briefing journalists during the COVI-19 awareness creation at the University.

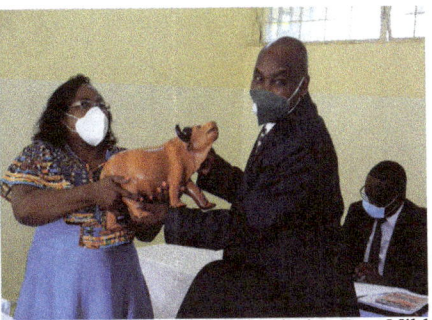

Kisii University Council Chair, Dr. Mildred Mudany hands a gift made from soapstone to a new member of Council, Nelson Koinet Kesei. Soapstone is a key resource in parts of South Mugirango, Kisii County.

Getting ready for a graduation ceremony.

During the 2020 graduation ceremony. Hundreds of graduands participated virtually due to COVID-19 pandemic.

Conferement of degrees at the University in 2020.

AWARD

The Article of the Year

2011

The Editors of *Tourism Recreation Research* (TRR) extend their congratulations to John S. Akama, Shem W. Maingi and Blanca A. Camargo for winning the Article of the Year Award 2011 for their contribution, *Wildlife Conservation, Safari Tourism and the Role of Tourism Certification in Kenya: A Postcolonial Critique*, published in TRR Volume 36(3), 2011. The judges ranked it high in Quality of Content and Practical Usability of Research.

John S. Akama holds PhD in Geography from Southern Illinois University. He has research interests in tourism policy, cultural tourism, wildlife ecology, park management and sustainable tourism. Dr. Akama was one of the academic staff who started tourism training at Moi University in the early 1990s. For several years he taught undergraduate and postgraduate courses in tourism in the same institution where he rose to the position of Professor of Tourism. In the beginning of 1994, Dr. Akama moved to Kisii University College as a Principal of the institution. Over the years, he has published widely in areas of tourism, wildlife ecology and park management.

Shem W. Maingi is a PhD Candidate at Kenyatta University. He holds a Master of Philosophy Degree in Tourism Management from Moi University (2007) and a B.Com Hons. (Management Science) from the University of Nairobi. His major research interests include tourism psychology, tourism certification, sustainable tourism within protected areas, particularly in Kenya and wildlife tourism development. He is a member of the Tourism thematic Group of the Kenya Climate Change Working Group.

Blanca A. Camargo is a Professor and Director of the International Tourism Program at University of Monterrey in Monterrey, Mexico. She has a doctoral degree in Recreation, Park and Tourism Sciences from Texas A&M University. Her area of specialization is sustainable tourism with a focus on cultural justice. Her research interests are in the areas of cultural heritage, cultural well-being, tourism pedagogy and accessible tourism.

Tej Vir Singh

(Tej Vir Singh)
Editor-in-Chief

5. THE WAY FORWARD

Corporate Social Responsibility

One may ask, who, between a university and the community needs the other more? For now, I will leave the question for you to answer. But my humble understanding is that a university cannot exist in a vacuum. Really, no institution can afford to exist as an ivory tower. A university, or any learning institution for that matter, is there for the good of the community around it and beyond.

With this understanding, Kisii University has over the years engaged in community service. This is what is sometimes referred to as Corporate Social Responsibility (CSR).

A major CSR activity that we have engaged in over the years in the nearby community pertains to the Kisii Soapstone Industry. This industry provides livelihood to thousands of residents in the Tabaka region of Kisii County and beyond. The industry has a lot of potential to enhance the social and economic development, especially, of the local people. Many of these people are engaged in carving activities; others own properties where the rock is mined while many others are involved in downstream value chain activities such as selling and marketing the soapstone products. Sadly, most of these people have not been able to maximize the economic benefits of the industry as they are always exploited by middlemen.

Within this socio-economic scenario, Kisii University has in the recent past engaged in empowering the soapstone producers through skills training to help enhance their levels and quality of production. The producers are trained on new production and marketing techniques, basic accounting and book keeping skills. The training is done through a programme that lasts one to two weeks, intended to equip the trainees with the relevant skills and competencies.

Another CSR initiative involves Kisii University staff engaging in the training of small scale farmers in Nyamira and Kisii counties on how to improve the production of indigenous vegetables. These indigenous vegetable varieties include the spider plant *(saga)* night shade *(managu)*, and the African spinach *(enderema)*, among others. We are driven by the realization that vegetables, and other indigenous crops, are of high nutritional value.

The small scale farmers also learn value addition and marketing skills. Also, in 2017, the university partnered with the United States Agency for International Development (USAID) to supply over thirty solar driers to women groups in the two counties. The beneficiaries use the driers to dry and store vegetables as a way of minimizing post-harvest wastage. Through these initiatives, small-scale farmers, who are mainly women, are able to sell their produce in other places of Western Kenya and other parts of the country.

As well, the university. in partnership with the Kenya Commercial Bank (KCB). has assisted farmers in the two counties to purchase high yielding dairy pedigree livestock through an initiative called *Mifugo ni Mali* (Animals are Wealth). In the arrangement, farmers are given interest free loans to purchase pedigree cattle through the supervision of the university. The Department of Animal Husbandry also provides extension services and training to the farmers free of charge. This is alongside offering subsidised Artificial Insemination (AI) services to the farmers in the region.

At the same time, over the years, the university has organized regular agricultural exhibitions. In these shows, latest farming techniques and technologies are showcased for the training of farmers. These activities are mainly undertaken by the School of Agriculture and Natural Resources Management and other identified stakeholders. Here, farmers learn how to use modern farm machinery, farm inputs and application of proper soil conservation techniques, to name just a few.

Further, the university understands well that young people are the cornerstone and future of any country. This is why the institution has undertaken various initiatives intended at empowering the youth. This happens through various forums such as short courses on entrepreneurship, provision of IT training and supporting youth business ventures. Examples include Kenyuni Self-Group and the Kisii Youth Sacco where over one hundred members have taken training in various business and entrepreneurship skills.

Overall, empowering the youth entails encouraging them to be wealth creators instead of being job seekers. The training offered assists the young people to identify viable business opportunities and link them to existing market opportunities for their products. They also learn to be risk takers and the knowledge gained enables them to bypass exploitative middlemen who purchase their products at throw away prices and end up making huge profits, thus disadvantaging the youth.

Moreover, one must appreciate the fact that the region where Kisii University is located is one of the most densely populated rural areas in Kenya, if not in Africa. The ballooning youthful population is not a bad thing. There is economic potential in having large numbers of people as producers and consumers. However, without proper planning and management, it could trigger many challenges including poverty, unemployment and environmental degradation. For instance, in many parts of Kisii and Nyamira counties, there is increasing land degradation, soil erosion and water pollution. This is occasioned by poor agricultural practices, and rapid population growth coupled with traditional land subdivision practices.

While Kisii Town is evidently an emerging regional economic hub, experts warn that existing practices, such as poor waste management and haphazard waste disposal have compromised the quality of the urban environment. For instance, the two rivers that pass through Kisii Town are highly polluted. This is notwithstanding the fact that, downstream, many people use the water from the rivers for domestic purposes.

Subdivision of land to small uneconomical portions also poses a great danger to farming in a region that was in the past regarded as one of Kenya's food baskets. When one adds these to the increasing problems of soil erosion and destruction of wetlands and riparian areas, things only get worse. It makes it obvious that the region is facing major and potentially catastrophic challenges of environmental and land degradation. In the end, the results include poor conditions of living, punctuated by preventable illnesses, poverty and malnutrition.

An example of the worst case scenario is what happened during the recent (2019) drought in the region. All the previously bountiful springs that had always existed in my home area dried up. In fact, many streams in the Kisii region have either dried up or have insignificant water flow. Worse yet, the existing springs, streams and rivers are highly polluted due to effluents from pit latrines and farm chemicals. These effluents get swept downstream during the rains. Furthermore, indigenous trees have been decimated and have been replaced by exotic species such as eucalyptus trees that are known to be water guzzlers and destroyers of waterbeds and rivers.

The university is well aware of such environmental challenges. For this reason, the institution is actively engaged in creating awareness concerning the dangers of growing eucalyptus trees in prohibited areas, especially along water beds and on wetlands. While initially people were reluctant to address the issue, they seem to have seen the light and are now slowly replacing the gum trees with water friendly plant species such as bamboo.

As part of environmental conservation initiatives, the University's Scouting Movement has played an active role in tree planting activities. As of 2019, the movement had planted close to one million indigenous trees and bamboo seedlings in both Kisii and Nyamira counties.

Also, as already shown, through our Department of Agriculture, the university trains farmers on modern methods of farming and land conservation techniques. The increasing subdivision of land is a complex social and cultural issue. But notwithstanding this, we are encouraging residents to shun or minimize the practice in order to enhance agricultural production.

Through these diverse socio-economic and environmental initiatives, the university is playing a role in transforming the livelihoods of Kenyans who live around it. These interventions also make the community claim ownership of the institution, and be part and parcel of its development, thus, promoting a win-win situation among various stakeholders.

Upholding Student Discipline

When one joins university, as a student, he or she is already a grown-up and capable of managing one's life. This is why we do not assemble outside the administration block every morning to issue instructions to students and reprimand those who have violated rules and regulations as it happens in primary and high schools. At university, students enjoy freedom, which sharply contrasts to what they experienced in their lower levels of schooling.

While this is the case, it happens that some students misuse the available freedom and end up dropping out of college or performing poorly in their studies. Thus, despite the fact that students have freedom and are expected to carry themselves with diligence and dignity, many face challenges of indiscipline, delinquency, and drug and substance abuse. Still others find themselves on a collision course with university authorities as they go on strike, and engage in other unbecoming behaviour.

On the whole, youth in Kenya face a myriad of challenges including problems that come with rapid social transformation and technological advancement. These technological transformations include increasing usage of the internet and social media. Coupled with this, our country has a major challenge of unemployment, underemployment and rising levels of poverty, with the youth taking the brunt of it!

The worst scenario pertains to the rising cases of suicide, manslaughter and murder where young men and women fall victim, become suspects, conduits or accomplices in the vices. The situation is so bad that a day hardly lapses without the media highlighting cases of murder or suicide, many of them involving the youth.

At Kisii University, we recognize these complex challenges confronting the youth. It is our tradition that when First Year students report to the university, they are taken through a rigorous induction programme that lasts for several days. In this elaborate orientation exercise, the students are systematically taken through the various aspects of university life. They are introduced to pertinent academic issues, and existing university rules and regulations. They are also taken through existing student welfare services, university social life and understanding diverse supportive services in and out of university.

From the very beginning of their university life, the students are encouraged to seek assistance whenever they are faced with academic and social challenges. They are also taken through virtues of positive character formation, good moral behaviour and responsiveness to the needs of other students and staff in the university environment and beyond.

As a matter of fact, at the university, we emphasise the understanding that we are one big family where each member should always care for the welfare of the other members, be they students, staff or other stakeholders, that is, being your neighbour's keeper. Students are urged not to be self-centred. They are persuaded to move away from the 'Me' syndrome and embrace the 'We' concept. This is where one understands that one's needs and expectations are closely intertwined with those of other people around one.

It is imparted upon the students that, as respectable and responsible human beings, they should always strive to make the university environment better than they found it. They are also encouraged to join various Christian and Muslim Associations to receive spiritual guidance and religious nourishment for the benefit of their overall welfare. In this connection, the university has very robust religious and interdenominational associations and a vibrant Students' Welfare Office. Students can receive prompt counselling whenever the need arises.

Perhaps more importantly, we have embraced an open door policy where our offices are accessible to students. This principle has become a major plank in our institution. Students are free to visit any office for service or advice. Even the Vice Chancellor's office is always open to the students or any other member of the university fraternity for that matter. Our understanding is that students are the most important members of Kisii University family. As such, the student welfare must be at the centre of university governance.

Through these forms of pro-active administrative approaches, we have managed to have relative peace and tranquillity within the university system. This is so despite the many challenges we have as a university, at the top of them being resource constraints.

We are very much aware of the fact that Kenyan universities receive thousands of young people from diverse social and economic backgrounds. We realize that most of the vices exhibited by the students are a manifestation of what is happening in the wider society. In this regard, it is true that in most instances, what happens in the university can be a reflection of what happens in the broader society.

As is the case with other Kenyan universities, at Kisii University, we have over the years experienced negative manifestations from some of our students. These include anti-social behaviour such as alcoholism, drug taking and petty theft. These are negative attributes with the potential of disrupting the smooth running of the university. If the trends were to be left unchecked, they could deny the university a chance of achieving its core objectives in teaching, research, innovation and community outreach. Further, such negative student activities stand to tarnish the institution's image that the university community has dedicatedly committed to build.

In particular, there is a common trend in Kenyan universities where students attempt to express their concerns through violent strikes and demonstrations. Most of these strikes usually lead to destruction of property, injury of students, staff and even bystanders. Temporary closure of institutions is often recommended as the best stop-gap measure in such situations so that calm can be restored. This affects the Academic Calendar and prolongs the time students take to complete their training.

As stated earlier, the Kisii University Management has come up with various strategies and mechanisms to reduce such incidents. This is why the university roots for holistic approaches to training. Hence, apart from academic training, students are provided with appropriate social, spiritual and life skills to enable them become better managers of their lives.

In this connection, the university has a fully established and functional Department of Students Guidance and Counselling. This is the office which handles diverse social, economic and other non-academic problems confronting the students. These holistic approaches help transform student lives to become productive citizens. By the time they finish their studies they are well equipped to take their place in the world. However, in extreme cases like psychiatric problems and extreme drug addiction, the students are referred to specialized institutions for appropriate treatment and rehabilitation.

Furthermore, in 2019, we established a Career Services and Placement Office. Here, students learn about existing career opportunities as relates to their areas of training. The career experts in the Department meet and give career advice to the students on a regular basis. The Department also invites specialized guest speakers to provide professional advice to students. They usually focus on trending thematic areas of career development and the evolving job market situation in Kenya and other parts of the world.

Perhaps the recent introduction of Mindset Education illustrates better our commitment to offering holistic training to our students. This is a programme, which is championed by the Office of the Dean of Students. Mindset or mind change training is widely applied in South Korea. In the

Asian country, this training has been central to the social and economic transformation of the Korean people. The mindset concept aims at transforming the whole thinking process and attitudes of the people especially the youth, to be positive in their approach to life. It particularly aims at making them always understand that people's abilities are boundless if positively applied.

Applying the mindset model, students and staff learn to have positive mindsets and change of heart. In the long run, this mindset empowerment should enable students to navigate and change their negative attitudes and overcome social barriers. The students and staff are also trained to always think positively about themselves, their colleagues, friends, the university and society in general.

Mindset Education emphasises the concept that, with a positive mind and a good heart, everything is possible. In fact, most human beings fail to succeed in their lives due to the barriers they build around their lives.

The South Korean experience clearly indicates that mindset training works and can transform people's lives and enhance their social, economic and cultural and technological wellbeing. For instance, the Gross Domestic Product (GDP) of the Asian country has grown rapidly and steadily in the last fifty years. This took place from the late 1960s when the South Korean Government took its citizens through a national transformative project called the 'New Village Movement'.

In this approach, the people of South Korea went through various ways of transforming their thinking that encouraged the people to work together and develop their communities and country. The results of this strategy are there to be seen today. In a period of less than four decades, the people of South Korea have managed to transform their country from an extremely undeveloped society to be one of the richest countries in the world.

The past poor economic state of South Korea can be demonstrated by the fact that in the late 1960s, Kenya's founding father Mzee Jomo Kenyatta gave a special grant to the South Korea Government. It is rather ironical that we are now looking to the same country to support us financially and for benchmarking on matters of development. One wonders where the rain started beating us.

Since the 1970s, the economy of South Korea has grown more than three hundred times, whereas ours is still stuck in the mud and struggling. For instance, South Korea does not produce any crude oil. The country imports crude oil from the Middle East and other parts of the world, which it refines and processes into high quality finished petroleum products. Currently, the country is the leading exporter of refined oil and finished petroleum products. South Korea is also the leading exporter of refined coffee products yet not even a single tree of the crop is grown within its borders. Of course, the Korean climate cannot allow the growing of coffee, a tropical plant.

The country is also a global powerhouse in electronic products including mobile phones, televisions sets and other appliances. It is also a major automobiles exporter. These mega industries are avenues of massive wealth creation.

I am convinced that the case of South Korea offers a lot for us to learn from. It shows that with positive thinking, hard work and commitment, Kenya can grow into an economic powerhouse in Africa. The continent is blessed with many natural resources and excellent climatic conditions, yet it is doing poorly as regards to economic growth and technological advancement. Consequently, the Korean example can serve as a major lesson for African countries including Kenya.

However, one may argue that while mindset training is a core aspect of national development, it is just one pillar. Some school of thought avers that the development of South Korea cannot solely be attributed to mindset education. Rather, other factors, key among them being good leadership, have also played a critical role. Other factors are historical for Korea as a former Japanese colony. It is argued that South Korea's nationalism spurred it to want to beat its former colonial master and hence the intense investment in areas where Japan was dominant such as electronics, automobiles, large-scale industrialization and manufacturing, among others.

We really need to change our mindset and it is with this understanding that Kisii University started programmes in Mindset Education to inculcate positive values to our students and staff.

When I Exit from Kisii University

Based on the preceding exposition, one can say that I have had an exciting, robust, fulfilling and equally challenging career at Kisii University. I joined the institution when it was a constituent college of Egerton University and witnessed its transformation into a full-fledged university. I have seen it crawl, stand, walk and run. I currently see the university vibrating with boundless opportunities for further growth. I would not have been part of the university's success story if God had not granted me this unique opportunity. I will be forever grateful to my family, colleagues, the Management and the Government of Kenya for according me the opportunity to serve the institution and, by extension, the Kenyan people in general.

I am now serving my second and last term as the Vice Chancellor of this great institution. My tenure draws to a close towards the end of 2022. However, before that period, I have some unfinished business. I trust that, by God's grace, I will accomplish a few more things before I exit from the scene. I am quite informed that this position that I have occupied for more than twelve years is contractual and whoever comes after me will be able to move the university forward to greater heights.

It is also important to note that, the Government of Kenya recognizes that education and training for Kenyans is fundamental to the national development agenda. Because of this, the country has consistently prioritized education at all levels. Over 30% of the National Budget is allocated to the sector. The Government of Kenya supports education not just as a key pillar for social prosperity but also as an impetus for national cohesion and economic transformation. In particular, the Government of Kenya envisions transforming the country into a prosperous and internationally competitive nation through education, training, and enhancing a knowledge-based economy.

As indicated earlier, universities do not operate in a vacuum. The country's university education system is expected to produce a large pool of well-trained and competent human resource, graduands equipped with the knowledge, skills and competencies required for the country to realize rapid socio-economic development and to remain globally competitive. Accordingly, education is a catalyst that should enable the country actualize the national ambition of a knowledge-based economy as envisaged in Vision 2030.

As a remedy for implementing Vision 2030, the Government of Kenya launched the Sector Performance Standards (SPS) in January 2010. Key measurable performance indicators for the higher education sub-sector include increasing the number of science parks, research output, registered patents, institutional research, and scientific publications. As already shown, since inception as a constituent college in 2007, Kisii University has proactively contributed towards the achievement of these national goals.

As part of promoting the National Government goals, at Kisii University, we are guided by the recently initiated 2019-2024 Strategic Plan. This is the blueprint guiding us as we seek to attain our overarching Vision and Mission and, in the process, do our bit to aid the government attain its set goals. In consequence, the document provides an impetus for institutional transformation and academic enhancement. However, to contextualize our transformation agenda towards the envisioned planning horizon of 2024, we have put into context, the role that Kisii University should play into the future. We are aiming to complement the government's broad agenda on national transformation as guided by Vision 2030 and the Big Four Agenda.

This is because, as a university, we have a responsibility to contribute to national development through the implementation of our core mandate namely; training, innovation, research and community extension. As a university, we continuously interrogate our strategic objectives to make sure that the institution is on the right trajectory as we move into the future.

Furthermore, in the broadest sense, it should be noted that the Sustainable Development Goals (SDGs), which is a collection of 17 goals set by the United Nations, form part of our guiding principles. We aspire to take Kisii University to higher heights. The goals were publicised in 2015 and cover social and economic development issues, including poverty, hunger, health, quality education, climate change, gender equality, water, sanitation, energy, urbanization, environment and social justice. Kenya as a member of the United Nations has fully subscribed to the SDGs. For instance, goal four (4) sets a target that by 2030, countries, Kenya being no exception, should ensure that all learners acquire knowledge and skills needed to promote sustainable development.

In tandem with its mandate, Kisii University therefore, has realigned its strategic objectives by focusing on delivering quality teaching, research, extension and innovation that would have a national and international impact. Consequently, we aspire to make Kisii University a world class institution renowned in academic excellence and promotion of social welfare. We intend to do this by reviewing and implementing our academic quality assurance regulations and guidelines. We will ensure that our schools consistently implement their documented operating procedures in line with the ISO 9001:2015, the International Standards Organisation's quality management system.

As I have already alluded, Kenya has undertaken an overall quest towards national prosperity. This quest, according to Vision 2030, includes the need to build a just and cohesive society. Hence, the country aspires to build a society which enjoys equitable social development in a clean and secure environment. This underpins the basis for social and economic transformation, where higher education plays a critical role. Along these lines, and as is the case with other Kenyan Public Universities, Kisii University promotes the National Government and the global agenda by training high level skilled human resource, and by engaging in research, innovation and community outreach initiatives.

The foregoing rationale underscores why the university reviewed its initial 10-year Strategic Plan. As I have noted, we are now working within the present Strategic Plan covering the period 2019-2024. The overall intention is to align our Vision and Mission with Vision 2030 and Third Medium Term Plan, whose implementation scope covers the year 2018-2022.

Further, the Government of Kenya introduced The Big Four Agenda on 12th December 2017. This strategy seeks to address the nexus between accelerated national economic development and the attainment of Vision 2030. The approach seeks to realign the country's development agenda for the period covered by the Third Medium Term Plan (2018-2022). Furthermore, the Big Four Agenda focuses on key tenets that are critical in uplifting the standards of living of Kenyans and transforming the country to become an upper-middle-income country by the year 2030. These key tenets include enhancing affordable universal and decent housing, affordable health care, employment creation through manufacturing and food security.

This national policy is supposed to bolster social cohesion and inclusive economic growth. In this context, through the revised Strategic Plan, Kisii University has realigned its objectives towards addressing these national development goals. This is as regards to national social and economic development, cohesion, industrialization and manufacturing, agriculture and healthcare. Also, the university, while reviewing its academic programmes and key policies, will ensure that the strategies are deliberately designed to address the Big Four Agenda.

The University of the Future

I am driven by the understanding that we can only transform Kisii University to become a beacon of excellence if we clearly identify and implement strategic objectives that are in line with national aspirations. As Management, we must also endeavour to showcase the institution to the immediate community, the entire country and the world as to why we exist as an institution of higher learning.

I emphasize that quality and relevance of education and training form the centre of Kisii University's revised 2019-2024 Strategic Plan. In Kenya, as is the case in most African countries, the recent rapid expansion of university education has raised pertinent questions as regards to quality of the graduates. To avoid this pitfall, Kisii University is continuously offering competitive, relevant and quality academic programmes. As Management, we will ensure that the programmes introduced are fully accredited and responsive to the needs of the dynamic job market and societal needs in general.

The programmes will be designed to have relevant content that aims at addressing national development goals. Similarly, the university will continually maintain a culture of academic excellence at all levels by ensuring that curricula, as well as learning and teaching methods, are developed as per the prescribed standards and international best practice.

The university has also placed the promotion of student affairs at the centre of its operations. We have embraced the students as key stakeholders. This will entail engaging them in critical areas such as lecturers' assessment and curricula and extra curricula development, policy formulation and other governance initiatives. Further, the university will progressively recruit, develop and retain highly skilled and competent staff within the timeframe of the strategic plan.

Furthermore, in modern times, universities cannot isolate themselves from society and the community where they are situated. This is particularly so due to the emerging trends in recent years, where universities are supposed to play a critical role in promoting the social and economic wellbeing of communities adjacent to the institutions and beyond.

Hence, some of the avenues for enhancing the relevance of higher education include participation in initiatives that address the practical needs and aspirations of the communities through research, extension and innovation. This demonstrates the critical role of institutions of higher learning in the design, development and dissemination of knowledge, skills, innovation and other specialized resources for the betterment of society.

As part of the transformation process, Kisii University will, during the five-year period of the Strategic Plan, continue to focus on innovation, research and extension services as enunciated in the long term national development goals as well as Vision 2030. This way, the university would have played its role in uplifting the social and economic welfare of the Kenyan citizenry.

Our research and extension programmes will be tailored to address priority strategic areas such as food security, healthcare, housing and unemployment within the Western Kenya region and beyond. Consequently, the university will endeavour to provide a conducive environment that recognizes and supports pragmatic and innovative research and extension initiatives.

Particularly, Science, Technology and Innovation (STI) are key to Kenya's socio-economic transformation as envisaged in Vision 2030. Indeed, those countries that have strong research and innovation systems have excellent science and technology programmes in institutions of higher learning. Similarly, new global indicators for sustainable development have been tied to investment in STI. Kisii University will therefore position itself towards making greater impact on the local and wider arena by providing tangible solutions that will enhance economic growth and industrialization.

Furthermore, the university will aim at becoming a beacon of excellence in the development of new technologies. This will entail providing innovative solutions to society and industry. Perhaps more importantly, the STI initiatives will at all times be realigned and driven by the national aspirations of the 'Big Four Agenda' (based on the MTP3) and Vision 2030.

As part of the implementation, we will also establish and implement a policy framework on STI. This will be in addition to establishing and supporting business incubation and innovation. This will help transform scientific knowledge and innovation into products and services for societal advancement. This innovation and technology initiatives will be based in our ultra-modern ICT Learning and Business Centre whose construction is now complete.

Leading universities world over are actively engaged in broad-based collaboration and partnerships with like-minded institutions. These partnerships are usually beneficial both to themselves and the broader constituents that they serve. Consequently, Kisii University seeks to position itself towards developing strong external linkages and partnerships. The relationships are expected to enhance mutual learning, research and innovation. This approach will provide opportunities for exposure to state-of-the-art knowledge, skills and competencies to students and staff through exchange programmes. We will also endeavour to enhance our linkages with industries, research institutes, international and multinational organizations, professional and regulatory bodies, county governments and our Alumni groups. This will allow our students and staff to acquire practical skills and knowledge in various spheres of academic and professional training.

Towards this end, during the five-year period, we will develop a policy framework and annual work plans on partnerships and collaboration. Further, we would ensure that the same is continually implemented in the subsequent years as we move towards the planning horizon of 2024. The results of this approach will determine our legacy when the strategic plan period comes to fruition.

****

Availability of requisite resources is one of the elements that characterize world-class universities. This is in response to the huge costs involved in running a complex, research-oriented university. Renowned world class universities have several sources of finances such as government budget allocation for operational expenditures and research, contract research and consultancy funding. Revenues can also come from established public organizations, private sector, financial returns from endowments and gifts, investments and tuition fees.

On the contrary, our university, as is the case with other Kenyan public universities, largely relies on government funding and internally generated revenue, mainly tuition fees, to fund expenditure and development. However, due to unfavourable economic conditions witnessed over the recent past, the government's support has steadily declined.

Due to this, the university has been conditioned to operate under a very constrained budgetary environment. Our competitiveness at Kisii University needs to be enhanced if the institution is to have a realistic chance of becoming one of the leading universities in the region. Such improved competitiveness may not really be anticipated without reconfiguration and expansion of the present income base. The university will therefore consolidate and diversify its resource base to enable it to be competitive.

By the end of the strategic planning period in 2024, it is projected that Kisii University would have enhanced its financial base to fully support its mandate. This is because teaching, research, innovation, and extension can only be achieved if adequate resources are available. To actualize this intent, the university will develop and implement a comprehensive Resource Mobilization Policy. In the same vein, the university will undertake prudent management of its financial resources. Already, the university has established an Income Generation Unit (IGU) which is now fully operational.

To attract the best staff and increase graduate and undergraduate student enrolment, the university will support the development of modern infrastructure and state-of-the-art facilities within the plan period. In the next five years, we will complete the development of ongoing projects which include Phase 2 of the ICT Learning and Business Centre, lecture theatres and Phase 2 of Office Block (Sakagwa Academic Block). We will also initiate the development of new projects such as the Administration Block, Student Centre, internal road network and a perimeter wall to enhance security.

A comprehensive Maintenance Policy for facilities and infrastructure will also be prepared and implemented during the strategic planning period. At the same time, comprehensive physical development Master Plans will be prepared for all parcels of land under the university. This will provide a clear spatial vision for the development of those properties. In addition, all infrastructural related issues would have usability and safety components as the core requirement.

More importantly, we have reviewed and improved our performance management systems. This has taken place through a deliberate transformative change management process. This happened with the understanding that, for optimal results, it was critical that all members of staff clearly understand their roles in the implementation of the Strategic Plan. The university will therefore continue preparing Annual Performance contracts with the National Government based on the strategic objectives and key performance indicators of the Strategic Plan.

As already indicated, in order to attain the intended outputs, the university will prepare Annual Work Plans guided by the key performance indicators as outlined in the Strategic Plan. It will further re-align the priority activities to be implemented in each financial year. Every Division, Campus, School and Department, will be required to prepare detailed Annual Work Plans, derived from the approved University Annual Work Plan. Additionally, all School Boards and Campus Boards will prepare and align their strategic plans with the University Strategic Plan.

As a strategy for operationalizing the five-year University Strategic Plan, every Head of Division will sign a performance contract with their respective Heads of Departments/Deans at the beginning of each Financial Year. This will be based on the University Performance Contract and Annual Work Plan as derived from the Strategic Plan. Heads of Departments/Deans will in turn sign Performance Appraisal instruments with their members of staff.

Further, every member of staff will draw their Individual Annual Work Plan from the Departmental Annual Work Plans. This will ensure each of them contributes to the achievement of the University Strategic Objectives. In this case, each Department will be responsible for the implementation of its work plans that will be tied into agreed performance contract indicators.

Through the Budget and Resource Allocation Committee, the university will prepare all budget proposals for submission to the National Treasury for allocation of the required financial resources. To ensure efficiency in budgeting and expenditure processes, the university's Budget and Resource Allocation Committee will, on a quarterly basis, review performance of the approved university budget.

Evaluation and review of the Strategic Plan will be carried out from time to time, using measures of relevance, efficiency, effectiveness, sustainability and impact. These parameters will gauge the extent of achievement of the intended results. The process will be undertaken after 2½ years period using internal evaluators. All Departments and Schools will hold quarterly departmental performance review meetings as stipulated in the university policies and guidelines. Reports from such meetings will be tabled for review and verification during the University Management Board meetings. In all these ambient, the University Council will play an oversight role.

****

In addition to Kisii University's Mission of training high level human resource that meets the development needs of the country and international labour market, we also aim at sustaining production of quality research and dissemination of knowledge, skills and competencies for the advancement of humanity. By 2024, the guiding principles for both students and staff of Kisii University will be the provision of a world-class education, in an atmosphere of academic freedom, civility, social responsibility, integrity and accountability.

It is expected that Kisii University graduates will espouse these principles in their work places and interactions with society. They will be clearly distinguishable as our products. Further, the university will have taken full advantage of its strengths and opportunities to develop and conduct learning, research and innovation programmes. These programmes will address the social and technological challenges of Kenya, the region, and the world at large.

Critical to the success of the university is the capacity to attract and retain students and staff of outstanding quality. The university, by 2024, therefore, aims to transform into a preferred destination with a supportive workplace for outstanding staff and students.

By 2024, I envisage that academic programmes offered at Kisii University will be among the most competitive not only in the country, but also globally. In this regard, Kisii University will be ranked among the most competitive institution of higher learning in the region.

In the same vein, the university will have one of the most competitive, skilled and competent staff. Here, emphasis is on academic members of staff who will be playing a critical role towards technological, social and economic development of the country. The university will also establish a strong quality management system that will ensure efficient and effective running of all its operations.

Best hiring policies and processes will be used to get the best academic and administrative staff for the institution. Continuous skills upgrading for the staff, curriculum review, updating of management systems and benchmarking with leaders in the university education sector will further ensure that we attain and retain the anticipated world class status.

The international reputation and competitiveness of universities, to a large extent, depend on the range and quality of their research and innovation performance. Kisii University aims to advance its reputation and performance as a major research and innovation university. We will do this by strengthening our role as a leading institution in research, training and innovation.

As a consequence, by 2024, I anticipate that Kisii University will be ranked among the leading institutions in research, innovation and extension. Excellence in these areas shall therefore be at the core of our operations.

I also expect that by this time, the university would have built superior capacity in teaching, research, innovation and extension. It will also have increased expenditure in research and extension, and fully implemented a research and extension policy framework. On top of this, we would have established research partnerships with strategic institutions in the country and across the world, diversified our sources on research funding, increased publications by staff and students, and continued to promote knowledge and skill transfer through workshops, conferences and seminars to disseminate knowledge and research findings.

Hence, by the end of the strategic planning period, I expect that Kisii University would have acquired and consolidated adequate resources to support its core mandate. It would have made a significant impact on the local and wider community through meeting the demands for the provision of tangible solutions that will enhance science, technology and innovation.

The university would have fully implemented a policy framework for Science, Technology and Innovation. It would also have increased the percentage of Science and Technology graduates. Further, it would have an established strategic partnership for Science, Technology and Innovation, and; provided adequate equipment and infrastructure to serve the teaching, learning, and management needs, and fully implemented the ICT policy framework.

The university would have also implemented its comprehensive ICT Policy. This will ensure that ICT infrastructure is maintained at a level permitting the institution to keep abreast of international 'best practice' in teaching, learning, innovation and research.

In this regard, by 2024, Kisii University would have actively engaged in broad-based partnerships. These partnerships will be beneficial both to the university community as well as the broader constituents it serves. The university would have positioned itself and developed strong external linkages and partnerships for mutual learning, research and innovation.

From the foregoing, the university would have realized strong linkages and partnerships with industries, research institutions and middle level colleges, international and multinational organizations, community, and relevant professional and regulatory bodies. Furthermore, by 2024, the university would have a vibrant Alumni Association. Linkages will be selectively done to ensure mutual benefit in teaching, research, learning and innovation.

Realizing the ambitious Vision reflected in our transformative agenda will largely depend on how we will translate our Strategic Plan through an efficient, effective, inclusive and resolute operational management system at all levels of the university's academic, administrative and governance structures. However, my message to the Kisii University family and other stakeholders is, we can only attain the envisaged transformation if we remain focused on our strategic objectives by working together as one cohesive entity.

Well, some of the wordings in this chapter and the next one may become stale by the end of 2024. However, the fact remains that the contents will influence the direction the university takes, going forward. It will also determine the legacy I would have left behind when my time to leave the university comes. My prayer is that as a university, we achieve and actualise the Strategic Plan in a visionary manner.

Biographer's Note

The University launched its Strategic Plan for 2019-2024 and unveiled Phase One of the ultra-modern and state of the art ICT Centre on March 6th, 2020. The ceremony was officiated by the Chairman of the Commission for University Education (CUE), Prof. Chacha Nyaigoti Chacha. Coincidentally, the chief guest served at the institution as the first Principal when it was elevated by the government from a teacher training college to a campus of Egerton University in 1994. Other guests included Chief Administrative Secretaries Zach Kinuthia (Ministry of Education) and Maureen Mbaka (Ministry of ICT, Innovation and Youth Affairs), members of the University Council, the University Senate and the University Management Board.

In his address, Prof. Chacha said a Strategic Plan was a roadmap that should guide the development of various facets of an institution. He emphasized the need for Kisii University to specialize in various niche areas of training where it has comparative advantage. This way, the university would be renown in the particular areas of interest and will be able to attract more students to those niche programmes.

The CUE Chairman said that the Strategic Plan should not lose sight of the emerging trends and challenges confronting university education and implored the Kisii University leadership to focus on transforming the institution into a high level training centre for human resource. He expressed optimism that this way, students graduating from the university will be abreast of critical problems and challenges the country is facing and be able to offer solutions. This, Prof. Chacha said, would be attained if the university put more emphasis on scientific and applied research in various fields.

It should be noted that when Education Cabinet Secretary Prof. George Magoha assumed office, newspapers reported that he was pushing for the merger of public universities. However, it did not take long before Prof. Magoha clarified that the government was not considering amalgamating the institutions. On August 9, 2019, Business Daily quoted him as saying that the government wants universities to specialize in academic programmes based on their strengths rather than duplicating programmes offered by others.

The Corona Virus Pandemic

This may appear misplaced here but it is not. I have to note that as I got into the homestretch in telling this story, tragic news of a new virus disease broke out. Initially, the outbreak of Corona virus disease (COVID-19) in China late 2019 did not make much sense to most Kenyans, I included. However, as days went by, it continued to be reported that the viral disease was giving China sleepless nights. I will not say much about the pandemic within the confines of this book but a small highlight will definitely be acceptable.

One thing stood out; the COVID-19 virus was spreading faster than initially fathomed. In a matter of days, the disease spread far and wide, affecting people of different races, nationalities and ages. By the end of 2020, the virus had infected more than 87million people globally and killed over 1.7 million. In Kenya, the first case was reported on March 13, 2020, reportedly imported from Europe. But by December, over 93,000 Kenyans had been infected. By this time, the disease had claimed the lives of over 1,600 Kenyans. There were over 75,000 recoveries.

With reality sinking in that the virus was here with us, the Government responded by putting in place various measures. These included closure of all learning institutions and public places of worship, imposing a partial lockdown and cessation of movement in hotspot areas such as Nairobi, Mombasa and Mandera. The Government also imposed a dusk to dawn countrywide curfew. Furthermore, the Government started creating awareness on hygiene and lifestyle measures like hand washing and/or sanitizing, wearing of facemasks, observing physical distancing and avoiding mass gatherings. The same guidelines have been recommended by the World Health Organisation (WHO).

At the start of July 2020, the Government relaxed some of the measures. Notably, President Uhuru Kenyatta lifted the lockdown of the three counties perceived as hotspots for the virus. Sadly, within a short time, the virus spiked.

By August, Kenya was reporting an average of 600 new infections daily. The country had done slightly more than

300,000 tests. This is a paltry number when compared to the total population. Perhaps this is why many people think that those who could have been infected by August were over three million, with a third of those cases being in the capital city, Nairobi.

From the look of things, this pandemic will have far reaching economic and social implications by the time it is contained. From where I view the situation, the full impact of COVID-19 disease will not be understood at this time. The virus has exposed the lack of preparedness and inadequacies of our medical facilities. It has shown our lack of adequate medical staff including doctors, nurses and lab technicians. So, we cannot accurately predict how many Kenyans will be affected even by the end of 2021.

However, our prayer is that through Government initiatives and individual responsibilities, the spread of the virus can be contained. The good news is that researchers all over the world are not in slumber land. Indeed, by the end of 2020 a number of vaccines had been approved and were being administered to protect people from the virus. In fact, Russia made the first pronouncement that it had found and approved a vaccine, although critics claimed that the country was by-passing the procedure of making a breakthrough in such undertaking. By January 2021, there was a glimmer of hope with reports that new vaccines had been developed and approved for use in the UK and USA. It is my hope that these vaccines will soon find their way to other parts of the world, including Kenya, so that precious lives can be saved.

Even so, there is no denying that the socio-economic impact of the pandemic is going to be huge. Already, as is the case in many countries, our economy is at a standstill. Thousands of Kenyans have lost their jobs and several businesses have closed down. This has especially affected the informal settlement the worst, particularly in our major cities such as Mombasa, Nairobi and Nakuru. The population that lives hand to mouth is now unable to raise any income. The activities that gave them a living have been crippled by COVID-19 epidemic.

Furthermore, the impact of the virus on education is also going to be huge. Since mid-March of 2020, our university remained closed in compliance with Government directive. It is only those in strategic areas of the university, including the Office of the Vice Chancellor, the Medical Department and the Security Department that remained partially open but with scaled-down operations. The workers in these critical Departments were required to follow the stipulated containment measures.

It is a fact that the university was hit badly with the disruption of the 2019/2020 Academic Calendar. When the pandemic hit Kenya, we had three weeks to finish the Academic Year. As much as we had finished the syllabus, our students went home without sitting for their end of semester examinations.

At the same time, internally generated income in terms of fees payment by the privately sponsored students went down almost to zero payment. This caused shortfalls in the university's budget. We started experiencing the challenge of balancing the books, including servicing our payroll and paying suppliers. We could also not effectively remit statutory deductions like Pay As You Earn (PAYE), staff loans and pension contributions by staff.

However, the university managed to roll out e-learning. This became a central part in the teaching and training of our students. In 2019, the university had developed the Learning and Management System (LMS) with efficient IT infrastructure. This is a versatile IT system which came in hand in supporting e-learning activities. Lecturers and students were trained on how to use the e-learning platform and other virtual training and research facilities.

With e-learning, we managed to start our Third Semester of the 2019/2020 Academic Year. Over 9,000 students could be taught on the LMS platform. They did the Continuous Assessment Tests (CATs) through the e-learning management system. With the use of technology, we were able to continue engaging with the students. I can see the full implementation of our e-learning management system, and I hope that we will continue exploiting it even way after the COVID-19 pandemic is contained.

The technology is ideal in teaching and conducting research by students and staff. Unlike in the past when all students and staff were required to have face to face contact, many are now engaged through this virtual technology. This is why I am optimistic that even when normalcy prevails once again, e-learning will still be used to minimize huge gatherings in the so-called blended learning initiatives.

It is important to note that as from October 2020, the National Government made announcement allowing partial and/or phased re-opening of universities. Thus, with strict adherence to the Corona virus prevention protocols, Kisii University started a phased re-opening of the institution as directed. Following a revised Academic Calendar, the university started by allowing close to 6,000 First Year students to report for initial orientation and eventual face-to-face teaching. In addition, all students taking physical sciences courses that required practical lessons were allowed back for face-to-face undertaking of the lessons in the university laboratories.

Also, from the start of October, the university managed to administer all pending end of semester examinations. This was done systematically, by allowing different cohorts of students, starting with Finalists or Fourth Years who reported on session for their tests that they missed as a result of closure of the university due to the pandemic. Gradually, other cohorts, all the way to the continuing First Year students, were able to report on session to do the examinations. Thus, as the university entered 2021, we had managed to cover all the courses and examinations that were disrupted by the outbreak of the pandemic.

It is also worth mentioning that at the end of 2020, the university managed to achieve another milestone. Through the dexterity and hard work of staff and students, the institution held a Virtual Graduation Ceremony on December 18th, 2020. We graduated 2,197 students. This was not a mean achievement under the existing situation of uncertainty brought about by the pandemic.

However, is important to emphasize that the overall impact of this pandemic cannot be fathomed in the course of finalizing this book. Still, we are trying to understand how University and individual staff and students are going to cope with the disease. What this pandemic has taught us is that, even as individuals, institutions, and as a country, as much as we may be having good strategic plans, they can be derailed by unforeseen exogenous factors like diseases and political unrest. Indeed, when we were planning for the 2019/2020 Academic Calendar, nobody ever anticipated that we were going to have a calamity of this magnitude. As is the case with other institutions globally, this pandemic has transformed the way we do business in the University.

This shows that when plans are made, risk management and development of pro-active contingency measures to confront the unforeseeable circumstances should be incorporated. In other words, universities and other institutions of learning should model and predict probable emergence of calamities with the aim of coming up with fundamental measures to assist in coping with such challenges.

However, there is always a glimmer of hope. In history, we have had pandemics such as the Bubonic Plague of the 14th Century and the Spanish Flu at the turn of the 20th Century. The two pandemics killed millions of people. Eventually, though, humanity was able to overcome them and thrive into the future. The same will happen with the Corona virus.

At Kisii University, we came up with an *ad hoc* committee consisting of fifteen members drawn from all academic sections, the Health Department and student representatives, among others. The committee was mandated to analyse the impact of the pandemic on University activities. They developed a clear roadmap for the eventual re-opening of the University at the right time. Indeed, the full extent and magnitude of the Corona virus pandemic is still unfolding. Its story will be told to completion much later from several perspectives.

Last Initiatives

When my second and last term as Vice Chancellor of Kisii University comes to an end in 2022, my life will continue but in a different context. God has been good to me, and I pray and believe that He protects me to continue to live a productive life, serve humanity and enjoy the exigencies of life. My exit from Kisii University will mark a culmination of a thirteen-year stint at the institution.

Having joined the institution when it was a Constituent College of Egerton University in January 2009 as the founding Principal, luck came my way again when it was elevated to a Chartered University in 2013 and I was appointed as the pioneer Vice-Chancellor. I have held this position and capacity, and given my best to date. This is no mean feat. However, it is clear in my mind that my life at Kisii University is a song worth singing.

As my term at the university comes to the end, I do not hesitate to say that we have laid a firm foundation for the university. This foundation is in the spheres of infrastructural and academic programmes. It also includes hiring, streamlining and empowering the human resource establishment. Further, it includes the creation of the requisite university governance structures, policies, rules and regulations.

As already discussed, the university has developed a revised 2019-2024 Strategic Plan with clear strategic objectives, performance indicators and targets that are being implemented. The five-year Strategic Plan has got well-articulated and implementable targets. I do not have any doubt that the plan will be implemented as required, God willing.

I believe that, with the support of critical stakeholders, I have put the university on the right trajectory to move to greater heights. It is worth noting that I am finishing my last term with a number of ongoing tasks. Fulfilment of some of these landmark initiatives will spill over beyond 2024 as stipulated in the Strategic Plan.

The construction and equipping of Phase 2 of the ICT Centre and the establishment of the business and incubation centre are very close to my heart. The development of the ICT infrastructure is a part of the ambitious Vision 2030 flagship project. Already, Phase 1 of the project is complete and launched for use. Our plans are that the remaining phase of the project will be completed within the period of the Strategic Plan, which draws to a close in 2024.

The ICT Centre is envisioned to be the hub of IT activities. These include Software Engineering, Computer Hardware Development and Installation, Information Science Technology and Business IT. It will also be linked to all university academic departments. This way, it will provide specialised IT services such as e-learning, internet connectivity, network design and e-resources. In this regard, we want to make IT the cornerstone of our academic activities. Primarily, every training programme will have aspects of IT usage and application.

The business and incubation centre will provide training and provision of hands-on skills and competencies on business entrepreneurship, project planning, development and risk management. This will entail the development of short tailor-made courses or training modules that we will benefit business people and entrepreneurs from the region. The courses are intended to empower trainees with entrepreneurship skills, development of business plan competencies, book keeping and marketing skills.

Further, emerging entrepreneurs will be assisted to develop, design and implement specific business projects. This also relates to business incubation initiatives where students, staff and other interested parties would be exposed to specific entrepreneurial skills. They will also be helped to enhance their business ideas and concepts at the business incubation centre.

As well, we plan to finalize other key futuristic projects. These include the construction of an ultra-modern Administration Complex, Student Centre and the Engineering and Technology complex. These will be state-of-the-art modern facilities intended to meet changing and evolving needs and demands of a university of the 21st century.

We will also build a modern Science Complex. The building will house various science laboratories and lecture theatres equipped with modern teaching and learning facilities. The university has also initiated alternative resource and income mobilization strategies. Here, the university plans to commercialise some of its programmes and activities. These include printing services, the cafeteria, a water processing plant and consultancy services offered by our senior academic staff, and students in different fields.

Furthermore, the university has started transforming the 70 acre Nyosia farm and the other parcels of land in Nyangweta (South Mugirango) and Kiamogake (North Mugirango) into income generating units. For instance, Nyosia Farm will become a dairy production unit where we will rear high quality pedigree dairy cows and establish a milk processing plant. The milk produced from the farm would go towards meeting the latent demand in Kisii region and beyond.

Through the various Schools, we have embarked on a plan to review and restructure our academic programmes with the objective of updating and making them competitive and able to meet emerging market demands. It is my conviction that this move will make our programmes more adaptive to the emerging trends in the development and dissemination of knowledge, skills and competencies.

There is more. The Senate and Management want to nurture a high level human resource that would guide the continuous academic development of the university. This will cover all disciplines and professions to attain the capability and capacity of providing solutions to existing and emerging problems and challenges confronting Kenya and the world in general.

Another area which has attracted our focus is the improvement of pedagogy. We aspire to come up with new teaching methods, incorporating modern technologies in the delivery of knowledge, skills and competencies.

In this respect, e-learning will be at the centre of training and research initiatives in our Schools, Faculties, Institutes and Directorates. This intends to place Kisii University in a good standing as an avenue of producing versatile, dynamic and adaptive manpower, capable of fitting into the post-modern society.

As a university, we always endeavour to hire the best staff, especially at the academic and administrative level. We value continuous staff development programmes where we allow our workers to go for specialised courses and engage in appropriate research. This process will be reinforced, so as to keep all staff relevant and abreast with emerging trends in their areas of specialization.

Consequently, we will continue motivating our staff by creating a good working environment. We will encourage merit-based staff promotions and enhanced remuneration within the scope of available financial resources. The staff will be, continuously, allowed to engage closely and regularly with the Management to offer their views, new ideas, and air their grievances. Thus, the staff will be encouraged to be part of the solutions of the challenges confronting them as individuals and as the Kisii University family.

In my career as a university manager, I have appreciated the fact that when one brings people together in a congenial atmosphere and have frank conversations, the staff gets motivated. This makes them feel part and parcel of the institution. Staff should be encouraged to always support their university, with the understanding that when it grows, they also grow and the reverse is true.

Brief on Succession

The beauty of rendering public service as a top manager is the fact that the position is transitory. In this regard, my tenure as the Vice Chancellor of Kisii University is drawing to a close and I am alive to this fact. More importantly, I am happy because the University Council and Management have come up with a clear succession plan for senior management and other cadres of senior staff. Recently, the university developed a staff establishment framework. It provides a clear vision and strategy on how the university should govern succession at various levels of administration and management.

Already, there are plans to identify, train and promote Kisii University staff to take over strategic academic and administrative positions. This includes those who are at high level leadership and management positions. It is assumed that by the time I exit as Vice Chancellor, the university would have developed a pool of experienced staff to take over and be part of a very effective University Management Board.

There are clear policies, rules and regulations on how senior management positions, including that of Vice Chancellor and Deputy Vice Chancellors, should be competitively filled. These policies have been derived from and guided by the universities' Act 2012 as reviewed in 2016, the University Charter and Statutes.

Based on the foregoing plans and guided by the related policies, law and regulations, Kisii University remains a stable and sustainable public entity raring to move ahead into the future. It is an institution for the present, the future and for generations to come.

When time comes for me to walk out of my current office, I will do so with my head held high. I foresee that in the next two decades, the university will be one of the best centres of academic and research, nationally and possibly internationally. In that league, it will play its enhanced role in the promotion of social and economic welfare of society.

Service to the Community

I have not hidden myself under the wraps of Kisii University's Corporate Social Responsibility (CSR) and avoided supporting society and the less fortunate. It seems that I acquired the trait of helping others from my late father. As much as he was not a wealthy person, my father was a philanthropist, at least as per our standards. He led a life based on African social principles of always being considerate. He helped and enhanced the lives of the less fortunate members of society.

As we grew up, I saw my father going out of his way to share his meagre resources with those in need. Some of the beneficiaries of his generosity were total strangers to us. My father treated every person equally. He was actually prone to giving more attention to the people in need even beyond his call, and to the disadvantage of his immediate family.

For instance, when we harvested foodstuff including maize, beans, potatoes and finger millet, he gave some to those who were experiencing food shortages. I can state that a large portion of our farm produce went to support those who were in need. Even the few farm hands we had were treated with a lot of respect and decorum by our father. They felt at home because they were treated as part of the immediate family. At the time, I thought that my father sometimes showed a softer heart to strangers than he did to his immediate family.

I can bet that if my father was mean with his resources, and unfortunately had my mother not fallen sick at an earlier age, we could have accumulated substantially more resources than we usually had. In fact, a self-centred person could say that my father wasted family resources by sharing them with people who were not members of his household. This is far from the truth. My father always lived to every word of the saying, 'tenda wema nenda zako' (always do good regardless of the pay back). I discovered from him that when one gave, one never lacked. Instead, there was satisfaction and God opened a floodgate of blessings to the family, perhaps fulfilling the saying that 'one gives to get'.

A pleasant example is when he brought a very sickly man to our home. That episode is permanently edged in my memory. When he did this, I was not amused. The man was very weak and, as young as I was, I waited until my father was out of sight and went against his wish. I chased the stranger out of our compound. The poor person died a few days later.

Looking at this unfortunate incident in retrospect, one can argue that this person would have lived had he received a bit of care that my father intended to provide him with. The downside is that the fellow would have died in our home. This would have brought serious complications with authorities, let alone the intricate spiritual cleansing as required in our people's culture.

Fast forward, as much as I have tried to avoid it, I have found myself doing things the same way my late father did. On this matter, I will again not want it to appear that I am blowing my own trumpet. However, this is my story and if I fail to say it, who would?

When I see people in problems, it touches my heart. I get touched when I see people suffering from sickness, malnutrition and other forms of want. My heart bleeds when I see orphans in distress, young people overwhelmed with poverty, unemployment and underemployment. I find myself very empathetic to the needy.

When I started working as a high school teacher, I found myself sharing my meagre resources with those in need. It became part of me and, over the years, I have used a significant portion of my income to pay school fees for students who are either orphaned or whose parents are unable to raise the money. I also give pocket money to some.

More importantly, in recent years, since I joined Kisii University, I have been engaged in several humanitarian and philanthropic activities. These include supporting the youth, the church and self-help groups. I try to assist members of these groups by providing advice and where possible financial support. This is to help them achieve their anticipated objectives of enhancing their livelihoods. In this regard, I provide the youth with counselling, mentorship and other forms of empowerment initiatives.

My home region is predominantly Christian, especially Catholic and Seventh Day Adventist (SDA) denominations. I have been involved in fundraising for churches to undertake their construction and other development projects. This happens almost fortnightly.

I have also been engaged in youth activities in the larger Gusii region. The youth face challenges of poverty, unemployment and underemployment. Without our support, their lives would continue being miserable. Definitely, this does not augur well with our conscience as human beings, and as society.

I regularly meet such youth outside the university environment. Some are school leavers while others are burdened with the yoke of drug and substance abuse, and alcoholism. I engage them with a view of creating awareness on how they can be involved in self-help initiatives that can improve their socio-economic wellbeing.

In particular, I have challenged the youth to move away from the elusive white collar job mentality. This attitude is partly to blame for the suffering they find themselves in. I encourage them to embrace wealth creation initiatives through engagement in small and micro-scale projects. Horticultural farming, value addition initiatives and marketing of locally produced farm products, among others, are some of the projects we have discussed with the youth in our interactions with them.

Further, I have engaged the youth to initiate small scale cottage industries, including banana and milk processing. For instance, in 2019, I engaged the Ministry of Agriculture and managed to source for a medium size milk cooler, which has been installed at Nyansakia village in Borabu Constituency. The 2,000-litre capacity cooler enhances milk preservation and decreases wastage, hence increasing earnings. The project would also assist in reducing the negative impact of middlemen who exploit farmers by buying their produce cheaply and selling it at astronomical prices. I almost single-handedly paid for the construction of the building where the cooler is installed.

I will not want to forget to mention what I did in 2012. For years, people in our home area in Borabu went to sleep as soon as dusk came because there was no electricity. This is why I brought together fifty families and created awareness on how we could get electricity to our homes. We agreed that each family contributes Kshs. 5000 for this strategic project so that households would abandon using kerosene and start using electricity.

However, carrying out this project became a tall order for us as much as I did not know this at first. Once we raised the money, I discovered that the Kenya Power and Lighting Company (KPLC) officers on the ground then were not forthcoming. This was sad to me, realizing that KPLC, which is the sole power supplier, and is a government parastatal whose role is availing power to Kenyans at affordable rates and in an efficient manner, was not living up to its noble mandate.

The process was basically prone to corruption due to intricacies perhaps occasioned by the monopoly enjoyed by the parastatal. I doubt that I would have initiated the project in the first place had I known that it would take a whole three years to accomplish. The project actually somewhat tainted my name, with speculation that I had squandered the money which my fellow home mates had given me with much trust.

In the course of implementing the project, I made several trips to the company's offices in Kisii and the headquarters in Nairobi, pursuing the matter. However, as time passed, I discovered that some people back home were pre-occupied with petty issues. Some expected their homes to be lit first, while others did not want the company to erect poles, which were going to connect the power line to their neighbours, on their farms.

This epitomized the kind of social and cultural intricacies that exist in an African setting. We in many instances tend to undermine others and destroy initiatives that could assist us all, as individuals and as communities. This indeed has been an inhibitor to fast development in many villages.

Also, I am alive to the fact that in recent years, access to clean water has increasingly become a challenge in Kisii and Nyamira counties. This is happening despite the fact that the region receives high amounts of rainfall in the better part of the year. Women and children walk long distances to fetch water from springs that are already contaminated by various effluents. It is with this understanding that I got involved in the drilling of a borehole in our home area to enhance the residents' access to clean water. The borehole project was a success. It was completed within a short time largely because we did not have to deal with bureaucracy as happened with the power project.

As already stated, many young people, especially in rural areas, appear frustrated. Sometimes they try to find imaginary shortcuts to succeed and be happy in life such as engaging in drug and substance abuse. They do this to build fantasies around them. Others opt for petty crimes such as theft. This is why I have made it a point that I always visit youth groups and have meetings with them whenever time allows. In the meetings, I create awareness on the dangers of these vices and offer alternatives. In a small way, these initiatives, as much as they are small and personalized, make positive impact in the social and economic empowerment of the youth.

My endeavour is to always encourage the youth to think positively, despite the challenges facing them. This is in addition to paying school fees for several young people, especially those who are orphaned and are pursuing their studies in high schools and universities. I get encouraged to do this because many of these disadvantaged youths end up being successful in life. I also encourage them to learn from my example and assist others in situations similar to the one I rescued them from.

More importantly, I want our young people to change their mindset. Many are preoccupied with negative thoughts and self-inflicted barriers. They believe that society is unfair to them and continue whining about it. I encourage such youths to re-evaluate their attitudes and be positive in their thinking.

A good number of them end up admitting that they are the ones who have been unfair to themselves and start charting new trajectories for their lives.

I tell the youth that we are all created uniquely and we are equal before God. They need to believe that something good can come out of each one of them. This is only possible when they stop doubting themselves and pointing fingers at society, which they are part of. When a young person believes and appreciates himself or herself and works hard and smart, he/she will end up succeeding in whatever endeavour he/she is engaged in.

Thus, my rallying point to the youth is that in whatever social and economic activities they are involved in, they should always have positive thinking. They should believe that their efforts are not in vain. If anything they should not lose sight to the fact that they are the most important resource in society.

World over, no country has ever succeeded while leaving its youth on the fringes. Indeed, without the youth, society has no future. Societies attain sustainable futures through what they are able to do with their youth. We cannot have successful families, communities, counties and a country if we neglect the needs of our youth. In other words, the problems of the youth are our problems. As parents and guardians, we have the capacity and obligation to mould today's youths to become successful young men and women of tomorrow.

When young people become drunkards, criminals and social misfits, the older generation should take the blame. We should ask ourselves if we have been good role models to our youth. How can the youth be good and morally upright when they see us engaging in corruption, drunkenness and other vices? They can only follow what we are doing and most likely beat us in our sinful game.

Kenyans should not be surprised when the youth copy their worst aspects of life and take them as the norm. How do we expect the youth to succeed when, in our schools and universities, we are bombarding them with negative thoughts? How will they succeed when we abuse, and show them that they are worthless or even brand them academic failures who are not capable of achieving anything good? How will they triumph when we are not there for them? Those are critical questions to ponder about.

However, notwithstanding what people like myself can do as individuals, these individual efforts when done without proper coordination often lead to fragmented results. It is important, therefore, to consider structured and collective action to handle the challenges youth face.

It is critical to note that society's problems are also structural and need solutions beyond what individuals can attain. Governments, both county and national, have the resources to invest in youth development. The government has the capacity to invest in counselling and creating an environment in which young people can thrive. A good start is the law on sourcing and allocating percentage of existing county and national resources to the youth. But structurally, the youth question requires more than throwing money at them. There is need for development of youth leadership skills far and beyond school; a national youth leadership academic model that brings the youth from all over the country or region to share their experiences and chat a common cause may trigger the unlocking of their untapped potential.

Furthermore, the issue of values and national ethos is a subject that needs to be inculcated into young people as they enter school. This is as much as the Competence Based Curriculum (CBC) identifies values as one of its pillars. We need to entrench core values of integrity, hard work, trust, reliance, among others. More importantly, we need to live up to the values we espouse.

Most of the time, we take an unfair advantage of our positions to enrich ourselves, to the detriment of the youth and society in general. These negative attitudes and behaviour are the easiest for the youth to copy. We are here because our parents, guardians and communities sacrificed and moulded us to become successful. So, adults must continually ask themselves what they can do for their children in order to make them better adults of tomorrow.

I will continue to undertake these charitable activities, God willing. When I retire from Kisii University, I will have ample time to do more. I believe it will be a fulfilling undertaking in retirement.

6. EPILOGUE

Broader Kenyan Perspective: My Personal Gaze

I have been around for a while and witnessed Kenya make strides albeit slowly since independence in 1963. Although I was a toddler at independence, I am in the list of those Kenyans who can proudly stand and be counted as having been alive and kicking at the start of the post-independence era. In particular, God has been good to me and I have seen Kenya in the hands of four Presidents.

When Mzee Jomo Kenyatta became President, excitement of immeasurable proportions swept through the country. Kenyatta made countrywide tours to familiarise himself with the nation that he was to steer forward in the formative years of self-rule. Kenya had been in bondage of colonialism for close to seventy years. Young as I was, I could feel that the country had been unchained and Kenyans were ecstatic about independence and charting their own destiny. The energy of nationalism was palpable across the country.

An incident that is still etched in my mind happened when I was a Standard One pupil at Changoi Primary School in the current Kericho County. On that day we were woken up very early in the morning. It was chilly and mist blurred our vision some fifty or so metres ahead of us. We walked to the main road near Kericho Town, duly informed by our teachers that President Kenyatta was going to pass-by in his seminal official visit to Western Kenya.

By 8 am in the morning, in the company of my elder sister Florence and the other pupils, we were already lined up along the main road, ready to receive President Kenyatta and his entourage. A wind of excitement engulfed us as we danced and hummed patriotic songs that we had been taught by our teachers.

However, as we stood by the roadside, the sun steadily rose in the sky and its rays burnt our foreheads. It was becoming hot and most of us removed our cardigans. I remember my friend Korir who was sweating profusely saying that he did

Epilogue

not see any hope of witnessing Kenyatta's entry in the town that day.

As we waited, and time passed, many of us, especially those in lower classes, were getting tired and hungry. Most of us had not carried any food with us. In my case, our parents had taken a precaution and given us a few coins before we left home that morning. There were many pupils who were not as lucky as we were and were carrying nothing. However, generosity among students did not allow some to swallow saliva as others ate. Instead, those who had some money purchased some snacks and shared with the rest. Despite our diverse ethnic backgrounds, there was a lot of generosity amongst pupils, which allowed us to share the little that we could afford.

I was lying down under a tree near the main road when I saw pupils jumping in excitement. A police siren could be heard, signalling that the President's motorcade was arriving. I stood up. But however much I tried to stretch my neck, I could not clearly see the President. He was atop his official car, brandishing his trademark flywhisk. We expected him to make a stop and address us. He never did so. We were disappointed to learn that he could not stop because time had ran out. He was going to spend the night in the Lake Town of Kisumu, which was quite a journey considering the speed at which vehicles moved at that time.

Soon after, we started a torturous journey back home. It was around 6 pm. I was exhausted, but happy that I had gotten a glimpse of the famed President. When the going got really tough and I was unable to walk, my sister carried me on her back for the rest of the journey home. We got home at almost 8 pm.

That encounter left a permanent impression. I can attest that the appearance of the founding father wearing glittering flowery African attire and his long and well maintained hair are still ingrained in my memory. It is as if I saw him the other day.

As much as I was young, I can relate very well to the early days of independence. Kenyatta ruled up to 1978 when he peacefully died in his sleep during a state-cum-holiday visit to the Resort Town of Mombasa. I remember when the news broke out; we were harvesting maize in our family farm in Borabu. We had loaded some of the harvest on a cart to be pulled by oxen.

As the tragic news spread like a bushfire in the Hammartan, adults and children who knew little about what the Head of State entailed were astounded. I believe that any Kenyan who was my age and above vividly recalls that the country literally came to a standstill and there was extreme anxiety and uncertainty in the entire Republic. In most African states, a scenario like that could easily be a recipe for chaos and social anarchy.

During Kenyatta's rule, indigenous Kenyans were allowed to settle on land previously grabbed by the white settlers. They were commonly termed as the 'White Highlands'. These included parts of the Rift Valley like Trans Nzoia, Uasin Gishu, Laikipia and parts of Central Kenya like Nyandarua and the Aberdares. My family was a beneficiary of this resettlement policy. It was a good initiative for Kenyan communities who had been forcefully displaced by colonialists who evidently displayed gluttonous tendencies.

As I can recall, the future looked promising when Kenyans started to undertake various farming activities in the settlements aimed at improving their livelihoods. It has been articulated by many other researchers such as Maina wa Kinyatti (2009), that when the founders of the independent Kenya were negotiating with the British Colonial Government at Lancaster House, there was extreme undue influence from the colonial masters. The negotiations did not taking place in a level playing ground. In particular, the British Government hoodwinked the new Kenyan leaders to take a huge loan from the United Kingdom to purchase the land, which had been unfairly taken away from their forefathers.

In fact and interestingly, during the Mau Mau uprising many Kenyans, especially from Central Province, took up arms and entered the forests from whence they launched vicious attacks against the colonial people. The fighters' major aim was to get back their land. Hundreds and perhaps thousands of these freedom fighters were killed during the struggle. Still others were dislocated from their homes and taken to concentration camps where they were subjected to torture and forced labour. Many died in the concentration camps due to the cruelty and the inhuman conditions they were subjected to. Meanwhile, the home guards acquired the land of those that had been detained or were in the forest fighting the colonizers.

However, another school of thought argues that the Settlement Trustee Funds (STF) was established and funded by the British to enable those obtaining the land 'buy out' the settlers. It is argued that there could have been friction were the settlers ordered out without compensation, hence the willing seller willing buyer policy. This way, the settler left peacefully while local people acquired the land albeit with an outstanding loan to repay. The compensation for settlers, it was argued, was for the 'development' they had established on the lands they occupied.

However, instead of resettling the neediest, political leaders and government officials grabbed the land for themselves. People who stood to suffer most were the Maasai and the Nandi who got displaced from their ancestral land through dubious means. As a result, Kenyatta could get farms in Nakuru, Coast and Taita Taveta using STF funds. This left out the more deserving and needy cases.

During the struggle, many top level Mau Mau leaders died. Dedan Kimathi, the leader of Mau Mau was captured, 'tried' and hanged at Kamiti Prison. Jomo Kenyatta and other leading independent luminaries were rounded up and imprisoned on trumped up charges. Ironically, the very land which the Kenyans fought and shed blood for, was eventually bought from the illegitimate owners, the White Settlers at exorbitant prices.

From my own perspective, when one looks at the issue of land ownership holistically, and in retrospect, it can be easily noted that land is an extremely finite resource. In other words, land cannot be expanded. It can only be utilized diligently to increase production. Indeed, the number of people who depend on land continues to increase exponentially. This demographic scenario quickly leads to land shortage as the people scramble to sub-divide and occupy what is available of it.

This scenario becomes even worse in developing countries such as Kenya where the majority of the people depend directly on the land for their livelihood. Thus, looking at this matter in retrospect, one can say that to a large extent, our post-independence leaders were driven by short-term economic interests. They did not have a clearly articulated land use policy upon which they could have based their decisions on land ownership and allocation. No wonder there was fallout among those in the political leadership class soon after independence.

Many top government officials and politicians took advantage and acquired large tracts of land in different parts of the country. This created a situation, which eventually degenerated into land grabbing. This situation led to some people owning too much land, which was not used efficiently for agricultural production. It also fated many people to live as squatters in their own country. To date, there are occasional removals of people who are deemed to be illegal settlers in parts of the country. This includes pastoralists who invade the large ranches in Laikipia to graze their livestock and the small scale farmers who illegally occupied land in Laikipia and Nyandarua regions in their effort to eke a livelihood.

Furthermore, it is critical to note that subdivision of land in different parts of Kenya into small plots is a phenomenon that is getting out of hand. Presently, many Kenyans own small pieces of land that are not suitable for sustainable agricultural production. The situation is worsening as years go by.

In this regard, it can be argued that in the Kenyan situation, the concept of individual land ownership and provision of private title deeds to individuals is the stroke that broke the camel's back.

The origins of land titles in Kenya go back to the early 1920s. From that period, a policy was introduced where the administration started issuing title deeds in the native reserves. They accelerated the process through to the 1960s. The idea was that a title deed could be leveraged for commercial farming financing or some other economic initiative. It meant that communal land ownership ended and those who were able or better informed managed to grab communal land for themselves at the expense of the other members of the communities.

Land is a unique, fragile and finite resource. As human population continues to increase exponentially, land is not expanding but is getting overused and exhausted in terms of fertility and capacity for agricultural production. For instance, there has been a significant drop, as high as 55%, in agricultural productivity in the Western Kenya region. This scenario is replicated in other parts of the country. The number of mouths to feed is increasing exponentially while the food available is diminishing at alarming rates.

Consequently, I have to state that from my own understanding, what is currently happening in Gusii perhaps provides the worst case scenario with respect to the misuse and/ or mismanagement of land resources. There was a paltry 300,000 people in Gusii at the time of independence in 1963. Right now, the population has exceeded 3.5 million people. There are also thousands of Gusii people who have moved and settled in different parts of the country and overseas. In other words, since independence, the population of the Gusii people has increased more than tenfold. With this demographic trend, it can be estimated that if everything remains constant, the Gusii population could exceed 20 million people in the next three decades. This figure is completely unsustainable in terms of available land and other requisite resources for development.

This scenario offers a worrying trend. More so, Kenya has not succeeded in becoming industrialised, as is the case in the West and in South East Asia. Approximately 75% of the Kenyan people live in rural areas where they depend on small scale peasantry farming for their survival. As is already shown, the available land has also been increasingly subdivided into smaller insignificant portions.

For instance, currently, my age mates in Kisi own less than a half an acre of land. These are pieces of land that they inherited from their parents. Here, they have built houses and other infrastructure, and also do farming. Natural fences, which run down and across the rolling hills of Kisii occupy substantial amount of land that cannot be used for food production. Clearly what remains for farming is not adequate for any meaningful farming. This is why issues of malnutrition and hunger are now becoming prevalent in many parts of Kisii, a region which was once one of the food baskets of Kenya.

But based on the highlighted issues, I may argue that in terms of national land policy or lack of it, the government made a strategic error that is haunting us to date. At independence in 1963 therefore, Kenya should have come up with a land policy where this critical finite resource should have been made a resource owned by the State. In this context, individuals could be given user-rights where the State allocates people specific acreage of land depending on their capacity and needs to make proper use of it.

This type of land ownership strategy could have been premised on the principle that one uses the allocated land resource effectively without causing degradation. The repercussions then would be having your user rights being revoked if you are not using the land efficiently and sustainably. Probably, if this was promulgated at independence, we would not be grabbling with a situation where productive land is being split into small and unsustainable pieces.

Looking at the long-term trajectory of Kenya's economy, one can argue that we started off the reconstruction of an independent Kenya on wrong tenets. This has been well captured by the seminal policy paper of African socialism. This policy realignment transfigured itself quickly into crude capitalism. In this form of socio-economic model, private individuals were encouraged to own huge properties especially land. This enabled them to undertake various economic activities and create wealth for themselves and the country. Also, the government came up with various policy statements on industrialisation, commercialisation and agricultural production. This is captured in Session Paper No 10 of 1965. It was particularly articulated that the existing developmental activities were to be driven by Kenyans through the broad policy of Africanisation of all sectors of the economy.

When I examine the political and economic paths Kenya and its neighbour Tanzania took after their independence, I agree with the contention that life can never be scripted. While Kenya walked on the capitalistic path, Tanzania opted for a socialistic model of development. In the Tanzanian scenario, the government owned the means of production including land. People in rural areas stayed in communal villages. This was called *Ujamaa,* which was rooted for and amplified by the founding President Mwalimu Julius Nyerere.

By implementing *Ujamaa,* Nyerere envisioned a country where land, industries and the commercial sector were to be owned by the national government. Following the promulgation of *Ujamaa,* under what is popularly known as *Azimio la Arusha* (the Arusha Declaration) in 1967, nobody in Tanzania exclusively owned any natural resource particularly land in the country. Wealth was created for the whole country and was supposed to be shared equitably among Tanzanians. As time went on, Nyerere looked at the Kenyan economic model and described Kenya as, "a man eat man society". This was due to wanton amassment of wealth by a gluttonous few at the expense of most Kenyans.

However, it did not take long before it emerged that the Tanzania model was not going to work. People became lazy because, basically, through the disorganized and unstructured communal activities, they lacked self-motivation to work hard and produce wealth. Probably, this can be said to be normal behaviour of human beings. In this regard, people were not properly harmonized and incentivised. The state failed to manage them under what appeared to be a Utopian ideological and philosophical model. Tanzanians did not see the essence of working hard to create wealth only to be shared and owned by an amorphous entity called the State or Commune. One other reason for the failure of the Tanzanian model was open sabotage by Western institutions like the World Bank (WB) and the International Monetary Fund (IMF). The international entities were bent on sabotaging the unique experiment as a way of demonstrating that socialism was inferior to capitalism.

The Kenyan model of capitalism appeared to work, albeit at a snail's pace and with several shortcomings. Individual Kenyans were able to transform their livelihoods through agricultural production, entrepreneurial activities and small scale processing industries. As time went on, many Kenyans were uplifted from poverty and were able to a larger extent lead sustainable livelihoods.

However, in the long run, these social and economic achievements were not going to be sustainable. This can particularly be seen today from the yawning gap between the haves and the have-nots. Unfortunately, the few rich Kenyans are a drop in the sea of a huge population living from hand to mouth.

To start with, for a capitalistic system to work, the government, from the local, regional and national level should create an enabling and level playing ground. This includes in farming, education, property ownership and factories ownership, among others. This is only possible when the government comes up with and implements appropriate policies, rules and regulations that govern the various sectors of the economy. Without a level playing ground, the people who control the social, economic and political means of production are most likely to unfairly accumulate huge amount of wealth to the detriment of the majority of the population.

For instance, due to lack of proper land policy, the powerful few ended up owning more land resources than they really needed, while many people ended up as squatters in their own country. Due to lack of a level playing ground, corruption is rampant in most sectors of the economy. However, it is the common man who feels the pinch the most. Public land has been privatised and with individual private title deeds, the land grabbers end up selling the land unashamedly at sky-rocketing prices, to the detriment of the whole society.

Furthermore, the founding fathers tried to bring various ethnic communities together in their nation building efforts. They also established civil structures from the national, provincial and grassroots level. This was to offer public services in education, health, administration and agriculture, among others. Unknown to them, this broad strategy to some extent ended up balkanising the young nation.

This happened because the established political and economic system was not well grounded on clear ideals of freedom, democracy and nation building. Thus, the founders of Kenya did not manage to create proper political institutions at the legislative, executive and judicial level. The three arms of government almost became one and the same thing, and multi-party democracy collapsed in favour of single party rule. Obviously, without well-grounded economic and political systems, there was no way the Kenyan society would thrive. It was not going to develop to be a nation-state where citizens are free to pursue their individual activities to promote their happiness and the overall wellbeing.

Due to lack of proper institutions of socio-political governance and development, people tend to turn to informal networks, usually based on ethnicity, to secure their interests. Such negative ethnic and racial networks become avenues of protecting and championing sectarian tribal interests. Particularly, the Kenyan politicians and the other elites have continuously taken advantage of existing loopholes to promote their personalized political and economic interests while flashing the tribal card to hoodwink their tribesmen that they are promoting their interests.

The Kenyan political elite have, in particular, notoriously refined their methods of using their tribes to promote their long-term and short-term personal interests. These unpatriotic leaders will always hide under the tag of their tribe to gain and enhance their economic and other forms of interests. When other Kenyans raise alarm about their wrong-doings, they quickly retreat to their tribal cocoons and claim that their tribe is being attacked. Interestingly, the poor masses come out guns blazing at the ready, arguing that their son is being finished. After the news runs in various media outlets, Kenyans go mute and wait for another day to go through a similar unwarranted and wasteful ritual.

It is rather interesting that in Kenya, when one joins national politics, one is very likely to step in there firmly never wanting to quit. Here, the aim is to position oneself to manage and control national resources for the benefit of a few of one's cronies. This is true in many cases since a few elites from the various tribes get to benefit while the majority continue to suffer. In fact, political parties in Kenya are majorly formed based on tribe and not ideological and philosophical principles.

In this regard, Kenya is governed by an elite consensus. The elite club is spread across ethnic groups. It is also a client-patron system where praise singers get rewarded for open support of their patron. The role of *mwananchi* (citizen) is that of a 'rubber stamp' to be manipulated and cajoled one way or the other, especially during elections. Indeed, *mwananchi* is poorly empowered to understand and actualize the concept of the 'social contract' and delegated authority. Hence, he can hardly exercise the immense power accorded to him/her in the Constitution. It has even been claimed that this has come about because the country got rid of civics in formal teaching in schools.

However, I have to state that Kenyatta's reign had some positive attributes that enhanced people's welfare. During that period, agricultural institutions such as the Kenya Cooperative Creameries (KCC), the Coffee Board of Kenya (CBK), and the Pyrethrum Board of Kenya (PBK) were well managed. They brought handsome financial returns that enabled parents to pay school fees for their children. For instance, my parents who grew tea and pyrethrum received relatively good proceeds that enabled them afford to pay my school fees and that of my siblings. Thus, we never experienced the unfortunate scenario of being sent out of school due to lack of fees.

Also in retrospect, I should note that on the education front, there were allegations that schools in Central Province where the President hailed from received more resources than was the case in other provinces. However, the introduction of free primary education in 1965 enhanced access for many youth to quench their thirst for education.

In the health sector, the introduction of free immunization programme was a brilliant idea. It ensured that more children survived to adulthood. The improved health conditions led to rapid population growth in the country.

The Nyayo Era

News of Jomo Kenyatta's death hit Kenyans like a hurricane. Many had not fathomed the possibility of the country's founding father dying anytime soon. People in the country were justified to be in a state of anxiety since they had not understood the provisions of the Constitution when such a sad eventuality arose.

At the time, Daniel Toroitich Arap Moi was the country's Vice President. The former primary school teacher, who reluctantly joined politics in the 1950s, was perceived to be indecisive and was not outspoken. Since his boss wielded total authority, Moi did not have room to brand himself as presidential material. As much as Kenyatta had laid the basis for the young nation to move on, he had not done so well in grooming his successor.

Indeed, on the political front, Kenyatta had completely emasculated democracy. This made the ruling party, Kenya African National Union (KANU) to be a monolithic political tool. The country was governed on personal control and self-aggrandisement instead of democratic principles. The executive arm of government was too powerful to be challenged, and there were no checks and balances. These provisions are central in any open democratic system of government.

Consequently, Vice President Moi worked under the heavy shadow of a powerful President. Previously, Kenyatta had sacked his VPs without much ado and Moi knew very well who the appointing authority was. This made Kenyans to see him as a stooge, an errand boy and a mouth piece of the President. Whenever he spoke in any public fora, he coloured his speech with the sycophantic phrase, "....*chini ya uongozi thabiti wa Mzee Jomo Kenyatta* (under the steady leadership of Mzee Jomo Kenyatta)."

This made Kenyans to believe that Moi was a total puppet to the powers that be and not a man of his own, politically speaking. He never cut the image of a leader who could stand on his own. So, Kenyans did not have Moi in the list of possible successors of Kenyatta. This was regardless of the Constitution dictating that he was the successor by virtue of his post as Vice President.

Charles Njonjo, the Attorney General when Kenyatta died was an eloquent, diligent and yet intimidating government officer. Some Kenyans thought that he was going to take over the presidency for he had had the ear of President Kenyatta all along. Also, names of Njoroge Mungai and Mbiu Koinange who were very close associates of Kenyatta were being touted as the possible heirs to the throne.

However, when Njonjo oversaw the swearing in of Moi as the second President of the Republic of Kenya, the sanctity of the law prevailed. The transition was successful and took some

Kenyans by surprise. Still, some said privately that Moi was merely a passing cloud. He ended up staying at the helm uninterrupted for a cool 24 years!

In his acceptance speech and other addresses to the nation, Moi said he was going to follow in the footsteps *(nyayo)* of his predecessor. He also started by going around the country to meet the people and familiarise himself with them. He spread what he termed as the Nyayo Philosophy of peace, love and unity. It did not take long before he started projects like providing free milk for primary school pupils, and constructing Nyayo wards in public hospitals.

Famed for his swagger stick and gigantic steps, Moi also started populist policies to endear himself to Kenyans. He painted an image of one who was in collegial leadership. He was always accompanied by a gentry clique of leaders like Charles Njonjo and Godfrey Gitahi (GG) Kariuki. They always stayed on his side to the extent of riding together in the presidential limousine. He was famous for his generosity in giving freebies such as money to people, even by the roadside. He also gave school buses and had many learning institutions, hospitals and major roads named after him.

It appeared like the stone, which had been rejected, had become the cornerstone of the 'building'. However, one of the worst legacies of Moi is the fact that people around him developed an insatiable appetite for public resources and took grabbing to new heights. Some of those he appointed to head government parastatals became extremely corrupt. Within a short time, flourishing public entities took to their knees. This happened because many of these cronies did not have adequate education, experience and expertise. They also lacked in integrity and patriotism. Not even the free school milk project survived the ugly trend of mismanagement of public resources.

Further, it should be remembered that Moi entrenched the single party rule. The KANU party promoted his political reign through its henchmen and the party came to be known as '*Chama cha Baba na Mama* (the father and mother of all political parties)'. KANU was entrenched as a *de facto* ruling party. Moi later made it a *de jure* ruling party. It was against this backdrop that there was an attempted coup to topple Moi and bring to an abrupt end the rule of KANU whose emblem was *jogoo* (cockerel) which epitomized power and authority. Luckily, the coup was extinguished at its initial stage, to the relief of peace loving Kenyans.

It seems to me that the aborted coup awakened Moi and made him change his political strategy and tighten his grip to power. He removed some people who surrounded him and brought in new ones mainly from his tribal backyard. He also mixed them with his loyalists from other ethnic groups, forming a mosaic of leaders who sung his music. Moi further weakened Parliament and the Judiciary. Moreover, he also used the excuse of the coup to reorganise government institutions and state parastatals.

It appears that this strategy of being surrounded by one's tribesmen, which is widespread throughout Africa, is based on a simple philosophy. The belief is that your kinsmen will stay loyal and you can use them to perpetuate your power. Those who came on board in this shakeup were generously rewarded in terms of monies and allocation of public land. They got almost free and unrestricted access to government resources. These included expansive tracts of land in the Coastal and Rift Valley regions, and other parts of the country.

It was during Moi's time that corruption became even more entrenched in all systems of government. It started flowing unchecked in the veins of a few individuals who were hell-bent on enriching themselves at all costs. Government parastatals and other state entities became sources of personal aggrandizement and primitive accumulation of wealth. Within a short time, some of these people became stinkingly rich and were untouchable. They became the power unto themselves and masters of total impunity.

In particular, Moi used his immense powers to reward the people of his community. He built many schools, hospitals and other viable economic investments in the South and

Epilogue

North Rift region, which is predominantly inhabited by his Kalenjin tribesmen. Thus, Moi used his powerful position to enhance the socio-economic standards of his tribesmen. Before he came to power, the Kalenjin nation was ensnared in relative poverty. His ascent to power became a stepping stone for individuals from his backyard to escape the enslavement of poverty.

Under his watch, he systematically elevated some members of his community into filthy rich individuals who became untouchable. This set the precedent of institutionalized tribalism. Maybe this is why many Kenyans now associate the institution of the presidency as the place where one's tribesmen have to eat as the rest of the people salivate from the flinches.

As such, during campaigns for the most powerful office of the land, presidential candidates retreat to their tribal cocoons. They marshal solid blocs with an assurance that the lives of their tribesmen would never be the same if they win. This has reduced what should be otherwise a democratic process to be a matter of life and death. Consequently, Presidential elections in Kenya are exceedingly emotive and often threaten to tear the country into pieces through ethnic flare-ups and skirmishes.

Frankly, I have to state that the 24 years of Moi rule made Kenya more impoverished economically. Perhaps the so called Goldenberg scandal, which involved foreign individuals in cohort with Moi's men, marked the pinnacle of shameless theft of public resources. This wastage and pillage of national resources took Kenya back many years, socially and economically. It will take many more years to recover and reach the league of its peers. Many of these resources were eventually siphoned out of the country to places that were perceived as safe havens. To date, hundreds and perhaps billions of dollars of tax payers' money, which should have unchained poor Kenyans, are still stashed in foreign accounts in the Western countries and elsewhere in the world.

However, I credit Moi for exhibiting a strong grip of the country during his reign. Every Kenyan in every part of the country felt his immense power. His political and administrative linkages right from the grassroots to the national level made him always updated on the goings-on in every part of the country. Some sources claim that Moi could wake up as early as 3 am to get briefs from Provincial Commissioners who were his eyes in the Districts and Provinces. It allowed him to have the pulse of the country at his fingertips.

Note that this mode of governance, through the provincial administration, was abolished in 2010, when the new Constitution was promulgated. We now have devolved units of governance through 47 counties.

Moi also made maximum use of government spies. These, according to grapevine, could be planted in all branches of government, offices and even university lecture halls. Their main mandate was to sniff any kind of opposition and resistance, real or imagined, and convey the message to the central government. By 8 o'clock every morning, Moi could have received all kinds of briefs from these intelligence networks. He also used the media to gather intelligence and spread government propaganda throughout the country. The Kenya Broadcasting Corporation (KBC), then known as the Voice of Kenya (VoK), radio and television earned notoriety through such ventures. Indeed, the state broadcaster was Moi's mouthpiece. It is interesting to note that the two stations have never recovered from this shame.

Whenever there was a political opposition and administrative conflict, Moi was always well informed in advance, and used state machinery to immediately restore tranquillity and stability. But during the sunset days of his reign, and with the reluctant introduction of multi-party democracy, there were seemingly stage-managed skirmishes in parts of the country. In these skirmishes, it so happened that communities perceived to be anti-Moi were the ones who were mostly attacked. This happened mainly in parts of Rift Valley. Communities such as the Gikuyu and Gusii were flushed out of their abodes in

Epilogue

Molo, Nakuru, Kitale and Cherangany, among other parts of the Rift Valley. This happened especially in 1992 and 1997/1998, prior to general elections.

Due to Moi's increasing tendencies of having a tight grip to power and ruling with an iron fist, Kenyans' agitation for multiparty democracy got intense towards the end of the 1980s. Some opposition luminaries such as Jaramogi Oginga Odinga, George Anyona, Martin Shikuku, Kenneth Matiba, Charles Rubia, James Orengo, Kijana Wamalwa and Raila Odinga started agitating for the introduction of democracy and multiparty state. They would later be joined by Mwai Kibaki who resigned before the elections of 1992.

Kenyans yearning for change believed that a united opposition would defeat Moi in the first multiparty elections of 1992. That never came to pass as they became fragmented, often along ethnic lines, and gave Moi another five years at the helm.

The same characters, now bereft of Jaramogi who was deceased by then, made another push to beat Moi in the 1997 elections. From the start, it appeared that the opposition was fighting a common enemy but it ended up approaching the poll, totally fragmented. The political parties went their different ways and as usual following tribal affiliations. Moi beat them once again, and affirmed himself as the 'Professor of Kenyan Politics'.

A crafty politician by any standards, he continually manipulated the Kenyan political landscape to his advantage. Interestingly, the influence of the independence party waned as time elapsed. His attempt to handpick his successor flopped in the 2002 general elections. A new fish in Kenya's turbulent waters of national politics, Uhuru Kenyatta, Moi's preferred successor, was handed a humiliating defeat in 2002. For the first time, Moi was beaten in his own game by a relatively united and impenetrable opposition.

Other critics contend that Moi would not have gone home a defeated man had the opposition not united against him at the eleventh hour. This probably was also going to be very unlikely because the world had changed. With the end of the cold war, he could not have gotten any super power to back him to stay on.

The political euphoria pulled firebrand politicians who were at the height of their career to one side. Raila Odinga who had previously contested for the Presidency and was a formidable force ditched his presidential ambition by his clarion call, '*Kibaki Tosha* (Kibaki is fit)'. Raila and Kibaki were joined by like-minded political colleagues including Musalia Mudavadi, Kalonzo Musyoka, Martha Karua and Charity Ngilu. Kibaki was overwhelmingly voted for as Kenya's third President.

Moi handed Kibaki the mantle, albeit with pain at heart in a chaotic ceremony at the historic Uhuru Park at the hip of the capital, Nairobi, where Moi was jeered and heckled by an ecstatic crowd. When he left State House, his close allies appeared orphaned and were captured on camera screaming and shedding tears uncontrollably. The country was, however, ecstatic that '*yote yawezekana bila Moi* (all was possible without Moi)'. When Kibaki assumed office, Kenyans were touted to be the most optimistic people in the world.

Biographer's Note

Although Moi handed over power to Kibaki peacefully, he left Uhuru Park a disappointed man. Cable News Network (CNN) reported on December 30, 2002 as follows: "...*Moi's swansong was marred by heckling from the vast crowd and clumps of mud thrown in his direction.*" CNN added that Moi's arrival at the park was greeted by chants of, "everything is possible without Moi" and "Moi must go."

The New Order of Governance

Kenyans had a lot of expectations and placed high hope in Mwai Kibaki's government. Kibaki is an economist of great repute who studied at Makerere University and the London School of Economics. Kibaki was not new in national politics; he had previously served as Minister under Jomo Kenyatta and later as Moi's Vice President. He also contested the Presidency in 1992 and 1997 and lost.

Epilogue

He cut an image of a visionary leader complimented by widespread administrative and political experience. He started parliamentary politics in Nairobi in the 1960s, but relocated to his rural home tuff and represented Othaya Constituency in Parliament for many years.

At the start of Kibaki's tenure as President, Kenyans were voted the most optimistic people in the world. Kenyans regarded his Presidency as a God-sent opportunity to rebuild their nation, which had been plundered for several decades. Kibaki started on the right footing by appointing competent and experienced people to take key positions in government. Apart from their political acumen, the appointees who included Raila Odinga, Anyang' Nyong'o, Mukhisa Kituyi, James Orengo, Musikari Kombo, Martha Karua and Koigi Wamwere were professionals in their own right.

Consequently, Kibaki did not disappoint, particularly in the initial years of his rule. Kenya was back in the right political and economic trajectory, with Kibaki at the wheel. By any standards, Kibaki delivered economically during his first term in office (2002-2007). He promoted self-reliance amongst Kenyans, with the mantra *"Tulipe Ushuru Tujitegemee* (Let's pay taxes to be self-reliant)". This was unlike Moi's time when the country depended on loans from international lenders to run its affairs.

Kibaki revamped the body responsible for tax collection, the Kenya Revenue Authority (KRA). He gave the taxman enhanced mandate to collect taxes to be used for social and economic development of the country. Through the raised funds, he started major projects countrywide under the Economic Recovery Strategy (ERRS) led by Planning Minister, Prof. Anyang' Nyong'o[1].These projects included hospitals, model schools and roads. The investments, alongside

---

1   **Editor's Note**: following the 2002 elections, Prof. Nyong'o appointed a 3-man Task Force that came up with the ERS which made recommendations for short, medium and long term action. ERS would later form the basis of Vision 2030.

the Constituency Development Fund[2] (CDF) accelerated development in all parts of the country.

It was during Kibaki's tenure that the Nairobi-Thika Super Highway, the first project of its kind in Kenya, was built and completed. The completion of the project drastically reduced traffic gridlock in the Nairobi-Thika area. The road was previously known for nothing big other than phenomenal traffic snarl-ups.

However, it did not take long before political cracks emerged and became visible for every Kenyan to see. Raila Odinga who had signed a pre-election Memorandum of Understanding (MoU) with Kibaki claimed that he had been given a raw deal. He accused Kibaki of failing to honour his part of the bargain. Odinga said that Kibaki had not given members of his party equal government appointments as per the pre-elections agreement. Specifically, according to Odinga, Kibaki had failed to create the position of Prime Minister where Odinga would serve. This occasioned a fallout. The NARC Government had promised Kenyans a new constitution. The divisions in the ruling coalition would play out openly in the subsequent referendum on the constitution.

Once again, Kibaki and Raila found themselves at an impasse. A draft of the Constitution, called the Bomas Draft had been put together. The Raila-allied faction in NARC supported this. Meanwhile, a section from the Kibaki wing retreated, made changes to the 'Bomas Draft' and produced what came to be known as the 'Wako Draft'. It is the latter document that was put to a vote.

Raila and his team opposed the draft Constitution that was put for the referendum in 2005. During that referendum, the now defunct Electoral Commission of Kenya (ECK) gave the

---

2 **Editor's Note:** the Constituency Development Fund (CDF) came by an Act of Parliament, passed in 2003, following the success of a motion by Muriuki Karue, MP for Ol Kalau. It was the MP's third attempt, having first moved the motion in 1999, during the Moi regime. Despite its passage, the government did not take it up for implementation. He followed up on the same in 2001 but, again, the Moi regime would have none of it! Only when Kibaki assumed power did the idea get government support.

'Yes' camp that was led by Kibaki the symbol of a banana. Raila's wing that was opposed to the draft had the symbol of an orange. Raila's side won in the plebiscite.

Out of the poll, a dynamic opposition captained by Raila formed a new party and named it the Orange Democratic Movement (ODM), a coinage from the symbol that was given to the opponents of the draft constitution. Consequently, Kenya went to the polls in 2007 with Raila and Kibaki having been politically divorced. At the time of voting, there were protestations accusing the party in power of massive theft of votes and other forms of electoral fraud.

Kibaki was controversially declared winner of the poll and was sworn in under the cover of the night. He was sworn in as President by Justice Evan Gicheru in the presence of ECK chairman Samuel Kivuitu. Kenya was immediately plunged into political turmoil. We stared at a civil war in the face.

The situation quickly degenerated into chaos in different parts of the country, especially in the North Rift that became the epicentre of the violence. Thousands of Kenyans were killed while others got displaced from their homes. The Kenyan media did not have the proper term or analogy to call those who were displaced from their homes and managed to escape with their lives. It is not clear how the term 'Internally Displaced Persons (IDPs)' was eventually coined by the foreign media, only for the local journalists to pick the term and run with it. It is unfortunate that to date, there are still many Kenyans who claim that they never got the opportunity to return to their homes nor were they resettled or compensated.

The world looked at Kenya and mourned. Kenya had been considered the beacon of hope, peace and democracy in a troubled continent. The world wondered why Kenyans were butchering each other and burning their properties that had taken years to build. Due to the chaos, the economy suffered a melt-down.

It took great effort from the United Nations and the African Union to bring Kibaki and Odinga to the negotiating table. This was despite the hard-line stance their close allies had expected the two to maintain. The two international bodies managed to broker a peace resolution for Kenya by appointing eminent persons including former United Nations Secretary General, Kofi Annan, former Tanzania President Benjamin Mkapa, and Graca Machel, wife of Nelson Mandela to spearhead the process. When Annan announced that the negotiations had borne a deal, Kenyans' hopes were rekindled. Kibaki and Raila agreed to work together in a power-sharing deal that extinguished the violence. Among the key deliverables for the Coalition Government was a new Constitution.

Perhaps the greatest achievement of Kibaki's Presidency was the promulgation of the current Constitution in 2010. Kibaki and Raila supported the passing of the draft Constitution in 2010, with the hope that it could undo the wrongs that precipitated the political chaos and other challenges that Kenyans faced over the years. William Ruto opposed the new Constitution but, as fate would have it, he became a key beneficiary following the 2013 elections.

The Kenyan Constitution has been hailed as one of the most progressive laws in the world. It has an elaborate chapter of human rights and individual freedoms that were previously trampled upon by the political elites. It also entrenches presidential democracy. However, soon after the promulgation of the Constitution, a section of Kenyans started pushing for its amendment. They argued that the 'winner takes all' mentality where the loser is totally excluded from apparatus of the reign of power must be reformed. This, critics say, brings inequality and/or exclusivity in social and economic development.

The 2010 Constitution paved the way for devolution. Kenya is now a unitary and indivisible nation with forty-seven County Governments. In the letter and spirit of the Constitution, resources are to be decentralised from the National Government and be taken to the grassroots to benefit all Kenyans. Several administrative and management functions were devolved to the County Governments. Furthermore, each County has its own economic and social blueprint. The Constitution has provided a clause for public participation so that Kenyans at the grassroots can have a say in their development agenda.

There is a lot one can say about the law. However, I do not wish to delve into the workability or otherwise of the County Governments at this stage. If I do, I will be going astray since that was not one of the intended reasons of writing this book.

Kibaki left power in 2013. He left Kenya relatively economically stable and politically sound. He handed over power peacefully to Uhuru Kenyatta after serving Kenyans for ten years. Kibaki definitely went home with his head held high, and he now leads a quiet life as an elder statesman enjoying his retirement.

President Uhuru Kenyatta is now serving his second and last term, which ends in 2022. William Ruto, his Deputy, has the ambition of succeeding the President in the fullness of time. When Raila Odinga disputed the presidential poll outcome in 2017, the Supreme Court nullified the exercise and ordered a repeat. Odinga boycotted the repeat poll, arguing that the playing field was tilted in favour of Kenyatta. Odinga and Kenyatta later struck a political rapport in the famous handshake. One cannot tell for sure the long-term viability of this arrangement but it has worked well so far.

In particular, Uhuru and Odinga drafted a list of key social, political and economic issues on what hails Kenya using identified technocrats from both sides of the political divide. One of the outcomes of this rapport was the launch of the Building Bridges Initiative (BBI). The BBI committee was supposed to, and indeed it did, carry out broad-based consultations with Kenyans. The committee came up with a report on how the Kenyan Laws including the Constitution can be amended to include the agreed upon resolutions, such as the elimination of the winner take all mentality of the current system of governance. In its place, Kenyans proposed an all-inclusive system of governance starting from the top national executive to the grassroots level. However, it should be noted that the democratic process of amending the Constitution appears to divide Kenyans ahead of the 2022 general elections.

Kenyans, especially the politicians, have a bad habit of being in an electioneering mood throughout. It is now 2021 but political temperatures in the country are already very high notwithstanding the fact that the next general election will be held in 2022.

In the overall, over the years, our country has been maturing politically, albeit slowly. Now, we do have a well-grounded Constitution, which advocates for promotion of individual freedom and democratic principles of governance. We live in a multiparty democracy with freedom of speech and association ingrained in the Constitution. Even so, political parties have their own challenges due to corruption, tribalism and personalized agenda. They are neither guided by clear ideological underpinnings nor do they have a defined developmental agenda.

That notwithstanding, currently, Kenyans are more informed about their rights than ever before. They freely engage in political discourse in various forums from the local, county and national level, airing their views freely. For instance, Kenyans can now criticise their leaders openly in exercise of the now entrenched freedom of expression and association.

Furthermore, Kenya now has one of the most vibrant media in Africa. Various media houses, electronic and print media, are actively engaged in informing, educating and entertaining Kenyans. The media space has opened and brought with it several investors who have provided employment for many as well as providing outlets for expression of various talents. We now have tens if not hundreds of community radio stations, television channels and newspapers. Kenyans are also very active in social media, exchanging all kinds of views.

It is the wish of many Kenyans of goodwill that through the Building Bridges Initiative (BBI), Kenya will refine its Constitution, especially on the entrenchment and implementation of various aspects of governance. For now, no one is certain if we will move away from presidential to parliamentary system of government. If we do, then probably, positions of Prime Minister and Deputy Prime Minister will be created.

Specifically, looking at our economic situation, one gets a feeling that we have not done well at all. Our agricultural sector, which is supposed to be the driving force of Kenya's economy, is doing poorly. As already shown, we lack dynamic land use policies to guide the sector. Because of this scenario, our agricultural production is fast declining against a rapidly increasing population. Our major export crops, tea and coffee, fetch very poor prices at the world market. As such, farmers are disenfranchised. In the worst case scenario, some farmers are now uprooting these crops.

In the recent past, particularly in 2019-2020, the Kenya Tea Development Agency (KTDA), a body mandated to manage the production, marketing and sale of tea has been in the news for the wrong reasons. Small scale farmers affiliated to the agency continue to cry foul over poor bonuses and monthly earnings. There is a general feeling that the agency is mismanaged and riddled with runway corruption that is hurting the farmer. The Tea Bill was passed in December and time will tell if it will restore the dashed hopes of the farmers.

On the other hand, rampant coffee theft and underpayment to farmers is the order of the day. Although we have rich potential to mint billions of dollars from the crop, we are unable to do so because, for one, Kenya has not prioritised value addition in coffee production. We have also not taken advantage of the global market network for strategic sales.

It is sad that as much as we are an agricultural country, we are not able to even feed ourselves. At my personal level, I appreciate that in President Kenyatta's Big Four Agenda, food security is aptly captured. Through national and county governments' efforts, I trust that our food production and the whole agricultural sector will be rejuvenated and enhanced. This will improve the economic standards of the Kenyan citizenry.

Perhaps the worst case scenario in our national development trajectory is in the area of industrialisation and manufacturing. After more than fifty years of independence, we have not undergone any major industrial transformation. We have been unable to come up with high level technology and skilled manpower to make Kenya industrialised. Today, Kenya, like most African countries, is industrially and technologically stunted. We have not leveraged existing forms of technologies and industries in manufacturing, food processing, pharmacology and ICT.

This is to the extent that we import almost everything, from cars to farm machinery, farm inputs and clothes. Furthermore, our country is increasingly flooded with second hand goods and low quality imitations. To the industrialised nations, we are a dumping ground for their used clothes, recycled electronics and reconditioned vehicles. At this rate, one can postulate that we are far from getting industrialized.

Countries such as China, Japan and South Korea, have in recent years managed to come up with clear industrialisation frameworks that are guided by clear policies. They have developed high skilled and technologically literate manpower. This has boosted strategic industrialisation in those countries. Furthermore, countries such as Japan and South Korea have managed to learn appropriate skills and technologies from the Western world. They have managed to develop, enhance and apply these technologies to advance their industrialization agenda. This is why countries in the Asian continent are currently the rising economic powerhouses of the 21st century.

But not all is lost. In the area of Information Technology (IT), our country is moving forward positively. In the recent past, we have witnessed technological innovations including mobile money systems like M-Pesa and other forms of electronic software systems that have revolutionized the way we do business in particular, and how we interact with one another, in general. However, these forms of IT innovations are being developed at individual capacities. They lack clear and well-articulated national policies, provision of financial support, investments to enhance production and marketing of IT products and services.

7. Reflections on Turning Points

What if I Was Not Born?

Looking back at my life history, and the struggles I have gone through, has made me understand and appreciate that I am not a perfect human being. This is not strange because I have never come across a perfect person on earth. We all have our hits and misses. Probably, there are a number of things that I could do differently if my clock were to be reversed. However, at this moment, I will not regret any plunders I made. Why should I, when I am aware that life is not a straight line and is full of pitfalls?

This life is a continuous struggle with ups and downs. In many instances, there are certain things, which happen in one's life that are beyond one's control. This can affect the person negatively or positively. The most important thing, however, is taking full responsibility for whatever happens in your life. Perhaps this is better articulated by Ock Soo Pack, in his book, *Navigating the Heart* where he says that, "When a person is wrong, makes mistakes, and realizes that he is much less than he thought, he becomes humble, sincere and diligent. People who are caught up in the taste of their own greatness do not listen to others and are busy putting forth their own opinions. Such people are high-hearted. They do not possess the ability to control themselves."

The Holy Bible is not devoid of appropriate examples applicable to our modern world. The book of Genesis says that when our original parents (Adam and Eve) went against the wisdom and plans of the Supreme Being in the Garden of Eden, God pronounced a mortal punishment on them. Adam, his wife and his offspring were cursed to go through challenges and eventual death. They were thrown out of the land of Eden to moil and toil in order to eat. They were to encounter other unfathomable challenges like disease, war and famine.

From this broad perspective, I argue that human life is full of problems and challenges. What makes the difference is the manner in which one responds to those challenges. With a positive attitude and hard work, the perceived challenges can become opportunities. These opportunities will be the positive that will nourish one's life and make it beautiful and worth living.

Interestingly for my case, based on lessons from my late mother, my challenges started way before I was born. My mother was very sickly throughout her pregnancy. Even so, she did not give up. She soldiered on and carried the pregnancy to its maturity. Her pregnancy sickening journey ended on a jubilant note when she gave birth to me.

My birth made her a happy and fulfilled mother. But over time, I have wondered if, to a certain extent, the pregnancy which led to my birth partly contributed to her sickness later on which ended her life before I could even reward her. However, I could be wrong because, immediately I was born, she recovered fully, albeit not for many years.

So, I can say that had my mother thrown in the towel at that earlier time, I could not have been born and you would not have encountered my story. What my mother went through can make one judge the world harshly. To a large extent, the world is unfair to women. Most societies are patriarchal in nature and do not appreciate the role of women in their existence.

Women undergo an agonising nine-month period carrying a pregnancy. They suffer extreme pain during delivery. Indeed, they are the instruments and givers of life. When they give birth, they nourish the children and take care of them through various stages of life.

Despite this sacrifice, society hardly celebrates women as the heroines of life. I have got to challenge men, especially in Africa, to change and transform ourselves in the manner we treat our womenfolk. A society which treats women as second class human beings will never succeed. Unfortunately, this is what is happening in most African societies.

Ideally, before we talk about problems in our local, regional and national institutions, we should reflect on how we treat our wives, sisters and daughters right from the family level. If we do not love and appreciate them, how can we talk about success? They are the nurturers of life and should be given their ample space at the table of life.

It is not a coincidence that societies where women are respected and their rights upheld do much better. Examples of such countries include the Nordic countries like Sweden, Norway and Finland.

Going back to my life story and especially looking in the manner in which I started my schooling at Changoi Primary School in the present Kericho County, I can say that my start was not promising. When I was in Standard One, my father wondered what kind of a son I was because I was unable to cope with school life and bolted out. It was until my elder sister joined us in Kericho that I had to restart my primary education.

It is true that I have scaled the heights of education. But when I examine my life, I find that my start was poor. I remember how my father used to spank me every time I got it wrong during remedial teaching in the house. True, I did not meet his expectations at the beginning, but in the long run, things took a different turn in my favour. My star shone as I travelled my academic journey to the pinnacle of academia.

This tells me that in life, what matters is how you finish and not so much how you start. It is the nature of human beings that whenever they start a new activity like studies, job or business, they face challenges. They may also feel that things are not going in the right direction. If you have a negative attitude, you can easily give up and say that life is unfair to you. In reality, you are the one who is unfair to yourself.

In life, you have to try without ceasing in order to succeed. In life, you should never give up, notwithstanding the odds. Instead, you should re-energise, gather courage, rebrand and continue fighting to overcome the challenges. Indeed, I should admit that Thomas Edison was right when he said, "genius is one percent inspiration, ninety nine percent perspiration."

People who succeed in life are not necessarily the very intelligent or exceedingly gifted. They are those ordinary human beings. What separates them from others who fail in life is that, they have positive thinking. They also have courage and put extra effort in whatever they are engaged in with a trust that they will eventually succeed.

As human beings, God has given us a lot of potential. All of us are created in His image. I believe that God did not create us to fail. He created us to succeed here on earth and join Him in the world hereafter. However, by doubting ourselves and putting artificial barriers before us, we are unable to achieve our full potential. But when one looks at success stories, like that of former US President Barack Obama, one realizes that one can overcome challenges and achieve one's dreams. This is why his remark, "I am a son of a black immigrant from Kenya. I graduated from Harvard and later on became a Senator in Chicago. I was also the President of the most powerful nation on earth," resonates well with people who are forward-looking like me.

And there are lessons in this respect from our past. If we look at our indigenous communities before colonialism, they had well established social and economic mechanisms. People were trained and empowered from a very early age to be courageous, hardworking and not to be quitters. This they were told to do, notwithstanding the many adversaries. Among the Gusii people, for example, one was exposed to various challenges of life from an early age and guided on ways of solving them, with determination and commitment.

The tractability of indigenous African education where the youth were instilled with virtues of perseverance, courage, commitment and selflessness was exemplified by the

Epilogue

traditional initiation and/or circumcision ceremonies. For instance, a traditional circumcision ceremony amongst the Gusii people was quite elaborate and traumatizing. It entailed pain and figurative songs that challenged one to be ready to die defending himself, family and community. One had to be ready to sacrifice for the good of one's loved ones and the wider society. This kind of training went on even after the initiation ceremony.

Indeed, after circumcision, the youthful males went to encampments (*ebisarate*) where they got trained in war skills and manoeuvres. At that age, if there was any form of attack on the community by the enemy, you were to come out to defend yourself and your people without fail.

In this regard, for the youth in Gusii, it was almost an abomination to give up. Such an act was a taboo that could bring a curse to oneself and the community. This is why when the Kings African Rival (KAR) soldiers invaded Gusii land in 1907 and attacked people and stole their livestock, Kisii warriors confronted them courageously. The warriors fought the colonial forces to the hilt, despite the invaders' sophisticated weaponry.

In the confrontation, the warriors were killed in their hundreds. This forced Gusii elders to order them to retreat, fearing that the community's young generation would be wiped out from the face of the earth.

The young warriors act shows that they were brought up to be forward-looking, courageous and ever ready to die protecting their community.

However, as one journeys along, some happenings can appear overwhelming. In my case, the death of my mother had serious ramifications on my life. The lady was the pillar upon which our family leaned on. It was through her struggles and sweat that, together with my siblings, we are where we are today. She worked hard to transform the life of our family. It was through her relentless ingenuity that she invested in a tailoring business from whence she made savings and managed to buy a relatively bigger piece of land in Borabu.

She did not stop at purchasing the land. Instead, she left my father behind in Kericho and moved to the virgin land to secure it, clear bushes, build a home and engage in meaningful agricultural activities. Maybe this straining for the good of her family contributed to her terminal illness and eventual death at the age of 48 years.

My mother took life with a stride and her death left a huge gap in the family which has never been filled.

*****

My mother died after we spent a whole day seeking treatment in the current Kisii Teaching and Referral Hospital, formerly known as Kisii District Hospital.

Sometimes, I wonder whether my mother would have survived longer had she got prompt treatment. Memories preceding her death are still in my mind. I remember that when we queued at the hospital for several hours, she did not show any signs of weakness. Perhaps she was suffering inwardly and, foreseeing her closeness to fate, she never revealed her emotions. Is it that she did not want to bother me?

Over the years, health services especially in rural areas of Western Kenya have remained wanting. In fact, for many years, the whole of Gusii (Nyamira and Kisii counties) had only one District Hospital serving hundreds of thousands of people. This hospital was built around 1918 as a treatment centre for British soldiers. It is obvious that, by the time of independence, it had become overwhelmed by the number of people it was meant to serve.

When I took my mother there, it had very few doctors, clinical officers, nurses and other medical personnel. It also lacked proper medical facilities such as labs and equipment needed for diagnosis. Notwithstanding the fact that we had arrived at the facility at 7 am, my mother was only attended to at around 5 pm. By that time, the medic was evidently exhausted. The

Epilogue

hospital lacked drugs too. In fact, we bought the prescribed drugs at chemists outside the hospital.

When I recall all that, I conclude that some patients die, not because their time has come but because they are not attended to promptly. To this day, Kenyans succumb to treatable and curable ailments like malaria, amoeba, typhoid and dysentery. In the Western Kenya region, we also have not had very successful privately owned hospitals like in other towns. Also, although we have a few private hospitals in the region, their charges are prohibitive and not affordable to many poor patients.

To a degree, devolution has reversed the narrative in recent years. There is notable and gradual improvement of health services in many parts of the country. In Kisii for example, the main hospital, in which my mother was attended forty years ago, has been improved in terms of personnel, physical infrastructure and diagnostic equipment. Residents of the county and its environs can now access services like dialysis in the hospital. Additionally, sub-county hospitals have been equipped and can even undertake minor surgeries like Caesarean Section (CS). This was unheard of in upcountry sub-district health facility before devolution.

But there is divided opinion whether health as a function is too delicate and complex to be managed by the counties. Those who hold this view say that the regional governments have several teething problems such as poor management of human resources and unreliable flow of funds. This scenario has seen some doctors and other heath personnel switch gears and look for greener pastures abroad or venture into private practice in silent protest.

My point of view is that the spirit of the Constitution to devolve health services is good. Because the services were centralised in Nairobi, people at the grassroots suffered for decades. Those who needed critical and quick specialised medical attention died on the way from the countryside while being evacuated to the city, typically in old vehicles or unroadworthy ambulances. This is no longer the case because, in times of need, most County Governments offer subsidised ambulance services using their fleets of new and well serviced vehicles.

Counties are now hiring more healthcare personnel. In the process, there are indications of enhanced healthcare services at the grassroots. An example is Makueni County, which has been hailed as a model county in the provision of medical services. Using minimal resources, Makueni's pioneer Governor Kivutha Kibwana has managed to build modern health facilities in all the sub-counties. These facilities are well equipped and have sufficient supply of medicine for all types of ailments. Makueni has become a reference point because it has succeeded in offering the much needed medical services to its people, for free. This has improved life expectancy of the Makueni people.

In Kisii, courtesy of devolution there are notable improvements in healthcare service provision. Compared to when my mother died in 1980, the situation has improved substantially. The County Government has developed and improved the main facility to the level of becoming a Teaching and Referral Hospital. The Kisii Teaching and Referral Hospital has modern diagnostic equipment. It also has several high level personnel, including specialist doctors.

Perhaps, even more importantly, the County Government and Kisii University have signed a Memorandum of Understanding (MoU) that allows the university to use KTRH as its practical skills training centre. Through the MoU, our students pursuing various healthcare related programmes use the hospital for hands-on practical training. This follows the accreditation of the University's Medicine and Surgery Programme by the Kenya Medical Practitioners and Dentists Board (KMPDB). The Board also accredited KTRH to be a Teaching and Referral Hospital.

As already stated, the National Government has also come up with a strategic policy called the Big Four Agenda. Free and quality healthcare is one of the pillars of this national policy. The collaboration between the two levels of government and institutions that are training high level personnel for the health sector such as Kisii University will highly improve the delivery of efficient and quality services to Kenyans from all walks of life. We want to make the lives of our children and grandchildren better than ours.

My mother worked to make my life better. It is my aspiration to make that of the current and the next generation even better.

Should I Have Married Earlier?

I am on the homestretch as far as telling my story is concerned. For me to proceed at this point in time, I am persuaded by my conscience to share the following poem. Titled *The Road not Taken*, it was written by Robert Frost.

> *Two roads diverged in a yellow wood,*
> *And sorry I could not travel both*
> *And be one traveler, long I stood*
> *And looked down one as far as I could*
> *To where it bent in the undergrowth;*
>
> *Then took the other, as just as fair,*
> *And having perhaps the better claim,*
> *Because it was grassy and wanted wear;*
> *Though as for that the passing there*
> *Had worn them really about the same,*
>
> *And both that morning equally lay*
> *In leaves no step had trodden black.*
> *Oh, I kept the first for another day!*
> *Yet knowing how way leads on to way,*
> *I doubted if I should ever come back.*
>
> *I shall be telling this with a sigh*
> *Somewhere ages and ages hence:*
> *Two roads diverged in a wood, and I—*
> *I took the one less traveled by,*
> *And that has made all the difference.*

Any young person who combines hard work, good behaviour and discipline has very high chances of succeeding in life despite the odds that one may encounter in one's way. I cannot therefore say that I am gifted more than others. The environment in my early life within my family played a critical role in making me. My basic beliefs and values came from the people I interacted with early in my life in my ancestral home of Nyansakia and later on in Borabu. These people included my parents, grandparents, playmates and teachers at school.

Added to this, I doubt I would have made it to where I have reached had I continued living in the ancestral village of Nyansakia. This is mainly because I compare myself with my cousins who had similar potential like mine. However, they never made it because, in the area, formal education was not a priority in the early years. The high incidents of alcoholism contributed to the low uptake of studies by the youth of my time in Nyansakia. This unfavourable environment denied many boys and girls an opportunity to explore formal education and reap its fruits. Moreover, parents were not able to motivate and encourage their children to soldier on with their studies.

I credit my parents for their bold decision to go against the grain and leave our ancestral home in search of greener pastures in Kericho. Out there, my father was able to mingle with people who knew the benefits of formal education and in the process became aware of the opportunities that came with formal education. This made him have a burning desire to educate his siblings as well as his children. However, as already presented elsewhere, his siblings disappointed him since they did not accord education the attention it deserved.

At a personal level, I can say in retrospect, yet without any regret, that I probably overindulged myself in educational matters at the cost of other life issues. I was probably over-ambitious on what I wanted to achieve. For example, when I graduated from university in 1984, I got employed immediately. As was the norm at that time, I could have gotten married and started raising a family. This is what most of my college mates did. Indeed, some graduated as couples; some with children.

Epilogue

So, I keep asking myself; what is this that made me not to do what was very normal during those days? Why didn't I marry at that particular time? These questions keep crossing my mind to date because I was under pressure then to marry soon after college. Most of my relatives and friends were of the opinion that, since I had lost my mother and had completed my undergraduate studies, I did not have any reason to stop me from marrying. They urged me to settle down and get children who would ensure the continuity of the family tree.

However, uniquely for my case, I had something different going on in my mind. I wanted to proceed with studies and, as such, I had applied for a Masters course at the University of Nairobi.

My failure to secure scholarship for the study at the University of Nairobi became a sad turn of events that made me to aggressively look for an opportunity for further studies out of the country. I ask myself, what would have happened if I had joined the University of Nairobi for my Masters? Could I have been able to scale the heights to the level I eventually reached? Is it possible that I could have dropped out of the Masters class the way many of my colleagues who received the scholarships did?

Regardless of what would have happened had I married early, yes that path that I did not tread, I am contented with where I am. I am blessed with supportive spouse and wonderful children. I believe that is what God willed for me.

Regarding Other Folks on the Road Travelled

To a certain extent, fate does determine one's destiny. As shown very early in the book, when I got sick after taking my CPE, I was unable to join Form One. This forced me to repeat and I did better and secured admission in a good school. One may say that the sickness could have hindered my advancement. However, it worked the other way round. It gave me an opportunity to retake my Standard Seven examination and get a better grade that guaranteed me a place at Itibo High School.

The same can be said of what happened to me when I completed my PhD training in the United States of America in 1993 and got a well-paying job in Washington, DC. In this connection, I ask myself several questions: what could have happened had I not fallen sick? What if I never returned to Kenya soon after due to the sickness? Could it be that I would have built a better career than I ended up doing?

They say that America is a land of opportunities. Maybe, I could have risen to the highest levels of American employment. However, could I have risen to the level of full professor or Vice Chancellor as I did in Kenya? Although, I hit rock bottom when I left a high paying job in the United States and returned to Kenya; I eventually rose to the level where I am today. The Kiswahili saying, *kuteleza sio kuanguka*, aptly applies in this case.

In life, you will face many challenges. Some situations will be good; others will be bad. There will be highs and lows in that journey of life. But in any situation, it is always good not to lose hope, for there will always be light at the end of the tunnel. As much as people may want to dim your God-given star, no one will dim it. As old wisdom holds, the darkest hour is just before dawn and for every door that closes, another one opens. In Gusii, our forefathers put it thus: "*gakiaborire inchera rogoro kerigerie inchera maate (when it fails in one place, always try an alternative)*".

This tells me that giving up should not be an option even when the odds are against one. Always soldier on. With the right mindset, tomorrow will be better. Keep hope alive and burning inside you. Hope is the fuel that will reignite your life engine to success.

As much as people say that I have managed to succeed, I went through Kenyan and American universities. In the USA, I was a beneficiary of government scholarships funded by the American taxpayer because I was an A-student. Interestingly, my encounter with students from all over the world surprised me that I could always emerge the best in our class, notwithstanding the stereotypes that black people are not good in academics.

On Kenya and Africa in the 'Global Village'

Many observers have said that when African students go to universities in the West, most of them do remarkably well in their studies. They are right. Many of these African students excel in their Bachelors, Masters and PhD training in universities in Germany, USA, Britain and elsewhere in the world.

The big question then is; what happens when these very scholars return to their home countries? When most of these promising men and women return to their home countries, usually, their impact is not felt. Why? How come that these young energetic and highly gifted Africans who return to their home countries with decorated higher education certificates are unable to distinguish themselves in service delivery to their countries? This is a topic that can form a book of its own and I choose not to delve into it now.

I have to admit that, to a large extent, we in Africa have not done well in many fronts. We have not done well economically, socially and culturally. Many African states are ranked amongst the poorest in the world. The majority of Africans live below the poverty line which is less than one dollar a day. Many African countries have over the years experienced political and civil strife and dictatorial rule.

Many theories have been advanced as to why we in Africa have not succeeded in many fronts. The worst-case conception is when it is said that Africans are an inherently inferior race, which is not capable of doing anything better. They say we Africans are inherently corrupt, innate and incompetent and there is nothing good to expect from us. All this is rubbish!

Some schools of thought argue that Africa is facing challenges because of the powerful forces of colonialism and neo-colonialism that have always worked against the interests of the African people. Proponents of this theory contend that colonialism made African societies to be underdeveloped. This conception was particularly articulated by Walter Rodney in his seminal book titled, *How Europe Underdeveloped Africa.* Proponents of this school of thought argue that the Europeans exploited and plundered African resources like minerals and converted Africans to work in crop plantations in the Western countries as slaves. The African resources were plundered and taken away to develop Western countries like Britain, France, Germany, Italy and the USA.

These scholars further argue that as much as African countries received their independence, this stage-managed freedom was and still is very superficial. Through neo-colonialism and internal under-developed capitalism, these former colonies continued being linked and exploited by their former colonial masters. Accordingly, in the global capitalism nexus, over the years, through neo-colonialism and post-colonialism, African states have been pushed to the periphery. They are far away from the centre of capitalism, which is based in Europe, North America, and other emerging economic power-houses.

Such arguments seem to validate Lord Macaulay's address to the British Parliament on 2nd February 1935 when he said;

> I have travelled across the length and breadth of Africa and I have not seen one person who is a beggar, who is a thief. Such wealth I have seen in this country, such high moral values, people of such calibre, that I do not think we would ever conquer this country, unless we break the very backbone of this nation, which is her spiritual and cultural heritage and therefore, I propose that we replace her old and ancient education system, her culture, for if Africans think that all that is foreign and English is good and greater than their own, they will lose their self-esteem, their native culture and they will become what we want them, a truly dominated nation.

I therefore understand that through international capitalistic manoeuvres, Africa continues to supply underpriced raw materials and labour to the global market. In this unequal global market situation, Western countries have exploited African states for hundreds of years. Through this exploitation, they have managed to advance technologically, industrially and in other spheres of life. These Western countries import raw materials from Africa at knocked down prices and export finished manufactured products that they sell to African countries at exaggerated prices. Thus, proponents of this line of thought argue that the world economic and political order is completely skewed against Africa and other third world countries.

I noted earlier that I will not delve into the merits and demerits of these schools of thought. But briefly stated, countries like Japan, India, Malaysia, Indonesia and Singapore experienced colonialism yet they are now in the right trajectory in all facets of life. They are stable economically and politically. Some like South Korea and Singapore are now some of the wealthiest states globally. We can therefore note that as much as there are elements of truth in the dependency theories, we cannot sit pretty and continue blaming other people for our predicaments. The buck must stop at our doorsteps.

The problems we face as Kenya, and as a continent, can only be solved by ourselves and not by any other external benevolent force. Thus, to a larger extent, most of the problems in Africa like poverty, unemployment, disease and political upheavals are of our own making. This does not mean that Africans are inherently inferior, corrupt and unable to do anything right. In fact, each person in Africa must ask himself or herself, "What role am I playing in solving the problems facing my country? Am I part of the problem or solution in what confronts us? What value have I added to the lives of people around me?"

Some people have argued that Africans and Kenyans in particular, are good at complaining and whining about their problems. Even when foreigners, especially white people come to Kenya, people spend hours on end complaining about our leaders, corruption, tribalism, and impunity, among other issues. But in those complaints, almost everybody, including those people in high positions who should take responsibility, keep talking about 'them'. "It is 'them' who are corrupt, tribal or egocentric."

You will find people in high positions always sitting around complaining. When they talk, they point the finger at others, not realizing that once you point your index finger at me, the other four fingers are pointing at you. I will not hesitate to once again quote former US President John F. Kennedy who famously told the Americans, "to ask themselves what they can do for their country and not what their country can do for them." This means that all of us must go an extra mile and give sacrifice for the betterment of our children and grandchildren's lives.

It is unfortunate that life is getting tougher for the younger generations. Youths in Africa are wallowing in abject poverty, extreme joblessness and insecurity. As the older generation, we cannot blame the youth. Let us blame ourselves. In any society, even in the animal world, the parents always aspire to leave the offspring leading a better life than theirs. For instance, in the elephant family, the matriarch goes out of the way to ensure that her young ones are comfortable and are protected from any danger. It leads them to places for water and pasture.

All of us need to introspectively reflect, own up and change our attitudes. This is how our societies are going to survive in a highly competitive and versatile globalised society. The fact remains that there is always light at the end of the tunnel. If we put our act together, we can change the prevailing sorry state within our lifetimes, and make the lives of our youths better.

In many instances, in recent years, we have been attending to symptoms of our problems. We first thought that changing the Constitution would solve the problems, which dogged us for years. Now, it is said that we have one of the most progressive constitutions in the world, which vividly captures democratic values, freedom and principals of human rights. But since the new Constitution was promulgated in 2010, are our lives becoming any better? Why is it that problems of corruption, impunity and poor governance at all levels still persist?

Sometimes, we argue that in Africa, we do not have good political leaders. We say that countries like South Korea, Singapore and India have had good leaders who spearheaded them to prosperity. But again, how are leaders made and sustained? As philosophers say, "people get the kind of leaders they deserve." You cannot expect the best Member of the County Assembly (MCA), Member of Parliament (MP), Senator, Governor or President when we as a people are not upright.

I get disappointed when I hear it said that most Kenyans are potentially corrupt but they lack the opportunity to exercise it. If Kenyans are willing to be bribed during campaigns by politicians driven by parochial interests, we will always get the worst leadership. What Kenya needs therefore is a total cultural and political revolution. We cannot advance economically, socially and politically if we do not examine our political and cultural values. Particularly, cultural values form the foundation, ladder and antenna, which give direction to peoples' lives.

Before the advent of colonialism, Kenyan communities were guided by clear indigenous cultural values. These values guided people at individual, family and broader community level. It is these values that made communities to survive for years notwithstanding the calamities and upheavals that the people faced from time to time. True, what differentiates human beings from other animals is their learnt culture. Without culture, you are no longer a human being but an animal, and a dangerous one at that.

Societies which have developed in all aspects of life are those that understand their culture, and appreciate and promote their core cultural values. In China, Mao Zedong launched the "Chinese Revolution" in the 1950s and 1960s. This "Cultural Revolution" came up with key cultural pillars upon which the development of China was to be hinged. For instance, through it, people were re-oriented to drastically change their family structures. This is how the concept of one child per family was ingrained in Chinese people's minds.

The revolution also helped the Chinese people to avoid blindly copying the Western cultural values. The Chinese rejected the Western model of democracy and went deeper into their culture to search for solutions to their social, political and economic challenges. Through their great thinkers such as Confucius, they were able to come up with their own model of governance. Indeed, their institutions have served them well if their prosperity is anything to go by.

Through the concept of Confucianism, corruption is highly discouraged in China. In China, they equate corruption to murder. This is why the corrupt are sentenced to death in broad daylight. Through their cultural values, the Chinese have managed to tame exploitation, dishonesty and use of shortcuts to amass wealth.

Due to the Cultural Revolution, China started to search for technology and scientific skills from all over the world. From the 1940s, they sent their talented youths to various parts of the world to learn. The youths ended up 'stealing' some technologies, returned to their home country, improved, domesticated and patented them. That is why countries like the USA are always worried when they think of technology espionage. Nevertheless, China is now highly developed and is politically stable. It is an emerging superpower, which has unsettled many countries. First nations had built themselves a comfort zone with the belief that they were the fulcrum upon which the world turned to for any form of idea or development. Evidently, the future of the 21st century is amongst the Asian Tigers.

Kenya too needs a cultural revolution. If someone asks you to state your unique Kenyan values, what will you tell him or her? One may ask how a country like Kenya can achieve a cultural revolution yet we have more than forty plus tribes. Well, China did it with its hundreds of tribes who form a total of over 1.4 billion people today. We are lucky to have these diverse cultures as a country. Through the Kenyan Cultural

Revolution, we can bring these cultures together and marry them in one rainbow Kenyan culture.

To my understanding, the issue of tribalism exists to divide us. What is needed is to distil cultural values from each of these Kenyan communities. We need a National Cultural Supreme Council to look into the positive cultural values of each Kenyan tribe. Our cultures have several positive commonalities. This tells me that if we systematically distil our values and combine them into one coherent Kenyan cultural system, it will provide the key principals that will guide the social, economic and political destiny of our country.

This is doable. We should think of making Kenya function like an organic body in which each organ contributes to the survivability or otherwise of the whole body. We need to seamlessly work like parts of a machine and shun working for personal and selfish interests. In this spirit, we should rebuke politicians for excelling in falsehoods and encourage them not to betray the trust Kenyans bestow upon them.

For instance, the Gusii were guided by a culture, which is summed up as *chinsoni*. *Chinsoni* simply means cherished core cultural values, which formed the basis for behaviour, relationships and wealth creation. Interestingly, just like the Gusii, every Kenyan community has its core cultural values. We cannot survive without such clear cultural values in the guise of baseless aping of Western cultural values. Ideally, you cannot be a Kenyan and pretend to be a Chinese or an American at the same time.

This is perhaps elucidated better by senior statesman Simeon Nyachae's foreword to my book, '*The Gusii of Kenya*', where he contends, "One should, however, avoid any tendency to romanticize past social norms and cultural values as were practised by our forefathers and foremothers. There is need to be pragmatic about identifying what from the past is of value today; that which advances the cause of humanity. We must understand that a people's cultural values and social systems are not static. They continually evolve and adapt to emerging social, cultural and economic trends as society matches into the future. Wholesale abandonment of people's cultural values and social norms and blind aping of alien cultural values, can have far reaching negative consequences as currently witnessed in many parts of Africa."

Hence, to wrap up, we need to shift from the fantasy world and find our national cultural compass to guide us towards the right direction.

-THE END-

REFERENCES

Books

Akivaga, S., K, & Bole, A. O.,1982. *Oral Literature; A School Certificate Course.* East African Educational Publishers, Nairobi.

Achebe, C., 1958. *Things Fall Apart.* Lagos. William Heinemann Ltd.

Akama, J. S., 2017. *The Gusii of Kenya: Social, Economic, Cultural, Political and Judicial Perspectives.* Nsemia Inc. Publishers, Nairobi.

Akama, J. S., 2019. *The Untold Story: Gusii Survival and Resistance to the Establishment of British Colonial Rule.* Nsemia Inc. Publishers, Nairobi.

Amateshe, A. D., 1988. *An Anthology of East African Poetry.* Longhorn, Nairobi.

Barclay, W., 1971. *Ethics In A Permissive Society.* London: William Collins Sons& Co Ltd, Glasgow.

Kenya Government. 2010. *The Constitution of Kenya, 2010.* Government Printer, Nairobi.

Park, O. S., 2011. *Navigating the Heart; Who Is Dragging You?* Seoul: On Mind.

Maina wa Kinyatti, 2009. *Kenya's Freedom Struggle.* Atlantic Highlands Press, London.

Ogot, B. & Ochieng, W. R. (Editors), 1995. *Decolonization and Independence in Kenya,* 1940-1993. Ohio University Press, Athens, Ohio.

Newspapers

Daily Nation: January 19, 2016. *Commission for University Education Orders Closure of 10 out of 13 Kisii University Campuses.* Nation Media Group, Nairobi.

References

Daily Nation: January 21, 2016. *CUE Revokes Degrees Awarded to Five Students by Kisii University.* Nation Media Group, Nairobi.

The Standard: September 12, 2019. *The Youth Should Try to Understand Their Ancestry and Build the Future.* The Standard Media Group, Nairobi.

People Daily: August 9, 2019. *There's no plan to merge universities, Magoha tells MPs.* Media Max Africa, Nairobi.

Daily Nation: January 21, 2016. *Varsity Vows to Defy Closure Notice".* Nation Media Group, Nairobi.

The Standard: January 26, 2016. *Education Team Must do More Than Just Close Universities.* The Standard Media Group, Nairobi.

Daily Nation: September 18, 2003. *University drops plan to move Kisii Campus.* Nation Media Group, Nairobi.

Kenya Times: June 16, 2003. *Controversy rocks Kisii Campus Over its Status.* Government Press, Nairobi.

www.ingramcontent.com/pod-product-compliance
Lightning Source LLC
Chambersburg PA
CBHW061702300426
44115CB00014B/2534